MasterChef
AT HOME

Be a winner in your own kitchen with
recipes and tips from the television series

CONTENTS

Oven temperatures
The oven temperatures given in this book are for conventional ovens. For fan-assisted ovens, reduce by 20°C, but please double check with your manufacturer's handbook.

JOHN TORODE

"Maybe just by cooking a few dishes from this book it could happen for you... go on: 'Change Your Life!'"

I sometimes sit in the MasterChef studio, glance over at Gregg and a huge grin starts on my face as I wonder how the hell did I get here? How am I so lucky to be doing this amazing thing: taking passionate amateurs and helping them to get better? If there is a way to do MasterChef forever, count me in, because as a television show it is extraordinary: thousands of people from around the country apply, a few get to cook, even fewer get to make it to the latter stages – and from then on the competition really hots up!

We try to give an insight into the world of the professional cook, which, for me, is the best industry in the world. The challenges they face are incredible. If anyone ever told me that I would be standing on the ramparts of a fort in the middle of India at sunrise watching three of the greatest amateur cooks MasterChef has ever seen, I would never have believed them. For both the contestants and myself, flying into Jodhpur and smelling the air, fragrant with spice and heady with humidity, was inspiring in a hugely different way to any task we have ever done. The lasting impression that trip had on me, both culinary and motivationally, will be one of those memories recalled to many around the dinner table.

MasterChef will always be a tough competition because it is about learning a new skill, and that is always hard, but with the added pressure of Gregg Wallace and myself peering over the cooks' shoulders, and the cameras as well – wow! Not only is it about a journey of food and cookery but one of real self-discovery. It's about people who have grown up, chosen a life, and then decided it's time to change and do something that they truly want to do for a lifetime, and because of that it's an emotional journey. For me this is the essence of MasterChef: people who truly care – Gregg, me, Karen Ross, and all the crew who make this wonderful programme what it is.

The result of all the blood, sweat and tears that come from MasterChef is a set of what we feel are the best cooks who know the secret of taking ordinary food to the extraordinary. Maybe just by cooking a few dishes from this book it could happen for you... go on: "Change Your Life!"

GREGG WALLACE

"Whatever the show, whoever the winner, one thing is obvious, that the contestants get better and better."

What an amazing year. The finals of this year's amateur competition were the best I have ever been involved in. The three finalists, Dhruv, Alex, and Tim, took the standard to heights I never dreamed of. Incredible guys, all three of them. Celebrity this year was a close run thing. For me, Lisa was one of the best winners we've had, but I have to say it was a tight call. MasterChef: The Professionals is completely different. All chefs talk of passion and commitment, but when you see that firsthand, when you work with people like Claire, David and John, who have devoted their lives to the pursuit of excellence, it can be breathtaking.

Whatever the show, whoever the winner, one thing is obvious, that the contestants get better and better with each lesson and each experience. This book brings a little of that experience into your home. All of the knowledge and the passion of the contestants is wrapped up in these recipes.

As you well know, me and my fellow judges don't always agree. The one and only thing that unites us in our judging is a standout dish. We've put them all here, in this book. They may be here for their technical brilliance or the beauty of their simplicity, what I can guarantee is that they taste heavenly.

MICHEL ROUX JR

"Some of the food I tasted was exceptional and worthy of the coveted Stars that professional chefs dream of."

I have always taken most pleasure out of my profession from teaching and helping chefs, whether amateurs or professionals, to achieve their goals.

The competition in MasterChef: The Professionals was again fierce and the standards as high as they get, for some of the chefs it really was an emotional rollercoaster.

The trend was for simpler food where the main ingredient can play its part, and where the skill of the chef is demonstrated by being bold enough to know when to stop adding more to the dish. We saw some use of the water bath and molecular cuisine, but the fundamental skills always shone through.

Some of the food I tasted was exceptional and worthy of the coveted Stars that professional chefs dream and work all their life for.

One of the high points for me was our trip to Noma and sampling René Redzepi's nordic cuisine. It's no surprise his restaurant has been voted the world number one. As a young chef I would have loved to have had the chance to work for him, and to see the faces of our three finalists when we told them where we were taking them, was priceless.

During the series the chefs evolve and grow in confidence. To be in part responsible for their future fills me with pride, and is one of the many reasons I love being a chef.

Michel

MONICA GALETTI

"We have discovered some brilliantly talented chefs that are sure to lead the way in the culinary future."

MasterChef: The Professionals 2010 was an absolute pleasure, and I am truly honoured to be a judge on this wonderful programme. Again, we have discovered some brilliantly talented chefs that are sure to lead the way in the culinary future, especially our amazing finalists Claire, David and John.

It is for me a very rewarding and proud feeling to watch the contestants battle it out and develop both as a person and a chef. In judging the semi-final with Michel, I was very pleased to see how the contestants that I put through the first tests had progressed. It was wonderful to see how much they had grown in confidence, enabling them to focus on their challenge and produce some fabulous plates of food.

What really stood out for me is how simplicity in a dish, both in appearance and combination of ingredients, can knock the socks of a dish that is too complicated and messy. One of my absolute favourites was "Pan-fried mackerel with à la grecque vegetables" – simple but delicious!

Basic kitchen skills are essential, they enable not just a professional but any cook to complete a task accurately, with ease and class. Follow my step-by-step skills guides in this book to sharpen up your techniques. The more you practise the skills, the easier it gets, and the more confident you will become. When you are comfortable making a recipe, you should try adding your own touch and change things to suit your own tastes – and most importantly, enjoy!

UTTERNUT SQUASH SOUP - BUTTERN
QUASH SOUP WITH SAGE AND PARME
AMPER - WHITING QUENELLES IN SH
ROTH - CELERIAC SOUP WITH CURRIE
CALLOPS - BILLY BY - CAULIFLOWER
ND BARBERRY FRITTERS WITH YOGU
AUCE - VEGETABLE TEMPURA WITH C
AYONNAISE - TOMATO SALAD IN A SA
UILLE BASKET TOPPED WITH A BASIL
ORBET - BEETROOT, WALNUT, AND G
URD SALAD, WITH A LEMON AND SHE
INEGAR DRESSING - GLASS NOODLE A
ERB SALAD - GOAT'S CHEESE AND ON
ARTS - BROAD BEAN AND PROSCIUTT
AVIOLI WITH A RED PEPPER SAUCE -
HEESE RAVIOLI WITH RAISIN, ROCKE
LMOND BEURRE NOISETTE - OPEN LA
F ROASTED SQUASH AND WILD MUSH

STARTERS

GAZPACHO SHOTS WITH TIGER PRAWNS
Dhruv Baker sales director and 2010 champion

PREPARATION TIME
35 minutes, plus chilling

COOKING TIME
2–3 minutes

MAKES 30 SHOTS

30 raw whole tiger prawns, peeled
  but tails left intact
lemon wedges, to garnish
salt and freshly ground black pepper

FOR THE GAZPACHO
15g (½oz) fresh breadcrumbs
1 egg yolk
1 small garlic clove, crushed
3 tbsp olive oil

1 tbsp tarragon vinegar, plus extra
  to season, if required
1 small onion, chopped
½ red pepper, deseeded and chopped
¼ small cucumber, chopped
½ red chilli, chopped
3 tomatoes, approx. 225g (8oz),
  chopped
230g can plum tomatoes
1 tsp tomato purée

MASTER TIP
TIGER PRAWNS

Tiger prawns are meaty, warm water or tropical prawns. Warm water prawns tend to be larger than their cold water cousins, and some varieties of tiger prawn can grow to 35cm (14in). They are harvested globally, and farmed extensively, raising some environmental issues, so check how responsibly the fish has been sourced when buying. Snip off the legs and antennae when preparing. The taste is mellow, honeyed, and succulent.

1 To make the gazpacho, mix the breadcrumbs with the egg yolk and the garlic in a bowl, then slowly add the olive oil, mixing as you do so. Transfer to a hand-held blender or food processor and add all the remaining gazpacho ingredients. Blitz until smooth.
2 Press the mixture through a fine sieve. Taste and adjust the seasoning with salt, pepper, and vinegar if necessary. Leave to chill for at least 2 hours or overnight.
3 Have ready a large bowl of iced water. Bring a pan of water to the boil, add a pinch of salt and the peeled prawns, and cook quickly at a rolling boil for 2–3 minutes, until they just change colour. Drain and plunge into the iced water. Swish them around a bit to cool, then drain again and set aside.
4 Pour the gazpacho carefully into large, chilled shot glasses and top each one with a prawn.

JOHN TORODE "Wow! That gazpacho is fabulous. It's rich. It's got the sweetness of the tomato, it's got a heat in there from a bit of spice, and it goes very, very well with the prawn."

BUTTERNUT SQUASH SOUP

Nihal Arthanayake radio and TV presenter and 2010 Celebrity contestant

PREPARATION TIME
20 minutes

COOKING TIME
30 minutes

SERVES 4

GREGG WALLACE

"It's got an earthy sweetness, with a hint of cumin, which is lovely. It gives it a different angle, gives it spice."

25g (scant 1oz) butter
1 onion, chopped
1 butternut squash, approx. 1kg (2¼ lb)
  in weight, deseeded and cut into
  large chunks

1 tsp ground cumin
750ml–1 litre (1¼–1¾ pints)
  chicken stock
salt and freshly ground black pepper
2–3 tbsp plain yogurt

1 Melt the butter in a large saucepan. Add the onion and cook over medium heat, stirring, for 4–5 minutes until it has softened but not coloured.
2 Add the squash with the ground cumin and cook for a further 1–2 minutes, stirring to coat.
3 Add the stock, bring to a simmer and cook for 15–20 minutes or until the squash is tender. Purée the squash using a hand-held blender or by transferring to a food processor, in batches, for a smoother result.
4 Season to taste and stir in the yogurt just before serving.

FLAVOUR COMBINATION
BUTTERNUT SQUASH AND CUMIN

Cumin is one of the foundations of savoury cookery East of Suez. That's because this sickle-shaped seed has amazing banks of taste and flavour. At the same time as being earthy, rich, and tangy it's balanced by a lemony citric bite. With so much to offer cumin picks up the smooth sweetness of butternut squash and takes it somewhere bigger and tastier. For greater excitement, scatter the soup with toasted whole cumin seeds.

BUTTERNUT SQUASH SOUP WITH SAGE AND PARMESAN DAMPER

Mark Little actor, comedian, and 2010 Celebrity contestant

90g (3¼oz) butter
3 shallots, finely chopped
1 butternut squash, approx. 1kg (2¼lb), peeled, deseeded, and diced
750ml (1¼ pints) chicken stock
250ml (9fl oz) cider
½ tsp freshly grated nutmeg

FOR THE DAMPER
225g (8oz) self-raising flour
sea salt and freshly ground black pepper

85g (3oz) butter, chilled and diced, plus extra for greasing
25g (scant 1oz) Parmesan cheese, grated
1 tbsp chopped sage

TO GARNISH
4 large sage leaves
4 tbsp soured cream

PREPARATION TIME
20 minutes

COOKING TIME
50 minutes

SERVES 4

1 Preheat the oven to 200°C (400°F/Gas 6). For the damper, sift the flour into a large bowl and season to taste, remembering the Parmesan is already salty. Rub in the butter until it forms a mixture resembling fine breadcrumbs. Then add the Parmesan and sage and bring together with 2–3 tbsp cold water to form a soft dough. Tip onto a board, knead briefly then shape into a round, flattening to form a circle about 14cm (5½in) in diameter. Transfer to a lightly greased baking sheet, cut a deep cross in the top of the damper, and bake for 30 minutes or until golden and the base sounds hollow when tapped. Cool slightly on a wire rack.

2 Meanwhile, make the soup. Melt 75g (2½oz) of the butter in a large saucepan over medium heat. Add the shallots and sauté for 3 minutes. Add the squash and sauté for a further 2 minutes and then add the stock, cider, nutmeg, and some seasoning. Bring to the boil, then reduce the heat slightly and simmer for 15 minutes or until the squash is tender. Blend using a hand-held blender or by transferring to a food processor until smooth. Season to taste.

3 Melt the remaining butter in a small frying pan over medium heat. Add the sage leaves for the garnish and cook for about 30 seconds or until crisp, turning halfway. Set aside on kitchen paper.

4 To serve, divide the soup between 4 warm bowls, top each with 1 tbsp of soured cream and garnish with a sage leaf. Break the damper into 4 and serve with the soup.

GREGG WALLACE
"I really like your soup. It's thick, it's rich, it's sweet, it's well-seasoned. And I'll tell you what, it looks refined."

WHITING QUENELLES IN SHELLFISH BROTH

Dick Strawbridge TV presenter and 2010 Celebrity finalist

PREPARATION TIME
45 minutes, plus chilling

COOKING TIME
55 minutes

SERVES 4–6

FOR THE QUENELLES
15g (½oz) butter, melted
40g (1¼oz) fresh breadcrumbs
100ml (3½fl oz) milk
225g (8oz) skinned whiting fillet,
   roughly chopped
2 tsp lemon juice
1 egg
salt and freshly ground black pepper
freshly ground nutmeg, to taste
100ml (3½fl oz) double cream

FOR THE BROTH
50g (1¾oz) butter
1 onion, chopped

1 celery stick, chopped
1 carrot, chopped
450g (1lb) raw whole prawns,
   peeled and roughly chopped
3 tbsp brandy
100ml (3½fl oz) dry white wine
3 ripe tomatoes, approx. 225g (8oz),
   chopped
1.5 litres (2¾ pints) fish stock
1 large leek, halved lengthways
   and sliced
1 large Maris Piper or King Edward
   potato, approx. 300g (10oz), diced
generous pinch of saffron
extra virgin olive oil, to garnish

MASTER TIP
WHITING

Whiting is undervalued by
many people as it has a light,
delicate taste, but it is very low
in fat and tends to be less
expensive than other members
of the cod group. The skin of
a whiting is particularly thin
and care should be taken when
skinning the fish, although
leaving the skin on, particularly
for grilling, protects the
delicate flesh. Always buy
fresh whiting and use quickly
as they can become almost
tasteless with age.

1 For the quenelles, mix together the melted butter, breadcrumbs,
and milk to make a coarse paste. Cover and chill for 30 minutes.
2 Put the whiting, lemon juice, and egg in a food processor with some
salt, pepper, and nutmeg to taste, and whizz to form a smooth paste. With
the motor running, gradually add the cream. Put into a bowl, sit this in
a larger bowl of iced water, cover, and set aside to chill and firm up.
3 To make the broth, melt half the butter in a large saucepan over
high heat. Add the onion, celery, and carrot and cook, stirring, for
5 minutes. Next, add the prawns and brandy and cook, stirring, for a
further 2 minutes. Then add the wine, tomatoes, and hot stock and
bring just to the boil. Reduce the heat and simmer for 30 minutes.
4 Blend the broth, in batches, in a hand-held blender or food
processor until smooth. Pass through a fine sieve into a large bowl,
using the back of a soup ladle to push out as much as possible. You
should end up with about 1.7 litres (3 pints) of broth. Set aside.
5 Return the stockpot to medium heat. Add the remaining butter,
leek, and potato and cook, stirring, for 3–4 minutes. Add the saffron
and broth and bring just to the boil. Reduce the heat so the mixture
is barely simmering. Season to taste.
6 For each quenelle, scoop a generous spoonful of the fish mixture
onto a dessert spoon. Then, with a second, equal-sized spoon, shape
the mixture into a rugby-ball shape, moving it from one spoon to the
other. Lower into the broth and repeat to make 4–6 quenelles. Poach
for 5 minutes, turning halfway. Divide between 4–6 warmed bowls and
spoon the broth all around. Drizzle with extra virgin olive oil to serve.

CELERIAC SOUP WITH CURRIED SCALLOPS

Tim Kinnaird paediatrician and 2010 finalist

PREPARATION TIME
15 minutes

COOKING TIME
40 minutes

SERVES 4–6

50g (1¾oz) butter
salt and freshly ground black pepper
1 large leek, finely sliced
1 medium to large celeriac, approx.
  550–600g (1¼lb–1lb 5oz) in weight,
  peeled and chopped into small cubes

1 litre (1¾ pints) chicken stock
4 large or 8 small scallops
1 tbsp good-quality curry powder
1 tbsp olive oil

1 Melt the butter in a large pan over medium heat, add a little salt and black pepper, and cook the leeks, stirring for 8–10 minutes or until softened but not coloured. Add the celeriac, pour in the stock, and bring to the boil.

2 Cover and simmer for about 30 minutes, until the celeriac is tender. Purée the soup using a hand-held blender or by transferring to a food processor, dividing it into batches for a smoother result. Season to taste then reheat gently.

3 Meanwhile, dust each scallop with a little curry powder and season with salt and pepper. Heat the oil in a frying pan over medium heat and quickly fry the scallops for 1–2 minutes only, turning once. Take care not to have the heat too high or the curry powder will burn and taste bitter.

4 To serve, ladle the soup into bowls and place a scallop or scallops in the centre.

MICHEL ROUX JR'S
BILLY BY

This is a beautiful, deep mussel broth that originated in one of Paris's finest restaurants. Although it looks simple, the flavours are rich and delicious and it's a wonderful start to a meal.

2 tbsp olive oil
25g (scant 1oz) butter
2 celery sticks, finely chopped
1 onion, finely chopped
2 sprigs of thyme
small handful of flat-leaf parsley
salt and freshly ground black pepper
150ml (5fl oz) white wine
400ml (14fl oz) fish stock
2kg (4½lb) mussels
1 carrot, finely chopped
1 leek, finely chopped
100ml (3½fl oz) double cream

FOR THE BREADED MUSSELS
2 tbsp plain flour, seasoned
1 large egg, beaten
40g (1¼oz) breadcrumbs, reserving
   1 cube of bread
groundnut oil, for deep frying

TO SERVE
1 leek, finely sliced
1 carrot, finely sliced
25–50g (scant 1oz–1¾oz) Parmesan
   cheese, grated

PREPARATION TIME
35 minutes

COOKING TIME
25 minutes

SERVES 4

1 Heat 1 tbsp of olive oil and the butter in a large, deep sauté pan. Add half the celery, the onion, the thyme, and a few sprigs of parsley, and season well. Fry, stirring, over medium heat for 5 minutes until softened but not coloured. Add the wine and bubble for a minute. Add the stock and the mussels, turn up the heat, cover with a lid and cook for 3–4 minutes or until all the mussels have opened. Discard any unopened mussels and pick the meat from the rest. Discard the shells. Strain the stock and discard the vegetables and herbs.

2 Heat the remaining olive oil in a large pan and add the other half of the celery, the carrot, the leek, and seasoning. Fry, stirring, over medium heat for 8–10 minutes or until softened. Add the mussels (reserving 12 for the breaded mussels), the reserved stock, and the cream. Blend until smooth. Season to taste and add a little more stock if necessary to thin it down. Chop the remaining parsley and stir in a tablespoonful.

3 Roll the reserved mussels in the flour, then in beaten egg, and finally in breadcrumbs. Pour groundnut oil into a small pan to a depth of 2cm (¾in) and heat until a small cube of bread turns golden brown in 30 seconds. Fry the mussels for 2–3 minutes or until golden. Remove with a slotted spoon and drain on kitchen paper.

4 To serve, pour the soup into 4 soup bowls, top each with 3 breaded mussels, and garnish with leek, carrot, and freshly grated Parmesan.

CAULIFLOWER AND BARBERRY FRITTERS WITH YOGURT SAUCE

Mitra Abrahams student and 2010 semi-finalist

PREPARATION TIME
20 minutes

COOKING TIME
15 minutes

SERVES 4

FOR THE YOGURT SAUCE
150g (5½oz) Greek yogurt
2 tsp chopped coriander
zest and juice of ½ lime
dash of olive oil
salt and freshly ground black pepper

FOR THE FRITTERS
1 small cauliflower, about 125g (4½oz),
   cut into small florets
60g (2oz) plain flour

1 tsp ground cumin
½ tsp ground cinnamon
½ tsp ground turmeric
2 large eggs, beaten
1 shallot, finely chopped
½ garlic clove, finely chopped
2 tbsp parsley, plus extra to garnish
30g (1oz) dried barberries, available
   from Iranian shops as zereshk
groundnut oil, for deep frying
1 cube of white bread

MASTER TIP
BARBERRIES

Harvested, often in the wild, from bushes of the *Berberis* and *Mahonia* genera, dried barberries have a soft texture and a pleasant, sweet-tart taste, with an underlying sharpness that derives from malic acid. Look for berries that are red rather than dark, as the latter may be older and will have less flavour.

1 For the sauce, place the yogurt, coriander, lime zest and juice, and olive oil into a small bowl. Season and mix together.
2 For the fritters, place the cauliflower florets in a small pan of boiling salted water and simmer for 3–4 minutes or until just tender. Drain and then refresh under cold water to stop the cauliflower cooking further. Set aside.
3 Place the flour and spices in a medium-sized bowl and mix together. Make a well in the middle, add the egg and beat with a whisk until smooth. Add the shallot, garlic, parsley, barberries, cooked cauliflower, and a sprinkling of salt and pepper, and mix well.
4 Heat the groundnut oil in a deep pan to about 190°C (375°F) or until a small cube of bread turns golden brown in 30 seconds. Take tablespoonfuls of the mixture in batches and carefully lower into the hot oil. Fry for about 2–3 minutes on each side or until golden brown. Remove with a slotted spoon and drain on kitchen paper. Repeat with the rest of the mix until you have 12 fritters.
5 Serve 3 fritters per person, scattered with chopped parsley, and with the sauce on the side.

VEGETABLE TEMPURA WITH GARLIC MAYONNAISE

Skills test for contestants in Celebrity MasterChef 2010

FOR THE MAYONNAISE
2 garlic cloves
½ tsp salt, plus extra to taste
2 egg yolks
1 tsp Dijon mustard
150ml (5fl oz) vegetable oil
150ml (5fl oz) olive oil
squeeze of lemon juice
freshly ground black pepper
groundnut oil, for deep frying
1 cube of white bread

FOR THE TEMPURA
85g (3oz) plain flour
1 tbsp cornflour
pinch of sea salt
100ml (3½fl oz) sparkling
  water, chilled
approx. 100g (3½oz) each of up to
  6 different vegetables, such as
  broccoli, carrots, courgettes,
  mushrooms, red peppers, and baby
  sweetcorn, cut into bite-size pieces

PREPARATION TIME
25 minutes

COOKING TIME
20 minutes

SERVES 4

1 To make the mayonnaise, crush the garlic with the salt in a pestle and mortar until you have a smooth paste, then set aside.

2 Place the egg yolks and mustard in a large mixing bowl and whisk together. Combine the oils in a jug then very slowly start to trickle into the egg yolks, whisking continuously. Continue slowly adding the oil while whisking until it is all incorporated and the mixture has thickened.

3 Add the garlic paste and a squeeze of lemon juice and combine thoroughly. Season to taste and set aside until needed. (See also MasterClass pp.24–25 for more advice on how to make mayonnaise.)

4 Heat the groundnut oil in a deep pan to about 190°C (375°F) or until a small cube of bread turns golden brown in 30 seconds. Put the ingredients for the tempura batter in a bowl and whisk together. Make the batter just before using and do not leave it to stand.

5 Dip the vegetables in batter and fry in small batches until crisp (about 2 minutes). Drain on kitchen paper then serve with the mayonnaise.

MONICA'S MASTERCLASS
MAKING MAYONNAISE

Perhaps the most popular of all cold sauces, mayonnaise is made by forming an emulsion of droplets of oil in vinegar, with egg yolks present to hold the emulsion stable and provide a rich flavour. This recipe makes 300ml (10fl oz).

1 **Prepare the ingredients**
Place 2 egg yolks, 1 tsp Dijon mustard, and 1 tsp vinegar in a mixing bowl, adding a pinch each of salt and pepper, if preferred. Make sure all ingredients are at room temperature before starting, especially the eggs and oil.

2 **Whisk in the oil**
Break up the egg yolks and vinegar with a whisk and then start to pour in 250ml (8fl oz) olive oil, drop by drop at first, whisking all the time. As the sauce thickens, increase the speed of pouring to a drizzle and then a steady stream.

Cold ingredients can make it more difficult to form an emulsion.

Whisk continuously to keep the emulsion stable.

"You can't beat a home-made mayo.
Experiment by adding different flavours
like a touch of lemon zest or spices."

 Stir in the lemon
Once all the oil has been incorporated
and the mayonnaise is thick, stir in 2 tsp
freshly squeezed lemon juice, or a little
more depending on how much you want
to offset the richness of the oil with the
sharpness of lemon. Season to taste.

4 **Rescuing curdled mayonnaise**
If the mayonnaise "splits" or separates
into eggs and oil it can still easily be
rescued. Place another egg yolk and
1 tsp mustard in a clean bowl, then
trickle in the curdled sauce, whisking
until it is all incorporated and smooth.

The extra yolk and mustard
will re-emulsify the sauce but
slightly change the flavour.

TOMATO SALAD IN A SAVOURY TUILE BASKET TOPPED WITH A BASIL SORBET

Tim Kinnaird paediatrician and 2010 finalist

PREPARATION TIME
30 minutes, plus chilling
  and churning

COOKING TIME
15 minutes

SERVES 8

25g (scant 1oz) basil leaves, plus extra
  shredded leaves to garnish
7–8 tbsp extra virgin olive oil
32 red cherry tomatoes
16 yellow cherry tomatoes

FOR THE SORBET
100g (3½oz) caster sugar
small bunch of basil leaves
squeeze of lemon juice

FOR THE BASKETS
1 small garlic clove
coarse sea salt
50g (1¾oz) unsalted butter
30g (1oz) plain flour
2 tbsp caster sugar
1 large egg, white only
100g (3½oz) Parmesan cheese,
  finely grated
1 tbsp finely chopped rosemary leaves

MASTER TIP

PEELING TOMATOES

To peel tomatoes, make small cuts in the skin around each tomato and put the tomatoes in a bowl of boiling water for 1–2 minutes. Use a slotted spoon to transfer to a bowl of cold water and then peel the skin.

1 To make the sorbet, dissolve the sugar in 200ml (7fl oz) water over moderate heat. Stir in the basil and lemon juice. Blend in a food processor, then pass through a fine sieve. Line a second sieve with muslin and set over a bowl. Pour in the basil syrup and leave to drain.

2 Pour the syrup into an ice-cream maker and churn for 1 hour. Line a baking sheet with baking parchment. Using 2 dessert spoons shape quenelles of sorbet, place on the tray, and freeze.

3 To make the baskets, preheat the oven to 200°C (400°F/Gas 6) and line 2 baking sheets with baking parchment. Grease the outsides of 8 medium dariole moulds and sit them upturned on another baking sheet. Crush and mince the garlic to a fine paste with the sea salt using the back of a knife. Beat the butter until pale and then beat in the flour, sugar, and garlic. Slowly beat in the egg white and Parmesan to form a sticky paste.

4 Draw four 12cm (5in) circles on each sheet of baking parchment, well spaced apart. Dollop 2–3 spoonfuls of the mixture into each circle and thinly spread with a palette knife to fill the circle. Sprinkle over some rosemary and bake for 6–8 minutes or until tinged brown around the edges. Drape over the moulds, and return to the oven for 3–4 minutes. Cool for a few seconds, then release from the moulds and leave to cool.

5 For the salad, blend the basil with 5–6 tbsp of the oil. Pour through a sieve set over a bowl. Peel the tomatoes (see left) and put into a bowl. Season with salt and a splash of olive oil.

6 To serve, carefully set a tuile basket on each plate and divide the cherry tomatoes between each. Put a quenelle of sorbet on top and garnish with the shredded basil leaves.

BEETROOT, WALNUT, AND GOAT'S CURD SALAD, WITH A SHERRY VINEGAR AND LEMON DRESSING

Neil Stuke actor and 2010 Celebrity semi-finalist

PREPARATION TIME
20 minutes

COOKING TIME
45 minutes

SERVES 4

3 beetroots, 1 each of red, white, and golden, approx. 500g (1lb 2oz) in weight, well washed
salt and freshly ground black pepper
40g (1¼oz) mixed salad leaves, such as chervil, rocket, and watercress
1 medium fennel bulb, trimmed

50g (1¾oz) walnut halves
200g (7oz) soft goat's curd cheese

FOR THE DRESSING
1 tsp sherry vinegar
1 tsp lemon juice
3 tbsp olive oil

GREGG WALLACE "All the ingredients work really, really well together. You've got smoky nuts, you've got sweet beetroot, you've got a lovely little sherry dressing. It's very good indeed."

1 Remove the stalks and leaves from the beetroot, leaving about 2.5cm (1in) of stalk on each beetroot, to prevent too much colour leeching out as they boil. Discard the stalks and leaves.

2 Place the red beetroot into one large pan and the white and golden beetroots into another. Cover with cold salted water, bring to the boil, turn down the heat, and then simmer for 30–45 minutes or until the beetroot is tender when pierced with a skewer or sharp knife.

3 As the beetroots are simmering, make the dressing. Whisk together the sherry vinegar, lemon juice, olive oil, and a pinch each of salt and black pepper. Add a pinch of sugar to taste.

4 When the beetroots are cooked, remove from the heat, drain, and then cool under cold running water. Remove the little stalk, peel the beetroot, and then thinly slice with a mandoline or sharp knife and set aside. Remember to use a separate board for each colour of beetroot to preserve the different colours.

5 Toss the salad leaves with a little of the dressing and place in the centre of a serving platter. Place the sliced beetroot on top of the leaves, layered up with the different colours.

6 Slice the fennel very thinly with a mandoline and place on top of the beetroot. Scatter the walnut halves over the top of the fennel, breaking them down slightly with a rolling pin beforehand, if necessary.

7 Scatter over the crumbled goat's curd, drizzle with the rest of the dressing, and serve.

JOHN TORODE'S
GLASS NOODLE AND HERB SALAD

Few recipes stick to the magic of great Thai cookery – one of the greatest cuisines in the world. The four essential elements are Sweet, Sour, Salty, and Hot – this salad ticks all the boxes and packs a punch. Make lots, there will never be enough.

150g (5½ oz) glass noodles
1 fat green chilli, deseeded and
    finely chopped
20g (¾ oz) palm sugar
1½ tsp nam pla (Thai fish sauce)
juice of 1 small lime
handful of mint leaves
handful of Thai basil leaves

handful of coriander leaves
½ cucumber, halved lengthways, seeds
    removed, and finely shredded
1 Thai pink shallot, very thinly sliced
½ long red chilli, deseeded and
    finely chopped
100g (3½ oz) fresh white crab
    meat, picked

PREPARATION TIME
20 minutes

SERVES 4–6

1 Place the noodles in a large bowl, cover with warm water, and leave for 4–5 minutes or until tender. Drain in a sieve and refresh under cold water.
2 Make a "*nam jim*" by pounding together the green chilli and palm sugar in a pestle and mortar, to form a paste. Add the nam pla and lime juice, then put to one side.
3 Mix the herbs with the cucumber, shallot, and red chilli, then combine with the noodles, crab meat, and *nam jim* to serve.

MASTER TIP
GLASS NOODLES

Glass noodles, or "*khanom jin*", are usually made from mung beans and are therefore also called mung bean thread. They are sometimes used in soups and similar dishes but they should never be fried. You could easily use rice noodles if you prefer. Glass noodles, Thai basil, and Thai shallots are commonly available from Asian food shops.

Celebrity 2010 Champion
LISA FAULKNER

"I put my heart and soul into those three final dishes. I really worked hard, and I was just so scared that John and Gregg weren't going to like it, and they loved it! I never expected the competition to be so tough. People think that when celebrities go on MasterChef everyone gives you a helping hand, but it's not like that at all: they all go and you're left to do it by yourself. I'm really proud of myself. I never thought – in my wildest dreams I never, ever thought – it was possible that I'd end up the winner."

MAIN

MONKFISH WITH BUTTERNUT SQUASH FONDANT AND SAUCE VIERGE p.94

"I thought this dish shouldn't work in any way, but Lisa pulled it together and it was just delicious. Very clever cooking." JOHN

STARTER
GOAT'S CHEESE AND RED ONION TART p.32

"The flavours and textures were wonderful, and the pastry was light as a feather. A fantastic dish."
JOHN

DESSERT
ALMOND PANNA COTTA WITH POACHED TAMARILLOS AND BERRIES p.304

"This dessert was a pudding man's heaven, I loved it! Soft, comforting cream and then the lovely tamarillos coming in."
GREGG

GOAT'S CHEESE AND RED ONION TART

Lisa Faulkner actress and 2010 Celebrity champion

PREPARATION TIME
25 minutes, plus chilling

COOKING TIME
55 minutes

SERVES 4

FOR THE PASTRY
small sprig of thyme
100g (3½oz) plain flour
25g (scant 1oz) butter
25g (scant 1oz) lard

FOR THE RED ONION JAM
25g (scant 1oz) butter
25g (scant 1oz) soft brown sugar
1 tbsp balsamic vinegar
1–2 tbsp cassis
salt and freshly ground black pepper
2 red onions, finely sliced

FOR THE GOAT'S CHEESE
175g (6oz) crumbly goat's cheese
1 egg yolk
1–2 tbsp double cream

FOR THE SALAD
handful of rocket leaves
2 tbsp olive oil
2 tsp lemon juice

JOHN TORODE "Light as a feather, the pastry crumbles in your mouth. Everything just sits beautifully like a little pillow. It's fantastic."

1 To make the pastry, strip the thyme leaves into a blender or a food processor and add the flour, butter, and lard. Mix on pulse setting to form crumbs. Gradually add enough cold water (about 2–3 tbsp) to form a soft dough. Wrap in cling film and chill for 30 minutes.
2 To make the onion jam, melt the butter in a sauté pan and add the sugar, vinegar, cassis, and some seasoning. Add the onions, bring to the boil and cook, uncovered, over very low heat for 30 minutes.
3 Heat the oven to 200°C (400°F/Gas 6). Place a sturdy baking sheet in the oven. Divide the pastry into quarters, then roll them out, and use to line four 10cm (4in) loose-bottomed tart tins. Line with greaseproof paper and baking beans. Place on the heated baking sheet and cook for 10 minutes. Remove the beans and lining paper and return to the oven for 5 minutes. Leave to cool for a few minutes.
4 Trim away any rind on the goat's cheese and crumble the cheese into a bowl. Mix with the egg yolk and a splash of cream. Season with salt and pepper.
5 Reserve about a third of the red onion jam to use as garnish, then divide the rest between the tartlets and spoon the goat's cheese mixture on top. Return to the oven for 7–8 minutes, or until the tops are bubbling and tinged with brown.
6 For the salad, rinse the rocket leaves and pat dry. Pour the olive oil and lemon juice into a bowl, and season with plenty of salt and pepper. Add the rocket and toss gently to coat.
7 To serve, place a spoonful of red onion jam on the centre of each plate. Carefully remove the tarts from their tins and sit them on top of the jam. Top with rocket salad and serve.

BROAD BEAN AND PROSCIUTTO RAVIOLI WITH A RED PEPPER SAUCE

Will Adams tailor and 2010 quarter-finalist

PREPARATION TIME
1 hour, plus chilling

COOKING TIME
20 minutes

SERVES 4

FOR THE RAVIOLI
300g (10oz) tipo "00" flour
salt
2 large eggs
4 large egg yolks
200g (7oz) frozen baby broad beans
50g (1¾oz) ricotta
1 sprig of mint, leaves finely chopped
1 tsp balsamic vinegar
about 2 tbsp extra virgin olive oil

2 slices prosciutto, finely chopped
salt and freshly ground black pepper
1 large egg, beaten

FOR THE PEPPER SAUCE
2 romano peppers, tops removed,
   halved lengthways, and deseeded
15g (½oz) butter
2 tbsp olive oil
a few sprigs of lemon thyme

MASTER TIP

MAKING PASTA DOUGH

To make pasta dough, put the flour and a pinch of salt into a food processor, add the eggs and egg yolks and pulse until the mixture is just coming together. Tip out onto a lightly floured board and knead well until you have a smooth, silky, and elastic dough and a clean surface. This will take about 10 minutes. Wrap the dough in cling film and rest in the refrigerator for about 10 minutes.

1 Make the pasta dough (see MasterTip, left). For the filling, place the broad beans in a saucepan of boiling salted water and boil for 2–3 mins or until tender. Drain and refresh in cold water then slip off and discard the outer skins. Place the beans in a blender or food processor with the ricotta, mint, vinegar, and olive oil and blitz for a few seconds. Add the prosciutto and blend again briefly. Season to taste with salt and pepper.
2 Divide the dough into 2 and roll into sheets (see MasterTip, opposite).
3 Lay one sheet of pasta on a flat surface, lightly mark twelve 6–7cm (2½–3in) circles with a pastry cutter and place 1 tbsp of the filling into each circle. Brush egg around the broad bean mixture and lay on a second sheet of pasta, gently shaping it around the mixture. Take care not to leave any air bubbles. Using a pastry cutter, cut out circles and then lift the ravioli and press the edges with your finger tips to seal. (See also MasterClass pp.126–7 for advice on how to make ravioli.)
4 For the sauce, place the peppers, skin side up, on a baking tray and place under a hot grill for 4–5 minutes or until the skin has charred. Remove from the oven, wrap in foil and leave to cool. Then peel off the skin and very finely slice one half of a pepper and set aside to use as garnish. Place the rest in a blender and blitz until smooth. Heat the butter and 1–2 tbsp of olive oil in a saucepan, add the pepper sauce, season well, add most of the lemon thyme leaves and warm through.
5 To cook the ravioli, bring a pan of water to the boil. Brush off the excess flour from the pasta, place in the water and boil for 4–5 minutes or until *al dente*. Remove with a slotted spoon and drain on a tea towel.
6 To serve, put a small spoonful of sauce onto 4 plates, top with 3 ravioli, drizzle with more pepper sauce and garnish with the thin pepper slices and a few lemon thyme leaves.

GOAT'S CHEESE RAVIOLI WITH RAISIN, ROCKET, AND ALMOND BEURRE NOISETTE

Claire Lara lecturer and 2010 Professionals champion

FOR THE RAVIOLI
300g (10oz) tipo "00" flour
salt and freshly ground black pepper
3 large eggs
4 large egg yolks
200g (7oz) Saint Maure de Touraine
 goat's cheese, rind and straw removed
1 shallot, finely diced

FOR THE ACCOMPANIMENTS
100g (3½oz) golden raisins or
 golden sultanas
300ml (10fl oz) chicken stock
30g (1oz) flaked almonds
75g (2½oz) butter
100g (3½oz) rocket
small handful of pea shoots

PREPARATION TIME
1 hour, plus chilling

COOKING TIME
20 minutes

SERVES 4

1 Make the pasta dough using 2 of the eggs (see MasterTip, opposite). For the filling, crumble the cheese into a bowl and soften it by beating with a wooden spoon. Add the shallot and season well.

2 Divide the dough into 2 and roll into sheets (see MasterTip, right).

3 Lay 1 sheet of pasta on a flat surface, lightly mark twelve 6–7cm (2½–3in) circles with a pastry cutter and place 1 tbsp of the filling into each circle. Brush the remaining egg around the filling and lay on a second sheet of pasta, gently shaping around the mixture. Take care not to leave any air bubbles. Using a pastry cutter, cut out circles and then lift the ravioli and press the edges with your finger tips to seal. (See also MasterClass pp.126–7 for advice on how to make ravioli.)

4 To cook the ravioli, bring a pan of water to the boil. Brush off the excess flour from the pasta, place in the water and boil for 1 minute. Remove with a slotted spoon and plunge into iced water.

5 To make the raisin purée, place the raisins and chicken stock in a saucepan on medium heat. Cover with a lid and bubble for 10 minutes or until softened. Tip into a blender and blitz until smooth. Pass through a fine sieve, add seasoning and set aside.

6 For the almond *beurre noisette*, toast the almonds in a dry frying pan for 2–3 minutes until golden. Tip into a bowl and set aside. Melt the butter over medium heat in a saucepan until it starts to turn nutty brown. Remove from the heat, leave to cool and add the almonds.

7 To wilt the rocket, put it into a large pan with a splash of water and stir for 30 seconds or until slightly wilted. Remove from the heat.

8 Just before serving, heat a large pan of boiling water, add the blanched ravioli and boil for another 2–3 minutes or until *al dente*. Drain on a tea towel. Gently reheat the purée and *beurre noisette*. Place a spoonful of the purée onto 4 plates, top with some wilted rocket, add 3 ravioli per person, and drizzle with the *beurre noisette*.

MASTER TIP

MAKING PASTA SHEETS

Working with one piece of pasta dough at a time (cover any other pieces to prevent them drying out), roll the dough a few times to flatten it slightly. Dust both sides of the sheet with flour and then run it through the thickest setting on a pasta machine. Fold the length in half and repeat this process about 5 times, always dusting both sides with flour and running it through the settings, making it thinner each time. Hang up the sheet to dry and repeat with any other balls of dough.

OPEN LASAGNE OF ROASTED SQUASH AND WILD MUSHROOMS WITH SAGE BUTTER

Tim Kinnaird paediatrician and 2010 finalist

PREPARATION TIME
1 hour 15 minutes

COOKING TIME
1 hour

SERVES 4

FOR THE PASTA
good pinch of saffron strands
150g (5½oz) tipo "00" flour
salt
1 large egg
1 egg yolk

FOR THE SQUASH
1 small Crown Prince squash, peeled
   and seeded, about 350g (12oz) peeled
   weight, and cut into bite-sized pieces
1 tbsp extra virgin olive oil
salt and freshly ground black pepper
¼–½ tsp chilli flakes

FOR THE MUSHROOMS
knob of butter
200g (7oz) mixed wild mushrooms,
   such as girolles, porcini, and pied
   blue, wiped and evenly chopped
1 garlic clove, finely chopped
3 tbsp Marsala wine
2–3 tbsp chopped flat-leaf parsley
100ml (3½fl oz) double cream

FOR THE SAGE BUTTER
75g (2½oz) unsalted butter
small bunch of fresh sage, leaves only

MASTER TIP
CROWN PRINCE SQUASH

Crown Prince is a renowned variety of winter squash with tender, smooth-textured, sweet flesh. Winter squashes are harvested in autumn and because of their maturity can be stored over winter. Crown Prince is also good roasted and puréed, then used in soups and cakes, or as a filling for ravioli. The tough, pale blue-grey skin can be difficult to peel.

1 Preheat the oven to 220°C (425°F/Gas 7). Soak the saffron in 2 tsp warm water for 10 minutes. Make the pasta dough (see MasterTip, p.34), adding the saffron and water to the dough with the eggs.
2 Put the squash on a baking tray, drizzle with the olive oil and scatter over the salt, pepper, and chilli flakes. Roast for 35 minutes or until soft and tinged with brown. Shake the tin occasionally for even roasting.
3 To cook the mushrooms, melt the butter in a large sauté pan until it foams, add the mushrooms and salt and pepper and fry over high heat for 4–5 minutes or until just turning golden. Reduce the heat to medium, add the garlic and fry for 1 minute. Add the Marsala and bubble for a few minutes. Stir in the parsley and cream and set aside.
4 For the sage butter, melt the butter in a heavy pan and cook gently until it turns a warm nutty brown. Take care not to burn it. Set aside.
5 Divide the dough into 2 and roll into sheets (see MasterTip, p.35).
6 Bring a pan of water to the boil. Brush off the excess flour from the pasta, place in the water and boil for 4–5 minutes or until *al dente*. Drain in a colander and then cut out twelve 8cm (3in) diameter circles using an oiled round pastry cutter. Brush with olive oil and set aside.
7 Just before serving, tear up nearly all the sage leaves and add to the cooled butter. Warm gently for 1–2 minutes and also warm the mushroom mixture and squash. Stack up the pasta separated by a layer of squash and a layer of mushrooms. Spoon over the sage butter and garnish with the remaining sage.

SEARED SCALLOPS WITH MINT AND PEA RISOTTO

Christine Hamilton TV personality and 2010 Celebrity finalist

PREPARATION TIME
15 minutes

COOKING TIME
35 minutes

SERVES 4

2 tbsp olive oil
75g (2½oz) butter
4 spring onions, finely chopped
1 large garlic clove, finely chopped
200g (7oz) risotto rice
200ml (7fl oz) white wine
900ml (1½ pints) chicken stock
150g (5½oz) frozen peas

small bunch of mint leaves,
   finely chopped, plus extra to garnish
25g (scant 1oz) Parmesan cheese,
   grated
salt and freshly ground black pepper
12 scallops, roe removed
   (see MasterTip p.42)
squeeze of lemon juice

1 Heat 1 tbsp olive oil and 15g (½oz) butter in a heavy saucepan, add the spring onions and fry over medium heat for 2–3 minutes until softened. Add the garlic and fry for 1 minute. Add the rice and fry, stirring, for 2–3 minutes or until translucent. Add the wine, turn up the heat and bubble for 3 minutes. Turn down the heat, then gradually add 700–800ml (1–1¼ pints) of the stock, one ladleful at a time, allowing all the stock to be absorbed before adding the next ladleful. Keep adding stock until the rice is *al dente* – about 20 minutes.

2 Heat the remaining stock in a small saucepan, add the peas, and bring to the boil. Mash slightly with a potato masher to release the flavour of the peas, then pour into the risotto. Add the mint, a knob of butter, and the Parmesan, season to taste and stir well.

3 For the scallops, heat a large frying pan until smoking hot. Brush the scallops with olive oil and season well. Imagining the pan is a clockface, place the first scallop at 12 o'clock and then add the others, working clockwise. Once you have placed the last scallop into the pan, the first one will be ready to turn over – they need 45 seconds' cooking on each side.

4 Add a knob of butter to the pan, and once it is foaming, use to baste the scallops. Add a squeeze of lemon juice and tip the scallops onto a plate. To serve, divide the risotto between 4 plates and top each with 3 scallops. Drizzle over a little of the scallop cooking juices, garnish with the mint and serve immediately.

PAN-FRIED SEA SCALLOPS WITH PEAS, CRISPY BACON, AND QUAIL'S EGG
John Calton head chef and 2010 Professionals finalist

50g (1¾oz) cubed pancetta
dash of olive oil
40g (1¼oz) girolles, brushed clean
  (see MasterTip, p.140)
15g (½oz) butter
150g (5½oz) fresh peas, shelled,
  blanched, and refreshed in cold water
3 Baby Gem lettuce leaves, shredded
4 thin slices of pancetta
4 quail's eggs
dash of olive oil

FOR THE PEA VELOUTÉ
40g (1¼oz) butter
1 small shallot, finely sliced

salt and freshly ground black pepper
1 garlic clove, finely chopped
2 sprigs of fresh thyme, leaves picked
200ml (7fl oz) chicken stock
200g (7oz) frozen peas
dash of sherry vinegar

FOR THE SCALLOPS
12 large scallops, prepared
  (see MasterTip, p.42)
1 tbsp olive oil
30g (1oz) butter
squeeze of lemon juice

PREPARATION TIME
20 minutes

COOKING TIME
30 minutes

SERVES 4

1   Preheat the oven to 200°C (400°F/Gas 6). To make the pea velouté, melt the butter in a medium saucepan, add the shallot and a little salt and pepper, and fry over low to medium heat for 5 minutes. Add the garlic and thyme and fry for 2–3 minutes. Add the stock, bring to the boil, and simmer for 5 minutes. Pass through a sieve into a clean pan, bring back to the boil, add the peas and boil for 2–4 minutes. Blend with a hand-held blender or transfer to a food processor. Add a dash of sherry vinegar, season to taste, then chill in a bowl over a bowl of iced water.
2   Fry the pancetta cubes in olive oil until starting to colour, add the girolles, reduce the heat, then add a little butter, the blanched peas, and about 50–75ml (1¾–2½fl oz) water. Bubble over medium heat, add the lettuce and leave to wilt for 1–2 minutes. Season well and set aside.
3   Place the pancetta slices between 2 baking sheets each lined with baking paper and bake in the oven for 4–5 minutes or until crisp and golden. Remove from the oven and set aside.
4   Pan fry the quail's eggs in a little olive oil for 1 minute or until the whites have just set, then put aside.
5   Brush the scallops with oil and season lightly. Heat a large frying pan until smoking hot, add the scallops, and fry for 45 seconds each side. Add the butter, cook until it foams, and baste the scallops with it. Swirl lemon juice around the pan and add a little more seasoning.
6   To serve, place 3 scallops on each plate, dot round with the peas, bacon, and girolles mix, drizzle with the pea velouté, and garnish with the fried quail's eggs, and crisp pancetta.

MICHEL ROUX JR
"I love the combination of bacon, scallops, and peas and you have made it work beautifully. Adding the lettuce, quail's egg, and the mushrooms has made it an even better dish."

TARTARE OF SCALLOPS WITH OYSTER BEIGNET

John Calton head chef and 2010 Professionals finalist

PREPARATION TIME
50 minutes, plus chilling

COOKING TIME
5–10 minutes

SERVES 4

8 large king scallops in their shells
2 tbsp mascarpone cheese
4 Greek-style yogurt
1 banana shallot, very finely chopped
2 lemons
salt
1 tbsp dill, finely chopped
1 tbsp chives, finely chopped
1 tbsp chervil, finely chopped
3 tbsp caviar
8 raw whole langoustines

FOR THE OYSTER BEIGNET
8 oysters
10g (¼oz) baking powder
100g (3½oz) self-raising flour
pinch of salt
100ml (3½fl oz) ice-cold water
about 300ml (10fl oz) vegetable oil,
  for deep frying
100g (3½oz) plain flour

FOR THE CUCUMBER SOUP (OPTIONAL)
3 cucumbers, halved lengthways
  and deseeded
175ml (6fl oz) whole milk
3 tbsp full fat crème fraîche
1 tbsp mascarpone cheese
25g (scant 1oz) horseradish, grated
1½ tsp salt

MASTER TIP
KING SCALLOPS

The king scallop is caught in the deep waters of northern Europe. The corrugated shell prevents it from closing very tightly, unlike other bivalves. King scallops are at their very best pan-seared, although intense heat makes the roe or coral pop. Take care not to overcook.

1 Prepare the scallops (see MasterTip, p.42 and left). Pat dry with kitchen paper and chill to firm them. Dice into 1cm (½in) pieces, place in a bowl set over ice, and mix with the mascarpone and yogurt to bind. Add the shallot and the finely grated zest of 1 lemon. Season with salt, the juice of half a lemon, and the finely chopped herbs. Reserving 2 tsp to decorate, mix in the caviar. Place in 4 small metal rings or round metal pastry cutters on a tray in the refrigerator and leave to set for at least 30 minutes.

2 Steam the langoustines whole in a bamboo steamer for 3 minutes, then remove the heads, peel the tails, and set aside to cool.

3 Remove the oysters from their shells and reserve the juices. Rinse the oysters and dry with kitchen paper. Combine the baking powder, flour, and salt. Add the water until a thick batter consistency is reached.

4 Heat the oil in a pan to a temperature of 190–200ºC (375–400°F). Dust each oyster in a little plain flour, then dip in the batter and deep fry for about 3 minutes until golden all over. Drain on kitchen paper.

5 Assemble the dish with the scallops tartare, oyster beignet, and a garnish of caviar and prawns.

Option This dish goes well with cucumber soup. Slice the cucumbers into a shallow dish. Sprinkle salt over, leave for 10 minutes, rinse, and drain. Add the reserved oyster juice to the cucumber and liquidize with the milk, crème fraîche, and mascarpone in a food processor. Add horseradish to taste. Pass through a sieve and serve in cups.

SCALLOPS WITH POTATO PANCAKES, PANCETTA, AND A SALSA VERDE DRESSING

David Coulson head chef and 2010 Professionals finalist

PREPARATION TIME
40 minutes

COOKING TIME
40 minutes

SERVES 4

4 large scallops
4 slices white bread, crusts removed
4–5 tbsp olive oil
200g (7oz) butter
10 shallots, halved
300ml (10fl oz) chicken stock
2–3 tbsp red wine vinegar
4 Maris Piper potatoes, peeled
  and chopped
3 eggs, separated
50g (1¾oz) plain flour
salt and freshly ground black pepper

250g (9oz) frozen peas
1 packet of pea shoots, lamb's lettuce,
  or baby salad leaves
4 rashers of pancetta
1 Baby Gem lettuce

FOR THE DRESSING
large handful of flat-leaf parsley
50g (1¾oz) cornichons
1–2 tbsp English mustard
50g (1¾oz) capers, rinsed if salted
250ml (8fl oz) vegetable oil

MASTER TIP
PREPARING SCALLOPS

To prepare scallops, prise them open slightly at the hinge with an oyster-shucking knife. Turn them flat side down and slide a flexible filleting knife across the flat side of the shell to release the scallop. Open out the shell and scoop the scallop out whole from the rounded side with a spoon. Pull off the frill around the edge and the black stomach contents, then wash in cold water.

1 Preheat the oven to 200°C (400°F/Gas 6). Prepare the scallops (see MasterTip, left) and lay them to rest at room temperature on a cloth. Cut the bread into croûton shapes, coat in olive oil, and roast in the oven for 15–20 minutes until golden. Crush into breadcrumbs.
2 Melt 50g (1¾oz) of the butter in a pan and lightly fry the shallots. Add 200ml (7fl oz) of the chicken stock and the red wine vinegar and simmer until the shallots are tender. Blend to a purée and keep warm.
3 Boil the potatoes in salted water for about 15 minutes until cooked, then drain and mash. Whisk the egg whites into stiff peaks. Add the yolks to the mash and fold in the egg whites and flour. Season with salt and pepper. Heat 50g (1¾oz) butter in a pan, spoon in tablespoons of the potato and fry until golden. Cut into rounds with a pastry cutter.
4 To make the dressing, put the parsley, cornichons, mustard, and capers in a food processor with 3 tbsp of oil and blitz to a paste. Add the remaining oil and blend well. Season and set aside.
5 Reduce the remaining chicken stock by a third, then add the peas. Cover, return to the boil and simmer for 3–4 minutes, then add 50g (1¾oz) butter. When cooked, add the pea shoots and stir through.
6 Put the pancetta between 2 baking sheets to keep it flat and roast in the oven for 15–20 minutes until crispy. Fry the scallops in a hot pan with 50g (1¾oz) of butter until golden, 1–2 minutes each side.
7 Lay the lettuce leaves on each plate. Add a potato cake and a spoonful of shallot purée. Top with a scallop and a rasher of crispy pancetta. Scatter the peas and pea shoots around the plate, and dress with salsa verde oil and a sprinkle of crushed croûtons.

SEARED ORKNEY SCALLOPS AND GLAZED PORK BELLY WITH SWEETCORN

Gary Cooke sous chef and 2010 Professionals quarter-finalist

200ml (7fl oz) Minus 8 Vinegar, or a very good sherry vinegar
16g sachet Vege-Gel
3 sweetcorn cobs, kernels cut off, cob chopped
200ml (7fl oz) fish stock
2 banana shallots, chopped
4 garlic cloves, chopped
4 tbsp chopped thyme
25g (scant 1oz) unsalted butter
3 tbsp vegetable oil
2 sheets of nori seaweed, shredded
1 tsp dried powdered scallop roe (see MasterTip, right)

150g (5½oz) caster sugar
salt and freshly ground white pepper
4 x 50g (1¾oz) cooked and pressed pork belly pieces, or thick unsmoked streaky bacon, or gammon
100ml (3½fl oz) pork demi-glace or concentrated pork stock
4 slices of imberico ham, 2mm (⅛in) thick, or pancetta
2 tbsp chopped chives
50g (1¾oz) maple syrup
4 XXL size hand-dived Orkney scallops
juice of 1 lemon

PREPARATION TIME
30 minutes, plus drying and chilling

COOKING TIME
40–50 minutes

SERVES 4

1 Put 100ml (3½fl oz) vinegar in a small pan, sprinkle the Vege-Gel into it and stir. Heat gently, stirring until thickened, then pour onto a plate and allow to set for at least 1 hour. Cut into rounds.
2 Preheat the oven to 200°C (400°F/Gas 6). Put the corn cob and kernels in a pan with the stock and 200ml (7fl oz) water and simmer for 10 minutes. Drain the liquid and reserve. Set the corn kernels aside.
3 Sweat the shallots, garlic, and thyme in a pan with the butter. Add the stock and cook until tender. Blend to make a purée. Set aside.
4 Heat 2 tbsp of oil in a pan and fry the seaweed for 2–3 minutes until crisp. Sprinkle with a pinch of powdered scallop roe, sugar, and salt.
5 Fry the pork for 4–5 minutes until crisp on both sides. Add 100ml (3½fl oz) vinegar, bubble for a minute, and then add the demi-glace. Reduce the sauce to a glaze, spooning over the pork occasionally.
6 Add the remaining sugar to 100ml (3½fl oz) water in a pan and heat until the sugar has dissolved. Add 50g (1¾oz) corn and boil for 4–5 minutes until caramel in colour. Drain and pat dry with kitchen paper. Heat 1 tbsp of oil in a pan and fry the corn for 2–3 minutes, until crisp.
7 Place the ham between 2 baking sheets in the oven for 15 minutes. Heat the remaining corn in a pan with 2–3 tbsp of purée, the chives, seasoning, and a little maple syrup. Season the scallops and sear in a frying pan for 2–3 minutes until golden. Finish with lemon juice.
8 Put a spoonful of corn and maple syrup, some pork and a scallop on each plate. Top with a round of vinegar jelly, the ham, and the crunchy sweetcorn. Add a smear of shallot purée and some seaweed.

MASTER TIP
POWDERED SCALLOP ROE

To make powdered scallop roe, preheat the oven to 150°C (300°F/Gas 2). Slice the roe in half, and place on a sheet of greaseproof paper on a baking sheet. Place in the oven for 2½–3 hours, turning occasionally, until dried through. Leave to cool, then blitz in a food processor to make a powder.

SAFFRON GLAZED SCALLOPS WITH APPLE AND PISTACHIO PURÉE AND PISTACHIO OIL

Dhruv Baker sales director and 2010 champion

PREPARATION TIME
40 minutes

COOKING TIME
20 minutes

SERVES 4

FOR THE PURÉE
1 tbsp light olive oil
1 cinnamon stick
6 whole cloves
1 star anise
2 Braeburn apples, peeled, cored, and chopped
50g (1¾oz) unsalted pistachios, shelled
juice of 1 lemon
salt and freshly ground black pepper

FOR THE OIL
50g (1¾oz) unsalted pistachios, shelled
3 tbsp extra virgin olive oil

FOR THE SCALLOPS
1 tbsp sherry or red wine vinegar
1 tbsp clear honey
small pinch of saffron strands
12 scallops, cleaned and corals removed (see MasterTip, p.42)

GREGG WALLACE

"I would eat the whole lot happily."

1   To make the purée, heat the olive oil in a saucepan with the cinnamon, cloves, and star anise, letting them fry gently for 2–3 minutes, or until they begin to release their aromas. Add the apples with 100ml (3½fl oz) of water and cook over low heat for 5–10 minutes, or until very soft. Remove the spices and add the pistachios. Cook for about 5 minutes, then transfer to a hand-held blender or food processor, and purée. Pass through a sieve into a bowl, add a little lemon juice and season to taste with salt and pepper. Cover and set aside.

2   To make the pistachio oil, put the pistachios into a clean blender or a food processor, and add the extra virgin olive oil. Blitz in brief bursts, so the nuts are chopped but not to a smooth purée as you want to retain some texture and bite. Spoon into a bowl and also set aside.

3   For the scallops, heat the vinegar in a small saucepan until reduced to about 1 tsp. Stir in the honey and saffron and keep warm over low heat.

4   Heat a large non-stick frying pan until searing hot. Season the scallops with salt and pepper and carefully place 6 of them around the edge of the pan, and cook for about 1 minute. Then turn over and cook for a further 1–2 minutes or until cooked through. Using tongs, dip each into the honey glaze on 1 side only and set aside to keep warm while cooking the remaining scallops in the same way.

5   Spoon 3 rounds of apple purée onto each serving plate and set a scallop on top, glazed side up. Spoon over a little pistachio oil, to serve.

LANGOUSTINE RISOTTO WITH COURGETTE AND ROASTED CHERRY TOMATOES

Neil Stuke actor and 2010 Celebrity semi-finalist

PREPARATION TIME
10 minutes

COOKING TIME
20 minutes

SERVES 4

3 bunches of cherry tomatoes on the vine, about 500g (1lb 2oz)
8 tbsp olive oil
salt and freshly ground black pepper
20 langoustines
3 banana shallots, finely chopped
300g (10oz) risotto rice
2 garlic cloves, chopped

100ml (3½fl oz) vermouth
50g (1¾oz) butter
juice of 1 lemon
2 courgettes, finely sliced
900ml (1½ pints) chicken stock
50g (1¾oz) Parmesan cheese, grated
1 bunch of basil leaves, sliced
pinch of saffron

GREGG WALLACE

"The dish is cooked perfectly, absolutely wonderful textures."

1 Preheat the oven to 200°C (400°F/Gas 6). Put the cherry tomatoes on a baking sheet with 2–3 tbsp of the oil and sprinkle with salt and pepper. Bake for 20 minutes or until soft.
2 Blanch the langoustines in a large pan of boiling water for 1–2 minutes. Remove from the water and when cool enough to touch, discard the heads and peel and devein the tails.
3 In a large sauté pan, heat 2–3 tbsp of the oil and add the shallots. Fry for 2–3 minutes until golden brown. Add the rice and half the garlic and stir well. Pour the vermouth into the pan and allow to bubble for a minute.
4 Add a ladleful of hot stock and stir well until the liquid is absorbed. Continue gradually adding two-thirds of the stock to the rice in the same manner.
5 Once two-thirds of the stock has been absorbed into the rice, add the roasted tomatoes, crushing them into the risotto, along with the courgettes. Add another ladleful of stock and stir well until the liquid is absorbed. Continue gradually adding the stock to the rice in the same manner until the rice is cooked *al dente* and all the liquid has been absorbed.
6 Add 25g (scant 1oz) of the butter and the lemon juice and stir well. Stir in the Parmesan, most of the basil (reserving some for garnish), and season to taste.
7 Heat a small pan with 2 tbsp of the oil and the rest of the butter. Add the remaining garlic and the saffron. Flash fry the langoustine tails in the flavoured butter for 2 minutes.
8 Serve the risotto in small bowls. Add 5 langoustine tails to each one and garnish with basil.

SALT AND PEPPER SQUID WITH CHILLI DIPPING SAUCE
Skills test for contestants in Celebrity MasterChef 2010

250g (9oz) fresh squid
4 tsp Szechuan peppercorns
4 tsp sea salt
4 tbsp plain flour
4 tbsp cornflour
groundnut oil for deep frying

FOR THE SAUCE
1 red chilli, finely chopped
2 tbsp rice wine vinegar
juice and zest of 1 lime
1 tsp fish sauce
2 tsp caster sugar

PREPARATION TIME
15 minutes

COOKING TIME
15 minutes

SERVES 4

1 For the dipping sauce, combine all the ingredients in a small bowl and stir until the sugar has dissolved. Set aside until needed.

2 Separate the tentacles from the squid. Lightly score the squid all over and cut into bite-sized pieces.

3 Crush the peppercorns in a pestle and mortar, then add to a bowl with the salt, flour, and cornflour. Toss the squid pieces and tentacles in the seasoned flour and shake to remove any excess.

4 Heat the oil in a deep frying pan and fry the squid in small batches until crisp and golden. Do not overcrowd the pan or they will not colour well. Remove from the oil using a slotted spoon and drain on kitchen paper.

5 Serve the crispy squid with the chilli dipping sauce.

MasterChef 2010 Champion
DHRUV BAKER

"Finding myself in the final was amazing but also hugely intimidating. Everything I had cooked up to this point was just to get here and I knew I had to show John and Gregg that I was worthy of that title. I also knew I had to really step it up competing against people like Alex and Tim, who had shown flair and excellent cooking throughout. I decided to have a little bit of fun with the pudding and also take a little bit of a gamble – especially with the masala tea ice cream. Thankfully, both John and Gregg got exactly what I was trying to do and the gamble paid off!"

STARTER

SPICED LOBSTER WITH FENNEL, CELERIAC PURÉE, AND A FENNEL CHILLI MAYONNAISE p.50

"Dhruv has a talent for cooking amazing fusion food, and this dish is wonderful with the salty lobster, mellow celeriac, and then the ginger coming through. I love it!" JOHN

MAIN

ROAST LOIN OF VENISON WITH CHESTNUTS, VENISON JUS, AND CHILLI CHOCOLATE OIL p.240

"Dhruv is probably one of the most amazing talents I have ever seen. He has the palate of an angel, and I fell in love with his food."
GREGG

DESSERT

MASALA TEA ICE CREAM AND SPICED SAUTERNES-POACHED PEAR WITH A CHOCOLATE TRUFFLE p.274

"This is a really clever dessert, even though it is cold it delivers an amazing warmth on your palate. I thought it looked stunning and tasted even better." JOHN

SPICED LOBSTER WITH FENNEL, CELERIAC PURÉE, AND A FENNEL CHILLI MAYONNAISE

Dhruv Baker sales director and 2010 champion

PREPARATION TIME
30–40 minutes

COOKING TIME
30 minutes

SERVES 4

1 small live lobster
1½ tsp fennel seeds
2 pinches of saffron
100ml (3½fl oz) dry white wine
10 black peppercorns
3 garlic cloves, 2 chopped
few pieces of dried fennel (optional)
6 baby fennel bulbs, halved
150g (5½oz) unsalted butter

FOR THE MAYONNAISE
2 egg yolks
2 tsp white wine vinegar
1 small red chilli, deseeded and
  finely chopped
½ tsp fennel seeds, finely crushed

¼ tsp caster sugar
200ml (7fl oz) groundnut oil
salt and freshly ground black pepper
juice of ½ lemon

FOR THE PURÉE
1 small celeriac, about 500g (1lb 2oz),
  peeled and diced
250ml (8fl oz) whole milk
1 tsp caraway seeds
2–3 tbsp double cream
freshly ground white pepper

TO GARNISH
1 tbsp chopped chives
handful of microgreens

JOHN TORODE "The saltiness from the lobster, sharpness of the fennel, a little warmth coming from the ginger, and a wonderful flavour of the celeriac sitting right at the back of your palate. I love it."

1 Put the lobster, 1 tsp of fennel seeds, a pinch of saffron, the wine, peppercorns, whole garlic clove, and dried fennel (if using) into a large pan and cover with boiling water. Cover and boil rapidly for 7–8 minutes. Lift out the lobster and when cool enough to handle, remove the claw meat. When cold, remove the meat from each half in one piece.
2 For the mayonnaise, put the egg yolks, vinegar, chilli, fennel, and sugar into a food processor. Mix briefly. With the machine running, gradually pour in the oil. Season with salt, pepper, and lemon juice. Set aside and chill.
3 Boil the celeriac and caraway in the milk for 15–20 minutes. Drain, reserving the milk. Purée the celeriac, adding a little of the milk and the cream, until smooth. Add seasoning. Blanch the fennel bulbs in boiling salted water for 5 minutes. Drain and refresh. Set aside.
4 Melt the butter in a pan. Spoon half into another pan. Add the remaining saffron and fennel seeds and the garlic to one pan, then add the lobster and spoon the butter over it. Heat the second pan of butter until foaming, then cook gently for 2–3 minutes until it turns nut brown.
5 Spoon the purée onto the plates. Top 3 with half a baby fennel and 3 with slices of lobster, alternately. Place a smear of mayonnaise in the centre, and put the lobster on top. Spoon the juices over. Reheat the *beurre noisette*, whizz to a foam with a hand-held blender, and spoon over the dish. Garnish with chives and microgreens.

SALAD OF LOBSTER, BASIL, MANGO, AND AVOCADO

John Calton head chef and 2010 Professionals finalist

PREPARATION TIME
50 minutes, plus chilling

COOKING TIME
15 minutes

SERVES 4

1 live lobster
1 ripe mango, chopped
grated zest and juice of 1 lime
1 large bunch of basil
360ml (12fl oz) olive oil
½ avocado

FOR THE BATTER
75g (2½oz) self-raising flour
25g (scant 1oz) baking powder
pinch of sea salt
200ml (7fl oz) sparkling water, chilled

FOR THE TIAN
2 plum tomatoes on the vine, halved,
 deseeded, and finely diced
1 ripe mango, finely diced
½ avocado, sliced into ribbons with
 a vegetable peeler
2 spring onions, finely sliced
2 tbsp olive oil
salt and freshly ground black pepper
1 bag of mixed salad
coarse and fine white and black pepper

GREGG WALLACE

"Absolutely lovely."

1 Plunge the lobster into boiling salted water and poach for 8–10 minutes until it is pink. Drain the lobster and carefully remove the meat from the claws and shell. Leave to cool, then chill. Reserve any small pieces of meat from the claws for the tian.
2 Place the mango in a food processor with the juice and zest of 1 lime and 12 basil leaves. Blend, slowly trickling in 50ml (1¾fl oz) of olive oil to make an emulsion. Transfer to a squeezy bottle, or set aside in a bowl.
3 Blanch half of the remaining basil leaves and refresh in cold water. Drain and pat dry with kitchen paper, then blend with 50ml (1¾fl oz) olive oil to make basil oil. Blend the avocado with the basil oil, place in a piping bag or a small bowl and set aside.
4 Make a tempura batter by mixing the flour, baking powder, salt, and sparkling water. Set aside.
5 Make the tian by binding the tomatoes, mango, avocado, spring onions, and any fragments of lobster meat from the claws with 2 tbsp of olive oil. Season, place in 4 metal rings and chill.
6 Heat the remaining olive oil in a pan. Dip the meat from the lobster claws in the tempura batter and deep fry for 2–3 minutes until golden brown. Lift out and drain on kitchen paper.
7 Dress the meat from the tail and the salad leaves with lime juice and seasoning.
8 On each plate, assemble the salad, the fried lobster claw, the tian topped with the dressed tail, a smear of basil and avocado oil, and the mango emulsion.

FISH PAKORAS WITH RAITA AND CORIANDER CHUTNEY

Nargis Chaudhary physiotherapist and 2010 semi-finalist

PREPARATION TIME
30 minutes

COOKING TIME
5–10 minutes

SERVES 4

250g (9oz) gram flour
1 tsp ground paprika
1 tsp ground cumin powder
1 tsp chilli powder
1 tsp garam masala
1 tsp salt
1 large cod loin, approx. 350g (12oz)
vegetable oil for deep frying

FOR THE CHUTNEY
1 large bunch of coriander
juice of 1 lemon
1 red medium-hot fresh chilli, deseeded
1 green medium-hot fresh chilli,
  deseeded

2 garlic cloves
3 tbsp oil

FOR THE RAITA
150g (5½oz) plain yogurt
salt and freshly ground black pepper
1 tsp mint sauce
½ cucumber, finely chopped
3 tbsp milk (optional)

FOR THE GARNISH
1 lemon, cut into wedges
bunch of coriander, chopped

JOHN TORODE

"I really like those little fish parcels: crispy on the outside and with a wonderful, spicy, big-flavoured chutney."

1 For the coriander chutney, put the coriander, lemon juice, chillies, and garlic in a blender or food processor. Add the oil and blitz until the mixture reaches a pesto consistency. Place in the fridge to chill while you make the rest of the dish.
2 To make the raita, put the yogurt in a bowl, add a pinch of salt and pepper, the mint sauce, and the cucumber, and mix together. If the mixture is too thick, add some milk. Place in the fridge.
3 Put the gram flour and all the ground spices and salt in a mixing bowl. Mix together then add 200ml (7fl oz) of water to make a fairly thick batter.
4 Wash the cod, cut it into small, even-sized squares measuring about 2cm (¾in), and sprinkle with salt.
5 Heat the oil in a deep fat fryer until it is very hot. Dip the fish into the pakora batter. Drop into the hot oil in small batches and cook for 3–4 minutes. When browned, remove and drain on kitchen paper.
6 Divide the pakoras between 4 plates, garnish with a thin wedge of lemon and the coriander, and serve with the two sauces.

SEARED PAVÉ OF BRILL ON PARSNIP PURÉE WITH RAISIN BUTTER SAUCE

Matthew Worswick sous chef and 2010 Professionals semi-finalist

500g (1lb 2oz) parsnips, cut into 3cm (1¼in) cubes
2 banana shallots or 4 small shallots, chopped
4 garlic cloves, sliced
1 bay leaf
2 sprigs of thyme
350ml (12fl oz) whole milk
salt and freshly ground white pepper
1½ tbsp olive oil
4 fillets of brill, approx. 80g (2¾oz) each

FOR THE SAUCE
100ml (3½fl oz) dry white wine
100ml (3½fl oz) white wine vinegar
500ml (16fl oz) double cream
150g (5½oz) chilled unsalted butter, cubed
3 spring onions, finely chopped
10g (¼oz) chives, finely chopped
50g (1¾oz) golden raisins, or large regular ones

PREPARATION TIME
30 minutes

COOKING TIME
40 minutes

SERVES 4

1 Place the parsnips in a medium saucepan with the shallots, garlic, bay leaf, and thyme. Pour in the milk and add some salt. Bring to the boil carefully and reduce the heat to a simmer. Cook the parsnips for 20 minutes, partially covered, taking care that the milk does not boil.
2 When the parsnips are cooked, remove the bay leaf and thyme and blend the parsnips, milk, shallots, and garlic using a hand-held blender or by transferring to a food processor until a really smooth purée is reached. Season with salt and white pepper. Place back in a clean pan and keep warm.
3 To make the sauce, place the wine and vinegar in a small saucepan and bring to a rapid boil. Reduce to a quarter of its volume, which will take about 5 minutes. Add the cream and bring back up to a rapid simmer. Reduce again for about 3 minutes until halved and starting to thicken.
4 Reduce the heat under the sauce and start to add the butter cubes, whisking them in to melt and thicken the sauce, making it really glossy. Add the spring onions, chives, and golden raisins, and season to taste.
5 Heat a large frying pan and pour in the olive oil. Season the brill fillets with salt and pepper, and when the oil is hot, fry for 2–3 minutes on each side, depending on thickness. The fish should flake easily.
6 Put some parsnip purée in the middle of each warmed plate and arrange a piece of fish on top. Spoon the sauce over the fish and serve.

MASTER TIP
BRILL

Also known as "kite" and "pearl", brill was at one time an underrated fish but is now well regarded. Similar in appearance to turbot, it has an equally fine, sweet flavour but is more flaky. Best pan-fried, grilled, or roasted.

DRESSING A COOKED CRAB

"Dressing" is the process of extracting the meat of a cooked crab. White meat is found in the claws, legs, and main body; brown meat (offal) in the carapace. Always cool crabs rapidly after cooking to help the meat draw away from the shell.

1 Separate the crab

Pull away the claws and legs and set aside, then twist off the apron or tail flap and discard. To separate the body from the carapace, first crack it under the tail then prise the two sections apart, holding the carapace in one hand and pulling the body from the tail end.

2 Remove the inedible parts

Remove the gills or "dead man's fingers" attached to the main body, and there may also be a few stray gills left in the carapace. Remove the stomach sac as well, which will either be attached to the body or in the carapace.

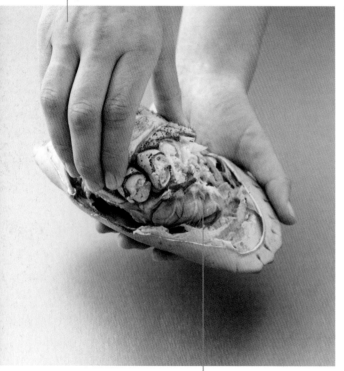

The body is firmly set in the carapace and needs a degree of force to remove it.

"One of my favourite crustaceans.
Pick through the meat carefully
to remove any shell as it's not
pleasant to chew on!"

3 Pick and scoop the meat

Cut the body of the crab into quarters and pick out the white meat, using a seafood fork or lobster pick. Take care to remove any shards of shell and pieces of membrane. Scoop out the brown meat from the carapace with a spoon.

4 Crack the claws and legs

Break the shell of the claws with a lobster or nut cracker. Extract the meat and remove the piece of thick cartilage, then check for any shell and membrane. Crack the legs across the narrowest part of the shell to avoid crushing the meat, then pick it out with a fork.

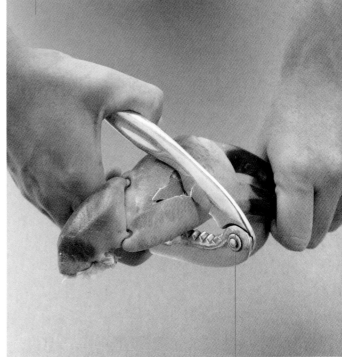

Avoid using too much force as this shatters the shell into lots of small pieces.

MONKFISH WRAPPED IN PANCETTA WITH BEURRE BLANC

Neil Stuke actor and 2010 Celebrity semi-finalist

PREPARATION TIME
30 minutes

COOKING TIME
30 minutes

SERVES 4

handful of chervil roots (optional),
  peeled and chopped into 1cm (½in)
  thick slices
12 Jerusalem artichokes, approx. 900g
  (2lb) in total, peeled and chopped into
  1cm (½in) thick slices
180g (6½oz) pack of thinly
  sliced pancetta
1 monkfish tail, approx. 400g (14oz),
  boned to give 2 fillets (similar to the
  thickness of one thick sushi roll)
1 tbsp olive oil

knob of butter
sea salt and freshly ground
  black pepper

FOR THE BEURRE BLANC
2 shallots, roughly chopped
150ml (5fl oz) dry white wine
2 tbsp white wine vinegar
2 tsp coriander seeds, crushed
100g (3½oz) unsalted butter, chilled
2 tbsp chives, snipped

JOHN TORODE

"Sweetness from the vegetables, then you get hit by the saltiness of the bacon, and then a richness that comes from the monkfish. That is delicious: it sang, it danced in my mouth."

1 Preheat the oven to 200°C (400°F/Gas 6). Bring a large saucepan of water to the boil and blanch the chervil roots (if using) and artichoke slices for 1–2 minutes.
2 Wrap the pancetta around the monkfish fillets and leave to rest.
3 Heat the olive oil and butter in a frying pan. Remove the artichokes and chervil roots from the boiling water, drain, and pat dry and then fry in the pan for 1–2 minutes or until golden brown. Season, transfer to a baking sheet and roast in the oven for 20 minutes.
4 Pan-fry the monkfish, turning it to brown the pancetta, and then place it in some buttered foil. Wrap it up and place on another baking tray and cook in the oven for 20 minutes.
5 Meanwhile, prepare the beurre blanc. Add the dry white wine, white wine vinegar, coriander seeds, and shallots to the pan, and season.
6 Bring the liquid to the boil and reduce by half. Then pass it through a sieve and bring the reduction back to the heat, adding cold cubes of butter and stirring constantly. Add the chives and take off the heat. Let it rest.
7 Take the fish and vegetables out of the oven, leaving the fish in the foil. Lay the roasted vegetables in a line down the centre of each plate. Open the foil, slice the monkfish and lay half over the roots on each plate. Then spoon over the beurre blanc, pour a little around the plate and serve.

MICHEL ROUX JR'S
STUFFED SEA BASS
WITH FENNEL AND TOMATO

This is a Roux family classic and is very close to my heart. The success of the dish rests on being able to fillet the fish without piercing the belly.

4 small sea bass
1 onion, finely chopped
2 fennel bulbs, 1 bulb finely chopped
3 tbsp olive oil, plus extra for greasing
100ml (3½fl oz) double cream
3 tbsp pastis
2 tbsp cornflour
salt and freshly ground black pepper

3–4 sprigs of thyme
2 bay leaves
100ml (3½fl oz) dry white wine
50g (1¾oz) dried tomatoes, finely chopped
12 baby onions or small shallots, peeled
knob of butter

PREPARATION TIME
25 minutes

COOKING TIME
25 minutes

SERVES 4

1 Preheat the oven to 200ºC (400°F/Gas 6), and place 2 large baking sheets in the oven. Prepare the fish by removing the scales, fins, and head. With a filleting knife, slit each fish along the backbone and remove the spine and guts, opening out the fish; take care not to pierce the belly. Remove the pin bones with tweezers, rinse in cold water, and dry.

2 Sweat the chopped onion in olive oil in a saucepan over low heat for about 5 minutes. Add the chopped fennel, cover, and cook for 2–3 minutes, stirring occasionally, until nearly tender. Pour in the cream and reduce the sauce until it starts to thicken.

3 In a separate small bowl, mix the pastis with the cornflour until smooth. Pour into the fennel mixture and whisk for 15 seconds, then remove from the heat. Season with salt and pepper and set aside.

4 Slice the remaining fennel lengthways into 1cm (½in) strips. Heat the oil in a frying pan and cook with the thyme and bay leaves for 1–2 minutes, or until browned. Add the wine and bring to the boil for 1 minute. Add the tomatoes and baby onions or shallots and 150ml (5fl oz) of water. Reduce the heat, cover, and simmer for about 10 minutes, or until the vegetables are tender. Remove the bay leaves and finish with the butter and some seasoning.

5 Place each fish on a sheet of oiled greaseproof paper. Stuff the fish with the fennel. Season and wrap in paper, twisting the ends to secure. Cook on the baking sheets in the oven for 8 minutes. Then turn the fish over and cook for a further 7–10 minutes or until cooked through.

6 Serve in the greaseproof paper, but unwrapped and with the fennel and tomato to garnish.

PAN-FRIED RED MULLET WITH FISH BONE SAUCE, FENNEL PURÉE, BUTTERED SPIDER CRAB, AND FENNEL AND ORANGE SALAD

Claire Lara lecturer and 2010 Professionals champion

PREPARATION TIME
30 minutes

COOKING TIME
20–25 minutes

SERVES 4

200g (7oz) unsalted butter
2 stalks of lemongrass, crushed
4 plum tomatoes on the vine, halved
  and deseeded
olive oil for frying, roasting, and
  salad dressing
salt and freshly ground black pepper
3 bulbs of fennel
2 shallots, sliced
200ml (8fl oz) Pernod
250ml (9fl oz) chicken stock

2 large or 4 small whole red mullet,
  cleaned, de-scaled, filleted, bones
  picked and set aside
  (see MasterTip, opposite)
200ml (8fl oz) white wine
300g (10oz) cooked spider crab meat
  (approx. 2 claws), picked
1 spring onion, chopped
1 blood orange, peeled and segmented
juice of 1 lemon
1–2 tbsp Chardonnay vinegar
bunch of dill, chopped

MICHEL ROUX JR

"It's a very complete dish. It's cooking of the highest order."

1 Make lemongrass butter by warming 125g (4½oz) butter in a pan. Add the lemongrass stalks and leave to cool and infuse for 20 minutes.
2 Preheat the oven to 200°C (400°F/Gas 6). To make the tomatoes confit, lay the tomatoes on a baking tray with a drizzle of oil and seasoning. Roast in the oven for 20-25 minutes, turning once half way through cooking. Allow to cool, remove skin, then dice. Set aside.
3 Finely slice 2 of the fennel bulbs and sweat with the shallot in a pan with 2 tbsp of olive oil. Add the Pernod and reduce by half. Add the stock and reduce by half again. Blend until smooth and season.
4 Fry the reserved fish bones in 50g (1¾oz) of butter. Once browned, add the wine and reduce by half. Pass through a fine sieve, then whisk the lemongrass-infused butter into the sauce. Pass through a sieve.
5 Finely slice the remaining fennel, reserving the fronds, and leave in iced water, so they don't discolour.
6 Warm the crab meat in 25g (scant 1oz) butter in a frying pan. Mix in the spring onions, tomato confit, and seasoning.
7 Heat 2 tbsp of the oil in a pan with a knob of butter and fry the fish fillets, skin side down, for 2–3 minutes on each side.
8 For the salad, cut the orange into cubes and chop the fennel tops. Make a dressing by combining 1 tbsp of vinegar for every 2 tbsp olive oil and add seasoning. Drain the fennel slices and mix in a bowl with the orange, dill, fennel tops, and the dressing. Reheat the fennel purée.
9 To serve, divide the tomato and crab between the plates. Top with the fish, and spoon the salad alongside. Drizzle over the fish sauce.

ROAST RED MULLET WITH PLUM TOMATOES AND TAPENADE

Lee Groves head chef and 2010 Professionals semi-finalist

700g (1lb 9oz) ripe plum tomatoes
  on the vine
about 100ml (3½fl oz) olive oil
salt and freshly ground white pepper
350g (12oz) wild garlic leaves with
  stems, or baby spinach leaves
4 small red mullet, approx. 300g (10oz)
  each, gutted, descaled, and filleted
  (see MasterTip, right)

pinch of saffron strands
  (see MasterTip, p.147)

FOR THE TAPENADE
100g (3½oz) pitted black olives
50g (1¾oz) anchovies in brine
1 garlic clove
bunch of basil

PREPARATION TIME
30 minutes

COOKING TIME
20 minutes

SERVES 4

1 Heat the oven to 200°C (400°F/Gas 6). Reserve 2 of the tomatoes, then halve and deseed the rest and place in a bowl. Toss in 2–3 tbsp of oil then put the tomatoes on a baking sheet and season. Bake for 15–20 minutes or until collapsed. Pour into a bowl and cover.
2 Score a cross in the top of the reserved tomatoes, blanch in boiling water for 2 minutes and then plunge into cold water. Peel off the skin, cut in half, scoop out the seeds, and cut out 8 small discs with a pastry cutter. Season and heat the discs gently under a low grill.
3 For the tapenade, put all the ingredients in a blender or food processor, reserving 4 basil leaves to garnish. Purée for 1 minute, then gradually add 60ml (2fl oz) of oil while the machine is running and blend until smooth. Season with pepper.
4 Wipe the blender or food processor and then blitz the baked tomatoes until they are smooth. Pass through a fine sieve, season, and keep warm.
5 Blanch the garlic or spinach leaves in boiling water for 1 minute and then plunge into cold water. Wipe the blender or food processor once again and blitz the garlic or spinach leaves with a little oil, until smooth.
6 Sprinkle the fish with 2–3 tbsp of oil, add a few saffron strands and then pan-fry, skin side down, for 1–2 minutes or until golden and crisp. Turn over and cook for 2 more minutes. When the fish is cooked, add the reserved basil leaves to the hot oil in the pan and fry until crisp. Set aside to garnish.
7 To serve, put a swipe of the garlic or spinach purée down 1 side of each plate and a swipe of tomato dressing up the other side. Overlap 2 tomato discs in the centre, lay a fish across and put a quenelle of tapenade on top. Garnish each serving with a deep-fried basil leaf.

MASTER TIP
RED MULLET

Delicately flavoured, the flesh of this highly-prized fish is off-white, becoming white when cooked. Red mullet is best cooked whole as it has many bones which can be located more easily after cooking. Trim and scale to prepare, but the liver of a red mullet is considered fine eating and should be left intact.

SMOKED HADDOCK TIMBALE WITH POACHED QUAIL'S EGG

Christine Hamilton TV personality and 2010 Celebrity finalist

PREPARATION TIME
15 minutes

COOKING TIME
30 minutes

SERVES 4

4 baby beetroots (or 1 mature beetroot, peeled and quartered)
salt and freshly ground black pepper
splash of olive oil
2–3 sprigs of thyme (optional)
butter for greasing
150g (5½oz) smoked haddock fillet, skin removed
400ml (14fl oz) double cream
4 egg yolks
2 tbsp chopped dill
2 tbsp chopped chives
4 quail's eggs

FOR THE SALAD DRESSING
1 tbsp lemon juice
½ tbsp olive oil
½ tbsp walnut oil
½ tbsp wholegrain mustard
1 tbsp caster sugar
ground black pepper

TO SERVE
small bag of rocket and watercress
50g (1¾oz) walnut pieces

1 Preheat the oven to 170°C (340°F/Gas 3–4). Season the beetroots with salt and pepper and wrap tightly in kitchen foil with olive oil and thyme (if using). Roast in a corner of the oven for 30 minutes.
2 Butter 4 timbale moulds. Poach the haddock lightly for 2–3 minutes in 200ml (7fl oz) of cream. Drain and reserve the cream.
3 In a bowl, whisk together the reserved and remaining cream, egg yolks, dill, chives, and a good pinch of black pepper.
4 Break the haddock into pieces with a fork and divide between the timbale moulds. Pour the cream mixture into each mould.
5 Place the moulds in a deep roasting tray or oven dish. Add 3–4cm (1¼–1½in) of water to the tray or dish before placing it in the preheated oven on a high shelf. Bake for 20 minutes, or until the timbales are set and do not wobble when moved.
6 Meanwhile, poach the quail's eggs by breaking each gently into a pan of just-simmering water and poaching for 30 seconds. When cooked, plunge into iced water.
7 In a small bowl, whisk together all the ingredients for the lemon and walnut dressing.
8 Remove the timbales from the oven and allow to cool before unmoulding. Arrange the dressed salad leaves on each plate, with the diced beetroot, and sprinkle over the finely chopped walnut. Position a timbale in the centre and place a poached quail's egg on top.

SMOKED HADDOCK FLORENTINE WITH POACHED EGG AND CHIVE BUTTER SAUCE

Alex Fletcher actress and 2010 Celebrity quarter-finalist

PREPARATION TIME
20 minutes

COOKING TIME
45 minutes

SERVES 4

375g (13oz) pack ready-made
  puff pastry
1 egg, beaten
4 pieces of undyed smoked haddock
  fillet, approx. 100g (3½oz) each,
  skinned and boned
600ml (1 pint) whole milk
1 fish stock cube

50g (1¾oz) unsalted butter
20g (¾oz) plain flour
1 tbsp malt vinegar
4 large eggs
150g (5½oz) young leaf spinach
15g (½oz) chives, finely chopped
salt and freshly ground black pepper

1 Preheat the oven to 200°C (400°F/Gas 6). Unroll the pastry on a lightly floured surface and cut twelve 6cm (2½in) discs, using a pastry cutter. Cut away one side of each disc to make a crescent shape. Place on baking parchment on a baking tray and brush with the beaten egg. Score a light criss-cross pattern on each one using a small kitchen knife. Bake for 20 minutes until puffed and golden.

2 Place the fish in a frying pan and add the milk. Dissolve the stock cube in a little boiling water and add to the pan. Cover the fish with a circle of greaseproof paper and the lid and heat to simmering point. Poach the fish gently for 6–8 minutes until it flakes easily.

3 Remove the fish from the milk and place in a warming oven. Sieve the milk into a jug, discarding all the bits. Measure out 300ml (10fl oz) of the milk. Melt 20g (¾oz) butter in a medium saucepan, stir in the flour, and cook for 1 minute. Gradually whisk in the milk and cook over gentle heat for 2–3 minutes to thicken. Remove from the heat, add cubes of the remaining butter over the top to prevent a skin forming, and leave at the back of the stove until ready to serve.

4 Put a deep frying pan on the heat, about two-thirds full of water with the vinegar added, and bring to simmering point. Reduce the heat slightly before adding the eggs, breaking each one into a cup or ramekin and gently lowering them into the water. Poach them for 4–6 minutes, depending on how set or runny you like your yolk. Dry each egg on kitchen paper as it comes out of the water.

5 While the eggs are cooking, wilt the spinach in a little water in a saucepan. Season and drain well. Reheat the sauce gently and reincorporate the melted butter. Add the chives and seasoning.

6 To serve, arrange the spinach in the middle of 4 warm plates, place the fish on top, and then an egg. Spoon over the chive butter sauce, and serve with 3 pastry crescents per plate on the side.

GRILLED SMOKED HADDOCK WITH BLACK PUDDING, POTATO CAKE, AND QUAIL'S EGG

David Coulson head chef and 2010 Professionals finalist

4 x 100g (3½oz) Maris Piper potatoes, peeled and halved
200g (7oz) black pudding, skinned and sliced
salt and freshly ground black pepper
40g (1¼oz) plain flour
1 large egg, beaten
50g (1¾oz) fresh white breadcrumbs
70g (2½oz) butter
4 pieces of undyed smoked haddock fillet, approx. 80g (2¾oz) each
150g (5½oz) baby spinach

freshly grated nutmeg
4 quail's eggs

FOR THE SAUCE
300ml (10fl oz) dry white wine
3 large sprigs of thyme
150ml (5fl oz) double cream
100g (3½oz) mature Cheddar cheese, grated
2 plum tomatoes, peeled, deseeded and chopped
10g (¼oz) chives, finely chopped

PREPARATION TIME
30 minutes, plus chilling

COOKING TIME
50 minutes

SERVES 4

1 Boil the potatoes in salted water until tender (20–25 minutes). Drain well, and leave to steam dry in the colander for 2 minutes. Mash with a potato ricer until smooth and leave to cool completely on a tray.
2 Transfer the potato to a bowl and crumble in the black pudding with some seasoning. Shape the mixture into 4 cakes. Coat each potato cake first in flour, shake off excess, then dip in the egg and finally the breadcrumbs to coat all over. Repeat with all the potato cakes and place on a plate in the fridge for at least 30 minutes.
3 Heat 30g (1oz) butter in a frying pan and fry the potato cakes over medium-low heat for 15–20 minutes until golden all over, turning frequently and cooking all around the sides too. Meanwhile, make the sauce by putting the wine and thyme in a pan and reducing by two-thirds over high heat. Add the cream and reduce again for 5 minutes. Remove from the heat, discard the thyme, and stir in the cheese, tomato, and chives. Season and keep warm on the back of the stove.
4 Preheat the grill to a high setting. Place the fish on a non-stick tray and dot with 15g (½oz) butter. Cook for 7–8 minutes under the grill.
5 Meanwhile, cook the spinach in 10g (¼oz) butter in a large saucepan to wilt it. Season with salt, pepper, and freshly grated nutmeg.
6 Heat the remaining butter in a small, non-stick frying pan, break in the quail's eggs, and cook for 1 minute. Reheat the sauce very gently.
7 To serve, divide the spinach between 4 warm plates, placing it in the middle. Place a potato cake on top, and then a piece of smoked haddock. Spoon the sauce over the fish and around the plate, and then finish each dish with a fried quail's egg.

MICHEL ROUX JR "That fish is cooked bang on, the cheese sauce is lovely, and that little Scotch egg made with the quail's egg and smoked haddock is divine."

MACKEREL WITH SMOKED BEETROOT, HORSERADISH CRÈME FRAÎCHE, AND SODA BREAD

Lisa Faulkner actress and 2010 Celebrity champion

PREPARATION TIME
45 minutes

COOKING TIME
45 minutes

SERVES 4

FOR THE BEETROOT
500g (1lb 2oz) small raw beetroot
3 tbsp basmati rice
2 tsp loose Earl Grey tea
1 tsp demerara sugar
1 tbsp olive oil

FOR THE SODA BREAD
200g (7oz) self-raising flour
200g (7oz) plain flour
25g (scant 1oz) butter, melted
½ tsp salt
1½ tbsp caster sugar
2 tsp bicarbonate of soda
400ml (14fl oz) buttermilk

FOR THE CRÈME FRAÎCHE
150ml (5fl oz) crème fraîche
1 generous tsp grated horseradish
squeeze of lemon juice
salt and freshly ground black pepper

FOR THE MACKEREL
2 fresh mackerel, filleted
  and pin-boned
1 tbsp olive oil

TO GARNISH
1 punnet each of micro beetroot,
  tarragon, and watercress

1 For the beetroot, preheat the oven to 180°C (350°F/Gas 4). Wrap the beetroot tightly in foil, place on a baking tray, and roast for 1 hour, or up to 1 hour 20 minutes if the beetroot is a bit larger. Test with a sharp knife – if it goes in easily without resistance, the beetroot is ready. Leave to cool slightly and then, wearing rubber gloves, trim off the ends, peel, and slice thickly.

2 To smoke the beetroot, place a piece of foil in the base of a smoker or wok and put the rice, tea, and sugar in the middle of the foil. Place a rack on top, cover with a lid, and place over high heat. Turn on the extractor fan and open a window. Leave for about 6 minutes, or until it is smoking well, then brush the beetroot slices with olive oil and put them in a single layer on the rack. Cover with a lid and smoke for 8 minutes. Remove and set aside, and repeat with the rest of the beetroot.

3 For the bread, preheat the oven to 220°C (425°F/Gas 7). Sift the flours into a large bowl and mix together. Pour the melted butter into the middle and rub with your fingertips until it is evenly distributed. Add the salt and sugar, sift in the bicarbonate of soda, and mix thoroughly. Make a well in the centre, pour in the buttermilk, and mix quickly with a fork to make a soft, very sticky dough.

4 Butter and lightly flour a 20cm (8in) loose-bottomed cake tin (at least 6cm/2½in deep), tip in the sticky dough, and smooth the top with a spatula. Cover loosely with well-oiled foil, place on a baking sheet, and bake in the oven for 20 minutes. Remove the foil, turn the heat down to 200°C (400°F/Gas 6), and bake for 15 minutes, or until golden brown on top and the loaf sounds hollow when tapped underneath. Tip out onto a wire rack and leave to cool.

5 To make the horseradish sauce, mix together the crème fraîche, horseradish, and lemon juice, and season to taste.

6 For the mackerel, score the skin with a sharp knife, brush with olive oil, and season well. Heat a large frying pan until hot, then add the mackerel skin side down and fry for 3 minutes. Turn over and take the pan off the hob – the residual heat will continue to cook the fish.

7 To serve, divide the smoked beetroot between 4 plates. Lay the mackerel on it, place a dollop of horseradish crème fraîche on top, and scatter with the microgreens. Serve with the bread alongside.

MACKEREL TARTARE AND SMOKED MACKEREL PÂTÉ WITH CUCUMBER PAPARDELLE

David Coulson head chef and 2010 Professionals finalist

PREPARATION TIME
15 minutes

SERVES 4

100g (3½oz) fresh mackerel, filleted, all bones removed
30g (1oz) creamed horseradish sauce
200g (7oz) crème fraîche
2 tbsp fresh dill, finely chopped
1 tsp lemon thyme leaves
juice of 2 lemons

100g (3½oz) smoked mackerel
3 tbsp double cream
1 egg yolk
1 medium cucumber
1 tsp apple vinegar
sprigs of thyme and dill, to garnish

MICHEL ROUX JR "Great combination of flavours. It works really well."

1 For the mackerel tartare, flake the mackerel and mix with the horseradish sauce, 150g (5½oz) of the crème fraîche, 1 tbsp of the dill, the lemon thyme, and half the lemon juice. Season and chill.
2 To make the pâté, blend the smoked mackerel, double cream, egg yolk, and remaining crème fraîche until smooth, using a hand-held blender or food processor.
3 Using a vegetable peeler, remove the skin from the cucumber and then cut long, thin strips of flesh using the same peeler. Mix in a bowl with the apple vinegar and the remaining lemon juice and dill.
4 To serve, divide the mackerel tartare between 4 plates, spooning it down the length of the plate. At one end top with a spoon of smoked mackerel pâté, then garnish with cucumber papardelle and sprigs of dill and thyme.

MI-CUIT SEA TROUT WITH APPLE PURÉE AND CIDER BEURRE BLANC

Claire Lara lecturer and 2010 Professionals champion

PREPARATION TIME
30 minutes

COOKING TIME
35 minutes

SERVES 4

2 Braeburn apples, peeled, cored, and chopped
3 tbsp apple juice
1 tsp caster sugar
juice of 1 lemon
1 Granny Smith apple
300ml (10fl oz) dry English cider
125g (4½oz) cold unsalted butter, cut into small cubes
2 shallots, finely chopped

2 tbsp cider vinegar
2 tbsp double cream
salt and freshly ground black pepper
8 baby leeks or spring onions, trimmed
1 tbsp olive oil
4 portions sea trout, approx. 90g (3¼oz) each
30g (1oz) watercress stems
1 tbsp chives, finely chopped

MICHEL ROUX JR
"Very elegant, very light, very appealing."

1 For the purée, cook the Braeburn apples with the apple juice and sugar in a covered pan, stirring frequently, for 15 minutes until they are very soft. Using a food processor or hand-held blender, blend the contents of the pan with lemon juice to taste until you have a smooth purée. Transfer the purée to a small saucepan to reheat later.
2 Using a melon baller, cut 12 ball shapes from the Granny Smith apple, leaving the peel on. Place 200ml (7fl oz) of cider in a medium saucepan and reduce over high heat for 3–4 minutes to about 3 tbsp. Gradually whisk in 50g (1¾oz) of the cold butter cubes. Add the apple balls and cook for 5 minutes until tender, turning occasionally. Remove the apple and set aside on a plate, leaving the sauce in the pan.
3 To make the beurre blanc, place half the shallots in a small pan with the vinegar and remaining cider. Reduce for 4–5 minutes until the liquid almost disappears. Add the cream then gradually whisk in the remaining butter. Add salt and pepper and a squeeze of lemon juice. While the beurre blanc reduces, steam the leeks for 4–5 minutes.
4 Heat a frying pan until hot. Rub the olive oil all over the fish with some salt and place the fish in the pan, skin side down. Cook on high heat for 1 minute only, then turn over and cook for a further minute.
5 Reheat the sauce that the apple balls were cooked in, adding some seasoning and the watercress stems. Just before serving, add the chives and remaining shallots to the gently heated beurre blanc to give a raw, clean flavour. Test for seasoning and adjust if necessary.
6 To serve, spoon some of the beurre blanc onto the middle of each plate, place the trout fillets on top, dot with the purée and a little of the sauce the apple balls were cooked in, then arrange the baby leeks or spring onions, apple balls, and watercress stems around the trout.

CONFIT OF SALMON AND ROASTED BABY BEETROOTS

Daniel Savage head chef and 2010 Professionals quarter-finalist

PREPARATION TIME
30 minutes

COOKING TIME
1 hour 10 minutes

SERVES 4

2 small golden beetroots
 (if unavailable, use purple), left whole
30g (1oz) sea salt
30g (1oz) caster sugar
large pinch of freshly ground
 white pepper
1 tbsp dill, chopped, plus 1 large stalk
salmon fillet, approx. 250g (9oz), skin
 on and pin-boned
2 tbsp finely grated horseradish

3 tbsp double cream
2 small purple beetroots, trimmed
 and peeled
3 tbsp white wine vinegar
300ml (10fl oz) olive oil
knob of butter
1 garlic clove, halved
3 tbsp crème fraîche
50g (1¾oz) baby watercress leaves

1 Cook the golden beetroots in simmering water for about 30–40 minutes until soft. Drain and leave to cool slightly, then slip off the peel.
2 Preheat the oven to 190°C (375°F/Gas 5). Mix the salt, sugar, pepper, and chopped dill in a small shallow dish and add the salmon. Press the mix into the salmon, rubbing in well all over. Marinate for 30 minutes in the fridge, flesh side down.
3 Place the horseradish and cream in a small pan. Bring to the boil and cook rapidly to reduce and thicken the mixture, about 2–3 minutes. Transfer to a bowl, cool to room temperature, then place in the fridge.
4 Peel the purple beetroots and slice very thinly on a mandolin. Place in a bowl with the vinegar and some seasoning and leave to pickle for 30 minutes. Meanwhile, cut the golden beetroots into wedges. Heat 2 tbsp of the olive oil and the butter in a frying pan and add the beetroots with some seasoning. Cook for a few minutes until brown all over and transfer to the oven to finish roasting for 15 minutes until golden.
5 Rinse the salmon with cold water and pat dry. Place the garlic, dill stalk, and remaining oil in a medium pan and add the salmon, making sure it is submerged in the oil – if not, add more. Heat the contents of the pan to 46–50°C (104–122°F). Maintain this temperature range for 18 minutes – you may need to turn the heat off for a while and back on again. Remove the salmon to a plate and discard the oil.
6 Fold the crème fraîche into the horseradish cream and test for seasoning. Take off the skin from the salmon, and gently scrape off the brown fat from the skin side.
7 Place the roasted beetroot in the middle of 4 plates and flake the salmon on top. Drain the pickled beetroot and arrange on the plate with watercress. Spoon the horseradish cream on the salmon to finish.

LIME AND CHILLI SALMON WITH CRÈME FRAÎCHE ON BLACK PEPPER OATCAKES

Alex Rushmer freelance writer and 2010 finalist

finely grated zest and juice of 4 limes
2 red chillies, deseeded
  and finely chopped
1 tsp salt
1 tsp caster sugar
salmon fillet, approx. 250g (9oz) ,
  skinned, pin-boned, and cut into
  1cm (½in) slices

FOR THE OATCAKES
250g (9oz) medium oatmeal
50g (1¾oz) medium rolled oats

¼ tsp bicarbonate of soda
¼ tsp salt
¼ tsp coarsely ground black pepper
25g (scant 1oz) duck fat,
  or 25ml (1½ tbsp) olive oil

TO SERVE
½ small red onion, finely chopped
150g (5½oz) crème fraîche
1 tsp nigella or black onion seeds
small bunch of sorrel leaves
  or wild rocket

PREPARATION TIME
20 minutes, plus marinating

COOKING TIME
10 minutes

SERVES 4

1 Pour the lime juice into a shallow dish and add the chillies, salt, and caster sugar. Mix well. Place the salmon in the marinade, making sure all the flesh is covered, and marinate for 30–60 minutes in a cool place.

2 Preheat the oven to 200°C (400°F/Gas 6). Line a large baking sheet with baking parchment. Mix the oatmeal, oats, bicarbonate of soda, and salt and pepper in a bowl. Rub in the duck fat, or mix in the olive oil. Gradually add 100–120ml (3½–4fl oz) freshly boiled water to form a dough. Knead on a floured surface for 2 minutes, then place between 2 sheets of cling film. Roll out to a thickness of 5mm (¼in) then remove the top sheet of cling film. Using a 3cm (1¼in) cutter (or a bite-size cutter of your choice), stamp out rounds and place them a little spaced apart on the baking sheet. You should have about 30–32 rounds of oatcakes, 3cm (1¼in) in diameter.

3 Bake the oatcakes in the oven for about 8–10 minutes, or until beginning to turn golden and crisp. Leave to cool on a baking sheet for 5 minutes, then transfer to a wire rack and leave until cold.

4 Stir the red onion into the crème fraîche and season with a little salt and pepper. Lift the salmon from the marinade, shaking off the excess, and then, using a very sharp knife, cut into tiny dice. Divide the salmon between the oatcakes and top with a blob of crème fraîche. Sprinkle on nigella or black onion seeds and garnish with sorrel or wild rocket leaves.

MASTER TIP
SORREL

Often found growing wild in meadowlands, there are two main culinary species: the common sorrel with an appearance like spinach and a refreshingly sharp, almost astringent taste; and the French sorrel, which has a milder, more lemony, more succulent flavour.

TWICE-BAKED SMOKED SALMON AND DILL SOUFFLÉ

Lisa Faulkner actress and 2010 Celebrity champion

PREPARATION TIME
20 minutes

COOKING TIME
55 minutes

SERVES 4

125g (4½oz) butter
75g (2½oz) plain flour
300ml (10fl oz) milk
3 eggs, separated
100g (3½oz) smoked salmon, chopped
1 tbsp dill, finely chopped
salt and freshly ground black pepper

FOR THE SAUCE
100ml (3½fl oz) dry white wine
125ml (4fl oz) double cream
1 tbsp dill, finely chopped

FOR THE SALAD
4 tbsp extra virgin olive oil
juice of ½ lemon
1 tsp Dijon mustard
1 tsp white wine vinegar
150g packet watercress, rocket,
  and spinach salad
1 lemon, cut into wedges, to garnish

1 Preheat the oven to 180°C (350°F/Gas 4). Melt the butter in a small saucepan and use to thoroughly grease four 200ml (7fl oz) ramekins, measuring 6cm (2½in) deep and 9cm (3½in) in diameter. Add the flour to the remaining melted butter and cook for 1 minute, stirring. Remove from the heat and gradually whisk in the milk. Return to the heat and bring to the boil, stirring all the time. Simmer for 1 minute, then pour into a mixing bowl and leave to cool slightly. Add the egg yolks, salmon, and dill and season with salt and pepper.
2 Whisk the egg whites in a separate glass or metal bowl until soft peaks form then fold into the salmon mixture. Divide the mixture between the ramekins and place these in a large roasting tin. Add just-boiled water from the kettle to come a third of the way up the sides of the ramekins. Place in the oven and cook for 25 minutes. Remove from the oven and carefully remove the soufflés from the tin to cool completely. (See also pp.312–13 for more advice on how to make soufflés.)
3 While the soufflés are cooking, make the sauce. Pour the wine into a pan and reduce by half. Add the cream, dill, and some seasoning.
4 Make the salad dressing by whisking together the olive oil, lemon juice, Dijon mustard, and vinegar, with some seasoning.
5 Increase the oven to 220°C (425°F/Gas 7). Run a knife around the edges of the soufflés and turn out into individual ovenproof gratin or other shallow dishes. Pour the cream sauce over them and reheat for 15 minutes.
6 To serve, toss the salad leaves with the dressing and position alongside the soufflés with a wedge of lemon.

SALADE NIÇOISE
Skills test for contestants in Celebrity Masterchef 2010

300g (10oz) baby new potatoes,
  scrubbed
2 eggs
100g (3½oz) fine green beans,
  with tails on
1 small heart of romaine lettuce, torn
50g (1¾oz) small cherry tomatoes,
  halved
50g (1¾oz) mixed pitted olives, drained

½ tbsp olive oil
4 tuna steaks, 80–100g (3–3½oz) each

FOR THE DRESSING
3 tbsp extra virgin olive oil
1 tbsp lemon juice
1 tsp Dijon mustard
salt and freshly ground black pepper

PREPARATION TIME
40 minutes

COOKING TIME
25 minutes

SERVES 4

1 Boil the potatoes in lightly salted water for 15–20 minutes until tender, then drain and refresh under running cold water. Cut in half.
2 Hard boil the eggs for 9–10 minutes in simmering water and refresh until cold in running water. Remove the shells.
3 Blanch the beans for 3 minutes. Refresh them in salted water until cold, then drain.
4 To make the dressing, whisk together the oil, lemon juice, mustard, and seasoning. Assemble the salad base on 4 plates. Start with the lettuce, then the potatoes, and then scatter over the beans, tomatoes, and olives. Slice the eggs in quarters and arrange them on the salad.
5 Preheat a large griddle pan until very hot. Rub a little oil on both sides of the tuna steaks, lightly season with salt, and sear on the griddle for 30–60 seconds on each side, depending on how rare you want them to be.
6 To serve, slice the steaks, arrange on the top of the salad, and drizzle the dressing around.

SALMON WITH CAVIAR VELOUTÉ AND POACHED QUAIL'S EGG

Chris Walker actor and 2010 Celebrity semi-finalist

PREPARATION TIME
20 minutes

COOKING TIME
1 hour 10 minutes

SERVES 4

4 salmon fillets, approx. 200g (7oz) each, cut from the middle
knob of butter, melted
1 tsp olive oil
1 tbsp malt vinegar
4 quail's eggs

FOR THE VELOUTÉ
1 tbsp olive oil
2 shallots, chopped
1 celery stick, chopped
1 carrot, chopped

2 garlic cloves, chopped
225g (8oz) fish trimmings
50ml (3 tbsp) Noilly Prat, or other dry vermouth
300ml (10fl oz) dry white wine, such as Sauvignon Blanc
salt and freshly ground black pepper
1 bay leaf
small bunch of dill, chopped
300ml (10fl oz) double cream
50g (1¾oz) salmon caviar

MASTER TIP
SALMON CAVIAR

Caviar is the "hard" eggs, or roe, of the female fish. The famously expensive black caviar comes from the sturgeon fish, whereas the bright orange keta caviar derives from the Pacific salmon keta (or chum). Use in small quantities as the eggs, once broken, release a rich salmon-oil taste that is quite exceptional.

1 First make the velouté. Heat the oil in a frying pan and fry the shallots, celery, carrot, and garlic for 10 minutes, or until softened but not browned. Add the fish trimmings, vermouth, and white wine and bring to the boil. Add about 600ml (1 pint) water and season with salt and pepper. Stir in the bay leaf and the dill, reserving some of the latter for a garnish, and return to the boil. Skim the surface, then simmer gently for 30 minutes, stirring occasionally.

2 Strain the stock into a clean pan and boil hard for about 12 minutes to reduce by half. Strain through a muslin-lined sieve into a pan, then stir in the cream. Boil for about 7 minutes until thickened slightly. Stir in the caviar, then taste and adjust the seasoning if necessary.

3 Brush the salmon fillets with a little melted butter, then add the olive oil to a large frying pan and cook the fillets for 8–10 minutes, skin side down first, turning once so that they cook evenly.

4 At the last minute, poach the quail's eggs. Set a shallow frying pan of water on the hob, add the malt vinegar and bring to a gentle simmer. Break the eggs into the pan and poach for about 30 seconds or until you see the whites are set.

5 To serve the dish, spoon a pool of velouté onto each serving plate and place the salmon on top, followed by the poached quail's egg. Sprinkle with dill to finish.

LAMB'S KIDNEYS WITH A VERMOUTH SAUCE ON CELERIAC ROSTI

Dick Strawbridge TV presenter and 2010 Celebrity finalist

PREPARATION TIME
25 minutes, plus marinating

COOKING TIME
15 minutes

SERVES 4

2 lamb's kidneys, whole
100ml (3½fl oz) whole milk
1 garlic clove, crushed
100ml (3½fl oz) vermouth
1 tbsp olive oil
15g (½oz) butter
150ml (5fl oz) double cream

FOR THE ROSTI
200g (7oz) celeriac, peeled and
  coarsely grated
finely grated zest of 1 lemon
2 tbsp plain flour
1 large egg, beaten
salt and freshly ground black pepper
1 tbsp olive oil
15g (½oz) butter

1 Remove the sinews from the centre of each kidney and slice the kidneys finely. Place in a small bowl and add the milk, garlic, and 2 tbsp vermouth. Cover and set aside for 10 minutes to marinate.
2 For the rosti, mix the grated celeriac with the lemon zest (reserving some for garnishing the dish later), flour, and egg. Season and mix well. Divide into 4 balls.
3 Heat 1 tbsp oil in a large frying pan. Place the celeriac balls in the hot pan, press down slightly with a spatula to flatten them, and fry over medium heat for 3–4 minutes or until golden on one side. Carefully flip over with a spatula and fry for another 2 minutes. Add the butter and swirl around the rostis to make them golden brown and crisp. Remove from the heat and drain on kitchen paper.

FLAVOUR COMBINATION
KIDNEYS AND CELERIAC

Celeriac is a knobbly, celery-flavoured root that can be eaten raw or cooked with little change in its comforting clear appeal. Kidneys have a gentle sweetness of taste and unusual flavour that can be made more palatable when combined with celeriac. In this recipe, white vermouth makes an inspired extra bridge of flavours between the two, because it adds the savour of dozens of herbs and spices and the lift of alcohol.

4 Strain the kidneys in a sieve, discarding the marinating mix, and pat dry with kitchen paper. Put the oil in a large frying pan over high heat. Season the kidney slices and then, when the oil is hot, fry for 45 seconds on each side. Add the butter and swirl around the pan. Tip the kidneys onto a warm plate and set aside.

5 Place the pan back on the heat. Add the rest of the vermouth and deglaze the pan – be careful, as the pan will be hot and could catch alight. Bubble for 1 minute to burn off the alcohol, remove from the heat, and add the cream. Stir well, season, and set aside.

6 To serve, place a rosti on each plate, divide the kidneys between the plates, and pour the cream sauce round the edges of the rosti (not on the top as this will make them soggy). Garnish with the reserved lemon zest.

GREGG WALLACE "It's an unusual looking plate of food, but the idea of those kidneys on a celeriac rosti was absolutely brilliant."

CARPACCIO OF BEEF SALAD WITH HORSERADISH TUILE, OYSTER EMULSION, AND "CHAMPAGNE" CAVIAR

Dick Strawbridge TV presenter and 2010 Celebrity finalist

PREPARATION TIME
2 hours

COOKING TIME
30 minutes

SERVES 4

225g (8oz) beef fillet,
  cut from the tapered end
salt and freshly ground white pepper
½ tsp cayenne pepper

FOR THE TUILE
100g (3½oz) plain flour
2 tbsp icing sugar
100g (3½oz) butter, melted and cooled
2 egg whites
30g (1oz) horseradish, finely grated

FOR THE SALAD
½ small celeriac, peeled and cut into
  julienne strips
1 small fennel bulb, thinly sliced
small bunch of radishes, thinly sliced

juice of 1 lemon
4–5 tbsp extra virgin olive oil
1 tsp finely grated horseradish,
  or to taste

FOR THE EMULSION
2 oysters with liquor
2 egg yolks
juice of ½ lemon
300ml (10fl oz) sunflower oil

FOR THE CAVIAR
750ml (1¼ pints) British pink
  sparkling wine
2 tbsp Sosa Vegetable Setting Powder
1 litre (1¾ pints) light vegetable
  oil, chilled

1 Trim the beef fillet completely of fat then wrap it in cling film and put it in the freezer for 45 minutes.

2 For the tuile, preheat the oven to 200°C (400°F/Gas 6). Line a large baking tray with non-stick baking parchment or a silicone sheet.

3 Mix the flour, icing sugar, and 1 tsp of salt in a bowl, then gradually beat the butter into the dry ingredients. Whisk the 2 egg whites in a separate bowl until soft peaks form when the whisk is removed. Whisk half of the egg white into the butter mixture then fold in the remainder with the horseradish.

4 Spread the tuile mixture in a thin layer on the baking tray and bake for about 8–10 minutes, or until pale golden-brown. Remove from the oven and allow to cool for a couple of minutes then, using a very sharp knife, cut into thin strips.

5 For the salad, mix together the celeriac, fennel, and radishes in a bowl. Put the lemon juice in a small bowl, add the olive oil, and whisk together well. Season to taste with salt and pepper and add the horseradish. Drizzle the dressing over the salad and toss .

6 For the oyster emulsion, carefully open up the oysters and lever out the meat and liquor into a food processor. Add the egg yolks and mix on pulse setting until just combined. With the machine running, gradually pour in the lemon juice and sunflower oil. Taste and season with salt and white pepper.

7 To complete the beef, remove from the freezer and discard the cling film. Heat some oil in a frying pan and season the beef with salt, white pepper, and cayenne pepper, then quickly sear it on all sides. Set aside to rest.

8 To make the "champagne" caviar, pour the wine into a pan and reduce by about half. Add the setting agent while the wine is hot then cool slightly and transfer to a bottle with a fine spout.

9 Drip very small drops of the wine reduction into a bowl of chilled oil set over iced water: the drops should resemble the size of a caviar egg and when they hit the chilled oil they will form tiny balls. Strain the caviar and then rinse with iced water. Repeat the process until all of the wine reduction has been used.

10 To serve, slice the beef across the grain into very thin slices and arrange on the side of the serving plates with a spoonful of caviar on top. Arrange a neat pile of salad and spoon a pool of oyster emulsion on the plate. Finish with a few pieces of horseradish tuile (any that you do not use can be stored in an airtight container for a few days).

FLAVOUR COMBINATION
BEEF AND OYSTERS

Oysters traditionally gave salt-sea richness to beef pies, suet puddings, and even Lancashire hotpots, so this recipe is a new look on an old favourite. The zingy result balances two heightened tastes. The oysters' complicated saltiness stimulates the taste buds to taste more of everything; the roasted crust of the beef has concentrations of gratifying *umami* taste. Together they make age-old magic in your mouth. Ensure you use every drop of the oyster liquor.

CREAMY MUSHROOMS WITH HAGGIS, POTATO CAKES, AND BLACK VELVET SAUCE

Dick Strawbridge TV presenter and 2010 Celebrity finalist

PREPARATION TIME
40 minutes

COOKING TIME
1 hour 10 minutes

SERVES 4

large knob of butter
1 fat garlic clove, crushed
1 sprig each of thyme and rosemary
150g (5½oz) mixed cultivated and wild
  mushrooms, thickly sliced if large
175ml (6floz) pale cream sherry
150ml (5fl oz) chicken stock
150ml (5fl oz) double cream

FOR THE POTATO CAKES
30g (1oz) butter
1 large or 2 small leeks, finely chopped
300g (10oz) mashed potato
salt and freshly ground black pepper
2 tbsp oil

FOR THE SAUCE
15g (½oz) dried mixed mushrooms,
  such as girolles, ceps, and morels
300ml (10fl oz) chicken stock
2 tbsp olive oil
2 shallots, finely chopped
80g (2¾oz) fresh mixed mushrooms,
  such as chestnuts and ceps, chopped
150ml (5fl oz) Guinness
150ml (5fl oz) champagne

FOR THE HAGGIS
1 good-quality haggis, skin removed
8 thin rashers of smoked streaky bacon
small knob of butter, melted

GREGG WALLACE "Dick being Dick, it was slightly unusual but I think he brought those flavours together very well."

1 First, make the potato cakes. Melt 15g (½oz) butter in a frying pan and fry the leek for 2–3 minutes until just softened. Mix with the potato and season well. Shape into cakes and chill to firm them.
2 For the sauce, soak the dried mushrooms in the stock for 10 minutes. Heat the oil in a pan and fry the shallots until softened. Drain the mushrooms, reserving the liquor, and chop finely. Add to the pan with the fresh mushrooms and fry for 2–3 minutes. Add the liquor and reduce almost completely. Pour in the Guinness and reduce to 6 tbsp, then repeat with the champagne. Pass through a sieve and set aside.
3 To cook the creamy mushrooms, melt the butter in a pan, add the garlic, herbs, and mushrooms, and cook until slightly softened and golden. Add the sherry and boil for 3–4 minutes until slightly reduced. Add the stock and cream and boil for 1–2 minutes, then turn the heat very low. When ready to serve, strain the mushrooms over a bowl and remove the herbs. Using a blender, whizz the sauce to a froth.
4 To cook the potato cakes, heat the remaining butter and 2 tbsp oil in a pan, dust the cakes with flour then fry for 5 minutes, or until golden-brown, turning once. Cut the haggis into 4 slices and wrap each one in 2 rashers of bacon. Brush with melted butter and cook in the same pan for 8–10 minutes or until heated through and the bacon is a little crisp.
5 Put the leek and potato cakes in the centre of each warm plate and top with the haggis and strained creamy mushrooms. Spoon a little of the sauce to one side and the creamy foam to the other.

SALAD OF WOOD PIGEON WITH A WARM BLACKBERRY VINAIGRETTE

Matt Edwards music executive and 2010 semi-finalist

2 whole oven-ready wood pigeons
3 tbsp olive oil
salt and freshly ground black pepper
6 large radishes, very finely sliced
1 banana shallot, very finely sliced
100g bag or bunch of watercress
2 tbsp walnut oil

FOR THE VINAIGRETTE
150ml (5fl oz) full-bodied red wine
150ml (5fl oz) chicken or
 vegetable stock

1 carrot, finely chopped
1 onion, finely chopped
2 celery sticks, chopped
small bunch of thyme
2 bay leaves
1 tsp juniper berries
grated zest of 1 orange
2 garlic cloves, crushed
1 tbsp red wine vinegar
1 tsp caster sugar
100g (3½oz) blackberries
2 tbsp olive oil

PREPARATION TIME
30 minutes

COOKING TIME
about 50 minutes

SERVES 4

1 Using a paring knife, remove the breasts from each bird, cutting closely along the breastbone and slicing the flesh downwards away from the bones. Remove any skin, season the breasts, and set aside.
2 Heat 1 tbsp olive oil in a large frying pan on medium heat. Add the pigeon carcasses and fry for about 15 minutes until well browned, turning frequently. Remove the carcasses from the pan and discard.
3 To make the vinaigrette, deglaze the pan by pouring in the wine and stirring over medium heat. Pour in the stock and 150ml (5fl oz) water and stir in the vegetables, herbs, juniper berries, orange zest, and garlic. Cook uncovered for 20 minutes until the vegetables are softened.
4 Strain the liquor, discard the vegetables and herbs, and return the liquor to the pan – there will be about 150ml (5fl oz). Bring to the boil on medium heat, reduce the heat slightly, and cook, uncovered, for a further 5–10 minutes until the liquor has reduced a little more. Add the vinegar, sugar, and 3 blackberries, crushing the berries with a wooden spoon. Whisk in the oil. Stir in the remaining blackberries, keeping them whole, then remove from the heat and keep warm.
5 For the salad, put the radishes, shallot, and watercress into a bowl. Add the walnut oil and lightly toss together until well coated.
6 Heat the remaining olive oil in a pan, add the pigeon breasts, and cook for 1–2 minutes on each side or until rare. Remove from the pan and leave to rest for 5 minutes, covering them with a sheet of foil.
7 To serve, slice the pigeon breasts thinly. Place a small pile of salad on each plate and arrange the pigeon breast on top. Drizzle vinaigrette around and scatter a few of the whole blackberries.

JOHN TORODE "The first thing you get is the sharpness of the raw onion against the sweet but sour blackberry, then you finish on the iron richness of the pigeon. There's lots of skill in this dish, that's for sure."

PHEASANT SALTIMBOCCA WITH BUTTERNUT SQUASH AND BEETROOT JUS

Alex Rushmer freelance writer and 2010 finalist

PREPARATION TIME
25 minutes

COOKING TIME
1 hour 10 minutes

SERVES 4

1 large butternut squash, peeled, cored, and diced
3 tbsp olive oil
150–200ml (5–7fl oz) chicken stock
200ml (7fl oz) beetroot juice
2 sprigs of thyme
4 pheasant breasts, skin removed

salt and freshly ground black pepper
handful of fresh sage leaves
12 rashers streaky bacon
50g (1¾oz) butter, plus 15g (½oz) for the beetroot leaves
10 baby beetroot leaves, to garnish (optional)

1 Preheat the oven to 200°C (400°F/Gas 6). Toss the butternut squash with 2 tbsp olive oil, place in a roasting tin, and cook in the oven for 25–30 minutes until softened. In a blender or food processor, blend the squash with enough chicken stock to give a smooth purée and set aside to keep warm.

2 Put the beetroot juice in a pan with the thyme, bring to the boil, and reduce to a glaze, which will take 5–10 minutes. Remove the thyme.

3 Season the pheasant breasts, place 4 sage leaves on one side of each breast, then wrap the breasts in the bacon. Wrap tightly in cling film to make a sausage shape and knot the ends. Poach in a large pan of gently simmering water for 10 minutes, then transfer to iced water.

4 To complete, unwrap the pheasant breasts and fry in 1 tbsp oil over high heat for 5–6 minutes, turning regularly until browned all over. Add butter to the pan halfway through the cooking time and baste the pheasant with the foaming butter. Remove from the pan and allow to rest before slicing. Wilt the baby beetroot leaves (if using) in a hot pan with the remaining butter.

5 To serve, place spoonfuls of butternut purée and a scattering of beet tops on each plate, then position the pheasant slices, drizzle a line of beetroot glaze down the centre, and finish with a scattering of sage leaves.

JOHN TORODE "The extraordinary flavour of the bacon and the rich depth that comes from that beet reduction brings the whole thing alive."

ITH FINES HERBES - CARDOON GRAT

LAIN CHAPEL WITH CRIQUE ARDÉCHO

PAN-FRIED COD WITH PROVENÇAL

EGETABLES IN A ROQUEFORT CHEESE

FRIED SEA BASS AND CLAMS WITH G

AUCE AND RICE - FISH STEW WITH RO

LMONDS, ROSEMARY, AND AÏOLI - MO

ITH BUTTERNUT SQUASH FONDANT A

AUCE VIERGE - JOHN DORY ON SPICE

ENTILS - SPICED BATTERED FISH AND

PAN-FRIED FILLETS OF SEA BASS WI

TRUS FRUITS, FENNEL, AND CORIAN

AN-FRIED SEA BASS WITH LANGOUST

ND FENNEL - SEA BASS WITH CRISPY

ROSCIUTTO AND CRUSHED NEW POTA

AKE WITH LEMON AND ANCHOVY POT

PAN-FRIED TURBOT WITH LANGOUST

ND TRUFFLED CELERIAC PURÉE - SE

VEGETABLES & FISH

JOHN TORODE'S
CLASSIC CHEESE AND MUSHROOM OMELETTE WITH FINES HERBES

This uncomplicated French classic, which should be cooked without colour, is light and beautiful and the fresh herbs take it to a different level.

PREPARATION TIME
10 minutes

COOKING TIME
10 minutes

SERVES 4

100g (3½oz) butter
24 button mushrooms,
  about 175g (6oz), sliced
salt and freshly ground black pepper
12 eggs
5 tbsp chopped mixed herbs such as,
  chives, flat-leaf parsley, tarragon,
  oregano, and chervil
200g (7oz) Gruyère cheese,
  finely grated

1 Heat a good omelette pan and melt half the butter. Add the mushrooms with a little salt and pepper and cook for 4–5 minutes, turning them until lightly golden all over. Using a slotted spoon transfer them to a foil-covered bowl to keep warm, leaving as much butter in the pan as possible.

2 For each omelette, break 3 eggs into a small bowl and beat them lightly with a fork (do not whisk them as they will scramble). Add some seasoning. Pour into the warmed omelette pan and sprinkle in 1 tbsp of mixed chopped herbs. As the omelette starts to set around the outside, draw the set egg into the centre and tilt the pan so that the raw egg fills the space. After a minute or so, when about half cooked, sprinkle over 50g (1¾oz) of the cheese with a quarter of the cooked mushrooms.

3 Fold the omelette by tilting the pan and shuffling the omelette forward – it should roll up like a large cigar. Roll it onto a warm plate and garnish with more herbs. Repeat for the remaining 3 omelettes, adding fresh butter before cooking as needed.

MICHEL ROUX JR'S
CARDOON GRATIN ALAIN CHAPEL WITH CRIQUE ARDÉCHOISE

This dish has been served for hundreds of years and is a true French classic. The cardoon is a great vegetable: the stalks look like celery, but it is part of the artichoke family.

PREPARATION TIME
20 minutes

COOKING TIME
30 minutes

SERVES 4

700g (1lb 9oz) cardoon stalks, cut into 3cm (1½in) lengths
2 tbsp plain flour
juice of 1 lemon
knob of butter
100g (3½oz) Gruyère cheese
2 truffles, thinly sliced into rounds
150ml (5fl oz) beef demi-glace, or concentrated beef stock
200g (7oz) beef marrow, soaked in tepid water for 30 minutes

FOR THE CRIQUE ARDÉCHOISE
300g (10oz) potatoes, peeled and grated
1 egg
50g (1¾oz) crème fraîche
2 tbsp chervil, chopped
2 tbsp chives, chopped
2 tbsp flat-leaf parsley, chopped
salt and freshly ground black pepper
1 tbsp olive oil

MASTER TIP
CARDOON

The cardoon looks like an overgrown thistle because that is what it is: a descendant of the same weed that gave us the globe artichoke. The edible parts of a cardoon are the long, central leaf stalks. These have a succulent but crunchy texture and a delicate flavour that combines artichoke and celery with a hint of aniseed.

1 Peel and cut the cardoon stalks as you would cut celery. Cook in a blanc by mixing together the flour and lemon juice to make a paste, then stirring into 1 litre (1¾ pints) boiling salted water. Add the cardoon and simmer for about 15 minutes, or until just tender. Drain well.

2 Layer the cardoon in a buttered gratin dish with three-quarters of the Gruyère and the truffle, demi-glace, and marrow. Finish the top with a final layer of cardoons and rounds of truffle and marrow.

3 Lightly sprinkle with the remaining Gruyère cheese and a little meat glaze. Finish under a hot grill.

4 For the crique ardéchoise, press the potatoes to remove excess moisture and pat dry. As the potato will discolour quickly, transfer immediately to a bowl and mix with the egg, crème fraîche, herbs, and a generous amount of seasoning. Fry the mixture for 8–10 minutes in a blini pan or in 8–9cm (3–3¾in) cooking rings until golden and cooked through, turning once.

PAN-FRIED COD WITH PROVENÇAL VEGETABLES IN A ROQUEFORT CHEESE SAUCE

Dean Macey Olympic decathlete and 2010 Celebrity quarter-finalist

6–8 tbsp extra virgin olive oil
1 aubergine, chopped
  into 2cm (¾in) pieces
salt and freshly ground black pepper
2 pinches of caster sugar
½ fennel bulb, sliced
2 courgettes, roughly chopped
1 red onion, roughly chopped
1 yellow or orange pepper, deseeded
  and roughly chopped
280g (9½oz) cherry tomatoes on the
  vine, halved

2 garlic cloves, finely chopped
80g (2¾oz) pitted black olives,
  quartered
80g (2¾oz) pitted green olives,
  quartered
4 fillets of cod, approx. 150g (5½oz)
  each
100g (3½oz) Roquefort cheese,
  crumbled
10g (¼oz) tarragon, chopped
10g (¼oz) basil, chopped

PREPARATION TIME
10 minutes

COOKING TIME
40 minutes

SERVES 4

1 Heat a large frying pan and add 4–6 tbsp of olive oil. Once hot, add the aubergine and cook uncovered over a fairly high heat for 5 minutes, turning, until golden. Season with salt and pepper and add the caster sugar.
2 Add the fennel, courgettes, red onion, and yellow or orange pepper, and cook uncovered for a further 10 minutes. Stir in the cherry tomatoes, garlic, and olives. Cover the pan and cook for 15 minutes, turning occasionally.
3 Halfway through the cooking time, preheat another frying pan with the remaining oil. Season the cod lightly and cook for 7 minutes skin side down. Turn and cook for a further 5 minutes or until cooked through.
4 Take the vegetables off the heat and add the cheese with the tarragon and basil. Check the seasoning.
5 To serve, distribute the vegetables on warmed plates and lay the cod on top skin side up.

FRIED SEA BASS AND CLAMS WITH GREEN SAUCE AND RICE

Neil Stuke actor and 2010 Celebrity semi-finalist

PREPARATION TIME
30 minutes

COOKING TIME
35 minutes

SERVES 4

4 tbsp extra virgin olive oil
1 banana shallot, or 3 shallots,
  finely chopped
2 garlic cloves, finely chopped
120g (4¼oz) chorizo picante, peeled
  and sliced
100g (3½oz) wild mushrooms, or 25g
  (scant 1oz) dried mixed mushrooms,
  reconstituted and drained
250g (9oz) paella rice
200ml (7fl oz) dry white wine
2 x 400g cans whole plum tomatoes,
  drained
500ml (16fl oz) hot chicken stock
pinch of saffron

250g (8oz) clams in shell
4 sea bass fillets, approx. 120g (4¼oz)
  each, boneless
1 lemon, halved
chilled Manzanilla, to serve

FOR THE GREEN SAUCE

40g (1¼oz) mixture of tarragon, mint,
  flat-leaf parsley, and chervil,
  leaves only
1 garlic clove, finely chopped
1 tbsp baby capers, rinsed and drained
2–3 marinated or tinned anchovy fillets
3–4 tbsp extra virgin olive oil
salt and freshly ground black pepper

MASTER TIP
CLAMS

The most common type of clam for cooking in the UK is the hard-shell clam. Small hard-shell clams can be eaten raw but the larger ones can be chopped or minced for chowder. The heavy shells open to reveal a sweet, tender, and pleasantly salty meat. Always check clams are alive before cooking.

1 Heat a deep-sided, large frying pan until hot and add 1 tbsp of the olive oil. Stir in the shallots, garlic, and chorizo and cook for 6–7 minutes, or until the shallot is golden and soft.

2 Add the plum tomatoes, crushing them in the pan, then add the rice and mushrooms and stir well. Pour in half the wine. Allow to cook down then start ladling in the stock. Add more each time it starts to reduce. This will take about 20 minutes. Add the saffron towards the end.

3 Make the green sauce by piling the herbs with the garlic, capers, anchovies, and some salt and pepper on a chopping board. Finely chop the ingredients with a large knife and transfer to a bowl. Stir in the oil and some seasoning.

4 Take the rice off the heat and leave, covered, to rest for 5 minutes.

5 Heat a small pan, add the remaining wine and the clams, and cook, covered, for 2 minutes. Turn off the heat but leave in the covered pan.

6 Preheat a large, non-stick frying pan. Oil the sea bass fillets and season. When the pan is very hot, sear the sea bass for about 5 minutes, skin-side down, until crisp. Turn the fish over, take the pan off the heat and leave the fish in the pan for 30 seconds. Squeeze the lemon juice over the fish.

7 To serve, place a line of the rice across the middle of each plate and lay a sea bass fillet on top. Drain the clams and scatter over the plates in a different direction. Then drizzle over some sauce. Serve with an ice-cold glass of Manzanilla.

FISH STEW WITH ROASTED ALMONDS, ROSEMARY, AND AÏOLI

Lisa Faulkner actress and 2010 Celebrity champion

15 saffron threads
2 tbsp olive oil
1 red onion, finely chopped
salt
2 garlic cloves, finely chopped
1 fennel bulb, chopped
1 dried red chilli, finely chopped
1 sprig of rosemary, finely chopped
1 bay leaf
1 tbsp sherry vinegar
125ml (4fl oz) dry white wine
1 x 400g can chopped tomatoes
40g (1¼oz) toasted flaked almonds
1 monkfish fillet, approx. 250g (9oz), skinned and boneless, cut into chunks

1 salmon fillet, approx. 250g (9oz), skinned and boneless, cut into chunks
12 whole clams (optional)
4 thick slices of sourdough
1 garlic clove, halved

FOR THE AÏOLI
2 large egg yolks
2 garlic cloves, crushed
4 tsp lemon juice
200ml (7fl oz) sunflower oil
100ml (3½fl oz) extra virgin olive oil
freshly ground white pepper

PREPARATION TIME
25 minutes

COOKING TIME
45 minutes

SERVES 4

1 To make the aïoli, put the egg yolk, garlic, and lemon juice in a food processor, together with a pinch of salt. Blitz for 1 minute to combine. Pour the oils into a jug. With the processor running, gradually add the oil through the funnel, initially to incorporate about a third. Then slowly increase the stream of oil until all the oil is added and the aïoli has thickened. Add salt and white pepper, and a little water to loosen if necessary. Store in the fridge for up to a week.

2 Put the saffron threads in a small jug with 125ml (4fl oz) boiling water and set aside to infuse.

3 For the fish stew, heat the oil in a wide deep saucepan and add the onion. Cover and cook to soften for 5 minutes. Add a little salt. Add the garlic, fennel, chilli, rosemary, and bay leaf and cook, covered, for about 10 minutes or until the fennel has softened. Then add the vinegar, wine, and saffron stock. Increase the heat and let it bubble for a few minutes. Add the tomatoes and cook gently for 20 minutes.

4 Pound or process the almonds in a pestle and mortar. Add them to the pan and check the seasoning. Discard the bay leaf. Add the monkfish, salmon, and clams (if using). Cook, covered, for 5–6 minutes or until the clams have opened and the fish is cooked.

5 Toast the bread and then rub both sides with the cut sides of the garlic clove. Place a piece of garlic toast in 4 serving bowls. Spoon over the stew, arranging the fish pieces and clams first, and then pour over the sauce. Add a dessert spoon of aïoli on the side or on top.

MONKFISH WITH BUTTERNUT SQUASH FONDANT AND SAUCE VIERGE

Lisa Faulkner actress and 2010 Celebrity champion

PREPARATION TIME
35 minutes

COOKING TIME
30 minutes

SERVES 4

50g (1¾oz) butter
300g (10oz) butternut squash, cut into
  rounds approx. 1.5cm (½in) thick
150ml (5fl oz) fish stock
salt and freshly ground black pepper
175g (6oz) French beans
4 slices wafer-thin pancetta
4 monkfish fillets, approx. 200g (7oz)
  each, skinned and cut into medallions
  approx. 2.5cm (1in) thick
1 tbsp olive oil
sprigs of basil, to garnish

FOR THE SAUCE VIERGE

3 tomatoes on the vine, skinned (see
  MasterTip, p.26), deseeded and
  finely diced
1 garlic clove, finely chopped
2 tbsp tarragon, chopped
2 tbsp basil, chopped
100ml (3½fl oz) olive oil, plus extra
2 tsp lemon juice

1 Preheat the oven to 200°C (400°F/Gas 6). Melt the butter in an ovenproof frying pan that is large enough to accomodate the butternut squash snugly. Add the squash, and cook over high heat for 2 minutes each side. Pour in the stock, season with salt and pepper, and cook in the oven for 20–25 minutes, or until tender.

2 For the sauce vierge, mix the tomatoes with the garlic and herbs, then moisten with olive oil and lemon juice. Season well.

3 Blanch the French beans in boiling salted water for 3–4 minutes. Drain and refresh under cold running water. Pat dry, then separate into little bundles and wrap each with a slice of pancetta. Secure with a cocktail stick. Place on a baking tray and put in the oven for about 5 minutes, or until the beans are heated through and the pancetta is crispy.

4 Brush the monkfish with olive oil and season well. Heat a non-stick frying pan and cook the fish for 3–4 minutes each side, or until cooked through.

5 Place the butternut squash on serving plates, arrange the monkfish around it and spoon the sauce vierge over and around. Place the beans on one side. Garnish with fresh basil.

GREGG WALLACE

"Lovely sauce vierge. The squash gives the monkfish an almost caramel softness. It is an utter delight. Absolutely brilliant."

JOHN DORY ON SPICED LENTILS

Ben Piette hospitality chef and 2010 Professionals semi-finalist

PREPARATION TIME
30 minutes, plus soaking

COOKING TIME
50 minutes

SERVES 4

4 John Dory fillets, approx. 200g (7oz)
  each, skinned
2 tbsp olive oil
sea salt and freshly ground black pepper
1 small banana leaf to line a 25cm
  (10in) bamboo steamer
200g (7oz) cockles
30g (1oz) butter
250g (9oz) baby spinach

FOR THE LENTILS
200g (7oz) black lentils, soaked
  for 30 minutes
1 bulb of galangal, finely chopped
1 red chilli, deseeded and finely chopped
1 small bunch of coriander, chopped
1 stalk lemongrass, finely chopped
2 kaffir lime leaves, finely chopped
50g (1¾oz) brown shrimps
1 garlic clove, crushed

1 tbsp vegetable oil
400ml can coconut milk
1 tbsp turmeric

FOR THE SHALLOT TEMPURA
50g (1¾oz) plain flour
50g (1¾oz) cornflour
200ml (7fl oz) sparkling water
1 small bunch of Thai basil,
  roughly chopped
1 banana shallot, cut into
  5mm (¼in) rings
200ml (7fl oz) vegetable oil

FOR THE GARNISH
2 tbsp coriander leaves
1 red chilli, deseeded and cut into
  julienne strips
½ small coconut, finely shredded
1 lime, quartered

MASTER TIP

JOHN DORY

John Dory has a wonderfully
sweet taste and firm texture,
highly prized for eating. The
skin is delicate and can be left
on if cooking the fish whole.
Extremely sharp barbs make
filleting hazardous: trim them
off with scissors.

1 Season the fish with 1 tbsp olive oil, salt, and pepper. Set aside.
2 Cover the lentils with water in a pan and simmer for 35 minutes or
until tender. Drain. Crush the herbs and spices, shrimps, and garlic
with a pestle and mortar to make a paste. Heat 1 tbsp of oil in a frying
pan and fry the paste over medium heat for 2–3 minutes. Pour the
coconut milk into the pan, add the turmeric, and cook over low heat
for 10 minutes until the sauce has thickened. Strain through a fine
sieve. Once the lentils have cooled, stir in the coconut sauce.
3 To make the tempura batter, mix the flour and cornflour with the
water, stir in the basil and shallot rings, and reserve in the fridge.
4 Line a bamboo steamer with the banana leaf and place the fish on
top. Cover the steamer and place over a pan of boiling water for 8–10
minutes or until the fish is cooked. Meanwhile, heat the oil in a pan
and deep fry the tempura until golden and crispy. Drain and keep warm.
5 Place the cockles in a hot pan with 1 tbsp of olive oil and seasoning,
then add just enough water to cover the bottom of the pan. Cover and
cook for 1–2 minutes until the cockles are all open. Drain and reserve.
6 Heat the butter in a pan and sauté the spinach for 1–2 minutes
until wilted. Season with salt and pepper. To serve, place the fish on
a bed of lentils and top with tempura. Garnish with coriander, chilli, and
coconut. Add the spinach and cockles and finish with a wedge of lime.

SPICED BATTERED FISH AND CHIPS

Dhruv Baker sales director and 2010 champion

4 John Dory fillets, or other white fish, approx. 150g (5½oz) each
handful of coriander, roughly chopped, to garnish

FOR THE MUSHY PEAS
250g (9oz) dried split green or yellow peas
2 onions, chopped
2 bay leaves
salt and freshly ground black pepper
handful of coriander, chopped
1–2 red chillies, deseeded and chopped
1–2 green chillies, deseeded and chopped
juice of 2–3 limes
300g (10oz) frozen or fresh peas

FOR THE BROWN SAUCE
2 tbsp tamarind paste
4 tsp caster sugar

juice of 2 limes
pinch of chilli powder

FOR THE BATTER
150g (5½oz) plain flour
2 tsp baking powder
½ tsp fennel seeds
¼ tsp turmeric
¼ tsp chilli powder
¼ tsp ground coriander
¼ tsp ground cumin
¼ tsp brown mustard seeds
½ tsp ginger paste, or freshly grated root ginger
½ tsp garlic paste, or 1 garlic clove, finely crushed

FOR THE CHIPS
4–6 large Maris Piper potatoes, peeled and cut into chips
corn oil for deep frying

PREPARATION TIME
40 minutes

COOKING TIME
50 minutes

SERVES 4

1 Put the dried peas in a saucepan with 1 litre (1¾ pints) of water, the onions, bay leaves, and some black pepper. Boil for 1¼ hours or until the peas are tender and mushy, adding more water if necessary. Add the coriander, chillies, and lime juice. In another pan, boil the frozen or fresh peas for 4–5 minutes or until just tender, then drain and crush, using a fork. Stir into the split peas and season with salt.

2 For the sauce, put the tamarind paste in a small pan with the sugar, lime juice, and 4 tbsp of water. Add the chilli powder. Boil over medium-high heat for 5 minutes or until reduced to a sticky sauce.

3 Parboil the chips in a pan of boiling water for 5 minutes, then drain. Preheat a deep-fat fryer or deep saucepan two-thirds filled with oil to 160°C (325°F). Cook the chips in batches for 5–6 minutes, then drain on kitchen paper. Increase the temperature of the oil to 180°C (350°F) and return the chips to the pan to crisp and turn golden. Toss in salt.

4 For the batter, mix the flour, baking powder, spices, ginger, and garlic with 150–170ml (5–6fl oz) iced water until smooth. Dip 2 pieces of fish in batter and deep fry for 7–8 minutes, turning once or twice. Drain and set aside to keep warm, then repeat with the remaining fish.

5 Serve the battered fish with the chips and mushy peas alongside. Drizzle a little brown sauce over and garnish the plates with coriander.

GREGG WALLACE

"The flavours are phenomenal. It just dances all over the place: coriander, fenugreek, and real sweetness in the sauce from the tamarind. I really like it, Dhruv."

PAN-FRIED FILLETS OF SEA BASS WITH CITRUS FRUITS, FENNEL, AND CORIANDER

John Calton head chef and 2010 Professionals finalist

PREPARATION TIME
1 hour

COOKING TIME
50 minutes

SERVES 4

1.5–2kg (3lb 3oz–4½lb) sea bass, scaled and gutted
2 tbsp coriander seeds, crushed
salt and freshly ground black pepper
1 tbsp olive oil
25g (scant 1oz) butter
juice of 1 lemon
3 plum tomatoes, skinned, deseeded, and cut into petals, to garnish

FOR THE BRAISED FENNEL
2 tbsp olive oil
50g (1¾oz) butter
2 shallots, finely sliced
1 garlic clove, finely chopped

2 fennel bulbs, trimmed and very finely sliced on a mandolin
100ml (3½fl oz) Noilly Prat vermouth
100ml (3½fl oz) Pernod
750ml (1¼pints) fresh orange juice
2 star anise
zest of 1 orange

FOR THE CITRUS VINAIGRETTE AND FRUITS
3 lemons, ideally Amalfi
1 red grapefruit
3 oranges
100ml (3½fl oz) extra virgin olive oil
1 bunch of coriander, leaves only

1 With a knife, score the skin of the fish in a diamond pattern. Press the coriander seeds on the skin, season, cover, and place in the fridge.
2 For the braised fennel, heat the olive oil and butter in a large sauté pan over gentle heat. Add the shallots, and fry for 1-2 minutes until softened but not coloured. Add the garlic and fry for 1 minute.
3 Add the fennel, stir into the softened shallots, then turn up the heat and add the Noilly Prat and Pernod. Bubble for 2 minutes to burn off the alcohol, then add the orange juice and star anise. Bubble over medium heat, stirring frequently until the orange juice has been absorbed and the fennel is tender and nicely glazed. This will take about 15 minutes. Add the orange zest, season well, and set aside.
4 For the vinaigrette, segment 2 lemons, the grapefruit and 1 orange, and place in a bowl. Juice 2 oranges into a small pan and bubble over high heat for about 15 minutes or until reduced to about 3 tbsp and syrupy. Add the juice of 1 lemon and the olive oil, season and set aside.
5 To cook the fish, heat a frying pan and add the olive oil. Add the fish skin side down, and fry for 3–4 minutes or until the skin is golden brown, then turn over and fry for another 2 minutes on the other side. Add the butter to the pan and baste the fish with the melted butter. Squeeze the lemon juice over the fillets and remove from the heat.
6 To serve, divide the braised fennel between 4 plates, top with a fillet of sea bass on each, scatter the fruits round the edges and drizzle with the citrus vinaigrette. Garnish with the tomato petals.

PAN-FRIED SEA BASS WITH LANGOUSTINES AND FENNEL

Tim Kinnaird paediatrician and 2010 finalist

75g (2½oz) butter
4 leeks, finely sliced
salt and freshly ground black pepper
2 tbsp olive oil
½ carrot, finely chopped
½ onion, finely chopped
½ celery stick, finely chopped
12 cooked shell-on Atlantic prawns, about 75g (2½oz)
50ml (1¾fl oz) brandy

200ml (7fl oz) white wine
4 star anise
pinch of saffron
8 fresh langoustines, peeled and deveined, heads and shells retained (see MasterTip, right)
200ml (7fl oz) double cream
1 fennel bulb, cut into 8 wedges
2 wild sea bass, scaled, filleted, and pin-boned

PREPARATION TIME
45 minutes

COOKING TIME
1 hour 10 minutes

SERVES 4

1 Heat 50g (1¾oz) of the butter in a sauté pan. When it is foaming, add the leeks, season well, and cover with a lid. Fry, stirring occasionally, for 15 minutes. Remove the lid and fry for a further 10 minutes.
2 Heat 1 tbsp of the oil in a medium pan, add the carrot, onion, and celery and fry over gentle heat for 10 minutes. Add the prawns and cook for 5 minutes, mashing them up with the back of a wooden spoon to extract as much flavour as possible. Add the brandy and bubble for a few minutes to burn off the alcohol.
3 Add the wine, star anise, saffron, and seasoning, and cook slowly, covered with a lid, for 5 minutes. Add the langoustine heads and shells to the pan and bubble, covered, for another 10 minutes. Pour into another pan through a fine sieve, pressing hard with a wooden spoon to extract as much flavour as possible from the solids. Discard the solids and place the sauce over medium heat. Add the cream and warm through for 3–4 minutes, or until slightly thick. Set aside.
4 Blanch the fennel wedges in boiling salted water for 3–4 minutes, then refresh in cold water.
5 Score the skin of the sea bass fillets with a sharp knife and season the fillets on both sides. Heat a large frying pan (or 2 if necessary), add the remaining butter and olive oil, and fry the blanched fennel for 3–4 minutes. Remove from the pan and set aside. Add the sea bass fillets to the pan, skin-side down, and fry for 3–4 minutes, or until golden. Turn them over carefully, add the langoustine tails and fry for another 2–3 minutes, or until they are just pink.
6 To serve, divide the leeks between 4 plates, top with a sea bass fillet, place the fennel wedges and langoustines round the edge, and drizzle with the sauce.

MASTER TIP
LANGOUSTINES

Also known as the Dublin Bay prawn and Norway lobster, langoustines have recently become highly prized for their sweet, tender meat. Unusually they do not change colour much when cooked, which can be confusing to the cook. To eat, crack open the claws and prize out the meat with a lobster pick, then pinch the tail until the underside cracks to expose the meat.

SEA BASS WITH CRISPY PROSCIUTTO AND CRUSHED NEW POTATOES

Alan Simpson medical insurer and 2010 contestant

PREPARATION TIME
30 minutes

COOKING TIME
10–12 minutes

SERVES 4

4 sea bass fillets, scaled and pin-boned
sea salt and freshly ground
  black pepper
750g (1lb 10oz) baby new potatoes,
  quartered

8 slices of prosciutto di Parma
1 tbsp olive oil
200g (7oz) unsalted butter
4 tbsp chopped chives
8 tbsp chopped parsley

1 Score the sea bass fillets on the skin side, being careful not to cut too deep into the flesh. Season the skin with salt and set aside.
2 Fill a large pan with cold water and add a little salt and the potatoes. Bring to the boil and cook for 8–12 minutes until tender.
3 Meanwhile, place the prosciutto slices in a cold non-stick frying pan; depending on the size of the pan, it may be necessary to do this in 2 batches. Turn on the heat and allow the ham to crisp up, turning once during cooking. Once cooked (about 3–4 minutes), remove from the pan and place on a sheet of kitchen paper to drain any excess fat. Set aside.
4 Wipe the pan clean and place it back on the hob over medium heat. Add a little olive oil and place the fish skin side down. Cook for 6–7 minutes on the skin side to allow this to crisp up. Turn and cook for a further 4–5 minutes on the flesh side until the fish is cooked through.
5 Drain the potatoes, add 50g (1¾oz) butter and the chives and crush them together. Once crushed, divide into quarters. Place into moulding rings in the centre of 4 plates and firm down. Remove each ring and add a slice of the prosciutto on top of the potatoes. Slice the sea bass fillets in half and add one half on top of the prosciutto with the skin facing up. Place the other slice of prosciutto on top and then the other half of the fish on top of this, again skin side up.
6 Wipe out the frying pan again, put it over gentle heat and add the remaining butter. Once the butter has nearly melted, add the parsley and mix it in.
7 Drizzle the butter and parsley over and around the potatoes, fish, and prosciutto. Serve immediately.

HAKE WITH LEMON AND ANCHOVY POTATOES
Tim Kinnaird paediatrician and 2010 finalist

2 tsp black peppercorns
2 tbsp chopped rosemary
2 tsp thyme leaves
1 bay leaf, finely chopped
1 tsp fennel seeds
1 tsp sea salt
4 x 150–175g (5½oz–6oz) portions hake
   fillet, from the thicker end, skin on
2 tbsp olive oil

FOR THE POTATOES
750g (1lb 10oz) Maris Piper potatoes,
   peeled and cut into 1.5cm (½in) cubes
6 anchovy fillets, chopped

1 unwaxed lemon
1 tbsp finely chopped rosemary
4 tbsp extra virgin olive oil
freshly ground black pepper

FOR THE SAUCE
2 vine tomatoes
1 shallot, finely chopped
1 small garlic clove, finely chopped
100ml (3½fl oz) extra virgin olive oil
1 tbsp lemon juice
small bunch basil leaves,
   finely chopped

PREPARATION TIME
40 minutes

COOKING TIME
25 minutes

SERVES 4

1 Grind the peppercorns in a pestle and mortar, then add the rosemary, thyme leaves, bay leaf, fennel seeds, and salt and mix together. Tip the herb mix onto a large plate and then roll the hake fillets in it, pressing to ensure all the fish is covered. Cover and place in the fridge while you prepare the sauce and potatoes.
2 Place the chopped potatoes in a large pan, cover with cold salted water, bring to the boil, and then simmer for 8–10 minutes, or until tender. Drain and set aside.
3 While the potatoes are boiling, grind the anchovy fillets into a pulp in a pestle and mortar. Add the grated zest of the whole lemon and juice of half the lemon, the rosemary, and the olive oil. Season with black pepper. Add the anchovy mix to the hot drained potatoes, mix well, and set aside.
4 For the sauce, place the tomatoes in a bowl of boiling water for 1 minute. Refresh in cold water and peel, deseed, and dice finely.
5 Place the shallot, garlic, olive oil, chopped tomato, and lemon juice in a small pan. Warm through over low heat for 3–4 minutes. Just before serving, add the basil and warm through.
6 To cook the fish, heat a large frying pan over high heat, add the oil, and then fry the hake skin side down for 3–4 minutes. Turn over and fry for 2–3 minutes or until just cooked through. If you have a thick piece of hake, place it on a baking sheet and finish in a preheated oven at 180°C (350°F/Gas 4) for a few minutes, or until just cooked through.
7 To serve, divide the potatoes between 4 plates, top with the hake, and pour the sauce around the edge.

JOHN TORODE
"I doubted you would be able to get that fish with all those heavy herbs to balance as one flavour. Why I doubted I have no idea. Because it's beautiful."

Professionals 2010 Finalist
JOHN CALTON

"MasterChef meant so much to me, it was an opportunity to realise my dreams and I felt so proud to get to the finals. The competition was mentally and physically tough but I kept it together and got better and better. The three dishes I made for the final were the best I'd cooked the whole time, and it was such a great feeling knowing that it had all come good in the end. I haven't reached where I want to be yet – I want to keep going, keep learning and hopefully one day I'll be as good as Michel."

MAIN

PAN-FRIED TURBOT WITH LANGOUSTINES AND TRUFFLED CELERIAC PURÉE p.104

"This looked beautiful, and tasted absolutely glorious. Wonderful combinations, and the celeriac and Bramley apple purée was just heavenly." MICHEL

STARTER

SALAD OF LOBSTER, BASIL, MANGO, AND AVOCADO p.52

"A beautiful starter
– fresh, almost sweet
lobster with the nice
tang of that basil and
the juicy sweetness
of the mango.
Absolutely lovely."
GREGG

DESSERT

**DARK CHOCOLATE MOUSSE,
GREEN TEA FINANCIER,
AND MILK ICE CREAM** p.320

"I think John excelled
with this – the milk ice
cream going into the
smooth, rich chocolate
is an absolute treat."
GREGG

PAN-FRIED TURBOT WITH LANGOUSTINES AND TRUFFLED CELERIAC PURÉE

John Calton head chef and 2010 Professionals finalist

PREPARATION TIME
1 hour 30 minutes

COOKING TIME
1 hour

SERVES 4

4 live langoustines (see MasterTip p.99)
1 celeriac, peeled and halved
85g (3oz) butter
700ml (1 pint 2fl oz) chicken stock
2½ tbsp olive oil
3 tbsp whole milk
2 tbsp double cream
2 tsp white truffle oil
1 small piece of truffle, finely
  grated (optional)
2 Braeburn or Granny Smith apples,
  peeled, cored, and finely diced

3 tbsp apple juice
juice of ½ lemon
1 banana shallot, finely chopped
1 garlic clove, finely chopped
250ml (9fl oz) white wine
bunch of flat-leaf parsley, chopped
salt and freshly ground black pepper
4 thick fillets of turbot, approx.
  150g (5½oz) each, skinned
200g (7oz) baby spinach
8 white asparagus spears, peeled

MICHEL ROUX JR

"Bang on the ticket. Wow! That's great. The langoustine with the celeriac and apple purée is heavenly. That is glorious."

1 Blanch the langoustines in boiling water for 1 minute. Refresh in iced water, then peel and set aside.

2 Cut 2 slices 3cm (1¼in) thick from half of the celeriac. Cut 4 rounds from them using a 4cm (1½in) cutter. Melt 15g (½oz) butter in a heavy pan and gently colour the rounds on both sides. Add 150ml (5fl oz) stock and 15g (½oz) butter, cover, and braise for 10 minutes. Turn and braise for another 5–10 minutes until cooked but with a bit of bite.

3 Finely chop the remaining celeriac. Heat 1 tbsp of olive oil in a pan and sweat the celeriac, covered, over medium heat for 5–10 minutes until softened but not coloured. Add 3 tbsp stock, the milk, and cream and cook for 5–10 minutes until soft. Purée in a food processor or with a hand-held blender and pass through a sieve. Season with ½–1 tsp truffle oil to taste and a little of the grated truffle (if using) and set aside.

4 Cook the apples with 15g (½oz) of butter and the apple and lemon juice for 5 minutes, then purée, sieve, and set aside.

5 Heat 1 tbsp olive oil in a pan and sweat the shallot and garlic until translucent. Add the wine, bring to the boil and reduce by half. Add 500ml (16fl oz) stock and reduce until syrupy, then whisk in about 25g (scant 1oz) cold butter until a rich emulsion sauce is achieved. Finish with grated truffle or 1 tsp truffle oil, parsley, and seasoning to taste.

6 Heat 15g (½oz) butter in a large frying pan and fry the turbot fillets for 4–5 minutes on each side. In another pan, heat ½ tbsp olive oil and wilt the spinach. Blanch the asparagus in boiling water for 2–3 minutes. Refresh and set aside.

7 Drop the langoustines into the sauce to warm through. Reheat all of the other components and serve as shown.

SEA BREAM WITH RATATOUILLE, TOMATO COULIS, CRISPY POTATO AND CHEESE BALLS

Nargis Chaudhary physiotherapist and 2010 semi-finalist

PREPARATION TIME
55 minutes

COOKING TIME
1 hour 30 minutes

SERVES 4

2 waxy potatoes, about 200g (7oz) each, peeled and halved
30g (1oz) butter
salt and freshly ground black pepper
120g (4¼oz) smoked mozzarella cheese or smoked Lancashire or Cheddar cheese, cut into small cubes
2 eggs, beaten
100g (3½oz) day-old breadcrumbs
500ml (16fl oz) sunflower oil
2 tbsp plain flour, seasoned
4 sea bream fillets, 140–150g (5–5½oz) each
15g (½oz) flat-leaf parsley, leaves only, to garnish

FOR THE RATATOUILLE
75ml (2½fl oz) olive oil
1 whole garlic bulb, halved horizontally
2 courgettes, chopped
1 large aubergine, chopped
2 red onions, chopped
1 large leek, chopped
1 red pepper, deseeded and chopped
1 green pepper, deseeded and chopped
1 fennel bulb, chopped
250g (9oz) cherry tomatoes

FOR THE COULIS
250g (9oz) cherry tomatoes
large pinch of caster sugar
1 tsp balsamic vinegar

JOHN TORODE "That piece of bream on top is cooked beautifully. Going very, very well with those sweet vegetables inside your ratatouille."

1 Place the oil and garlic for the ratatouille in a small pan. Heat gently for 10 minutes, then leave to infuse for at least 30 minutes.
2 Preheat the oven to 220°C (425°F/Gas 7). Boil the potatoes in salted water for 20 minutes until soft. Drain, add the butter, and mash with some salt and pepper. Transfer the mash to a bowl and leave to cool slightly, then add the cheese to the mash and mix well. Shape into 28 walnut-sized balls. Dip the balls in egg first, then breadcrumbs. Place in the fridge for about an hour to firm up.
3 Place the vegetables for the ratatouille in a large roasting tin. Add the infused oil, discarding the garlic, season, and mix well. Roast in the oven for 40 minutes, until the vegetables are tender and roasted.
4 For the coulis, blend the tomatoes with the sugar and vinegar. Strain through a fine sieve, season, and set aside.
5 Heat the oil to very hot and fry the cheese balls in 3–4 batches for 3 minutes, turning frequently until golden. Drain on kitchen paper.
6 Place the flour on a plate. Preheat a large frying pan. Add a little oil, coat the fish in the flour, and add it to the oil, skin side down. Cook for 4 minutes over medium heat until the skin is crispy. Turn and cook for a further 2–4 minutes depending on how thick the fish is.
7 To serve, place a mound of ratatouille in the middle of warmed plates, then arrange the fish on top and the crispy potatoes around. Spoon the tomato coulis over and scatter with parsley leaves to serve.

BLACK BREAM WITH BROAD BEANS, MUSSELS, AND SALSIFY

Matt Edwards music executive and 2010 quarter-finalist

2 medium black bream or sea bream, scaled, gutted, and filleted
1 carrot, chopped
1 fennel bulb, chopped
1 small onion, chopped
large bunch of flat-leaf parsley, chopped
1 fresh bay leaf
50ml (3 tbsp) dry vermouth
175ml (6fl oz) dry white wine
400g (14oz) mussels, cleaned and barnacles removed

500g (1lb 2oz) Jersey Royal potatoes (see MasterTip, p.200)
salt and freshly ground black pepper
100g (3½oz) butter
2 tbsp olive oil
200g (7oz) salsify, peeled and sliced
6 shallots, finely chopped
175g (6oz) baby broad beans
squeeze of fresh lemon juice
small handful of tarragon leaves, chopped
2 tbsp plain flour

PREPARATION TIME
45 minutes

COOKING TIME
1 hour

SERVES 4

1 Score the skin of the fish fillets with a sharp knife and set aside. Place the fish bones in a pot with the vegetables, half the parsley, the bay leaf, and vermouth, and cover with cold water. Bring to the boil, then simmer gently, covered, for 20 minutes. Strain, place back on the heat, and bubble for 10 minutes.

2 Bring the wine to the boil in a wide, heavy pan. Add the mussels, cover, and cook for 3–4 minutes, or until they have all opened. Discard any that have not. Remove the meat from the shells, reserve the cooking liquor, and discard the shells. Set aside.

3 Boil the potatoes in salted water for 15 minutes, or until tender. Drain, and then roughly crush with a small handful of parsley, salt, pepper, and 25g (scant 1oz) butter.

4 Heat 1 tbsp of olive oil in a large sauté pan, add the salsify, and fry over medium heat for about 5 minutes, or until golden brown on all sides. Add the shallots and fry for 2–3 minutes. Blanch the broad beans in boiling salted water for 1–2 minutes, then refresh in cold water. Slip off the skins, add the beans to the sauté pan, and fry for 1–2 minutes. Add 25g (scant 1oz) butter, the lemon juice, a small handful of parsley and tarragon, and stir. Add 200ml (7fl oz) fish stock and the mussel cooking liquor and bubble for 3–4 minutes. Season.

5 Season the fish fillets with salt and pepper and dust with flour. Heat a large frying pan until hot, add the remaining olive oil and butter, and place the fish skin-side down in the pan. Fry for 3–4 minutes, turn over, and fry for another 2–3 minutes on the other side.

6 To serve, divide the potatoes between 4 plates, spoon the bean and salsify mix round the potatoes, and top with the fish.

MASTER TIP
BLACK BREAM

Also known as "old wife", the black sea bream is considered to be one of the finest of the bream family for the table, and its firm, white-textured flesh is particularly admired in the Mediterranean. Bream require careful trimming and scaling.

PAN-FRIED HALIBUT WITH SAUTÉ POTATOES AND A CREAMY CLAM SAUCE

Dhruv Baker sales director and 2010 champion

PREPARATION TIME
40 minutes

COOKING TIME
55 minutes

SERVES 4

500g (1lb 2oz) white fish bones
  (no oily fish bones)
1 carrot, chopped
1 celery stick, chopped
1 leek, chopped
½ bulb fennel, chopped
1 sprig each of thyme and parsley
600g (1lb 5oz) Maris Piper potatoes,
  thickly sliced
100g (3½oz) unsalted butter
3 tbsp olive oil
salt and freshly ground black pepper

50g (1¾oz) piece of chorizo, peeled
  and finely chopped
250g (9oz) clams in shells
2 shallots, finely chopped
125ml (4fl oz) dry white wine
125ml (4fl oz) dry vermouth
large pinch of saffron
125ml (4fl oz) double cream
125ml (4fl oz) single cream
4 halibut fillets, approx. 150g (5½oz) each
250g (9oz) bag baby spinach
1 lemon, halved

GREGG WALLACE

"The flavours are absolutely superb. It's salty, it's almost caramelly sweet, and it's got those nice deep bits of clam in there as well."

1 For the fish stock, place the fish bones in a large saucepan with 1.5 litres (2¾ pints) of water and the carrot, celery, leek, fennel, and herbs. Bring gently to the boil and simmer for 30 minutes. Drain the stock into a jug and discard the flavourings and bones.

2 Parboil the potatoes in salted water for 12–15 minutes, until just beginning to yield but holding their shape. Drain well and leave to steam dry for a couple of minutes. Melt a third of the butter with half the olive oil in a frying pan and add the potatoes. Sauté for 15 minutes, turning them every 4–5 minutes. Sprinkle with seasoning.

3 Dry fry the chorizo in a small frying pan for 3–4 minutes, or until crispy. Transfer to a plate lined with kitchen paper.

4 Cook the clams in a little water in a covered saucepan for 3–4 minutes and drain. Remove the clams from the shells and retain both.

5 In a medium saucepan, heat half of the remaining butter and cook the shallots, covered, for 5 minutes. Add the wine, vermouth, and 250ml (9fl oz) of the fish stock and reduce by about three-quarters. Add the saffron and creams and cook for about 5 minutes until the sauce has thickened. Strain through a sieve into a clean pan.

6 For the halibut, heat the remaining butter and oil in a frying pan and place the halibut fillets in, skin side down. Cook for 3–4 minutes on each side, depending on their thickness, or until cooked through.

7 Lightly steam the spinach and season to taste.

8 Reheat the sauce with the clams and finish with a squeeze of lemon.

9 To serve, put the potatoes in the centre of 4 plates with the halibut on top. Put some spinach to 1 side and the clam shells around the plate, filling each with the chorizo. Spoon the cream sauce over.

HALIBUT IN CHERVIL SAUCE WITH MINTED PEAS, FENNEL, AND SAUTÉED POTATOES
Christine Hamilton TV personality and 2010 Celebrity finalist

500g (1lb 2oz) baby new potatoes
3 tbsp olive oil
75g (2½oz) butter
5 shallots, finely chopped
salt and freshly ground black pepper
125ml (4fl oz) vermouth
250ml (8fl oz) fish stock
150ml (5fl oz) double cream
2 lemons, halved

dash of Pernod (optional)
1 bulb fennel, diced
300g (10oz) shelled or frozen peas
15g (½oz) sprigs of mint
3 tbsp plain flour
4 halibut loins or fillets, approx.
  150g (5½oz) each, skinless
3 tbsp fish stock
1 tbsp chopped chervil or chives

PREPARATION TIME
30 minutes

COOKING TIME
1 hour 25 minutes

SERVES 4

1 Cook the potatoes in salted boiling water for 15 minutes and drain. Heat 2 tbsp of the oil and a knob of the butter, and add one of the chopped shallots. Cook for 3–4 minutes to soften and add the par-cooked potatoes with seasoning. Continue to cook over medium heat for 15–20 minutes, shaking the pan regularly, until golden.
2 For the sauce, cook the remaining 4 shallots in 15g (½oz) of the butter in a wide deep frying pan for 5 minutes to soften. Add the vermouth and reduce by half. Add the stock and reduce by half again. Finally, add the double cream and reduce again to the consistency of double cream. Pour through a fine sieve into a small saucepan and season to taste with salt, pepper, and lemon juice. Add a dash of Pernod (if using). Strain the sauce through a fine sieve and set aside.
3 Preheat the oven to 200°C (400°F/Gas 6). In a saucepan, melt 25g (scant 1oz) of the butter and add the fennel. Cook for 20–25 minutes until softened. Add a squeeze of lemon and some seasoning.
4 Cook the peas in salted boiling water with 2 sprigs of the mint. Drain and discard the mint. Put the peas back in the pan and crush. Roughly chop the remaining mint leaves (off the stalk) and add to the peas to taste. Add seasoning. Stir in the fennel with a knob of butter.
5 Put the flour on a plate and add seasoning. Dip the halibut in the flour and coat all over. Preheat an ovenproof frying pan and melt a knob of butter and the remaining 1 tbsp of oil. When it's hot, add the fish and cook for 2 minutes to seal. Turn the fillets over and add the stock. Finish roasting the fish in the oven for 4–5 minutes.
6 To serve, arrange the peas and fennel in a small mound on each plate, or lightly press into a 7.5cm (3in) diameter ring then remove the ring. Place the fish on top and arrange the potatoes around the outside. Spoon the sauce over and garnish with the chervil or chives.

MASTER TIP
HALIBUT

Also known as the "cow of the sea", halibut has a dense, white, firm-textured flesh and is the largest of all the flat fish. Halibut flesh is moist and very lean with a sweet, mild taste; take care when cooking as the lack of fat makes it easy to over-cook.

MONICA'S MASTERCLASS
FILLETING A FLAT FISH

Flat fish can be filleted into four small "quarter cross-cut" single fillets or two larger "cross-cut" double fillets, as shown here. The key point to remember is to keep the knife close to the bone and to use long, sweeping strokes.

1 | Slice along the head

Start with a whole fish, skinned and gutted; a Dover sole is shown here. Trim the fins and remove the gills with scissors, if they haven't already been. Slice all the way across the base of the head, down to the backbone, to separate the fillet from the head.

2 | Cut into the sides

Starting at the head end, cut along one side of the fish, a short distance in from the edge, slicing just above the bone and keeping the knife almost flat. Turn the fish around and make the same cut along the outer edge of the other side.

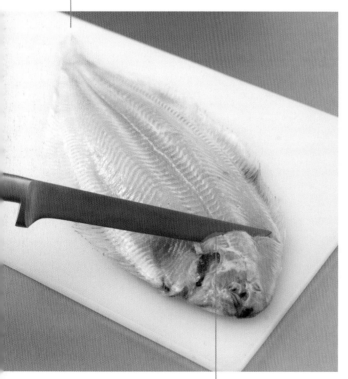

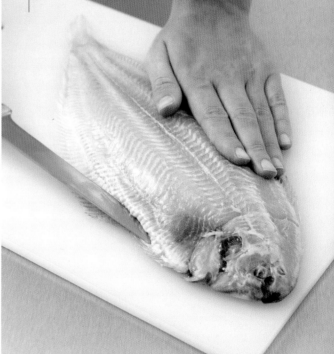

Cut close to the head so there is minimal waste.

"Flat fish, such as Dover sole,
are very versatile and wonderful
pan-fried, steamed, or poached.
They're also great for fish mousse."

3 Release the fillet

Returning to the first side, insert the knife and this time cut all the way across the fish, with a long stroking action. Release the fillet at the backbone and continue cutting to the other side, until the whole fillet is released.

4 Lift and repeat

Lift off the fillet in a single piece and then turn the fish over to repeat the process. Smaller types of flat fish, such as Dover sole, are more commonly cut into whole fillets and a single fish will be enough to feed two people.

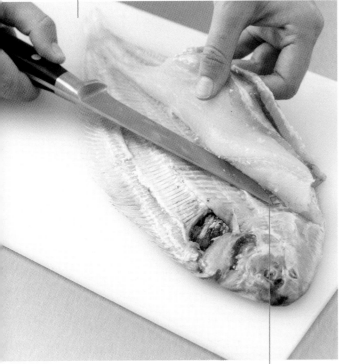

Cut gently and keep the knife close to the bones, almost flat.

MICHEL ROUX JR'S
SOLE CANCALAISE

This is a beautiful seafood dish that has the wonderful flavours of Dover sole, oysters, and prawns, all held together in a rich yet light, creamy white wine sauce. Absolute heaven on a plate!

PREPARATION TIME
25 minutes

COOKING TIME
55 minutes

SERVES 4

2 whole Dover sole, approx. 350g (12oz) each, skinned on both sides
60g (2oz) butter, softened
2 shallots, finely chopped
200ml (7fl oz) dry white wine
500g (1lb 2oz) baby new potatoes
salt and freshly ground black pepper

8 whole raw oysters in their shells
8 whole raw prawns in their shells
100ml (3½fl oz) double cream
½ lemon
1 Romaine lettuce, leaves separated
1 tbsp chopped parsley

1 Preheat the oven to 190°C (375°F/Gas 5). Butter an ovenproof dish, large enough to hold both fish, with 20g (¾oz) of the butter. Place the Dover soles in the dish and scatter over the shallots. Pour over the wine and loosely cover with foil. Bake in the oven for 35–40 minutes.
2 Meanwhile, place the potatoes in a saucepan of salted water and bring to the boil. Cook them for 20 minutes. Drain and add 20g (¾oz) of the butter with some seasoning, cover and leave to keep warm.
3 Open each oyster and sieve the liquid into a bowl. Put the oysters in a separate bowl and discard the shells. Peel the prawns and place the heads and shells in a saucepan. Add the reserved oyster water.
4 When the fish is cooked, strain the wine into a saucepan with the prawns and bring to the boil. Cover the sole with foil to keep warm. Boil the stock and wine rapidly to reduce by half. Add the cream and reduce by half again. Pass the sauce through a fine sieve into another pan. Discard the shells. Season to taste and add a squeeze of lemon juice.
5 Blanch the lettuce in salted boiling water for 30 seconds and drain in a colander, cooling under running cold water. Cut out the stem of each leaf and then wrap a leaf around each oyster to make little parcels.
6 Preheat a small frying pan and add the remaining butter and the prawns, and cook for 2–3 minutes, turning until they have turned pink and feel firm. Meanwhile, steam the oyster parcels for 3 minutes. Reheat the potatoes with the parsley.
7 Use a palette knife to carefully take the fillets off the sole from both sides of the fish. Discard the bones. Serve 2 fillets of sole per person with the potatoes. Place 2 oyster parcels on each plate with the prawns. Reheat the sauce and spoon it over the fish.

PAN-FRIED DOVER SOLE WITH PEA AND BROAD BEAN STEW AND QUAIL'S EGGS

Stacie Stewart PA and 2010 semi-finalist

4 Dover sole fillets, approx. 120g (4¼oz) each
seasoned plain flour for dusting
knob of clarified butter
4 tbsp olive oil

FOR THE TARTARE SAUCE
2 egg yolks
2 tsp white wine vinegar
2 tsp freshly squeezed lemon juice
good pinch of salt
300ml (10fl oz) groundnut oil
1 tsp Dijon mustard
2 small shallots, very finely chopped
4 small gherkins, finely chopped
1 tbsp capers, roughly chopped

1 tbsp parsley, chopped
1 tbsp chives, chopped
freshly ground black pepper

FOR THE QUAIL'S EGGS
8 quail's eggs
1 egg, beaten
50g (1¾oz) day-old white breadcrumbs
200ml (7fl oz) groundnut oil

FOR THE STEW
200g (7oz) fresh or frozen broad beans
500ml (16fl oz) chicken stock
225g (8oz) frozen petits pois
25g (scant 1oz) unsalted butter

PREPARATION TIME
35 minutes

COOKING TIME
40 minutes

SERVES 4

1 To make the tartare sauce, put the egg yolks, vinegar, lemon juice, and salt into a blender or food processor. Mix briefly to combine. With the machine running, gradually trickle in the oil to form a smooth mayonnaise. Scrape into a bowl and add the remaining ingredients. Season with salt and pepper to taste. Cover and chill until required.
2 Hard boil the quail's eggs for 3 minutes. Place them in iced water and then peel. Dry the eggs on kitchen paper and coat in egg and then in the breadcrumbs. Repeat, pressing the mixture firmly around the egg. Place the eggs in the fridge to set for about 30 minutes.
3 For the stew, preheat the oven to 200°C (400°F/Gas 6). Cook the broad beans in the stock for about 10 minutes. Transfer half the beans to a food processor and add the peas to the pan. Return to the boil and simmer for 5 minutes. Blend the broad beans with a little of the cooking liquid, until smooth. Return to the pan to thicken the stew.
4 Dust the fish with flour. Heat the butter and 2 tbsp of the oil in a large frying pan. Add the fish and cook for 3–4 minutes. Pour over the remaining oil, flip over the fillets, and cook for a further 3–4 minutes. Transfer to the oven for about 8 minutes to complete cooking.
5 Heat the groundnut oil in a large saucepan and deep-fry the quail's eggs for 4 minutes, or until crispy and golden. Drain on kitchen paper.
6 To serve, reheat the stew and stir in the butter. Spoon into bowls and top with the fish. Add the eggs on the side and serve with the sauce.

RAGOUT OF FISH WITH CUCUMBER AND BASIL CREAM SAUCE AND PARMESAN TWISTS

Christine Hamilton TV personality and 2010 Celebrity finalist

PREPARATION TIME
20 minutes

COOKING TIME
35 minutes

SERVES 4

FOR THE TWISTS
125g (4½oz) all-butter puff pastry
1 egg, lightly beaten
20g (¾oz) Parmesan cheese,
  finely grated
large pinch of cayenne pepper

FOR THE RAGOUT
20g (¾oz) butter
2 x 150g (5½oz) fillets of salmon,
  skinned and left whole
150g (5½oz) monkfish fillet, skinned
  and cut into 3cm (1¼in) cubes
4 plump scallops, roes removed
  (see MasterTip, p.42)

12 large raw tiger prawns, peeled
salt and freshly ground black pepper
200ml (7fl oz) fish stock
75ml (2½fl oz) dry vermouth
100ml (3½fl oz) dry white wine
100ml (3½fl oz) double cream
10cm (4in) piece of cucumber, peeled,
  halved lengthways, deseeded,
  and sliced
20g (¾oz) basil leaves, chopped
½ lemon
125g (4½oz) samphire or
  fine asparagus
200g (7oz) long grain and wild
  rice, cooked

MASTER TIP

SAMPHIRE

Growing along seashores and river estuaries, samphire has thin, fleshy leaves and an appetizing salty flavour. It is best lightly steamed or pickled. Rock samphire is similar in appearance, but grows only on rocky beaches. It has a strong, resinous, slightly lemony taste.

1 Preheat the oven to 200°C (400°F/Gas 6). Lightly grease an 8cm (3in) ring mould and line a large baking tray with parchment.
2 To make the twists, roll the pastry on a floured surface to 30 x 12cm (12 x 5in). Brush the pastry with the egg, and sprinkle over the cheese and cayenne. Press the cheese into the pastry. Cut into 4 strips and twist each one into a circle. Brush with more egg and transfer to the baking tray. Cook in the oven for about 15 minutes, or until golden.
3 For the ragout, melt the butter in a large frying pan and add the salmon, monkfish, scallops, and prawns. Sprinkle with salt. Cook the fish for 3–4 minutes, turning once or twice, to cook through. Remove the monkfish, scallops, and prawns to a warming dish, cover in foil, and keep warm. Cook the salmon for a further 2–3 minutes, keeping it a little underdone in the middle. Gently flake and keep warm.
4 Add the fish stock to the pan, and boil until it has reduced by half. Add the vermouth, wine, and cream, and boil again until it has reduced by about half and begins to thicken slightly. Strain the sauce to remove the cooking residues, and place back in the wiped out pan.
5 Add the cucumber and gently cook for 2 minutes. Then add most of the basil with a good squeeze of lemon juice and seasoning to taste.
6 Steam the samphire or asparagus for 2–3 minutes, and strain.
7 To serve, place a portion of rice on the centre of each plate, top with a Parmesan twist and spoon round the ragout, garnishing with a sprig of basil.

PAN-FRIED MACKEREL, SHALLOT PURÉE, AND À LA GRECQUE VEGETABLES

Claire Lara lecturer and 2010 Professionals champion

PREPARATION TIME
35 minutes

COOKING TIME
55 minutes

SERVES 4

4 mackerel fillets, approx.
  170g (6oz) each
1 tbsp olive oil
knob of butter
1 lemon, quartered, to garnish

FOR THE SHALLOT PURÉE
25g (scant 1oz) butter
1 tbsp olive oil
6 banana shallots, finely sliced
200ml (7fl oz) hot chicken stock
salt and freshly ground black pepper

FOR THE VEGETABLES
1 tbsp olive oil
1 tsp coriander seeds

4 sprigs of thyme
4 bay leaves
large pinch of saffron
  (see MasterTip, p.147)
1 small garlic bulb, cloves separated,
  peeled, and left whole
300ml (10fl oz) dry white wine
1 tsp red wine vinegar
4 celery sticks, peeled and sliced
½ head of cauliflower, cut into florets
6 baby carrots
6 spears of asparagus, trimmed
  and halved
250g (9oz) shelled broad beans
2 plum tomatoes, cut into wedges
20g (¾oz) basil, leaves torn

1 To make the shallot purée, heat the butter and oil in a saucepan and cook the shallots covered over medium heat for 10 minutes. Pour in the stock and bring up to a simmer. Cook for 20 minutes until the shallots are soft and the liquid has reduced. Transfer to a food processor, whizz to a purée, and season to taste.

2 For the vegetables, heat a large saucepan and add the oil. Add the coriander seeds, thyme, bay leaves, saffron, and garlic and cook for 1–2 minutes. Add the wine and vinegar and bring to the boil.

3 Add the celery, cauliflower, carrots, asparagus, and broad beans to the stock and simmer, covered, for 8–10 minutes. Once they are almost cooked, remove them from the pan with a slotted spoon into a bowl. Add the tomato wedges and basil to the bowl, stir to mix and taste for seasoning. Add 2–3 tbsp of the cooking liquid from the saucepan too.

4 For the mackerel fillets, heat the oil in a large non-stick frying pan. Season the fillets and cook them, skin side down, for 5 minutes. Turn them, add the knob of butter, and continue cooking for 3–4 minutes, basting the flesh with the butter.

5 To serve, spoon some purée onto 4 plates and place the mackerel on top. Arrange the vegetables around the edges, discarding any of the whole spices or herbs. Garnish with the lemon wedges to squeeze over.

PAN-FRIED SEA TROUT WITH CRUSHED NEW POTATOES AND BABY LEEKS

Lisa Faulkner actress and 2010 Celebrity champion

500g (1lb 2oz) baby new potatoes
500g (1lb 2oz) cherry tomatoes
2 tbsp olive oil, plus a little for the fish
sea salt and freshly ground
  black pepper
1–2 tsp sherry vinegar
large pinch of caster sugar
3 tbsp double cream

25g (scant 1oz) unsalted butter
300g (10oz) baby leeks, trimmed
4 spring onions, green and white parts
  finely sliced
1 tbsp French vinaigrette dressing
4 sea trout or salmon fillets,
  approx. 175g (6oz) each
15g (½oz) basil, finely chopped

PREPARATION TIME
20 minutes

COOKING TIME
40 minutes

SERVES 4

1 Preheat the oven to 190°C (375°F/Gas 5). Put the potatoes in a large pan of boiling salted water and cook for 15–20 minutes or until tender. Drain, transfer to a bowl and cover to keep warm.
2 Take half of the tomatoes, slice them in half and arrange, cut side up, on a roasting tray. Drizzle with 1 tbsp of the oil, season well and then roast in the oven for 5–10 minutes until softened.
3 Heat the remaining oil in a saucepan and add the rest of the tomatoes. Cook them, covered, over medium heat for 8–10 minutes until softened. Add the vinegar (to taste), seasoning, and sugar. Transfer to a hand-held blender or food processor, whizz to a purée.
4 Pass the tomato sauce through a fine sieve into a clean saucepan and discard the skin and seeds in the sieve. Add the cream and butter to the sauce, check for seasoning and set aside until needed.
5 Meanwhile, place the baby leeks inside a steamer and cook for 8–10 minutes until tender.
6 Lightly crush the cooked potatoes with the back of a fork and then toss with the spring onions and vinaigrette to taste.
7 Heat a non-stick frying pan over medium heat. Rub the skin of the fish with a little oil, season well and then fry, skin side down, for 3–4 minutes until the skin is crisp. Carefully turn the fish and cook for a further minute or so for a rare-to-medium cooked fish. If you like the fish more cooked, give it a further 2 minutes.
8 When ready to serve, reheat the sauce and add the basil. Arrange a stack of crushed potatoes on 4 plates, then lay some leeks over the top and spoon on the roasted tomatoes. Place a piece of trout, crispy skin side up, on the tomatoes. Spoon most of the tomato basil sauce on the edge of the plates, with a small amount on the fish itself.

MASTER TIP
SEA TROUT

Sea trout, also known as salmon trout, is the migratory form of the brown trout. It has a particularly sweet and fine flavour that is not as intense as that of salmon. Poach it whole or in fillets.

SEA TROUT WITH BEETROOT PURÉE

Alex Rushmer freelance writer and 2010 finalist

PREPARATION TIME
15 minutes

COOKING TIME
1 hour 20 minutes

SERVES 4

4 sea trout or salmon fillets, approx.
  175g (6oz) each, pin boned
2 tbsp olive oil
knob of butter
juice of ½ lemon
sprigs of watercress, to garnish

FOR THE PURÉE
12 baby beetroots
small bunch of thyme sprigs
splash of olive oil
sea salt
splash of balsamic vinegar

FOR THE MASH
4 potatoes, chopped
100ml (3½fl oz) single cream
50g (1¾oz) butter

FOR THE HORSERADISH CREAM
1 banana shallot, finely diced
1 garlic clove, finely chopped
1 tbsp olive oil
250ml (9fl oz) fish stock
100ml (3½fl oz) single cream
1 tsp grated horseradish

FOR THE KALE
200g (7oz) kale
knob of butter

1 For the beetroot, preheat the oven to 200°C (400°F/Gas 6). Put the beetroot on a sheet of foil, add the thyme and oil and season with salt. Scrunch up the foil to seal then bake for 45 mins–1 hour, or until very soft. Remove from the oven, but keep the oven turned on.

2 Leave the beetroot to cool, then peel away the skins. Put into a blender or food processor and whizz with a little vinegar to form a purée. Spoon into a sheet of muslin and squeeze out the juice into a bowl. Reserve the juice and put the purée into a clean pan.

3 Cook the potatoes in boiling salted water for 15–20 minutes or until tender. Drain and press through a ricer. Heat the cream and butter and stir into the potatoes with plenty of seasoning. Keep warm.

4 For the horseradish cream, cook the shallot and garlic in the oil for 5 minutes to soften. Add the stock, bring to the boil, and reduce by half. Stir in the beetroot juice and reduce by half again. Strain into a pan and stir in the cream, horseradish, and seasoning to taste. Keep warm.

5 Blanch the kale in boiling salted water for 6–8 minutes, then refresh under cold running water and pat dry.

6 Put the oil in a heavy ovenproof pan to heat. Add the fish fillets, skin side down, for 3 minutes. Flip over and add the knob of butter to the pan. Spoon over the buttery juices once melted, then transfer to the oven for 5 minutes to complete the cooking. Squeeze over a little lemon juice.

7 Reheat the kale tossing it in melted butter. Divide the mash between 4 plates and top with the kale, fish and purée. Spoon the horseradish cream around the edge and garnish with the herbs.

SALMON MARINATED IN LIME, CHILLI, AND CORIANDER WITH BEETROOT RELISH

Dhruv Baker sales director and 2010 champion

PREPARATION TIME
25 minutes

COOKING TIME
10 minutes

SERVES 4

FOR THE SALMON
2 garlic cloves, finely chopped
5cm (2in) piece of fresh ginger, peeled
  and finely chopped
½ tsp sea salt
1 lime
500g (1lb 2oz) salmon fillet, skinned
  and pin-boned

FOR THE MARINADE
50g (1¾oz) spinach leaves
20g (¾oz) bunch coriander, leaves
  and stalks
10g (¼oz) bunch of mint, leaves only

2–3 green chillies, deseeded
  and roughly chopped
1 tsp lime juice
1–2 tbsp vegetable oil
1 tbsp chickpea flour (gram flour)
2 tbsp Greek yogurt
salt and freshly ground black pepper

FOR THE RELISH
340g jar pickled baby beetroot
2 shallots, sliced
1 tsp caster sugar
1 tsp lime juice
10g (¼oz) coriander leaves

JOHN TORODE

"The rich salmon against the lime, and the heat of the chilli with all those herbs I really like. And then the crunch of that onion on top. I think it's delicious."

1 For the salmon, pound the garlic and ginger with the salt in a pestle and mortar to form a smooth paste. Spoon into a shallow dish and squeeze in juice from the lime. Cut the salmon into 2.5cm (1in) cubes and add to the dish. Mix gently to coat evenly in the mixture and leave to marinate for about 10 minutes.
2 Preheat the oven to 220°C (425°F/Gas 7). Put the spinach, coriander, and mint in a blender or food processor, then add the chillies, lime juice, and a trickle of vegetable oil. Blend until smooth, adding a little more oil if the mix is too thick. Add the chickpea flour and yogurt, and blitz again to combine. Season with a little salt and add the salmon, gently turning to coat evenly.
3 Transfer the salmon to a large ovenproof dish and cook for 8–10 minutes on the top shelf, or until just cooked through and slightly browned around the edges.
4 Meanwhile, make the beetroot relish. Drain the beetroot, retaining 2 tbsp of the liquid from the jar, and cut the beetroot into tiny dice (wear gloves for this, as it stains). Put in a small bowl with the reserved liquid, shallots, sugar, lime juice, and coriander leaves. Taste for seasoning, adding salt and pepper if necessary.
5 Serve the salmon pieces topped with a generous spoonful of the beetroot relish.

MICHEL ROUX JR'S
ESCALOPE DE SAUMON À L'OSEILLE ET BOUQUETIÈRE DE LEGUMES

This is a legendary dish from the culinary dynasty of the Troisgros family, and allegedly won them their third Michelin star – a truly great dish.

4 salmon fillets, skin on
salt and freshly ground black pepper
½ tbsp olive oil
2 shallots, finely chopped
10g (¼oz) butter
200ml (7fl oz) dry white wine

100ml (3½fl oz) double cream
large handful of sorrel, or baby spinach
  leaves or dill, roughly chopped
½ lemon
choice of spring vegetables, to serve

PREPARATION TIME
20 minutes

COOKING TIME
35 minutes

SERVES 4

1 Preheat the oven to 220°C (425°F/Gas 7). Score the skin of the salmon fillets and sprinkle with some salt.

2 Heat the oil in a large non-stick pan until hot, and sear the salmon, skin side down, for about 30 seconds. Remove from the pan and carefully peel away the skin. Place the skin between 2 sheets of buttered greaseproof paper or foil, lay on a baking sheet and weigh down to press. Then cook in the oven for 10 minutes or until crisp. Remove from the oven and set aside to drain on kitchen paper. Turn off the oven.

3 Season the salmon on both sides with a little salt and pepper and cook in the same pan for about 5 minutes or until the flesh is pink. Remove the salmon from the pan and keep warm in the oven, which should still be fairly hot.

4 Drain the pan of any leftover fat and cook the shallots in the butter for about 5 minutes, or until soft, then deglaze with the white wine and quickly reduce by about half. Add the cream and again reduce until the sauce is a slightly thicker consistency. Finish with the herbs, a squeeze of lemon juice, and season to taste.

5 Serve the salmon with spring vegetables, cooked until tender, but still vibrant, and decorate with the crispy skin.

ROASTED SALMON WITH CLAMS, BROAD BEAN PURÉE, AND HORSERADISH BROTH

Alice Churchill chef de partie and 2010 Professionals semi-finalist

PREPARATION TIME
1 hour 10 minutes

COOKING TIME
50 minutes

SERVES 4

300g (10oz) frozen broad beans
sea salt and freshly ground white
  pepper
1 small onion, diced
3 fennel bulbs, cut into eighths and
  trimmings reserved
2 tbsp grated horseradish
300ml (10fl oz) whipping cream
100ml (3½fl oz) crème fraîche

600g (1lb 5oz) salmon, skin on and cut
  into 12 even-sized pieces
24 clams (see MasterTip, p.92)
300ml (10fl oz) white wine
300g (10oz) baby carrots
6 small turnips, cut into quarters
25g (scant 1oz) butter
small handful of flat-leaf parsley,
  chopped

MICHEL ROUX JR

"It's delicious.
I'd eat the lot."

1 Preheat the oven to 200°C (400°F/Gas 6). Skin the broad beans and put into boiling water to cook for 3–4 minutes, or until soft. Drain off most of the water and blitz the broad beans to a purée with a hand-held blender or by transferring to a food processor. Pass through a fine sieve and season well.

2 To make the broth, sweat the onion in a pan with the fennel trimmings. Add the horseradish. Then add the cream and crème fraîche and allow the broth to reduce for 10–15 minutes until thickened (it will have reduced by almost a half). Season well. Set aside and then heat and whisk lightly to make it frothy just before serving.

3 Place the salmon pieces in a non-stick roasting tin, skin-side up, and roast in the preheated oven for 10 minutes.

4 Put the clams into a saucepan with the wine and simmer for about 5 minutes, or until the clams have all fully opened.

5 Cook the carrots and turnips in lightly salted water for 5 minutes.

6 Gently melt the butter in a saucepan and add the parsley.

7 Reheat the bean purée gently in a pan, adding some of the vegetable cooking liquid to make it easier to reheat, if necessary.

8 To serve, divide the salmon and clams between 4 plates, toss the vegetables in the parsley butter and place alongside, then spoon over the warmed broth.

CHAUD-FROID OF SALMON ON PEAS AND BROAD BEANS WITH LEMON HOLLANDAISE

Ben Piette hospitality chef and 2010 Professionals semi-finalist

6 salmon fillets, skin on
1 tsp Dijon mustard
1 tbsp white wine vinegar
½ small lemon
handful of dill, roughly chopped
salt and freshly ground black pepper
300g (10oz) peas
300g (10oz) broad beans, podded
a little olive oil
50g (1¾oz) unsalted butter

punnet of salad cress or similar, such as red amaranth or purple shiso

FOR THE HOLLANDAISE
250g (9oz) unsalted butter
2 tbsp white wine vinegar
2 bay leaves
1 tbsp white or black peppercorns
4 egg yolks
½ small lemon

PREPARATION TIME
30 minutes

COOKING TIME
55 minutes

SERVES 4

1 Skin 2 of the salmon fillets for the tartare, about 150g (5½oz). Dice the salmon into small cubes and put in a bowl, then add the mustard, vinegar, a generous squeeze of lemon, the dill, and seasoning to taste. Cover with cling film and reserve in the fridge until serving.
2 Blanch the peas and broad beans for 1–2 minutes in boiling water, then refresh in iced water and drain. Pop the broad beans out of their skins and mix in with the peas in a bowl. Set aside until needed.
3 Prepare the hollandaise by melting the butter in a saucepan. Skim any white solids from the surface and keep warm.
4 Put the vinegar in a small saucepan with the bay leaves and peppercorns. Bring to the boil and simmer for a minute. Let this cool a little, then strain the peppercorns and bay leaves from the reduction.
5 Put the egg yolks in a metal or glass bowl and add the vinegar with a pinch of salt. Place over a pan of barely simmering water and whisk continuously for 3–5 minutes or until pale and thick.
6 Slowly whisk in the melted butter, bit by bit, until it is incorporated and has reached ribbon stage (if it gets too thick, add a splash of water). Remove from the heat and add a squeeze of lemon juice, to taste. Keep warm until needed.
7 Place the 4 whole salmon fillets in a frying pan on high heat, skin-side down, and add a little oil. After 2–3 minutes, add half of the butter, bit by bit. Reduce the heat to medium and continuously baste the fish with the butter. Cook for 6–8 minutes, depending on the thickness of the fish, until cooked through.
8 Put the peas and beans in a saucepan and sauté in the remaining butter until hot. Season to taste. Serve the salmon on a bed of peas and broad beans and with the hollandaise and tartare sauces alongside.

MICHEL ROUX JR
"The salmon has a nice crispy skin. The hollandaise I really like, the tartare is nice and fresh."

CORNISH SEAFOOD RAVIOLI WITH CRAB SAUCE AND SAMPHIRE

Dick Strawbridge TV presenter and 2010 Celebrity finalist

PREPARATION TIME
45 minutes, plus chilling

COOKING TIME
40 minutes

SERVES 4

500g (1lb 2oz) strong plain flour
  or "00" pasta flour
½ tsp salt
5 large eggs, beaten
25g (scant 1oz) butter, melted

FOR THE MOUSSE
85g (3oz) scallops, white only
1 small cooked crab, dressed and white
  and brown meat separated (see
  MasterClass, pp.56–7)
1 small egg, separated
1 tbsp double cream
salt and freshly ground white pepper

FOR THE SAUCE
225g (8oz) fish trimmings
150ml (5fl oz) dry white wine
1 garlic clove

6 vine-ripened tomatoes, chopped
1 tbsp tomato purée
small bunch of dill, separated into
  stalks and fronds
150ml (5fl oz) double cream

FOR THE FISH
100g (3½oz) monkfish fillet, sliced into
  medallions 1cm (½in) thick
4 scallops, with their coral
knob of butter
1 tbsp olive oil

FOR THE SAMPHIRE
large bunch of samphire, rinsed well
  to remove sand
1 tbsp olive oil
juice of ½ lemon
50g (1¾oz) goat's cheese

GREGG WALLACE

"Really good pasta, it's packed full of crab."

1 For the pasta, sift the flour and salt into a bowl and gradually add the eggs one at a time to form a soft dough. Knead thoroughly for at least 10 minutes or until smooth and silky. Do not be tempted to add extra flour to the dough if it seems sticky: it will become smoother as it is kneaded. If it adheres to your hands, moisten them with a little oil. Wrap the dough in cling film and set aside.

2 For the mousse, put the scallops in a food processor with the white crab meat, egg white, and double cream. Reserve the brown meat for the sauce and the egg yolk for the ravioli. Mix on pulse setting until just combined. Season with salt and white pepper. Scrape into a bowl and chill.

3 For the sauce, put all the ingredients except the dill fronds, cream, and cheese into a saucepan with 100ml (3½fl oz) water. Bring to the boil. Skim the surface with a slotted spoon, reduce the heat, and simmer for 30 minutes. Remove from the heat, stir in the brown crab meat, then pass through a sieve into a clean pan. Stir in the cream. Set aside.

4 Separate the corals from the scallops, then halve the scallops through the middle. Quickly fry in butter and olive oil for 2 minutes. Season well, then leave to cool.

5 For the ravioli, halve the pasta dough. Wrap one half in cling film and reserve for another time. Take lemon-sized pieces of the remaining dough and, one at a time, roll through a pasta machine, starting at the thickest setting and working through to the thinnest. Alternatively, use a rolling pin to roll it out extremely thinly. Stamp out 16 large discs of pasta, about 10–12cm (4–5in) wide. Moisten the edges with the reserved egg yolk.

6 To assemble the ravioli, place a spoonful of mousse on 8 discs of pasta. Top with slices of scallop, coral, and monkfish. Season and sandwich together with another pasta disc. Using a fork, press the edges firmly to seal. Place on a tray lined with cling film and chill for 30 minutes. Remove from the cling film and cook the ravioli in a large shallow pan of boiling salted water for about 5 minutes or until the pasta is cooked and the filling is thoroughly heated through. Lift out very carefully with a slotted spoon and drizzle with melted butter.

7 Blanch the samphire for 3–4 minutes in boiling salted water, then drain and toss in olive oil and lemon juice. Reheat the sauce and stir in the goat's cheese and chopped dill fronds. Spoon into a small sauceboat. Place a ravioli on each plate with a spoonful of samphire. Slice the ravioli in half or into quarters, drizzle over a little of the sauce, and serve the remainder separately.

Note For a lighter supper dish or starter, omit the monkfish and scallop halves and make smaller ravioli using only the mousse, as shown in the MasterClass pp.126–7.

FLAVOUR COMBINATION

SCALLOPS, SAMPHIRE, AND TOMATO

Scallops are the sweetest and most sensual of seafood. Serving them warm increases their sweetness. Here balanced by samphire, thin green barrels that explode in your mouth with crunchy saltiness, a proper reminder of the sea. A brilliant combination already, but the addition of tomato means there's the elusive savouriness of *umami*, the fifth taste that's known also to add a distinct feeling of comfort and well-being.

MONICA'S MASTERCLASS
ASSEMBLING RAVIOLI

The taste of fresh, home-made pasta is simply unbeatable and making your own stuffed pasta, such as ravioli, is sure to impress. The hardest part is mastering the pasta machine (see page 35); forming the ravioli is a relatively simple task.

1 Mark out the shapes

Roll out a thin sheet of pasta using a pasta machine and divide it in half into two equal lengths. Take one of the sheets and mark out the number and shape of ravioli, as specified by the recipe, by lightly scoring the pasta using a pastry cutter.

2 Place the filling

Take teaspoonfuls of the filling mixture and carefully place them in the centre of each scored raviolo half. Brush on beaten egg or a little water, to help bind the edges of the ravioli, as specified in the recipe you are following.

Lightly flour the work surface to prevent the dough from sticking.

Do not skimp on the filling but equally take care not to overload the ravioli.

"Prepare ravioli on a cold work
surface, and it's very important to
roll the pasta out thin. Have fun
trying different fillings."

3 | Position the second sheet

Take the second length of rolled-out
pasta and carefully lift it over the first
sheet, check for alignment, and then
place on top. Gently shape round
each dollop of filling, getting rid of
any air bubbles.

4 | Cut out and seal

Take the pastry cutter and run it
round the outside edges of the ravioli
sheet to form a neat edge, then cut out
each individual raviolo. Press round the
edges with your finger tips to seal but
avoid pressing so hard that the pattern
of the edge is spoilt.

WITH CELERIAC MASH – POACHED CHI
WITH SPINACH, MUSHROOMS, AND BR
EANS IN A CREAMY SOMERSET CIDER
ANCETTA-WRAPPED CHICKEN WITH
INE NUT, AND BASIL STUFFING – BLA
E VOLAILLE – CHICKEN ROULADE WIT
SAFFRON POTATOES AND A HONEY, W
ND PINE NUT SAUCE – BALLOTINE OF
WITH POMMES PURÉE, SAVOY CABBAG
IROLLES, AND MADEIRA SAUCE – CHI
ND MUSHROOM "PIE" – THAI GREEN
URRY – MURG SAAG ON PILAU RICE –
UCK LEG POORI, SAFFRON RAITA, AN
UCUMBER SALAD – PAN-ROASTED BR
F DUCK, RAINBOW CHARD, CARROTS
OLENTA – DUCK WITH SPICED TOBAC
ARAMEL, POTATO ROSTI, PICKLED C
ND DUCK HEART SALAD – PAN-ROAS

POULTRY

CHICKEN BRAISED IN CIDER AND CHORIZO WITH CELERIAC MASH

Lisa Faulkner actress and 2010 Celebrity champion

PREPARATION TIME
20 minutes

COOKING TIME
1 hour 15 minutes

SERVES 4

1 tbsp olive oil
4 chicken legs, skin on
4 chicken thighs, skin on
200g (7oz) chorizo, chopped into 2cm (¾in) pieces
1 large shallot, finely chopped
2½ tbsp plain flour
600ml (1 pint) dry cider

1 tbsp Dijon mustard
salt and freshly ground black pepper
1 large celeriac or 900g (2lb) potato or sweet potato, peeled and cut into medium-sized chunks
100ml (3½fl oz) double cream
50g (1¾oz) butter
fine green beans, to serve

1 Preheat the oven to 200°C (400°F/Gas 6). Heat the oil in a roasting tin or large pan over medium heat, then add the chicken and brown for 5–10 minutes or until golden. Remove from the tin and set aside.
2 Add the chorizo and shallot and cook for a further 5 minutes. Stir in the flour and cook for 1 minute, then gradually add the cider. Simmer for a few minutes before stirring in the mustard and seasoning to taste.
3 Return the chicken to the roasting tin and cover loosely with foil. Bake in the oven for 40 minutes, or until the chicken is cooked all the way through.
4 Meanwhile, simmer the celeriac (or potato) in water for 12–15 minutes or until tender. Drain and mash with the cream, butter, and plenty of salt and pepper. Serve with fine green beans.

FLAVOUR COMBINATION
CHORIZO AND CIDER

Chicken is extraordinary. It marries with every ingredient, fruit or vegetable, sweet or savoury, herbal or spicy. Here chef's choices make a gratifying, tightly knit combination. Apple-based cider perfects paprika-spiked chorizo sausage made from pork; who doesn't like the light acidity of apple with the sweetness of pork? Haunting and earthy paprika, whether hot or sweet, underpins the dish with welcoming "look at me colour" and bold flavour. But beware, paprika easily dominates.

POACHED CHICKEN WITH SPINACH, MUSHROOMS, AND BROAD BEANS IN A CREAMY SOMERSET CIDER SAUCE

Stacie Stewart PA and 2010 semi-finalist

90g (3¼oz) unsalted butter
2 shallots, finely chopped
1 garlic clove, finely chopped
4 sprigs of thyme
1 bay leaf
75ml (2½fl oz) Somerset cider apple brandy or Somerset cider
350ml (12fl oz) chicken stock

3 tbsp double cream
4 skinless chicken breasts
salt and freshly ground black pepper
150g (5½oz) shelled broad beans
200g (7oz) girolles or chestnut mushrooms, cleaned and sliced (see MasterTip, p.140)
200g (7oz) baby spinach leaves

PREPARATION TIME
40 minutes

COOKING TIME
1 hour 20 minutes

SERVES 4

1 Melt 25g (scant 1oz) of butter in a saucepan over low–medium heat. Add the shallots and garlic and sweat for 10 minutes, or until very soft, but not coloured. Add the thyme and bay leaf and cook for 2 minutes. Add the brandy or cider, increasing the heat a little, and simmer until the liquid is reduced by half. Stir in the stock and reduce again by half, then stir in the cream. Finally whisk in 25g (scant 1oz) of the butter, bit by bit, then set aside.

2 Season the chicken with salt and pepper, then wrap each breast in cling film. Poach in boiling water for 20–25 minutes or until cooked through. Remove and set aside to rest.

3 Cook the broad beans in a saucepan of lightly salted boiling water for 5 minutes, then drain and refresh in iced water. Melt another 25g (scant 1oz) of the butter in a frying pan. Unwrap the chicken and pan fry, turning occasionally for 10 minutes, or until golden on all sides. Remove from the pan and rest on a clean board.

4 Meanwhile, cook the mushrooms in the same pan, adding a little more butter if needed, for 5 minutes, then stir into the cider sauce with the broad beans and begin to reheat. Finally, in a separate pan, wilt the spinach leaves with the remaining 10g (¼oz) of butter, season well and drain on kitchen paper.

5 To serve, spoon the spinach on to the centre of 4 plates. Slice each chicken breast into 5 pieces and arrange on top of the spinach, placing the mushrooms, broad beans, and cider sauce around and on top of the chicken.

GREGG WALLACE

"Beautiful looking bowl of food. It looks fantastic. It looks professional. That chicken is really moist."

Celebrity 2010 Finalist
CHRISTINE HAMILTON

"By the final cook-off I was 'punch drunk' by the whole experience and chose simple food – by MasterChef standards. I decided not to overload plates, to demonstrate I had learnt something, but I didn't quite succeed. Clearly, it'll take more than John and Gregg to change this Battleaxe! Taking part was an extraordinary experience. It was more stressful than I could possibly have imagined but I am grateful that MasterChef forced me to expand my culinary horizons. I learned lessons which will stay with me for the rest of my life."

STARTER

SMOKED HADDOCK TIMBALE WITH POACHED QUAIL'S EGG p.62

"I really enjoyed the lovely combination of smoky fish and the sweet, earthy beetroot. I thought it was a good dish."
GREGG

MAIN

PANCETTA-WRAPPED CHICKEN WITH TOMATO, PINE NUT, AND BASIL STUFFING p.134

"This dish sums Christine up – she collects flavours like a magpie, and kept adding one or two more than was probably necessary!"
GREGG

DESSERT

CITRUS MERINGUE TART WITH CINNAMON CREAM AND PASSION FRUIT p.290

"This is exactly what I want in a dessert, gloopy and delicious with a zing of lime. And as an Aussie I love those wonderful tropical flavours!"
JOHN

PANCETTA-WRAPPED CHICKEN WITH TOMATO, PINE NUT, AND BASIL STUFFING

Christine Hamilton TV personality and 2010 Celebrity finalist

PREPARATION TIME
1 hour, plus chilling

COOKING TIME
1 hour 20 minutes

SERVES 4

50g (1¾oz) pine nuts
2 tbsp olive oil
4 shallots, finely chopped
2 small garlic cloves, finely chopped
50g (1¾oz) breadcrumbs
handful of basil, roughly chopped
1 egg, lightly beaten
salt and freshly ground black pepper
20–24 slices of pancetta
4 skinless chicken breasts
75g (2½oz) sunblush tomatoes in oil

FOR THE SAUCE
4 sprigs of thyme
500ml (16fl oz) vermouth
100ml (3½fl oz) double cream
1 tbsp clear honey
50g (1¾oz) unsalted butter

TO SERVE
300g (10oz) new potatoes
300g (10oz) baby carrots, peeled
knob of butter
2 Baby Gem lettuces, quartered
pinch of caster sugar

JOHN TORODE "I'm getting the rich sweetness of those tomatoes, a really lovely, rich sauce and the chicken flavour is still standing proud."

1 Preheat the oven to 180°C (350°F/Gas 4). Toast the pine nuts in a dry pan for a few minutes until golden and set aside in a large bowl. Add 1 tbsp of the oil to the pan and, on medium heat, cook 2 of the shallots and the garlic for 5 minutes. Add to the pine nuts and then add the breadcrumbs, basil, egg, and some salt and pepper. Stir to combine.
2 On 4 sheets of foil, lay 5–6 pancetta slices so they are overlapping and in a rectangle slightly larger than the chicken breasts. Make a few slashes in the thickest part of each breast, and lay between 2 sheets of cling film. Use a rolling pin to bash the chicken until about 1cm (½in) thick and then arrange over the pancetta.
3 Spoon the tomatoes and stuffing over the chicken in a strip along one of the shortest sides, and roll into a log shape. Wrap tightly in foil, twisting the ends to secure, then chill in the fridge for at least 1 hour.
4 Place the chicken parcels on a roasting tray. Cook for 30 minutes, then unwrap the foil (reserving any juices left in the foil parcels) and cook for a further 15 minutes or until cooked.
5 Meanwhile, make the sauce by cooking the remaining shallots in a little olive oil with the thyme sprigs for about 3 minutes or until soft. Add the vermouth and simmer until reduced by half, then stir in the cream, honey, and any reserved juices. Reduce the sauce again by half and remove from the heat before whisking in the butter.
6 In separate pans, boil the potatoes and carrots in salted water until tender. Melt the butter in a frying pan, then gently braise the lettuce with a pinch of sugar and some seasoning for 5–8 minutes, until golden. Slice the chicken and serve alongside the vegetables, spooning over the sauce.

MICHEL ROUX JR'S
BLANQUETTE DE VOLAILLE

This is an especially rich and delicious chicken dish. The name translates as "white meat in white sauce", so the finished dish should have no colour in it at all, except for the crisp, golden crouton.

PREPARATION TIME
30 minutes

COOKING TIME
55 minutes

SERVES 4

2 skinless chicken breasts, halved
2 chicken legs, skinned
2 chicken thighs, skinned
1 large carrot, quartered
2 onions, 1 cut into quarters and
  1 studded with a whole clove
1 bouquet garni (see MasterTip, left)
1 litre (1¾ pints) chicken stock
125ml (4fl oz) double cream
1 large egg yolk

salt and freshly ground black pepper
juice of ½ small lemon

TO SERVE
knob of butter
2 thick, crustless slices of bread, cut
  into large rounds
12 baby onions, peeled
125g (4½oz) small button mushrooms
cooked pilau rice, to serve

MASTER TIP
BOUQUET GARNI

A bouquet garni is a bundle of herbs that is usually tied together with a piece of string and then used to flavour stews, stocks, and soups. It is removed after cooking and before eating. For this recipe, use ½ celery stick, ½ small leek, and herbs such as a sprig of thyme, flat-leaf parsley stalks, and 1 bay leaf.

1 Place all the chicken pieces into a large saucepan with the carrot, onion, and bouquet garni. Add the chicken stock, making sure all the chicken is covered by the liquid, adding more stock if necessary. Cover with a piece of baking parchment cut to fit the pan; there's no need to add the pan lid as well. Bring to the boil, then reduce the heat and simmer for 25–30 minutes or until the chicken is cooked through.
2 Remove the pan from the heat, and set aside. Ladle 250ml (9fl oz) of the stock into a small pan. Bring up to a simmer and reduce by half. Then add 100ml (3½fl oz) of the cream and reduce again.
3 Meanwhile, in a bowl, mix together the egg yolk and the remaining double cream. Remove the pan from the heat and stir in the egg and cream mixture. Stir until incorporated and the sauce thickened slightly. Season to taste and flavour with lemon juice.
4 For the croutons, melt the butter in a separate pan and fry the round bread until golden and crisp.
5 Meanwhile, put 500ml (16fl oz) of the stock from the chicken pan into another pan along with the baby onions. Bring the liquid to the boil, reduce the heat, and simmer for 10–15 minutes or until the onions are tender. Add the mushrooms, cover, and simmer for a further 10 minutes. Drain the onions and mushrooms and keep warm until serving. Remove the chicken from the stock.
6 Divide the chicken between 4 plates. Pour over the sauce and add the onions, mushrooms, and croutons. Serve with pilau rice.

CHICKEN ROULADE WITH SAFFRON POTATOES AND A HONEY, WALNUT, AND PINE NUT SAUCE

Tim Kinnaird paediatrician and 2010 finalist

PREPARATION TIME
1 hour

COOKING TIME
1 hour 50 minutes

SERVES 4

5 unsmoked streaky bacon rashers, sliced into small pieces
2 chicken thighs, skinless and boneless, chopped into small chunks
2 tbsp olive oil
3 shallots, finely chopped
50g (1¾oz) chestnut mushrooms, diced into 1cm (½)cubes
1 tsp chopped sage leaves
salt and freshly ground black pepper
4 skinless chicken breasts

25g (scant 1oz) walnuts
15g (½oz) pine nuts
250ml (8fl oz) chicken stock
2 tbsp clear honey
3 tsp Dijon mustard
75g (2½oz) unsalted butter
3 bay leaves
1 large sprig of thyme
large pinch of saffron
650g (1½lb) waxy potatoes, such as Desirée or Maris Piper, sliced

JOHN TORODE

"The flavour combinations zing around in your mouth and test your mind and your palate."

1 For the stuffing, put the bacon and chicken thighs into a blender or food processor and pulse until combined (no more than 10 seconds). Heat 1 tbsp of the oil in a pan and cook 1 shallot for a few minutes, or until softened. Add the mushrooms and sage and cook for 7–8 minutes. Season well and allow to cool, then stir into the minced meat.
2 Flatten each chicken breast between 2 sheets of cling film. Divide the stuffing between each, roll up, tuck in the ends, and wrap tightly in cling film. Poach in simmering water for 15–20 minutes.
3 Meanwhile, blanch the walnuts in boiling water for 30 seconds. Drain and remove as much of the skin as possible. Toast the pine nuts for a few minutes until golden, then grind the walnuts and pine nuts together in a pestle and mortar. In a small pan, add 100ml (3½fl oz) of the stock with the honey and mustard and stir in the nuts. Bring up to the boil, then remove from the heat and keep warm.
4 Using a large, wide-based pan, sauté the remaining shallots in 25g (scant 1oz) of the butter for 5 minutes or until a pale gold. Melt the remaining butter with the bay leaves, thyme, and saffron, then add the potatoes, pour over the remaining stock, and bring to the boil.
5 Reduce the heat, cover with greased greaseproof paper and a lid, and cook gently for 20 minutes or until tender. Remove the lid and paper and simmer for 35–40 minutes, or until the liquid has mostly been absorbed. Remove the bay leaves.
6 Unwrap the chicken. Heat the remaining oil in a pan and cook the chicken for 8–10 minutes, turning frequently until evenly golden. Slice and serve with the potatoes and nut sauce.

ROASTED CHICKEN BREAST WITH THYME RISOTTO AND PAN-FRIED CHANTERELLES

Alex Rushmer freelance writer and 2010 finalist

2 chickens, about 1kg (2¼lb) each
salt and freshly ground black pepper
bunch of thyme
2 small onions, roughly chopped
1 tbsp olive oil
250ml (8fl oz) dry white wine
2 good-quality chicken stock cubes
15g (½oz) dried porcini
2 garlic cloves, bruised

splash of light soy sauce
4 shallots, finely chopped
50g (1¾oz) unsalted butter
200g (7oz) Vialone Nano risotto rice
150ml (5fl oz) dry white vermouth
finely grated zest of 1 unwaxed lemon
25g (scant 1oz) Parmesan cheese,
   finely grated
100g (3½oz) chanterelles, sliced

PREPARATION TIME
20 minutes

COOKING TIME
1 hour 15 minutes

SERVES 4

1 Preheat the oven to 180°C (350°F/Gas 4). Season the chickens and place in a roasting tin. Put 3 thyme sprigs and the onions in the cavities. Drizzle the skin with oil. Pour the wine into the roasting tin and cover the tin tightly with foil. Roast for 45 minutes, then remove the foil, baste with the juices, and roast for another 15 minutes or until the skin is golden and the breast just cooked through. Remove from the oven, cover with foil, and leave to rest for 15 minutes.
2 Dissolve the stock cubes in a pan with 1.2 litres (2 pints) boiling water. Add the porcini, garlic, a sprig of thyme, and the soy sauce, and bring to the boil. Leave to simmer gently for 10 minutes to infuse.
3 Sauté the shallots gently in half the butter for 5 minutes. Stir in the rice and mix to coat in the buttery shallots. Pour in 75ml (2½fl oz) vermouth and boil over high heat until evaporated away. Place a sieve over the risotto and gradually stir in the stock a ladleful at a time, making sure it is fully absorbed before adding the next. Place the flavourings caught in the sieve back into the simmering stock so that the flavour keeps intensifying. Once the rice is cooked but still retains some bite (at least 30 minutes), stir in the lemon zest and some thyme leaves. Stir in the Parmesan, then taste and season.
4 Lift the chickens onto a warmed plate. Pour off excess fat from the roasting tin then set the tin over the hob. Stirring continuously, add 75ml (2½fl oz) vermouth and deglaze the pan over high heat. Strain into a clean pan and bubble for 10–15 minutes or until reduced by a third.
5 In a frying pan, sauté the chanterelles in the remaining butter over high heat until golden brown. Season well and set aside. Carve off the chicken breasts and slice each into 6–8 pieces.
6 Spoon the risotto into warmed dishes and place the chicken on top. Spoon the mushrooms over, drizzle with jus, and garnish with thyme.

GREGG WALLACE

"Mmm, that's lovely. I love the deep, deep taste of that sauce around the perfectly cooked rice, specks of thyme, and really moist chicken."

BALLOTINE OF CHICKEN WITH POMMES PURÉE, SAVOY CABBAGE, GIROLLES, AND MADEIRA SAUCE

Dhruv Baker sales director and 2010 champion

PREPARATION TIME
1 hour 45 minutes

COOKING TIME
1 hour

SERVES 4

300g (10oz) pork belly
1 tsp tarragon leaves
1 tsp fennel seeds
finely grated zest of 1 small lemon
salt and freshly ground black pepper
4 Maris Piper potatoes
100ml (3½fl oz) full-fat milk, warmed
100g (3½oz) butter
6 shallots, chopped
olive oil for frying
1 sprig of thyme, leaves only
1 bay leaf
75ml (2½fl oz) red wine
75ml (2½fl oz) Madeira wine
250ml (8fl oz) pork demi glace or
   beef stock
2 skinless chicken breasts

FOR THE CABBAGE
½ small Savoy cabbage, halved, cored,
   and leaves shredded
85g (3oz) smoked bacon lardons
100g (3½oz) cooked chestnuts
   (vacuum packed are fine), sliced
1 small carrot, finely diced
75ml (2½fl oz) single cream

FOR THE MUSHROOMS
100g (3½oz) girolle mushrooms,
   brushed clean
2 garlic cloves, peeled and left whole

MASTER TIP
GIROLLES

Highly-prized girolles or chanterelles have smooth, tender flesh and a noticeably nutty, fruity flavour. They are best sautéed. The trumpet shape and concave cap make girolles easy to recognize. The striking yellow colour fades as the mushroom matures.

1 Mince the pork in a blender or food processor until coarsely chopped and then stir in the tarragon, fennel seeds, and lemon zest. Season well with salt and pepper and chill until needed.
2 Boil the potatoes whole in their skins for 20–25 minutes or until tender. Drain and, when cool enough to handle, peel off the skins and press through a potato ricer. Mix in the warmed milk and 25g (scant 1oz) of butter with plenty of seasoning. Set aside.
3 Sauté the shallots in a large frying pan in 25g (scant 1oz) of butter and 1 tbsp of oil for about 5 minutes, or until softened. Add the herbs and season with a twist or two of pepper.
4 Pour in the red wine and reduce by half. Add the Madeira wine and reduce again by half. Stir in all but 1–2 tsp of the demi glace or stock and reduce by about a third or until the sauce is glossy and thickened. Strain into a clean pan.
5 Flatten the chicken breasts evenly between 2 sheets of cling film with a rolling pin, taking care not to tear the flesh. Divide the pork mixture between each and roll up, tucking in the ends. Wrap tightly in cling film and then foil. Poach in simmering water for 15–20 minutes. Remove from the pan and leave to cool.

6 To cook the cabbage, blanch the leaves in boiling salted water for 3 minutes, drain and refresh in iced water.

7 Heat a frying pan, add the bacon lardons and cook over medium heat, stirring frequently. As they brown and release their fat, add the chestnuts and carrot. Sauté for about 2 minutes, then stir in the cabbage and sauté for another 2–3 minutes. Stir in the single cream and remaining demi glace.

8 Meanwhile, melt half the remaining butter in another frying pan and add 1 tbsp of the oil. Unwrap the chicken and fry for 10 minutes, turning and basting frequently so they are golden all over. Remove from the pan and keep hot. Add the remaining butter and sauté the mushrooms with the garlic for 5 minutes. Season well.

9 To serve, reheat the potatoes and taste and season again if necessary. Slice each chicken roll in half. Pile the cabbage mixture in the centre of each plate and lay the chicken on top. Put the potatoes on the side, scatter the mushrooms over, and spoon the sauce over and around.

JOHN TORODE "The dish works very well because you have the crunch of the cabbage and the saltiness of the bacon with the sweetness of the chestnuts. I think it's a pretty good dish."

CHICKEN AND MUSHROOM "PIE"
David Coulson head chef and 2010 Professionals finalist

PREPARATION TIME
1¼ hours, plus chilling

COOKING TIME
3¾ hours

SERVES 4

1 whole chicken
salt and freshly ground black pepper
vegetable oil for frying and brushing
200ml (7fl oz) chicken stock
150ml (5fl oz) Madeira wine

FOR THE "PIES"
4 large flat cap mushrooms
1 celery stick, finely diced
1 carrot, finely diced
1 small leek, finely diced
1 shallot, finely diced
1 garlic clove, crushed
100g (3½oz) wild mushrooms, 4–8
  kept whole, the remainder chopped

100ml (3½fl oz) white wine
2–3 tbsp double cream
1 tsp dried chervil
1–2 tsp chopped thyme leaves
100g (3½oz) ready-made puff pastry
plain flour, for dusting
1 egg, beaten

FOR THE CREAMED POTATO
500g (1lb 2oz) Maris Piper potatoes,
  chopped
50g (1¾oz) butter
100ml (3½fl oz) milk
chervil or flat-leaf parsley,
  to garnish

MICHEL ROUX JR

"Wow! I've never seen a chicken pie like that. It just brings a smile to my face. I think it's great."

1 Preheat the oven to 190°C (375°F/Gas 5). Cut off the chicken legs, wings, and breast meat. Remove the skin from the breast and reserve. Wrap the breast in cling film and twist the ends to secure. Chill for 1 hour then poach in simmering water for 20 minutes, or until cooked.
2 Put the legs into a roasting tin. Season, drizzle with oil, and roast for 20–30 minutes or until the meat is cooked. Leave to cool, then remove the chicken skin, cut into strips and reserve. Shred the meat.
3 Remove the tip of the wing joints and cut each wing into 2. Scrape the meat away from the tip of the single-boned pieces. Brown the wings in a little oil in a saucepan. Pour over the stock and Madeira. Bring to the boil, cover, and simmer for 15 minutes. Uncover and reduce the sauce. Remove the wings, keep warm. Strain the sauce.
4 Remove the mushroom stalks, chop, and reserve. Brush the mushrooms with oil and place on a baking sheet. Heat a little oil in a pan and fry the celery, carrot, leek, shallot, garlic, and chopped wild mushrooms and mushroom stalks. Cook for 8–10 minutes to soften.
5 Add the wine, bring to the boil and reduce for about 5 minutes. Stir in the cream, chervil, and thyme and add the shredded leg meat. Season to taste. Pile the chicken mixture onto the mushroom caps.
6 Roll out the pastry. Cut out 4 discs and place on a baking sheet and glaze with egg. Lay the chicken breast skin on the tray to crisp also. Cook the mushrooms, pastry, and chicken skin for 10–15 minutes until the pastry and the skin are crisp and the mushrooms softened.
7 Boil the potatoes for 10–15 minutes until tender. Drain, roughly mash, then pass though a sieve. Beat in the butter and milk. Fry the

remaining whole wild mushrooms in a little oil until softened.
To serve, cut each chicken breast in half and place on a spoonful of the potato on each plate. Add a filled mushroom with a pastry disc on top to make the "pie". Place 1–2 whole mushrooms and a chicken wing on each plate, and reheat and drizzle on the reduced Madeira sauce. Garnish with the crispy chicken skin and chervil or parsley.

THAI GREEN CHICKEN CURRY

Nargis Chaudhary physiotherapist and 2010 semi-finalist

PREPARATION TIME
30 minutes

COOKING TIME
50 minutes

SERVES 4

1–2 tbsp vegetable oil
2 x 400g cans coconut milk
400g (14oz) chicken breast and thighs, skinless and boneless, cut into cubes
1 aubergine, cut into 8 large cubes
210g jar pea aubergines, drained
15g (½oz) fresh root ginger, grated
small handful of lime leaves
1 tsp palm, gran, or granulated sugar
1 tbsp nam pla (Thai fish sauce)
salt
225g (8oz) Thai jasmine rice
knob of butter

FOR THE CURRY PASTE
1 tbsp coriander seeds
1 tbsp white peppercorns
1 tbsp cumin seeds

50g (1¾oz) green bird's eye chillies, deseeded and chopped
50g (1¾oz) long green chillies, deseeded and chopped
2 red chillies, deseeded and chopped
1 garlic bulb, cloves peeled
3 lemongrass stalks
3 tsp ground turmeric
handful of coriander
60g (2oz) galangal, grated
8 red or white shallots, chopped
grated zest of 1 lime
30g (1oz) shrimp paste

TO SERVE
basil leaves
red chillies, left whole

MASTER TIP
THAI PEA AUBERGINE

A miniature green aubergine, this Thai variety has a slightly bitter flavour and crisp texture. The high seed-to-flesh ratio makes the aubergines pleasantly crunchy, and they do not soften with cooking.

1 For the curry paste, place the coriander seeds, peppercorns, and cumin in a large pestle and mortar and grind to a fine powder, then blitz with the remaining ingredients to form a smooth paste.
2 Heat the oil in a large pan or wok and add 4 tbsp of the curry paste. Cook, stirring continuously, over medium heat until the mixture begins to smell fragrant. Stir in 2–3 tbsp of the coconut milk and cook for 5 minutes. Then stir in the remaining coconut milk.
3 Add the chicken to the pan with the fresh and drained aubergines. Simmer for 15 minutes and then stir in the rest of the ingredients and cook for another 5 minutes. Taste and add a little salt if necessary.
4 Meanwhile, cook the rice following the packet instructions and with the addition of the butter.
5 Garnish with basil leaves and red chillies and serve with the rice.

MURG SAAG ON PILAU RICE

Nargis Chaudhary physiotherapist and 2010 semi-finalist

2 tbsp vegetable oil
3 large white onions, finely chopped
1 large garlic bulb, finely chopped
2 x 5cm (2in) pieces of fresh ginger,
  peeled and finely chopped
1 or 2 green bird's eye chillies, to taste
1 tsp ground coriander
1 tsp ground cumin
1 tsp ground paprika
1 tsp ground garam masala
1 tsp ground chilli powder
1 tsp ground turmeric
salt
400g can chopped tomatoes
2 tbsp plain yogurt
squeeze of lemon juice

450g (1lb) skinned chicken wings
150g can spinach in water, drained and
  extra water squeezed out
4 chicken breasts, skinned, with whole
  wings attached
4 large tomatoes, roughly chopped
4 tbsp chopped coriander

FOR THE PILAU RICE
1 tbsp vegetable oil
½ tsp cumin seeds
2–3 cloves
3 bay leaves
¼ tsp garam masala
180g (6½oz) white basmati rice

PREPARATION TIME
30 minutes

COOKING TIME
1 hour

SERVES 4

1 Heat the oil in a large saucepan. Add two-thirds each of the onions, garlic, ginger, and the chillies and cook over moderate heat for 10 minutes, stirring occasionally. Add the ground spices and 2 tsp of salt. If the mixture is sticking to the pan, add some water. Cook for 1 minute.

2 Stir in the tomatoes. Once the tomatoes are heated, add the yogurt and lemon juice and add all but 1 of the chicken wings. Bring to the boil, cover with a lid, reduce the heat, and simmer for 25–30 minutes.

3 Divide the spinach leaves between the chicken breasts, placing them at one end of the meat and roll up, closing with cocktail sticks.

4 Add the stuffed chicken breasts to the curry, cover again and leave to cook for 12–15 minutes, or until the chicken is cooked through.

5 For the pilau rice, heat the oil in a saucepan, add the remaining onion, garlic, and ginger along with the cumin, cloves, bay leaves, garam masala, and the remaining chicken wing.

6 Add the rice and 375ml (13fl oz) of water. Bring to the boil, cover with a lid and leave to simmer for about 10 minutes, or until cooked. Strain if necessary.

7 Remove the cocktail sticks from the chicken, transfer to a plate, and keep warm. Add the chopped tomatoes to the curry and heat through for 2–3 minutes.

8 To serve, place a 10cm (4in) metal ring on 1 of the serving plates, fill with rice and press to shape. Remove the ring and repeat on the other 3 plates. Top each pile of rice with a chicken breast and spoon over the sauce. Garnish with coriander.

SPICED DUCK LEG POORI, SAFFRON RAITA, AND CUCUMBER SALAD

Dhruv Baker sales director and 2010 champion

PREPARATION TIME
30 minutes, plus chilling

COOKING TIME
2 hours 35 minutes

SERVES 4

FOR THE RAITA
250g (9oz) plain yogurt
½ cucumber, peeled and grated
½ tsp salt
½ tsp ground cumin
1 tsp caster sugar
good pinch of saffron
juice of 1 lime

FOR THE DUCK
5cm (2in) piece of root ginger, peeled
   and roughly chopped
4 garlic cloves, peeled
½ tsp nigella seeds (black onion seeds)
½ tsp black mustard seeds
½ tsp fenugreek seeds
1 tsp fennel seeds
1 tbsp vegetable oil
1 dried red chilli
⅛ tsp asafoetida powder
¼ tsp red chilli powder
¼ tsp garam masala

½ tsp ground turmeric
¼ tsp salt
2 whole duck legs
250ml (8fl oz) chicken stock, plus
   extra if required

FOR THE POORIS
250g (9oz) wholemeal flour
1 tsp salt
½ tsp baking powder
vegetable oil for deep frying

FOR THE SALAD
½ cucumber, finely chopped
1 small red onion, chopped
3 tomatoes, chopped
½ green chilli, deseeded and chopped
½ bunch of coriander leaves
1 tsp caster sugar
½ tsp salt
juice of 2 small limes
about 4 tsp olive oil

1 Mix all the ingredients for the raita in a bowl. Cover and chill until required; this can be made a day in advance.

2 For the duck, mix the ginger and garlic with 2 teaspoons water in a mini food processor, or by using a sharp knife on a board, to form a paste. Coarsely crush the nigella, mustard, fenugreek, and fennel seeds in a pestle and mortar.

3 Heat the oil in a frying pan and cook the chilli for 1 minute, or until it darkens. Add the ginger and garlic paste and cook for 1–2 minutes, then sprinkle in the coarse ground spices and stir for 1 minute. Add the remaining spices and salt and cook the mixture for a further 1–2 minutes.

4 Add the duck to the pan, coating it thoroughly in the spice mix, then pour in the stock. Bring to the boil, cover partly with a lid, reduce the heat and simmer for 2–2½ hours or until the duck is beginning to soften away from the bones. Check occasionally that the pan is not boiling dry. If this is happening, add a little more stock.

5 Meanwhile, make the pooris. Sift the flour, salt, and baking powder into a bowl. Stir in 150–175ml (5–6fl oz) cold water to form a smooth dough. Knead lightly, then cover with damp muslin and leave in the fridge for 1 hour.

6 Take small portions of dough, about the size of a ten pence coin, and roll out each to a thickness of 3mm (⅛in). Deep fry in batches for 2–3 minutes, or until puffed up and golden. Drain on kitchen paper. When cooled, make a small hole in the base of each poori ready for the stuffing.

7 Shred the duck meat and moisten with some of the cooking liquor. Taste and season if necessary. Use this to fill the pooris. Handle gently as the pooris will be quite delicate.

8 For the salad, mix the cucumber, red onion, tomatoes, and chilli in a bowl with the coriander leaves. Sprinkle over the sugar and salt, then dress with the lime juice and oil. Toss everything together and serve with the pooris and raita.

MASTER TIP
SAFFRON

The most expensive spice in the world, saffron is the dried stigma of the saffron crocus flower. The taste is delicate yet penetrating, warm, earthy, musky, and lingering. For most dishes, saffron threads are infused in liquid. If an infusion is added in the early stages of cooking it will impart more colour; added later it contributes aroma.

PAN-ROASTED BREAST OF DUCK, RAINBOW CHARD, CARROTS, AND POLENTA

John Calton head chef and 2010 Professionals finalist

PREPARATION TIME
30 minutes

COOKING TIME
45 minutes

SERVES 4

500g (1lb 2oz) carrots, tops still on
4 duck breasts
1 tbsp extra virgin olive oil,
  plus extra for dressing
200g (7oz) clear honey
200ml (7fl oz) balsamic vinegar
200ml (7fl oz) soy sauce
sprig of rosemary
200g (7oz) chard, plus baby chard
  to garnish
squeeze of lemon juice

FOR THE POLENTA
knob of butter
splash of olive oil
1 banana shallot, finely chopped
1 garlic clove
250g (9oz) polenta
about 500ml (16fl oz) carrot juice
100g (3½oz) mascarpone cheese
100g (3½oz) Parmesan cheese, grated
1 bunch of chives, chervil, and
  coriander, chopped
salt and freshly ground black pepper

GREGG WALLACE

"It tastes fantastic. Really nice meaty dish with little zingy notes in it as well."

1 Trim and cook half the carrots in boiling water for about 10 minutes or until soft. Transfer to a blender or food processor and blend to a purée.
2 Preheat the oven to 200°C (400°F/Gas 6). Heat the olive oil in a large, heavy frying pan and pan-fry the duck breasts for 7–8 minutes until pink. Transfer to a roasting tin and cook in the oven for about 10 minutes to finish. Transfer the duck to a plate and leave to rest.
3 To make the polenta, heat the butter and olive oil in a saucepan and then sweat the shallot and garlic over low heat for about 5 minutes or until soft. Stir in the polenta and cover with the carrot juice. Bring to the boil and cook for 5–10 minutes, stirring continuously, until the polenta is soft and the liquid absorbed. Add the cheeses and the chopped herbs (reserving some for garnishing). Correct the seasoning to taste.
4 Meanwhile, make a sauce by combining the honey, vinegar, soy sauce, and rosemary in a saucepan. Bring to the boil and reduce by half.
5 Blanche the chard in boiling water for about 2 minutes. Drain and dress it with extra virgin olive oil, lemon juice, and seasoning.
6 To serve, cut the duck breasts into slices. Divide the polenta between 4 plates. Top with the chard and slices of duck and add spoonfuls of the carrot purée on each side. Pour the sauce around each plate and garnish with the reserved herbs and baby chard.

DUCK WITH SPICED TOBACCO CARAMEL, POTATO ROSTI, PICKLED CUCUMBER, AND DUCK HEART SALAD

Alex Rushmer freelance writer and 2010 finalist

PREPARATION TIME
35 minutes, plus infusing

COOKING TIME
45 minutes

SERVES 4

4 duck breasts, approx. 175–200g
 (6–7oz) each, skin on

FOR THE CARAMEL
125g (4½oz) caster sugar
125ml (4fl oz) still mineral water
2.5cm (1in) stick of cinnamon
1 star anise
5 cloves
2 black peppercorns
pinch of smoky rolling tobacco such as
 Drum or Golden Virginia

FOR THE CUCUMBER
1 large pickling cucumber
1 tsp caster sugar
4–6 tbsp white wine vinegar

FOR THE ROSTIS
4 large baking potatoes,
 approx. 200g (7oz) each
sea salt and freshly ground
 black pepper
8 spring onions, finely chopped
olive oil for frying
unsalted butter for frying

FOR THE SALAD
8 duck hearts or 4 livers
olive oil for frying and dressing
100g bag of watercress
1 lemon

MASTER TIP
PICKLING CUCUMBERS

Pickling cucumbers are
typically stubby in shape with
solid, crisp flesh that keeps
its texture when pickled.
Remove the peel if eating
pickling cucumbers raw, as
it is bitter and indigestible.

1 To make the caramel, gently heat the water, add the sugar, and
stir to dissolve. Then add the spices and tobacco and leave to infuse
for 30 minutes.

2 For the pickled cucumber, first peel the cucumber and discard the
peel, then use the peeler to remove 12–16 ribbons lengthways from
the cucumber. Place these "ribbons" in a shallow container, sprinkle
over the sugar and add enough vinegar to cover. Leave for 30 minutes
then remove to fresh water and leave to sit until ready to serve.

3 Preheat the oven to 150°C (300°F/Gas 2). Remove the skin from
the duck breasts, salt the skin generously and place between 2 baking
sheets with a lip to catch the fat. Cook in the oven for 30 minutes.
Then increase the temperature to 180°C (350°F/Gas 4), remove the
top baking sheet and cook the skin for a further 15 minutes.

4 Meanwhile, make the rostis. Peel and grate the potatoes. Put
them into a colander, sprinkle with sea salt and leave for 10 minutes.
Tip the potato into a tea towel and squeeze out as much water as
possible. Place the grated potato into a bowl, add the spring onions,
season with pepper, and mix.

5 Heat a large frying pan or griddle and add a dribble of oil and four 10cm (4in) rosti rings. Divide the potato and spring onion between each ring. Press down with the back of a spoon and leave to fry for 3–4 minutes. Remove the rings and flip the rostis. Then add a knob of butter and fry for a further 5 minutes or until browned on both sides and cooked through. Keep warm.

6 While the rostis are cooking, season the duck breasts and fry over high heat in an ovenproof pan for 5 minutes. Turn and then place in the oven with the crackling for the last 10 minutes of cooking time. Remove the duck and crackling from the oven and leave the duck to rest for at least 5 minutes. Let the crackling cool and cut each piece of skin in half.

7 For the salad, slice the duck hearts or livers in half, season with salt and pepper, then fry in a little oil for 30 seconds on each side. Dress the watercress with 2 tbsp of oil to each 2 tsp of lemon juice and salt and pepper. Add the fried hearts or livers and toss together.

8 Strain the infused tobacco mixture into a saucepan, then boil hard for 5 minutes until reduced and caramelized.

9 To serve, spoon a generous tbsp of the caramel onto each plate. Place a rosti just off centre and top with the watercress and heart salad. Dry 3–4 slices of the cucumber and place next to the potato and watercress. Slice the duck into 5 or 6 pieces and place on the cucumber. Season with a little sea salt and a tiny drizzle of caramel. Top with 2 slices of the duck crackling.

JOHN TORODE "The look of the dish is that of a French classic. The flavour is something of the Orient. It's fantastic: there is a sweetness from that tobacco sauce against a sharpness of cucumber, with little subtle notes of smokiness."

PAN-ROASTED DUCK IN PICKLING SPICES WITH CARROT PURÉE AND PLUM SAUCE

Dhruv Baker sales director and 2010 champion

PREPARATION TIME
30 minutes

COOKING TIME
1 hour

SERVES 4

1 Gressingham duck, plus
  2 duck breasts
knob of butter
handful of chopped coriander leaves,
  plus extra to garnish
pickling spice mix (see MasterTip)

FOR THE SAUCE
100g (3½oz) plums, stones removed
50g (1¾oz) caster sugar
1 black or green cardamom pod
5cm (2in) stick of cinnamon
½ tsp paprika
1 tsp fennel seeds
pinch of salt

FOR THE PURÉE
2 carrots, chopped
3 tbsp white wine vinegar
½ tsp coriander seeds
2 dried red chillies
pinch of caster sugar
salt and freshly ground black pepper
½ bunch coriander, leaves only
2 tsp desiccated coconut
4 tbsp double cream

FOR THE PILAU RICE
½ tbsp vegetable oil
5cm (2in) stick of cinnamon
2 cloves
2 green cardamom pods
100g (3½oz) basmati rice

MASTER TIP

PICKLING SPICE MIX

Blend 4 garlic cloves and 5cm (2in) peeled fresh ginger to a paste in a small blender or food processor. Coarsely grind 1 tsp fennel seads with ½ tsp each of nigella (black onion), fenugreek, and black mustard seeds. Mix ½ tsp red chilli powder with ¼ tsp garam masala, ¼ tsp turmeric and ⅛ tsp asafoetida. Heat 1 tbsp vegetable oil in a large frying pan and fry ½ tsp dried chilli flakes. Add the garlic paste and fry for a further 1 minute. Then add the ground seeds and, after another minute, add the remaining spices and mix together thoroughly.

1 To make the plum sauce, put the plums in a small saucepan and add the remaining ingredients with a splash of water. Cook over low heat for 15 minutes, then remove from the heat and allow to cool. Blend and pass through a sieve into a clean pan. Keep warm.
2 For the carrot purée, place the carrots in a saucepan with the vinegar, spices, sugar, and some salt and pepper. Cover with water and bring to the boil. Cover with a lid, reduce the heat and simmer for about 30 minutes, or until cooked through. Once cooked, drain, discard the chillies and then purée with the remaining ingredients.
3 Remove the duck breasts from the carcass and set aside. Remove the legs and chop up the meat. Mix the pickling spices (see MasterTip, left) and transfer to a pan with the leg meat. Cook for 2–3 minutes, then add 250ml (8fl oz) of water and cook for 20 minutes, stirring occasionally. Place the breasts in a separate frying pan, skin side down, on moderate heat. Spoon off some of the excess fat. After 5 minutes, turn them over and add a knob of butter and a few spoons of the spice mixture. Cook for 10–12 minutes until the duck is rosy pink.
4 For the pilau rice, heat the oil in a saucepan with the spices. Add the rice and fry briefly, then cover with water and bring to the boil. Reduce the heat, cover, and cook for 10–15 minutes, until tender.
5 Reheat the carrot purée and slice the duck breasts. Serve as shown.

SOY-BRAISED DUCK WITH GREENS AND A PARSNIP AND TURMERIC PURÉE

Dhruv Baker sales director and 2010 champion

PREPARATION TIME
40 minutes

COOKING TIME
1½ hours

SERVES 4

2 Gressingham ducks
2 tbsp caster sugar
5 slices galangal
3 garlic cloves
3 tbsp dark soy sauce
800ml (1¼ pints) chicken stock
1 tbsp rice vinegar

FOR THE PARSNIP PURÉE
1 tbsp vegetable oil
3 slices of fresh or dried galangal
1 lemongrass stalk
2 x 5cm (2in) pieces turmeric or 1 tsp ground turmeric

1 red chilli, halved and deseeded
1 garlic clove, finely chopped
4 parsnips, chopped
400ml can coconut milk
salt and freshly ground black pepper

FOR THE GREENS
4 pak choi, white part removed
2 banana shallots or 4 shallots, finely chopped
2 tbsp vegetable oil
2 garlic cloves, finely chopped
400g bag spring greens
100ml (3½fl oz) chicken stock

JOHN TORODE

"It looks lovely, and it tastes even better than it looks."

1 Carefully remove the duck breasts from each bird. Take off the legs and keep for another time. Score the skin on each breast with a sharp knife, then set aside. Using a cleaver, chop up the carcass into smaller pieces.

2 Heat a large wok, add the sugar and, as it begins to caramelize, add the galangal and garlic. Reduce the heat and cook for 1 minute, taking care not to let it burn. Stir in 400ml (14fl oz) cold water (it will splutter a bit), then add the soy sauce. Put in the chopped duck carcass and bring to the boil. Stir in the stock and vinegar, reduce the heat, and let it simmer gently for about 50 minutes, stirring frequently.

3 Meanwhile, make the parsnip purée. Heat the oil in a pan, add the galangal, lemongrass, turmeric, chilli, and garlic. Cook gently for 5 minutes.

4 Add the parsnips to the pan. Cook, stirring, for 2–3 minutes. Pour in the coconut milk, bring to the boil, then reduce the heat and simmer for 15–20 minutes or until the parsnips are tender. Fish out and discard the galangal, lemon grass, 1 piece of turmeric (if using), and chilli.

5 Strain the mixture through a sieve, collecting the liquid in a bowl underneath. Purée the parsnips using a hand-held blender or transferring to a food processor, adding enough of the reserved cooking liquor to form a smooth mixture that will just hold its shape.

6 Spoon the purée into a small saucepan, taste and season with salt and pepper, if necessary.

7 Heat a large frying pan and cook the duck breasts, skin side down, over low heat for 8–10 minutes. As the fat begins to run, drain it off. Turn the duck over and add 2 ladlefuls of the simmering stock from the wok into the frying pan. It should come three-quarters up the meat without covering the skin. Cook for a further 6–7 minutes, then lift out the duck onto a plate and leave to rest in a warm place.

8 Strain the wok mixture through a fine sieve into the pan used for frying the duck. Skim off the fat and reduce the stock by about two-thirds.

9 Fry the shallots in the oil for 5 minutes. As they begin to colour, add the garlic and stir-fry for 1 minute. Scatter in the green tops of the pak choi and all the spring greens. Stir-fry for 2 minutes then pour in the stock, season with salt and pepper and cook for 5 minutes, or until the spring greens are just cooked. Gently heat the parsnip purée.

10 Slice each duck breast lengthways into 1.5cm (½in) pieces. Divide the greens between 4 plates and fan out the meat on top. Spoon the parsnip purée around the side and pour over a little of the duck sauce to moisten.

FLAVOUR COMBINATION

DUCK, SOY SAUCE, AND GALANGAL

Soy sauces are magical because they are loaded with *umami*, the fifth basic taste in food. Found particularly in the savouriness of roasted meats, in tomatoes, and potatoes, it also gives a sense of gratification. Dark soy sauce is sweetened and so befriends many sweet ingredients in this exotic recipe, including the duck. The galangal from Thai cooking counters this sweetness. Less biting than ginger, its haunting effect includes overtones of camphor.

TEA-SMOKED DUCK WITH LOBSTER, APPLE PURÉE, MAPLE JELLY, AND BITTER LEAVES

Alex Rushmer freelance writer and 2010 finalist

PREPARATION TIME
30 minutes, plus chilling

COOKING TIME
1 hour 30 minutes

SERVES 4

FOR THE JELLY
100ml (3½fl oz) maple syrup
1 star anise
2.5cm (1in) stick of cinnamon
3 cloves
2 leaves of gelatine

FOR THE PURÉE
3 Braeburn apples, peeled, cored,
   and finely chopped
3 tbsp apple juice
3 tbsp sparkling white wine
juice of 1 lemon
2–3 tsp sugar, to taste

FOR THE DUCK
4 duck breasts, skin on
salt and freshly ground black pepper
150g (5½oz) brown rice
150g (5½oz) soft dark brown sugar
100g (3½oz) Darjeeling tea leaves

FOR THE SALAD
1 small lobster, cooked
knob of butter
4 tbsp sunflower or groundnut oil
1–2 tsp lemon juice
100g (3½oz) mixed bitter leaves, such
   as chicory, radicchio, and endive

1 To make the maple jelly, warm the maple syrup in a saucepan with 3 tbsp of water and all the spices. Leave to infuse for 15 minutes. Meanwhile, soak the gelatine in cold water to soften. Strain the maple syrup, then pour it back into the pan and heat gently. Shake off the excess water from the gelatine and stir into the maple liquor. Stir continuously over medium-low heat until the gelatine has completely dissolved. Pour the mixture into a small shallow dish and chill for at least 3 hours (preferably overnight) until firm.

2 For the apple purée, cook the apples in a pan with the apple juice for about 10 minutes, stirring frequently until completely soft. Stir in the wine, lemon juice, and sugar, then use a hand-held blender or food processor to blitz to a purée. Press through a sieve into a bowl and chill until needed.

3 Using a very sharp knife, score the fat on each duck breast in a diagonal pattern. Take care not to cut through to the flesh and season well. Mix together the rice, sugar, and tea leaves and scatter in the base of a smoking pan or wok. Set over medium-high heat for 5–10 minutes and, when the mix begins to smoke, place the duck on a rack in the pan. Cover the pan with foil and a lid, reduce the heat, and smoke for about 20 minutes. Turn off the heat and leave until cool.

4 For the salad, carefully pick out the meat from the lobster. Try to keep it in large pieces so you can cut it up neatly. Pan-fry the lobster meat in butter for about 3 minutes and cut into slices. Pour the oil and lemon juice into a bowl, then whisk in plenty of seasoning. Add the leaves but do not toss together yet.

5 Put the duck breasts, skin-side down, in a cold frying pan. Place over medium-high heat and cook for 6–8 minutes, or until the fat starts to run. Cook for a further 4–5 minutes, basting the meat continuously, until the skin is golden and crisp. Turn over and cook for 3–4 minutes more, or longer if you prefer your meat less pink.

6 To serve, cut the jelly into tiny cubes. Toss the salad and arrange on 4 plates with the lobster. Slice the duck and place on top of the salad and then finish with a swirl of apple purée.

FLAVOUR COMBINATION

DUCK, LOBSTER, AND MAPLE SYRUP

Smoking duck develops a full array of basic tastes: sweet, salt, bitter, and acid – all deliciously carried into the flesh by its fat. This perfectly partners lobster's natural sweetness Then woody-rich maple syrup underpinned with spices completes a stage of different sweet tastes on which more feral flavours of duck, smoking, and spices can all show off. The less sweet the apple sauce, the more fireworks of flavour there will be on your tongue.

ABBAGE, AND SWEET CHESTNUTS -
ITH LIVER AND SWEETBREAD - PAN-
RIED LAMB SWEETBREADS WITH BAC
AULIFLOWER PURÉE, HAZELNUT BRI
ND BLACKBERRY COULIS - LAMB LOI
N A PEA PURÉE WITH A MINT SAUCE
ONFIT TOMATOES - CHARGRILLED RA
F LAMB AND CONFIT OF SHOULDER V
AUTÉED POTATOES, TOMATOES, AND
AYONNAISE - ROAST RACK OF LAMB
PARSNIP PURÉE, CABBAGE IN YOGU
ND A CURRY-SCENTED SAUCE - SPIC
AMB CURRY WITH WILD RICE AND TO
LMONDS - MUSALLAM LAMB TWO WA
AFFRON POMMES ANNA AND A BEET
HUTNEY - LAMB STEW WITH APPLE A
OUR PLUMS - ROAST LAMB WITH OLI
AUCE AND ANCHOVY TEMPURA - RUM

MEAT

FIG AND CHILLI LAMB WITH CHAMP, CABBAGE, AND SWEET CHESTNUTS

Dick Strawbridge TV presenter and 2010 Celebrity finalist

PREPARATION TIME
45 minutes

COOKING TIME
45 minutes

SERVES 4

2 eye of loin of lamb,
   450g (1lb) each, boneless
salt and freshly ground black pepper
½–1 dried chilli

FOR THE CHAMP
800g (1¾lb) potatoes, peeled and diced
5 spring onions, sliced
50g (1¾oz) butter
100ml (3½fl oz) whole milk

FOR THE BAKED FIGS AND JUS
8 figs
4 tsp honey

1 tbsp olive oil
3 shallots, chopped
120ml (4fl oz) port
1 small red chilli,
   deseeded and finely chopped
1 tbsp fig jam
1–2 tbsp red wine vinegar, to taste
1–2 tbsp chilli chutney, to taste

FOR THE CABBAGE
½ Savoy cabbage or 400g (14oz) cavalo
   nero, finely shredded
140g (5oz) smoked pancetta
200g (7oz) sweet chestnuts

MASTER TIP
SWEET CHESTNUTS

To cook fresh sweet chestnuts, score an "X" on the flat side of each nut, soften in a hot oven for 15–25 mins, or until the "X" opens up a little, then use a small, sharp knife to remove the shell and papery inner skin while still warm. Marrone del Mugello (pictured) is a Tuscan variety particularly prized for its sweet taste.

1 Preheat the oven to 200°C (400°F/Gas 6). To make the champ, place the potatoes in a pan, cover with water, and bring to the boil. Cook for 8–10 minutes until tender. Drain and rice in a potato ricer or mash.
2 Soften the onions in a pan with 20g (¾oz) butter. Pour in the milk, bring to the boil, and simmer for a couple of minutes. Add the milk and onion mix to the potatoes and whisk until smooth.
3 Season the lamb and rub in the chilli. Heat a pan until hot then seal and brown the lamb on all sides for 6–8 minutes. Transfer to a roasting tray and bake for 18–20 minutes. Remove and rest for 10 minutes.
4 Cut a cross in the tops of 4 figs and place them on a roasting tray. Drizzle with honey and cook in the oven for 10–15 minutes until soft but not falling apart.
5 Meanwhile, heat the oil in a pan. Add the shallots and sauté for 2–3 minutes to soften. Chop the remaining figs and add them along with the port, chilli, and jam, then cook for 10–15 minutes until the figs have completely fallen apart. Add vinegar to taste. Strain and reduce to a coating consistency. Season with salt and pepper.
6 Add the cabbage to a pan of boiling water and cook for 3–4 minutes until wilted. Drain and set aside. Fry the pancetta in its own fat until crisp, then add the chestnuts and cook for 2–3 minutes to heat. Add the cabbage and heat through for 2–3 minutes.
7 Carve the lamb and divide between the plates, served on a bed of the cabbage and champ. Place a fig alongside, top with a little chilli chutney, and drizzle with the fig and port jus.

LAMB WITH LIVER AND SWEETBREAD

Claire Lara lecturer and 2010 Professionals champion

30g (1oz) rosemary leaves, finely chopped
4 tbsp olive oil
2 boneless loins of Welsh lamb,
   450g (1lb) each, trimmed and tied
2 large garlic bulbs, separated
½ bunch of flat-leaf parsley
salt and freshly ground black pepper
100g (3½oz) lamb's sweetbread
100g (3½oz) lamb's liver
600g (1lb 5oz) asparagus, trimmed
150g (5½oz) unsalted butter
300g (10oz) morel mushrooms

FOR THE JUS
1 tbsp vegetable oil
500g (1lb 2oz) lamb trimmings

2 shallots, roughly chopped
5 button mushrooms, halved
3 garlic cloves
2 sprigs of fresh rosemary
1 large bay leaf
2 large plum tomatoes on the vine,
   roughly chopped
1 tbsp sherry vinegar
175ml (6fl oz) Madeira wine
375ml (13fl oz) full-bodied red wine
500ml (16fl oz) good-quality lamb stock
100g (3½oz) unsalted butter
2 tsp cornflour

PREPARATION TIME
30 minutes, plus marinating

COOKING TIME
45 minutes

SERVES 4

1 Mix the rosemary and oil together and rub into the lamb. Chill and marinate in the fridge for 2–3 hours or overnight. Return to room temperature before cooking.

2 Place the garlic in a bowl and cover with boiling water. Leave for 10 minutes, then peel. Place in a pan and cover with cold water. Bring to the boil, discard the water, and repeat 6 times. Place the garlic in a food processor with the parsley and blend until smooth. Season.

3 Preheat the oven to 200°C (400°F/Gas 6). Place the sweetbread and liver in a pan, cover with water and bring to the boil. Simmer for 3–4 minutes, then drain and cool briefly. Remove any scum and peel off the membranes. Dry on kitchen paper and set aside in the fridge.

4 Place the asparagus in a pan of boiling water and cook for 5–6 minutes until just tender. Refresh and set aside. Make the jus (see MasterTip, right).

5 Place the lamb on a roasting tray and cook in the oven for 20 minutes. Remove from the oven and leave to rest for 10 minutes.

6 Heat 50g (1¾oz) butter in a frying pan until it is foaming, add the garlic purée, and toss the asparagus in foaming butter until hot. In another pan, heat 50g (1¾oz) of the butter and fry the sweetbreads and liver for 5–7 minutes until golden and cooked through. Remove and allow to rest. Add another 50g (1¾oz) of the butter, allow to foam, then add the morels and cook for 6–8 minutes until tender.

7 Serve the lamb on the asparagus and sauce. Arrange the livers, sweetbreads, and morels around it and spoon over the lamb jus.

MASTER TIP

MAKING THE JUS

Start the jus by heating the oil in a large saucepan, adding the lamb trimmings, and stirring until golden and browned. Add the shallots, mushrooms, garlic, rosemary, and bay leaf. Stir until aromatic. Add the tomatoes and stir until the sauce has completely reduced, then deglaze with the sherry vinegar.

Add the Madeira and reduce by half. Add the red wine and stock and reduce by a quarter. Sieve the sauce, then return to the pan over high heat to reduce to the desired consistency. Mix the butter with the cornflour and chill. Whisk into the jus just before serving to gloss it.

PAN-FRIED LAMB SWEETBREADS WITH BACON, CAULIFLOWER PURÉE, HAZELNUT BRITTLE, AND BLACKBERRY COULIS

Alex Rushmer freelance writer and 2010 finalist

PREPARATION TIME
1 hour 10 minutes

COOKING TIME
30–45 minutes

SERVES 4

4 small sweetbreads, about 75g (2½oz) each, soaked in cold water
2 tbsp white wine vinegar
8 rashers of smoked streaky bacon
15g (½oz) seasoned flour
1 tbsp vegetable oil
30g (1oz) butter
mixed microgreens, to garnish

FOR THE PURÉE
400ml (14fl oz) whole milk
200ml (7fl oz) double cream

1 cauliflower, about 600g (1lb 5oz), broken into florets
salt and freshly ground white pepper

FOR THE BRITTLE
50g (1¾oz) hazelnuts
200g (7oz) caster sugar

FOR THE COULIS
100g (3½oz) blackberries
50g (1¾oz) caster sugar (or to taste)

MASTER TIP

HAZELNUT BRITTLE

To make hazelnut brittle, first line a baking sheet with a silicon mat. Preheat a heavy frying pan and dry roast the hazelnuts over medium heat, shaking the pan from time to time so that they brown evenly. Remove and crush lightly in a pestle and mortar. Add the sugar to the pan and melt over low heat, stirring. Increase the heat and as soon as the sugar turns to a golden caramel, scatter the nuts in and then pour in a thin layer onto the mat. Leave until cold, then break into shards.

1 Preheat the oven to 220°C (425°F/Gas 7). Blanch the sweetbreads, uncovered, in boiling water with added vinegar for 3–4 minutes. Drain and refresh in iced water. Remove the outer membrane and set aside.
2 For the purée, pour the milk and cream into a pan. Bring to the boil and add the cauliflower florets. Boil steadily for 10–12 minutes or until tender. Drain, reserving the cooking liquor, and purée with 2–3 tbsp of the liquor using a hand-held blender or by transferring to a food processor. Pass through a fine sieve and season with salt and pepper.
3 Make the hazelnut brittle (see MasterTip, left). For the coulis, cook the berries with the sugar and a little water for 5 minutes, or until they begin to break down and release their juice. Break up with the back of a spoon, cook for 2–3 minutes more, then pass through a sieve and set aside.
4 Sandwich the bacon between 2 heavy baking sheets to keep the rashers flat and cook in the oven for 10 minutes, or until crispy.
5 Coat the sweetbreads in the seasoned flour. Heat the vegetable oil in a frying pan and cook the sweetbreads for 4–5 minutes over medium heat, turning once. Add the butter to the pan and, once it is melted, add the bacon and cook for 2–3 minutes, basting the sweetbreads continually.
6 Reheat the cauliflower purée and spoon onto warmed plates. Top with sweetbread and bacon. Drizzle a line of coulis to one side and garnish with hazelnut brittle and microgreens.

LAMB LOIN ON A PEA PURÉE WITH A MINT SAUCE AND CONFIT TOMATOES
Stacie Stewart PA and 2010 semi-finalist

PREPARATION TIME
45 minutes, plus marinating

COOKING TIME
45 minutes

SERVES 4

2 anchovy fillets, canned in oil
2 large sprigs of rosemary, leaves picked and finely chopped
2 large garlic cloves, crushed
2 tbsp olive oil
2 boneless fillets of lamb loin, weighing about 250g (9oz) each
12 baby carrots with green tops
12 asparagus spears
knob of butter

FOR THE MADEIRA SAUCE
1 tbsp vegetable oil
500g (1lb 2oz) lamb trimmings (offcuts from lamb: a mix of bone, meat, and skin)
2 shallots, roughly chopped
5 button mushrooms, halved
3 garlic cloves
2 sprigs of rosemary
1 large bay leaf
2 large plum tomatoes on the vine, roughly chopped
1 tbsp sherry vinegar

175ml (6fl oz) Madeira wine
375ml (13fl oz) full-bodied red wine
500ml (16fl oz) good-quality lamb stock
100g (3½oz) unsalted butter
2 tsp cornflour

FOR THE PURÉE
250g (9oz) frozen petit pois
3 tbsp double cream
25g (scant 1oz) unsalted butter
salt and freshly ground black pepper

FOR THE MINT SAUCE
2 tsp sugar
1 large bunch of mint, leaves picked and finely chopped
2 tsp white wine vinegar

FOR THE TOMATOES
20 cherry tomatoes on the vine
2 sprigs of thyme
1 tsp caster sugar
2 tbsp balsamic vinegar

1 Crush the anchovies in a pestle and mortar with the rosemary, garlic, and oil to form a paste. Coat the lamb in the paste and marinate overnight.

2 Preheat the oven to 190°C (375°F/Gas 5). Make the Madeira sauce by heating the oil in a large saucepan, adding the lamb trimmings, and stirring until golden and browned. Add the shallots, mushrooms, garlic, rosemary, and bay leaf. Stir until aromatic. Add the tomatoes and stir until the sauce has completely reduced, then deglaze with sherry vinegar.

3 Add the Madeira and reduce by half. Add the red wine and stock and reduce by a quarter. Sieve the sauce, then return to the pan over high heat to reduce to the desired consistency. Mix the butter with the cornflour and set aside in the fridge to chill.

4 Meanwhile, for the pea purée, cook the peas in boiling water for 3–4 minutes then briefly refresh in ice water. Blitz with the cream and butter, using a hand-held blender or by transferring to a food processor. Pass through a fine sieve, season, and set aside to be reheated later.

5 For the mint sauce, add 1 tsp of sugar to the mint. Blanch it in 4 tbsp of boiling water, then add the remaining sugar and enough white wine vinegar to give it a tang. Season and set aside.

6 To make the confit tomatoes, put the tomatoes, thyme, sugar, and balsamic vinegar in an ovenproof dish. Toss to coat the tomatoes.

7 Heat a large cast iron pan and brown the lamb on all sides for 2 minutes, basting it with the rendered fat in the last 30 seconds. Put the lamb and tomatoes in the oven and cook for 10–12 minutes. Remove the lamb from the oven and set aside to rest, leaving the tomatoes to cook in the oven for a further 10 minutes.

8 Meanwhile, place the carrots and asparagus in a pan of boiling water and cook for 4–5 minutes, until just tender. Drain, add a knob of butter and cook for 1–2 minutes to glaze. Reheat the sauces, whisking the chilled butter into the Madeira sauce to gloss it.

9 To serve, slice the lamb and place on a smear of pea purée. Drizzle the mint sauce over it. Arrange the carrots, tomatoes, and asparagus around the lamb and drizzle with the Madeira sauce.

CHARGRILLED RACK OF LAMB AND CONFIT OF SHOULDER WITH SAUTÉED POTATOES, TOMATOES, AND GARLIC MAYONNAISE

Ben Piette hospitality chef and 2010 Professionals semi-finalist

PREPARATION TIME
1 hour

COOKING TIME
2 hours

SERVES 4

½ large bunch of rosemary
100ml (3½fl oz) extra virgin olive oil
salt and freshly ground black pepper
3 x 4-rib rack of spring lamb,
  French trimmed
  (see MasterClass pp. 170–171)
250g (9oz) unsalted butter
500g (1lb 2oz) Désirée potatoes, peeled
  and cut into 4cm (1½in) cubes
1 small bunch of baby watercress

FOR THE TOMATOES AND MAYONNAISE
100g (3½oz) each red, green, yellow,
  and baby plum cherry tomatoes
1 smoked garlic bulb
15g (½oz) pickling spices
100ml (3½fl oz) cider vinegar
pinch of caster sugar

250ml (8fl oz) vegetable oil
2 egg yolks
1 tbsp Dijon mustard
1–2 tsp cider vinegar
100ml (3½fl oz) groundnut oil

FOR THE CONFIT
300g (10oz) lamb shoulder on the bone
1 carrot
1 onion
1 celery stick
1 leek
2 bay leaves
25g (scant 1oz) black olives
½ large bunch of rosemary
750ml (1¼pints) Merlot or Burgundy
  red wine
1 tsp redcurrant jelly

1 Finely chop the leaves of 3 sprigs of rosemary. Mix with 3 tbsp of olive oil and season well. Marinate the lamb in the mixture and chill for at least 30 minutes.

2 Preheat the oven to 150°C (300°F/Gas 2). Cut the red tomatoes in half and season. Place on a greased baking tray. On another tray, break up the garlic bulb into individual cloves. Place both in the oven for 20 minutes, by which time the garlic should have a soft paste consistency. Remove from the oven and set aside to cool.

3 Pierce or halve the green tomatoes and place in a jar. Mix the pickling spices, vinegar, sugar, and 100ml (3½fl oz) water and pour over the tomatoes

4 Put the baby plum tomatoes in a pan of boiling water for a few seconds, then place in an iced bath and remove the skins. Heat the vegetable oil in a deep pan. Carefully lower the yellow tomatoes into the oil and cook briefly until the skin pops and crisps up.

5 To make the mayonnaise, place the egg yolks, Dijon mustard, and cider vinegar in a bowl. Whisk, slowly adding the groundnut oil, until the mayonnaise is formed. Stir in the roasted smoked garlic and chill until needed.

6 For the confit, place the lamb, carrot, onion, celery, leek, bay leaves, olives, and half the rosemary in a pressure cooker. Season well. Add the wine, redcurrant jelly, and 750ml (1¼ pints) water and cook for about 40 minutes until the meat is tender. Then strain the liquor into a pan, discard the vegetables, and transfer the meat to a board. Shred or dice the meat and set aside. Reduce the remaining liquor by boiling it until it coats the back of the spoon. Return the meat to the pan.

7 To cook the potatoes, preheat the oven to 200°C (400°F/Gas 6). Heat 25g (scant 1oz) butter in an ovenproof frying pan until it is bubbling, add the potatoes and cook on medium heat. Add 200g (7oz) butter and baste continuously for 10–15 minutes until golden, then place in the oven for 15 minutes until tender.

8 Heat a large frying pan, place the rack of lamb skin side down and cook for 4–5 minutes on each side until brown. Transfer to an oven tray and roast for about 10–12 minutes. Remove from the oven and rest for 8 minutes.

9 Meanwhile, warm the remaining olive oil in a pan with the remaining rosemary. Remove from the heat and allow to infuse for at least 10 minutes.

10 Heat a small pan with 25g (scant 1oz) butter, add the watercress, season, and cook for about a minute to wilt. Remove from the pan.

11 Place the lamb shoulder and jus in the oven for 5–8 minutes until heated through.

12 Carve the rack of lamb into chops. Divide the sauté potatoes and confit shoulder between plates and place a chop on top. Pour the jus over, and serve with garlic mayonnaise and the medley of tomatoes. Drizzle over the rosemary oil to serve.

MONICA'S MASTERCLASS
FRENCH TRIMMING A RACK OF LAMB

A rack of lamb uses the best end cut of meat and French trimming is a traditional way of making the rack look attractive. This can be expensive for a butcher to do and is a simple enough technique for the more confident home chef.

1 Chop off the backbone

Remove the blade bone, under the skin along the edge of the cut. To remove the backbone, first slice horizontally from the skin side tight against the bone, down to the ribs. Turn the cut vertically and, with a large knife, chop down along the edge of the backbone.

2 Expose the rib

Trim off the elastin (along the edge opposite the backbone) and any flank meat. To form the "rack", expose about 5cm (2in) of the bone at the thin end of the ribs. Make a horizontal cut down to the ribs at this point, all the way across, and then slice away the meat above.

Use a vigorous action, keeping the meat stable and fingers clear of the blade.

"Best served pink, lamb is a lovely reminder of spring. Remember to rest the meat after roasting, it makes a huge difference."

3 | Cut between the ribs

Remove the meat between the ribs by cutting down the length of the exposed portion of rib, getting the knife tight against the bone, then cut across and slice up the other side along the edge of the next rib.

4 | Prepare for the oven

Score the skin in a criss-cross pattern. If serving two people, a traditional method of roasting is to form a "guard of honour" by chopping the rack in two and intersecting the bones. To serve four, take two racks of lamb and tie them together, skin-side in, to form a "crown".

Once you've finished, tidy up the ribs by cleaning away any stray bits of meat.

ROAST RACK OF LAMB WITH A PARSNIP PURÉE, CABBAGE IN YOGURT, AND A CURRY-SCENTED SAUCE

Daniel Howell sous chef and 2010 Professionals quarter-finalist

PREPARATION TIME
30 minutes

COOKING TIME
1 hour 15 minutes

SERVES 4

6 large parsnips, trimmed and peeled
25g (scant 1oz) butter
1 tsp ground cumin
1 tbsp clear honey
50g (1¾oz) dried good-quality
   breadcrumbs
4 garlic cloves, crushed
15g (½oz) mint, leaves picked and
   finely chopped
3 tbsp olive oil
3 x 4-rib rack of lamb, trimmed
1½ tbsp English mustard
150ml (5fl oz) red wine

1 tbsp redcurrant jelly
4 curry leaves
500ml (16fl oz) lamb stock

FOR THE CABBAGE
1 tbsp olive oil
1 onion, very finely sliced
1 tsp turmeric
½ Savoy cabbage, shredded
150ml (5fl oz) white wine
150ml (5fl oz) plain yogurt
salt and freshly ground black pepper

GREGG WALLACE

"I love that lamb with those flavours. There's a taste almost like piccallili in the cabbage. That's great."

1 Preheat the oven to 200°C (400°F/Gas 6). Using a potato peeler, shave 2 parsnips into ribbons, place on a greased baking tray, and reserve until later. Chop the remaining parsnips, place in a foil parcel with the butter, cumin, and honey, and roast for 20–25 minutes until soft and caramelized. Transfer to a food processor, purée until smooth, amd then set aside.
2 To cook the cabbage, heat the oil in a large frying pan and fry the onion with the turmeric, stirring, for 5–6 minutes until soft. Add the cabbage and wine and sweat on medium heat until wilted. Add the yogurt and season with salt and pepper.
3 Mix the breadcrumbs with the garlic and mint. Season well.
4 Heat 1 tbsp oil in a large frying pan. Seal and brown the rack of lamb, skin side down, for 6–8 minutes until golden. Remove from the pan, spread the fat with mustard and cover with the seasoned breadcrumbs. Transfer to a roasting tin and cook in the oven for 15–20 minutes. Remove and allow to rest for 8–10 minutes.
5 Place the lamb pan over high heat, pour in the red wine and allow to bubble. Add the redcurrant jelly, curry leaves, and stock, then boil to reduce until the jus coats the back of a spoon.
6 Meanwhile, drizzle the shaved parsnips with 2 tbsp of olive oil and roast for 8–10 minutes until golden.
7 Carve the lamb and serve on the parsnip purée and cabbage. Top with parsnip crisps and drizzle with red wine jus.

MOROCCAN SPICED LAMB WITH WILD RICE AND TOASTED ALMONDS

Christine Hamilton TV personality and 2010 Celebrity finalist

150ml (5fl oz) dry white wine
150g (5½oz) sultanas
100g (3½oz) dried apricots, chopped
100g (3½oz) pancetta, diced
1kg (2¼lb) lamb shoulder, diced
1–2 tbsp olive oil
1 large onion, thinly sliced
4 garlic cloves, crushed
3 tsp ras-el-hanout (harissa
  spice powder)
1 tsp ground cinnamon
1 tbsp sherry vinegar

1.2 litres (2 pints) lamb or
  vegetable stock
6 large plum tomatoes, chopped,
  or 400g can plum tomatoes
250g (9oz) mixed wild and
  long grain rice
100g (3½oz) slivered almonds
1 small bunch of mint, roughly chopped
1 small bunch of parsley,
  roughly chopped
1 small bunch of coriander,
  roughly chopped

PREPARATION TIME
15 minutes

COOKING TIME
1 hour 30 minutes

SERVES 4

1 Preheat the oven to 150°C (300°F/Gas 2). Heat the wine in a small pan until simmering, turn off the heat, and add the sultanas and chopped apricots. Set aside.
2 In a large frying pan, fry the pancetta for 1–2 minutes until the fat releases. Divide the lamb into 4, and fry along with the pancetta in batches for 4–5 minutes, turning only once – add a little olive oil if the fat from the pancetta is not sufficient. Transfer to a covered casserole.
3 Add a little oil to the frying pan, then add the onion, garlic, ras-el-hanout, and cinnamon and fry until fragrant. Pour the vinegar over to deglaze the pan and let it bubble for a minute, then tip in the sultanas, apricots, and wine and stir well.
4 Pour the onion, sultana, and apricot mix over the meat. Add 500ml (16fl oz) stock and the tomatoes and bring to a simmer. Cover the casserole and place in the oven for an hour until the meat is tender.
5 Meanwhile, cook the rice following pack instructions, using the remaining stock instead of water.
6 While the rice is cooking, tip the almonds into a large frying pan and gently toast for 3–4 minutes.
7 Sprinkle the herbs over the lamb and serve with rice sprinkled with the toasted almonds.

MASTER TIP
WILD RICE

Although they look elegant, wild rice grains are too spiky to eat when undercooked. Boil until the skins split and they will have a pleasing chewy texture. The intense grassy, tea-like flavour of wild rice means a little goes a long way.

MUSALLAM LAMB TWO-WAYS WITH SPICED POMMES ANNA AND BEETROOT CHUTNEY

Dhruv Baker sales director and 2010 champion

PREPARATION TIME
1 hour

COOKING TIME
3 hours

SERVES 4

FOR THE CHUTNEY
1 large onion, chopped
1 large cooking apple, peeled, cored, and sliced
finely grated zest and juice of 1 lemon
200ml (7fl oz) distilled malt vinegar
1 tsp ground ginger
1 star anise
½ tsp salt
70g (2¼oz) sugar
450g (1lb) cooked beetroot, peeled and diced

FOR THE SHOULDER OF LAMB
4 tbsp ghee
1 large onion, thinly sliced
45g (1½oz) flour
20 almonds, blanched and peeled
15 green cardamoms, peeled and ground
6 tbsp thick natural yogurt
6 tsp ground coriander
4 tsp ground ginger
2 tsp garam masala

1 tsp chilli powder
1 tsp ground mace
pinch of saffron, soaked in 1 tbsp of warm water (see MasterTip, p.147)
1½ tsp salt
20g (¾oz) black peppercorns, crushed
4 drops of Kewra water
1.5kg (3lb 3oz) shoulder of lamb
25g (scant 1oz) butter

FOR THE RACKS OF LAMB
1 rack of lamb, 8 ribs, French trimmed (see MasterClass, pp.170–171)
1 rack of lamb, 4 ribs, French trimmed
2 tbsp olive oil
25g (scant 1oz) butter

FOR THE POMMES ANNA
50g (1¾oz) ghee (see MasterTip, left)
1 tsp ground cumin
½ tsp ground turmeric
700g (1lb 9oz) Maris Piper potatoes, peeled and thinly sliced
salt and freshly ground black pepper

MASTER TIP
GHEE

An Indian product, ghee is made by clarifying and cooking butter to remove its excess water content. Once solidified, the resultant smooth, creamy paste has a rich, nutty flavour.

1 Put all the ingredients for the chutney except the beetroot in a large pan or preserving pan. Bring to the boil, stirring occasionally. Reduce the heat and simmer for 30 minutes. Add the beetroot, return to the boil, and simmer for about 1 hour, stirring now and again, until the chutney is thick.

2 To cook the shoulder of lamb, preheat the oven to 180°C (350°F/Gas 4). Heat the ghee in a pan and fry the onion for 10 minutes, or until golden brown. Remove with a slotted spoon and drain on kitchen paper. Put into a blender or food processor and blitz briefly. Mix together with all the remaining ingredients except the lamb and the butter.

3 Prick the shoulder of lamb all over with a metal skewer. Give the marinade a good stir. Prick the meat again, place in a roasting tin, and rub in the marinade. Pour the ghee remaining in the pan over the meat and cover with foil. Place in the oven and cook for 1 hour. Uncover the lamb and, using a very sharp knife, cut the meat away from the bone in large chunks. Cover again and cook for 2 hours, turning and basting the meat every 25 minutes.

4 Meanwhile, cook the potatoes. Preheat a second oven to 200°C (400°F/Gas 6). Grease a non-stick ovenproof frying pan. Melt the ghee in a separate pan with the spices. Layer the potatoes in the ovenproof pan, brushing with the spiced ghee and seasoning with salt and pepper as you go. Pour over any remaining ghee then place over medium heat for about 5 minutes to brown the base. Cover with baking parchment and bake in the oven for about 50 minutes, or until tender.

5 In a clean frying pan, fry the racks of lamb in oil and butter for 15 minutes or until sealed on all sides. Transfer to a roasting tin, retaining the buttery juices in the frying pan, spoon over 2 tbsp of the sauce from the shoulder of lamb and cook in the oven for 15 minutes. Remove from the pan, slice into cutlets, and return to the frying pan to fry briefly until browned. Keep in a warm place to rest.

6 Remove about three-quarters of the sauce from the roasting tin in which you cooked the shoulder of lamb and blend until smooth, adding a little water if the mixture is too thick. Spoon into a pan. Lift the lamb onto a board and, using 2 forks, shred the meat. Melt 25g (scant 1oz) butter in a large frying pan and, when bubbling, sit 8 chef's moulds about 4cm (1½in) in diameter and 5cm (2in) deep in the pan. Pack in the shredded meat, pressing it down firmly with the back of a spoon. Fry for 2–3 minutes on each side to crisp. Gently reheat the sauce.

7 Using a fish slice, transfer the lamb to warmed serving plates. Sit the chops by the side, along with a spoonful of pommes Anna and some chutney. Spoon the sauce over and lift off the chef's moulds just before serving.

MASTER TIP
LAMB AND BEETROOT

Beetroot has greater culinary potential than expiring in vinegar. Yet, it's at its very best when its coarseness combines with vinegar and spices into a vibrant relish. Normally this is too extreme with the subtle flavours of lamb, but here shoulder of lamb is cooked with more spices, their intensity diluted by heat and cooking time. The relish thus refreshes the flavours of the shoulder, and the racks provide bright contrast that's better with the potatoes.

LAMB STEW WITH APPLE AND SOUR PLUMS

Mitra Abrahams student and 2010 semi-finalist

PREPARATION TIME
30 minutes

COOKING TIME
1 hour 45 minutes

SERVES 4

3 tbsp olive oil
2 large onions, sliced
800g (1¾lb) neck of lamb, cut into
 1.5cm (¾in) slices
20 Iranian dried sour plums, soaked in
 hot water for 30 minutes
pinch of saffron
1 tbsp groundnut oil

2 apples, peeled, cored, and sliced
 into thin wedges
1 tsp ground cardamom
dash of rosewater
1 tbsp sugar
salt and freshly ground black pepper
200g (7oz) basmati rice
sprigs of chervil, to garnish

1 Heat the oil in a large flameproof casserole dish over medium heat. Fry the onions until golden, then remove from the casserole and set aside. Fry the lamb in small batches until brown, adding more oil if necessary.

2 Stir in the onions and drained plums. Grind the saffron stems with a pestle and mortar, add to the casserole, and cover the contents with boiling water. Bring to the boil and simmer, covered, for 1½ hours.

3 When the lamb is ready, heat the groundnut oil in a frying pan and sauté the apples until lightly golden. Drain on kitchen paper. Add the apples, cardamom, rosewater, and sugar to the lamb. Season with salt and pepper and cook for a further 10 minutes.

4 Put the rice in a pan and add 400ml (14fl oz) boiling water, a dash of olive oil, and some salt. Bring to the boil and simmer with the lid on for 15–20 minutes, or until cooked.

5 Shape the rice in a ramekin or cup and turn out on serving plates. Arrange the lamb, fruit, and sauce next to the rice and garnish with some chervil.

JOHN TORODE "The sour plums are really sour, the apples are really sweet, your lamb is cooked perfectly and the spices you've got running through it are really subtle."

ROAST LAMB WITH OLIVE SAUCE AND ANCHOVY TEMPURA
John Calton head chef and 2010 Professionals finalist

PREPARATION TIME
1 hour

COOKING TIME
1 hour 15 minutes

SERVES 4

4 rumps of lamb, about 250g (9oz) each, trimmed and tied
1 punnet of basil cress, to garnish

FOR THE AUBERGINES
2 aubergines, halved lengthways
2 garlic cloves, thinly sliced
2 tbsp olive oil
zest of 1 Amalfi lemon
2 tsp mild curry powder

FOR THE LAMB JUS
500g (1lb 2oz) lamb trimmings and bones
2 banana shallots
1 small bunch of thyme
250ml (8fl oz) dry white wine
250ml (8fl oz) Noilly Prat
600ml (1 pint) lamb stock
salt and freshly ground black pepper

FOR THE ROASTED GARLIC
1 garlic bulb
3–4 tbsp olive oil

FOR THE CHEESE SAUCE
200g (7oz) good-quality soft goat's cheese
5–6 tbsp olive oil

FOR THE OLIVE SAUCE
200g (7oz) pitted Kalamata olives
1 tbsp superfine capers
1 garlic clove, crushed
2 white anchovy fillets
6–8 tbsp olive oil
1 small bunch of basil
2 plum tomatoes

FOR THE TOMATOES
200g (7oz) baby plum tomatoes on the vine
1–2 tbsp oil
50g (1¾oz) dry breadcrumbs
50g (1¾oz) Gruyère cheese, grated

FOR THE MEDITERRANEAN VEGETABLES
1 medium fennel bulb, finely sliced
sea salt
juice of 1 Amalfi lemon
7 tbsp olive oil
1 red pepper, diced
1 yellow pepper, diced
1 courgette, cut into ribbons with a potato peeler

FOR THE TEMPURA
100g (3½oz) self-raising flour
20g (¾oz) baking powder
500ml (16fl oz) sparkling water
150ml (5fl oz) vegetable oil
4 white anchovy fillets

1 Preheat the oven to 200°C (400°F/Gas 6). Begin with the aubergines, slashing them several times on the cut side. Spike the garlic into the aubergines, then drizzle with the olive oil. Place on an oven tray, wrap in foil, and bake for 40 minutes. Remove from the oven, scrape out the flesh, and chop it roughly. Place the aubergine in a pan and heat gently to remove excess moisture. Stir in the lemon zest and curry powder. Set aside.

2 Meanwhile cook the lamb jus. Place the lamb bones in a baking tray along with the shallots and thyme and roast for 25 minutes. Remove from the oven, place on high heat, and pour the wine and Noilly Prat into the pan. Stir and bring to a simmer. Add the stock, bring to the boil, and reduce the jus until it clings to the back of a spoon. Strain through a fine sieve. Season with salt and pepper and set aside.

3 For the roasted garlic, break up the garlic bulb into individual cloves. Place in a small roasting tin, drizzle with 3–4 tbsp oil, and roast in the preheated oven for 15–20 minutes until soft and tender.

4 Meanwhile, make the cheese sauce. Place the goat's cheese in a food processor and process until creamy. With the motor running, trickle in the oil until a piping consistency is reached. Season well and set aside.

5 To make the olive sauce, reserve 4 olives and, using a food processor, blend the rest with the capers, garlic, anchovies, oil, and a few basil leaves. Transfer to a bowl. Score a cross in the base of the tomatoes, place in a bowl, and cover with boiling water for 1–2 minutes until the skin begins to peel. Drain and peel off the skin. Cut into quarters and remove and discard the seeds. Finely dice the flesh and stir into the sauce with the olives to serve.

6 Next, season the rumps of lamb. Heat a large frying pan and brown the lamb for 3–4 minutes on each side, then transfer to a roasting tin and cook in the oven for 12–14 minutes. Remove from the oven and leave to rest for 10 minutes.

7 Place the baby plum tomatoes in a roasting tin, drizzle with the oil and roast for 15 minutes until tender. Sprinkle with breadcrumbs and cheese and return to the oven for another 10 minutes until golden.

8 For the Mediterranean vegetables, season the fennel with sea salt, drizzle with lemon juice and 3 tbsp of olive oil, and set aside. Heat 2 tablespoons of oil in a pan, add the red and yellow peppers, and cook slowly for 10–15 minutes until tender.

9 Meanwhile, make the tempura. Whisk together the flour, baking powder, a pinch of salt, and the sparkling water to make the batter. Heat the vegetable oil in a deep pan. Drop a spoonful of batter into the oil to test if it is hot enough – it should bubble. Dry the anchovies on kitchen paper then dip them in the batter and fry for 3–4 minutes until golden. Remove with a slotted spoon and set aside.

10 Place the courgette in a pan of boiling water for 1 minute and drain. Season and drizzle with 2 tbsp olive oil.

11 Spoon the aubergine onto the centre of each plate. Pipe or spoon the goat's cheese sauce over it and place the lamb rump on top with some fennel. Arrange the roasted tomatoes, peppers, and roasted garlic around the lamb and drizzle with the olive sauce. Pour the jus over the lamb and serve with tempura anchovies and basil cress.

RUMP OF NEW SEASON LAMB WITH CRUSHED SPRING VEGETABLES

Neil Mackenzie sous chef and 2010 Professionals quarter-finalist

PREPARATION TIME
45 minutes

COOKING TIME
45–60 minutes

SERVES 4

4 rumps of lamb, approx. 250g
  (9oz) each
salt and freshly ground black pepper
114g can anchovies, drained
4 sprigs of rosemary, approx. 5cm (2in)
  long, plus extra for roasting
1 large garlic clove, sliced
3 tbsp olive oil

FOR THE VINAIGRETTE
3 tbsp balsamic vinegar
1 tsp chopped rosemary leaves
4 tbsp grain mustard
2–3 tbsp olive oil
juice of 1–2 lemons

FOR THE VEGETABLES
200g (7oz) broad beans, shelled weight
  (3kg/6½lb unshelled)
400g (14oz) shelled peas
  (800g/1¾lb unshelled)
4 tbsp chopped mint
25g (scant 1oz) butter

FOR THE CARROTS
500g (1lb 2oz) Chantenay carrots,
  halved lengthways if large
3 tbsp olive oil
2 tbsp clear honey
25g (scant 1oz) butter

1 Preheat the oven to 200°C (400°F/Gas 6). Using a sharp knife, score the fat of the lamb in a criss-cross pattern. Season well with salt and pepper, rubbing the salt into the fat, then make a cut about 5cm (2in) long right the way through each lamb rump and use your finger to open it up a little. Set aside.

2 Lay 3–4 anchovy fillets on the chopping board, slightly overlapping each other. Place a sprig of rosemary on top and gently roll up the anchovy fillets to encase the rosemary and form a neat cigar shape. Repeat with the other 3 sprigs of rosemary. Insert the rosemary wraps into the incisions in the lamb and add a few slices of the garlic.

3 Place the broad beans in a pan of boiling water for 2 minutes. Rinse and refresh in cold water, then peel off the grey-green skin to reveal the tender bright green beans.

4 Heat 2 tbsp of oil in a frying pan and sear the lamb rumps for 4–5 minutes on all sides, fat side first, until golden brown. Pour 1 tbsp of oil into a baking tray, scatter in a few extra sprigs of rosemary, 3–4 anchovy fillets, and any leftover garlic. Place the lamb on top of the herbs. Pour any cooking juices from the frying pan over the lamb and roast in the oven for 12–14 minutes until just cooked. Remove the lamb from the baking tray and set aside to rest.

5 To make the vinaigrette, drain any fat from the baking tray and pour the remaining cooking juices into a jug. Place the hot baking tray over medium to high heat and deglaze the pan with the vinegar. Add the rosemary, mustard, and oil and whisk together. Add the lemon juice and finally pour in any resting juices from the lamb. Give the vinaigrette a final whisk and then strain into the jug of reserved cooking juices. Mix thoroughly before serving.

6 Steam the peas and blanched broad beans in a steamer placed over boiling water for 3–4 minutes until tender. Add the mint and butter, season to taste, and lightly crush the mixture in the pan.

7 Place the carrots in a pan of boiling water and cook for 5–6 minutes, then drain. Heat the oil in the pan. Add the carrots, stirring to coat, then add the honey and season with salt and pepper. Cook over moderate heat, turning the carrots frequently, for 2 minutes. Add the butter at the end to glaze.

8 Carve each stuffed rump into approximately 5 thick slices and serve on top of the crushed greens. Arrange the carrots around the dish with a drizzle of the vinaigrette.

HERB-CRUSTED RUMP OF LAMB WITH CELERIAC PURÉE, BALSAMIC-ROASTED BEETROOT, AND A TOMATO HERB JUS

Dhruv Baker sales director and 2010 champion

PREPARATION TIME
50 minutes

COOKING TIME
30–45 minutes

SERVES 4

1 tsp coriander seeds
1 tsp fennel seeds
¼ tsp white peppercorns
4 lamb rumps or thick lamb steaks,
   approx. 175g (6oz) each
1 tbsp olive oil
2 tbsp vegetable oil
1 garlic clove
1 sprig of thyme
1 sprig of rosemary
salt and freshly ground black pepper

FOR THE BEETROOT
12 baby beetroots
1 tsp caraway seeds
4 tbsp olive oil
1 tbsp balsamic vinegar
½ tsp salt
½ tsp sugar

FOR THE PURÉE
1 celeriac, weighing about 500g
   (1lb 2oz), peeled and chopped
400ml (14fl oz) whole milk
100ml (3½fl oz) double cream
1 tsp salt
½ tsp freshly grated nutmeg
knob of butter

FOR THE JUS
1 tbsp olive oil
4 shallots, chopped
2–3 tomatoes, chopped
1 sprig of rosemary
1–2 sprigs of oregano
3 garlic cloves, chopped
300ml (10fl oz) lamb stock
20g (¾oz) butter

1 Preheat the oven to 200°C (400°F/Gas 6). Crush the spices for the lamb in a pestle and mortar or using a spice grinder. Rub each rump or lamb steak with olive oil and then press them in the spice mix to coat evenly. Set aside.

2 Parcel up the beetroots in a sheet of foil with the caraway seeds, oil, vinegar, salt, and sugar. Place on a baking tray and cook in the oven for about 30–45 minutes, or until soft. Remove the beetroots from the oven and reduce the temperature to 180°C (350°F/Gas 4).

3 While the beetroots are cooking, put the celeriac in a pan with the milk and cream and bring to the boil. Season with salt and nutmeg and simmer for 20–25 minutes, or until tender. Drain, reserving the cooking liquor. Blend the celeriac using a hand-held blender or transferring it to a food processor, adding the butter and enough cooking liquor to form a smooth purée. Taste and adjust the seasoning.

4 To make the jus, heat the olive oil in a large saucepan and gently fry the shallots and tomatoes with the herbs for 10 minutes. Add the garlic and fry for 5 minutes. Stir in the stock and slowly bring to the boil. Bubble until the stock is reduced by two-thirds. Strain through a fine sieve into a clean pan.

5 To cook the lamb, heat the vegetable oil in an ovenproof frying pan, add the herb-coated rumps or steaks and fry them on each side for 3–4 minutes to seal. Add the garlic, thyme, and rosemary. Season with salt and pepper and cook in the preheated oven for 10–12 minutes – the lamb should still be pink in the centre. Leave to rest in a warm place. Reheat the jus, adding any juices from the lamb, and also reheat the celeriac purée.

6 To serve, spoon the purée onto warmed plates and top with the lamb. Spoon a puddle of jus over and serve with the baby beetroots.

RUMP OF HOGGET WITH LENTIL RAVIGOT AND STUFFED BABY ARTICHOKES

Claire Lara lecturer and 2010 Professionals champion

PREPARATION TIME
1 hour 10 minutes

COOKING TIME
25–35 minutes

SERVES 4

25g (scant 1oz) butter
1 garlic clove, crushed
sprig of thyme
1 rump of hogget, approx. 800g (1¾lb)
salt and freshly ground black pepper
450g (1lb) baby carrots

FOR THE ARTICHOKES
8 baby artichokes
2 tbsp lemon juice
2 tbsp plain flour
sprig of thyme
1 bay leaf
4–5 black peppercorns
2 tbsp Chardonnay or
   white wine vinegar
50g (1¾oz) butter

1 onion, finely chopped
1 tsp caster sugar
300ml (10fl oz) lamb stock
2 lamb's kidneys
200g (7oz) lamb's sweetbreads
50g (1¾oz) parsley, finely chopped
100g (3½oz) wafer-thin pancetta

FOR THE RAVIGOT
300g (10oz) Puy lentils
25g (scant 1oz) butter
½ carrot, finely diced
½ celery, finely diced
½ leek, finely diced
1 tsp ground cumin
1 garlic clove
1 star anise

BABY ARTICHOKES

Artichokes have an earthy, nutty flavour with a slight astringency. Only very small artichokes can be eaten whole or stuffed. The baby purple artichoke (pictured) has a mild flavour with a hint of sweetness. It can also be deep-fried, either whole or sliced into wedges.

1 Preheat the oven to 180°C (350°F/Gas 4). Prepare the artichokes by cutting the outer leaves down to two-thirds and removing the stalks. To prevent them from discolouring, place them in a bowl of cold water with the lemon juice until you are about to use them. Mix the flour with enough water to make a paste and add to a pan of boiling water with the artichokes, thyme, bay leaf, peppercorns, and Chardonnay or vinegar. Bring to the boil and simmer for 10–15 minutes until tender. Drain, then remove the choke and any papery leaves from the centre of the artichokes. Set aside.

2 To cook the meat, melt the butter in an ovenproof frying pan, add the garlic and thyme and cook the hogget on all sides for 4–8 minutes to seal. Season and cook in the oven for 25–35 minutes for meat that is still pink. Remove from the oven and leave to rest in a warm place. Increase the oven heat to 200°C (400°F/Gas 6).

3 While the meat is cooking, make the stuffing for the artichokes. Melt half the butter in a frying pan, add the onion and caramelize it by sprinkling it with sugar and cooking gently for 10–15 minutes until brown. In a saucepan, bring the stock to the boil and simmer for 10–15 minutes to reduce it. Meanwhile, melt the remaining butter in another frying pan and seal the kidneys and sweetbreads for a few minutes. Cool and chop finely.

4 To make the ravigot, place the lentils in a saucepan with 600ml (1 pint) of water, bring to the boil, then simmer for 15–20 minutes until *al dente*. Drain if necessary. Melt the butter in a frying pan over low heat and sweat the vegetables with the cumin, garlic, and star anise for 10 minutes. Remove the garlic and star anise and add the vegetables to the lentils.

5 Place the onions, kidneys, sweetbreads, and parsley in a bowl, then mix together with the lamb stock reduction and season to taste. Spoon the stuffing into the centres of the artichokes. Place in an ovenproof dish and wrap pancetta around each artichoke to keep it moist. Cook in the oven for 15–20 minutes. Meanwhile, boil or steam the baby carrots until tender, about 10 minutes.

6 Remove the pancetta from the artichokes. Slice the hogget and serve with the lentil ravigot, carrots, and artichokes.

GREGG WALLACE "The whole thing is a beautifully seasoned meaty feast, absolute feast."

BEEF WRAPPED IN COPPA DI PARMA WITH SWISS CHARD AND SOFT POLENTA

Neil Stuke actor and 2010 Celebrity semi-finalist

PREPARATION TIME
20 minutes

COOKING TIME
40 minutes

SERVES 4

1kg (2¼lb) beef fillet
100g (3½oz) fat from Prosciutto di parma
2 garlic cloves, finely sliced
1 sprig of rosemary, leaves and stalks separated
sea salt and freshly ground black pepper
10 thin slices Coppa di Parma
2 tbsp olive oil
2 sticks celery, chopped
1 red onion, chopped
2 sprigs of thyme

1 bay leaf
360ml (12fl oz) full-bodied red wine such as Barolo
200ml (7fl oz) beef stock
30g (1oz) butter
200g (7oz) polenta

FOR THE CHARD
450g (1lb) Swiss chard, stalks removed
2 tbsp olive oil
2 garlic cloves, finely chopped
1 dried chilli, crushed

JOHN TORODE

"I actually think this beef dish was better than good. The chard with that spike of chilli, I think that was great."

1 Using a sharp knife, make small incisions all over the beef fillet, following the grain of the meat, and insert a sliver each of prosciutto fat, garlic, and rosemary leaves. Season with salt and pepper.
2 Wrap the fillet in the Coppa di Parma and tie evenly with string. Heat the oil in a deep sauté pan and sear the beef on all sides. Reserve.
3 Add the celery and onion to the pan and sauté, stirring, for 5 minutes, or until softened. Stir in the thyme, bay leaf, and rosemary stalks. Pour in the wine and beef stock, bring to the boil, and return the beef to the pan. Place some damp greaseproof paper over the pan, and then cover with the lid. Simmer for 20–30 minutes. Lift out the beef, transfer to a warm plate, and leave to rest.
4 Strain the cooking juices into a clean pan, discard the vegetables, and simmer the liquid until it has reduced by half. Season with salt and pepper to taste, stir in 15g (½oz) butter, and keep hot.
5 To prepare the polenta, cook in a pan of boiling water as directed on the packet to end up with a soft consistency. Add the remaining butter and season well with salt and pepper to taste.
6 For the Swiss chard, blanch the leaves in a saucepan of boiling salted water for 2–3 minutes, and drain well. Heat the oil in a frying pan, add the garlic and chilli and cook for 1–2 minutes, stirring. Add the chard and stir-fry quickly for 2 minutes.
7 To serve, remove the string and slice the beef fillet into thick slices. Spoon the polenta just off centre in large serving bowls and place the Swiss chard on top. Rest a thick slice of the beef on top, then spoon the sauce over it and around the bowl.

ROAST FILLET OF BEEF WITH VANILLA MASH AND SHALLOT JUS

Stacey Warr chef de partie and 2010 Professionals semi-finalist

PREPARATION TIME
30 minutes

COOKING TIME
40 minutes

SERVES 4

600ml (1 pint) chicken stock
400g (14oz) frozen peas
16 Chantenay carrots
15g (½oz) butter
2 tbsp sugar
salt and freshly ground black pepper
4 beef fillet steaks, about 175g (6oz)
   each and 2.5cm (1in) thick, trimmed
1 tbsp olive oil
50g (1¾oz) pea shoots, to garnish

FOR THE JUS
2 tbsp olive oil
8 banana shallots, finely chopped

4 garlic cloves
4 sprigs of rosemary
4 sprigs of thyme
150ml (5fl oz) ruby port
150g (5½oz) redcurrant jelly
600ml (1 pint) beef stock

FOR THE MASH
800g (1¾lb) Maris Piper potatoes,
   peeled and quartered
½ vanilla pod, halved lengthways
100ml (3½fl oz) whole milk, warmed
20g (¾oz) butter
2 tbsp clotted cream

CHANTENAY CARROTS

Carrots are never better than in the late spring when they are young and tender. Chantenays are short and stubby when fully grown. They have a rich flavour and there is no need to peel them before use.

1 To make the jus, heat the oil in a large frying pan, add the shallots and sauté for 5 minutes until golden. Add the garlic, rosemary, thyme, port, and jelly, and caramelize over moderate heat until the liquid reduces by half. Add the beef stock to the pan, bring to the boil, then turn the heat down to simmering and reduce the sauce by half again. Season with salt and pepper then pass through a sieve.

2 For the mash, boil the potatoes in salted water for 20 minutes until cooked. Drain, pass through a potato ricer, and return to the saucepan.

3 Scrape the seeds out of the vanilla pod. Add the pod and seeds to the milk and infuse for 5 minutes. Strain the milk through a fine sieve and add to the potatoes with the butter and cream. Beat in the pan over low heat until the butter melts and the mash is heated through.

4 To prepare the peas, pour the chicken stock into a small pan and bring to the boil. Add the peas and simmer for 3 minutes. Drain the peas, reserving the stock. Blend the peas in a blender or a food processor, adding some hot chicken stock to produce a purée.

5 Blanch the carrots whole in boiling salted water for 3 minutes, drain well, and pat dry with some kitchen paper. In a large frying pan, melt the butter then add the sugar and carrots and sauté for 15–20 minutes over moderate heat, until the carrots are caramelized.

6 Season the steaks and heat the oil in a pan. For rare steaks, cook for 1–2 minutes each side; rest for 6–8 minutes. For medium, cook for 3 minutes each side then rest for 4 minutes. To serve, spoon sauce on the plates, then add the beef and vegetables. Garnish with pea shoots.

FILLET OF BEEF WITH WILD MUSHROOMS, DAUPHINOISE POTATOES, AND MADEIRA SAUCE

Chris Walker actor and 2010 Celebrity semi-finalist

4 beef fillet steaks, approx. 175g (6oz)
   each and 2.5cm (1in) thick
salt and freshly ground black pepper
1 tbsp olive oil
30g (1oz) butter
16 wild mushrooms, such as girolles
140g (5oz) button mushrooms
45g (1½oz) dried wild mushrooms,
   reconstituted

FOR THE SAUCE
2 tbsp grapeseed oil
2 shallots, finely chopped

1 celery stick, diced
1 carrot, diced
200ml (7fl oz) Madeira wine
600ml (1 pint) fresh beef stock
1 bay leaf
2 sprigs of rosemary
10g (¼oz) butter

FOR THE POTATOES
500ml (16fl oz) double cream
3 garlic cloves
4 large King Edward or Maris Piper
   potatoes, peeled and thinly sliced

PREPARATION TIME
20 minutes

COOKING TIME
35 minutes

SERVES 4

1 Preheat the oven to 190°C (375°F/Gas 5). To make the sauce, heat the oil in a frying pan, add the shallots, and sauté, stirring, for 5 minutes until soft. Add the celery and carrot, and continue to cook over moderate heat for a further 5 minutes. Add the Madeira and then reduce the liquid by half.

2 Add the stock to the pan with the bay leaf and rosemary, bring to the boil and then simmer until reduced by half again. Pass the sauce through a sieve and discard the vegetables and herbs. Season with salt and pepper and then whisk the butter through the sauce.

3 To make the dauphinoise potatoes, place the cream and garlic in a large saucepan and bring to a simmer. Add the potatoes and simmer for 3–4 minutes, until they are just tender. Remove the potatoes from the pan with a slotted spoon and transfer to an ovenproof dish, then pour the infused cream over, discarding the garlic. Bake in the oven for about 30 minutes, or until the potatoes are tender and browned.

4 Season the fillet steaks with salt and pepper. Heat the oil in a large frying pan. For rare steaks, cook for 1–2 minutes each side then rest for 6–8 minutes; for medium, cook for 3 minutes each side then rest for 4 minutes. Add the butter to the same pan and sauté the mushrooms for 3 minutes, until cooked.

5 To serve, pool the sauce onto the warmed plates and then add the steak, potatoes, and mushrooms.

ROASTED BEEF FILLET WITH A BLACK OLIVE EMULSION, CONFITS, AND A SOCCA AND SWISS CHARD MILLEFEUILLE

Renaud Marin head chef and 2010 Professionals quarter-finalist

PREPARATION TIME
1½ hours

COOKING TIME
30 minutes

SERVES 4

2 tbsp olive oil
900g (2lb) 28-days old mature beef fillet
30g (1oz) butter
1 garlic clove, crushed
1 sprig of thyme

FOR THE SAUCE
3 tbsp vegetable oil
1 white Spanish onion, chopped
2 garlic cloves
250ml (8fl oz) red wine
500ml (16fl oz) veal stock
500ml (16fl oz) chicken stock
2 sprigs of thyme
1 tsp black peppercorns

FOR THE EMULSION
100g (3½oz) pitted black olives
2 tbsp mineral water
4 eggs, separated and egg yolks
  gently whisked
450ml (15fl oz) grapeseed oil

FOR THE CONFITS
500ml (16fl oz) olive oil
6 sprigs of thyme
2 sprigs of rosemary
2 garlic cloves, crushed
2 bay leaves
4 large banana shallots, finely chopped
1 garlic bulb, separated
15 cherry tomatoes on the vine

FOR THE MILLEFEUILLE
115g (4oz) chickpea flour
sea salt and freshly ground black pepper
4 tbsp olive oil
300ml (10fl oz) whole milk
grapeseed oil for frying
1 head French Swiss chard
200g (7oz) flat-leaf parsley
½ bunch sorrel, cut into julienne strips

TO SERVE
200g (7oz) wild rocket

MICHEL ROUX JR
"I love that, I think that's delicious. I love the socca and the Swiss chard."

1 To make the sauce, heat the oil in a hot frying pan and add the onion and garlic and sauté gently for 10 minutes or until the onion is caramelized. Deglaze the pan with red wine and, when the alcohol has evaporated, add the two stocks, thyme, and peppercorns. Leave to simmer until reduced by half.
2 Meanwhile, make the olive emulsion. Blitz the olives and mineral water in a blender or food processor until smooth, then transfer to a heatproof glass bowl. Place the bowl over a pan of simmering water and gradually whisk in the egg yolks, then slowly add the grapeseed oil, whisking until emulsified. When cool, transfer to the fridge.
3 For the confits, heat the oil to 120°C (250°F) in the pan and add the thyme, rosemary, garlic cloves, and bay leaves. Turn off the heat and then divide the infused oil among 3 separate pans.
4 Add the shallots to one of the olive oil pans. Return to the heat and leave to simmer for about 10 minutes or until soft. Take off the heat.

Add the garlic cloves to another of the pans. Bring to a simmer for about 7 minutes or until the garlic is soft, then take off the heat.

5 Separate all the tomatoes with a pair of scissors, keeping the calyx on each tomato. Add to the remaining pan of infused oil and simmer for about 8 minutes until the skin splits. Take off the heat, transfer the tomatoes with a slotted spoon to a bowl and keep warm.

6 For the millefeuille, mix the chickpea flour with salt and pepper. Then add 2 tbsp of the oil and gradually pour in the milk, beating well to form a "socca" batter. Allow the batter to rest for 15 minutes in the fridge.

7 Clean and separate the green from the white of the Swiss chard, then cut the green part into julienne strips and finely dice the white.

8 Heat the remaining oil in a pan, add the white Swiss chard and sauté for 2–3 minutes. Season to taste, then add the green Swiss chard and flat-leaf parsley. Cook for a further 2 minutes. Take off the heat, add the sorrel and confit shallots drained from the oil.

9 In a hot non-stick pan, about 15cm (6in) in diameter, cook thin crêpes from the the socca batter until used up. Keep warm. When ready to serve, alternate the socca crêpes with the Swiss chard mix to create small millefeulles 4cm (1½ in) high. Press gently and cut each one into a neat square. Keep warm in a low oven.

10 Heat the oil in a pan and sear the beef until brown all over. Add the butter and, when foamy, add the garlic and thyme. Cook to your preference: for rare beef, cook for 4 minutes, rest for 6–8 minutes; for medium beef, cook for 6 minutes, rest for 4 minutes.

11 To complete the sauce, strain the liquid into a pan and reheat.

12 Place a tear drop shape of the olive emulsion on 4 plates and put the tomatoes and rocket inside the tear. Add slices of the beef and a millefeuille, drizzle some jus over the beef and top with a garlic clove.

FLAVOUR COMBINATION
BEEF AND OLIVES

Choose naturally black olives for their succulent oiliness, saltiness and dark flavours, for even in an emulsion of egg yolk and oil they'll stay lively, producing tastes rather like a better-behaved anchovy sauce, traditionally a British favourite. Eaten with the savoury, *umami*-taste of the seared beef crust, the olive emulsion switches on every taste bud and runs it at maximum. The beef gives all its got and you will taste depths you never imagined.

FILLET OF BEEF WITH TWICE-BAKED CHEESE AND LEEK SOUFFLÉ, POTATO ROSTI, AND SAUTÉED SPINACH AND WATERCRESS

Christine Hamilton TV personality and 2010 Celebrity finalist

PREPARATION TIME
25 minutes

COOKING TIME
1 hour

SERVES 4

FOR THE SOUFFLÉS
75g (2½oz) butter
45g (1½oz) plain flour
250ml (8fl oz) full-fat milk
60g (2oz) Lancashire cheese, grated
200g (7oz) soft goat's cheese,
  any rind removed
4 baby leeks, finely chopped
small bunch of tarragon, chopped
salt and freshly ground black pepper
4 eggs, separated, plus 1 egg white
juice of ½ lemon
60ml (2fl oz) single cream

FOR THE ROSTI
4 baking potatoes
oil, for frying

FOR THE BEEF
15g (½oz) dried porcini mushrooms,
  soaked in 150ml (5fl oz) boiling water
  for 30 minutes

2 tbsp olive oil
2 shallots, finely chopped
1 clove garlic, finely chopped
4 flat mushrooms, finely chopped
½ lemon
sea salt and freshly ground
  black pepper
12 air-dried bacon rashers (or similar)
900g (2lb) centre-cut fillet of beef
sprig of rosemary, finely chopped
2 sprigs of thyme, finely chopped
30g (1oz) butter
200ml (7fl oz) Madeira wine
450ml (15fl oz) beef stock

FOR THE SPINACH AND WATERCRESS
1 tbsp olive oil
200g (7oz) spinach
75g (2½oz) watercress
1 nutmeg

1 Preheat the oven to 190°C (375°F/Gas 5). For the soufflés, melt 45g (1½oz) of the butter in a saucepan, and use some of it to thoroughly grease four 200ml (7fl oz) soufflé dishes. Place them in the fridge to chill. Stir the flour into the pan and return to the heat. Cook for 1 minute. Gradually stir in the milk, and keep stirring over low heat until the sauce thickens and is smooth. Stir in half of the Lancashire cheese and all of the goat's cheese. Leave to cool.

2 In another pan, heat the remaining butter and add the leeks. Sauté until soft and golden, then add the tarragon, and season.

3 Beat the eggs yolks into the cheese sauce. Stir in the leeks, and season, adding a squeeze of lemon juice. Set aside to cool. Whisk the egg whites in a clean bowl until soft peaks form, then fold them into the leek mixture.

4 Fill the prepared ramekins about three-quarters full with the cheese and leek mixture. Place them in a roasting tin and fill with

boiling water to come halfway up the sides. Bake for 8–10 minutes, or until well risen, golden-brown and cooked through. Set aside.

5 To make the rosti, place the potatoes in their skins into a pan of boiling water, then reduce the heat and simmer for 10 minutes. Place the potatoes in cold water until they are cool enough to handle, then peel and finely grate them. Sprinkle the potato with salt and place in a clean tea towel or cloth. Squeeze firmly to remove excess moisture.

6 Heat some oil in a frying pan, and then place four 10cm (4in) chef rings into the pan and press the potato into each ring. Cook the rostis on medium heat for 2–3 minutes until golden on one side. Remove the rings, turn the rostis over, and cook for 2–3 minutes until browned on the other side. They can be re-heated just prior to serving.

7 To prepare the beef, first drain and finely chop the mushrooms. Heat 1 tbsp of the oil in a frying pan, add the shallots and garlic, and sauté for about 5 minutes until the shallots are soft. Add the dried and flat mushrooms, and cook for a further 2–3 minutes, then add a squeeze of lemon juice and season with salt and pepper. Set aside.

8 Lay the bacon rashers on an oiled piece of baking parchment so they are slightly overlapping with no gaps. The bacon needs to be slightly wider than the beef fillet and long enough to wrap around the beef with a 2cm (¾in) overlap. Spread the mushroom mixture along one end of the bacon so that it is in a neat line across each rasher. Season the beef, roll in the chopped herbs, and then place on top of the mushroom mixture. Roll up the beef from the mushroom end, remove the paper and tuck in any excess bacon at each end of the fillet, then secure with string.

9 Increase the oven temperature to 200°C (400°F/Gas 6). Heat 1 tbsp of oil and the butter in an ovenproof pan and brown the meat on all sides, then transfer to the oven and cook for 15–18 minutes. Remove the meat from the pan, cover, and rest in a warm place.

10 Meanwhile, to make the sauce, add the Madeira wine and deglaze the pan until the alcohol has evaporated. Then add the stock and reduce until the sauce thickens and is approximately half the volume.

11 Carefully remove the soufflés from the ramekins and place in an ovenproof dish. Brush with the cream and sprinkle the remaining Lancashire cheese on top. Bake for 5 minutes, or until the cheese has melted and is bubbling, and the soufflés are heated through.

12 For the sautéed spinach and watercress, heat the oil in a pan and sauté the spinach and watercress for about 2 minutes or until the leaves are wilted. Season with salt and pepper and grated nutmeg.

13 To serve, remove the string from the beef, carve it into slices, and arrange on 4 plates with a warm soufflé, potato rosti, and a portion of sautéed spinach and watercress. Drizzle with the sauce.

OSSO BUCO, SAFFRON FONDANT POTATO, PEA GREMOLATA, AND SWEDE PURÉE

Alex Rushmer freelance writer and 2010 finalist

2 tbsp olive oil
4 veal shanks, dusted in plain flour
1 carrot, diced
2 sticks celery, diced
1 red onion, diced
2 large garlic cloves, finely chopped
3 tbsp tomato purée
1 bay leaf
100ml (3½fl oz) dry white wine
500ml (16fl oz) dark veal stock
30g (1oz) butter

FOR THE POTATOES
4 sprigs of thyme
good pinch of saffron
  (see MasterTip, p.147)

1 chicken stock cube dissolved
  in 400ml (14fl oz) boiling water
100g (3½oz) butter
4 large baking potatoes, peeled and
  cut into fondant barrel shape

FOR THE PURÉE
1 swede, approx. 500g (1lb 2oz), diced
20g (¾oz) butter
salt and freshly ground black pepper

FOR THE GREMOLATA
200g (7oz) frozen peas or petits pois
handful of flat-leaf parsley
1 small garlic clove, finely chopped
finely grated zest and juice of ½ lemon

PREPARATION TIME
25 minutes

COOKING TIME
2 hours

SERVES 4

1 Heat the oil in a pan and brown the veal. Remove from the pan and add the vegetables and garlic and cook for 5 minutes until golden. Stir in the purée and bay leaf. Cook for 2 minutes.

2 Add the wine and stir in, scraping up all the meat residue. Then add the stock and bring to the boil. Return the veal shanks, cover with a damp sheet of parchment paper and a lid, then simmer very gently for about 2 hours. Stir occasionally and add to the stock if necessary.

3 For the potatoes, add the thyme and saffron to the stock and leave to infuse. Melt the butter in a pan and brown the potatoes all over. Add the stock, cover, and cook gently for about 30 minutes or until tender.

4 Cook the swede in boiling salted water for 20–25 minutes or until tender. Drain, then using a hand-held blender, blend until puréed. Pass through a sieve, add the butter, season well, and reserve.

5 For the gremolata, add the peas to a pan of boiling water and cook for 2–3 minutes or until *al dente*. Refresh in iced water. Put in a blender with the parsley, garlic, and lemon zest and juice. Season and blitz briefly in bursts to produce a fairly rough texture.

6 Lift the veal shanks from the pan. Strain the liquor back in. Discard the vegetables. Reduce to a glaze. Return the veal to a pan, add the butter and fry on both sides for 1 minute. Reheat the gremolata.

7 Divide the swede between 4 dishes and top with a potato. Sit the veal on the side and top with the pea gremolata. Glaze with the jus.

MASTER TIP
OSSO BUCO

Osso buco is the Italian name for bone-in slices of veal (calf) hind shank. The sinews in these cuts of meat produce a succulent texture when cooked, and the marrow from the bone enriches the sauce. Osso buco is best braised or cooked in a stew.

JOHN TORODE'S
GNUDI

There's pasta and meat sauce – everyone loves it – but then there really is pasta and meat sauce... Try this combination of soft little ricotta dumplings with my version of what a true meat sauce should taste like, and you'll never look back.

PREPARATION TIME
20 minutes, plus chilling

COOKING TIME
2½ hours

SERVES 4

FOR THE DUMPLINGS
250g (9oz) fine semolina flour
250g (9oz) ricotta cheese
50g (1¾oz) Parmesan cheese,
  finely grated

FOR THE BEEF STEW
750g (1lb 10oz) shin or skirt of beef or
  ox cheek, cut into bite-sized chunks
salt and freshly ground black pepper
4 tbsp olive oil
200g (7oz) thick bacon, cut into
  big chunks
2 carrots, halved and cut in half
  lengthways

2 leeks, cut into strips the same
  size as the carrots
2 celery sticks, cut into strips the same
  size as the carrots
2 x 400g cans chopped tomatoes
2 bay leaves
small bunch of flat-leaf parsley
small bunch of sage
350ml (12fl oz) red wine

TO SERVE
handful of parsley, chopped
Parmesan cheese, grated

1 About 24 hours ahead of cooking the dish, coat a flat tray with a layer of semolina flour. Mix the ricotta with a fork and add the Parmesan cheese. Roll into a long log and then into dessert spoon-size balls. Roll each ball in the semolina flour and place each one on the tray so they do not touch. Pour the rest of the semolina over so that the balls are almost completely covered. Place in the fridge, uncovered, and leave overnight.

2 When you are ready to cook the dish, preheat the oven to 190ºC (375ºF/Gas 5).

3 To make the ragout, season the meat well and heat the oil in a flameproof casserole dish. Add the bacon, cook it for 2 minutes and then add the meat. Leave it to sit and sizzle until the chunks are well browned underneath, when they will naturally lift and come away from the pan. Turn them over and cook for a further 10 minutes, making sure to move the bacon so it does not burn. You can always take the bacon out and return it to the sauce at the next step.

4 Add the vegetables and pour in the tomatoes. Add the bay leaves, parsley, and sage and season well with salt and pepper. Then add the wine and bring to the boil, increasing the heat so the alcohol

evaporates. Let it bubble for about 10 minutes, scraping the sticky bits of meat from the bottom of the pot.

5 Add about 500ml (16fl oz) of water so that it almost covers the meat. Cover and place in the oven for 1 hour, then take the lid off, give the meat a good stir, and pop it back in to cook for another hour, so that a lot of the liquid can evaporate. Reduce the oven temperature to 170°C (325°F/Gas 3) for the second hour.

6 Leave the sauce to cool for about 30 minutes and then, using two forks, pull the meat apart and shred it well. If the sauce is too thin, return it to the boil and reduce, but remember this will be served with pasta or bread so it doesn't want to be dry. Taste, season and discard the herbs.

7 To cook the dumplings, bring a large saucepan of water to the boil with a good amount of salt. Dust off the excess semolina flour and drop the dumplings into the water. Let them float to the top and cook for 3 minutes. Then, using a slotted spoon, drop them into the ragout and gently stir. Add the chopped parsley and stir through as well.

8 Spoon the ragout and dumplings into bowls and top with the grated Parmesan. Serve with chunks of bread or freshly-cooked pasta.

BEEF AND CHORIZO WITH HORSERADISH MASH AND ROASTED ROSEMARY DUMPLINGS

Dick Strawbridge TV presenter and 2010 Celebrity finalist

900g (2lb) shin beef, cut into 5cm (2in) chunks
30g (1oz) plain flour, seasoned
salt and freshly ground black pepper
2 tbsp olive oil
1 onion, chopped
300g (10oz) carrots, cut into large chunks
300g (10oz) parsnips, cut into large chunks
750ml (1¼ pints) red wine
225g (8oz) chorizo

FOR THE MASH
900g (2lb) King Edward or Maris Piper potatoes, chopped
100g (3½oz) butter
100ml (3½fl oz) milk, warm
2 tbsp creamed horseradish

FOR THE DUMPLINGS
175g (6oz) self-raising flour
75g (2½oz) shredded suet
1 tbsp very finely chopped rosemary

PREPARATION TIME
20 minutes

COOKING TIME
3–4 hours

SERVES 4

1 Preheat the oven to 140°C (275°F/Gas 1). Coat the beef thoroughly in the seasoned flour. Heat the olive oil in a flameproof casserole dish and brown the meat.

2 Add the onion and cook for 5 minutes. Add the carrots and parsnips and continue to cook, stirring for a further 5 minutes.

3 Add any remaining seasoned flour, cook for a further 5 minutes, stirring well so the meat and vegetables brown evenly. Add the wine and chorizo and stir again.

4 Transfer the dish to the oven and cook for 3–4 hours, or until the meat is cooked through. Remove the casserole from the oven and increase the temperature to 200°C (400°F/Gas 6).

5 For the mash, cook the potatoes in boiling water in a covered pan for about 15 minutes or until tender. Drain and return to the pan over gentle heat. Mash with the butter and warmed milk. When smooth, beat in the horseradish and season to taste. Cover and keep warm.

6 To make the dumplings, sift the flour into a bowl and add the suet and rosemary. Season with salt and pepper, then add enough water (about 3–4 tbsp) to make a soft, but not sticky, dough. Using a knife, work the ingredients together and finally bring it to a soft dough with your hands.

7 Divide the dough into 12 dumplings, each about the size of a medium egg. Place on a baking tray and bake in the oven for about 15 minutes until cooked through.

8 Serve the beef and chorizo with the roasted dumplings on top and the horseradish mash.

PAN-ROASTED CALF'S LIVER WITH CRUSHED JERSEY ROYALS AND SPRING BROTH

Claire Lara lecturer and 2010 Professionals champion

PREPARATION TIME
15 minutes

COOKING TIME
30 minutes

SERVES 4

3 plum tomatoes on the vine
125g (4½oz) shelled peas
85g (3oz) shelled broad beans
150g (5½oz) fine asparagus
12 small Jersey Royal potatoes
600g (1lb 5oz) calf's liver, sinew
  removed and liver thinly sliced

salt and freshly ground black pepper
115g (4oz) unsalted butter
1 garlic clove, chopped
1 sprig of thyme, leaves removed
500ml (16fl oz) chicken stock
1 tbsp chopped parsley
½ lemon

MASTER TIP
JERSEY ROYALS

This famous heritage variety from the Channel Islands is one of the first to arrive in the spring. The smooth, waxy flesh has a distinctive rich, buttery flavour. Waxy potatoes are ideal for boiling, steaming, and in stews as they keep their shape when cooked.

1 Put the tomatoes in a bowl and cover with boiling water. Leave for 1 minute, then remove from the water, skin, and chop.

2 Cook the peas and broad beans in an uncovered pan of boiling water for 5 minutes. Drain and refresh in iced water for 5 minutes to keep a good colour.

3 Prepare the asparagus in the same way as the peas and beans and cut into 2.5cm (1in) pieces when cool.

4 Boil the potatoes in a covered saucepan of boiling salted water for 10–15 minutes or until soft.

5 Season the liver with salt and pepper, cover, and leave in the fridge until needed.

6 Melt 15g (½oz) of the butter in a saucepan and sweat the garlic and thyme for about 10 minutes, or until translucent. Then add the stock and boil rapidly to reduce by half to make a broth.

7 Crush the potatoes, add 60g (2oz) of the butter and all the parsley. Season with salt and pepper and cover to keep warm.

8 Add the vegetables to the chicken broth and simmer for 8 minutes to thicken the broth and ensure the vegetables are tender. Just before serving, add a squeeze of lemon juice to the broth and adjust the seasoning to taste.

9 Heat the remaining butter in a large frying pan until foaming and lightly cook the liver for 3–4 minutes, turning halfway through. Remove it from the pan, cover and leave to rest for few minutes.

10 To serve, divide the crushed potatoes between 4 plates, top with the calf's liver and spoon the vegetable broth around the plate.

LOIN OF PORK IN A BLACK PUDDING CRUST

Chris Walker actor and 2010 Celebrity semi-finalist

1 litre (1¾ pints) extra virgin olive oil
900g (2lb) pork loin joint
100g (3½oz) black pudding, chopped
85g (3oz) panko breadcrumbs
grated zest of 1 unwaxed lemon
1 tbsp finely chopped fresh sage
salt and freshly ground black pepper
2 eggs, beaten
2 Granny Smith apples, peeled, cored, and diced
2 tbsp pure maple syrup

FOR THE LENTILS
1 tsp olive oil
1 large banana shallot, finely chopped
1 garlic clove, crushed
100g (3½oz) smoked back bacon, cut into small cubes
1 celery stick, chopped
1 large carrot, chopped

150ml (5fl oz) chicken stock
1 tbsp sherry vinegar
225g (8oz) cooked Puy lentils (100g/3½oz dry weight)
1 tbsp chopped parsley

FOR THE CELERIAC MASH
175g (6oz) celeriac, peeled and cut into cubes
350g (12oz) Désirée potatoes, peeled and cut into cubes
30g (1oz) butter
4 tbsp double cream

FOR THE SAUCE
300ml (10fl oz) ready-made pork demi-glace or concentrated pork stock
2 tbsp Calvados
2 tbsp dry scrumpy cider

PREPARATION TIME
45 minutes

COOKING TIME
50 minutes

SERVES 4

1 Pour the oil into a deep pan, heat to simmering point, and poach the pork in it for 3 minutes. Remove from the oil and set aside to cool.
2 For the lentils, heat the oil in a sauté pan, add the shallot and garlic and sauté, stirring, until soft. Add the bacon, celery, and carrot and cook for 5 minutes. Pour in the stock and vinegar and simmer, uncovered, until the vegetables have softened. Add the Puy lentils and simmer, uncovered, until the liquid has been absorbed.
3 Put the black pudding, breadcrumbs, lemon zest, and sage in a food processor. Process to make fine crumbs, then season well.
4 Preheat the oven to 200°C (400°F/Gas 6). Dip the pork in egg and then coat in breadcrumbs. Repeat, then shallow fry on all sides and roast for 15 minutes. Reduce the heat to 180°C (350°F/Gas 4) and cook for a further 45–50 minutes until cooked through. Leave to rest.
5 Boil the celeriac and potatoes in salted water for 15–20 minutes. Drain and mash. Beat in the butter and cream and season well.
6 For the sauce, reduce the pork demi-glace and add the Calvados and scrumpy. Simmer until syrupy. Put the apples in a pan with the maple syrup and cook quickly over high heat to caramelize.
7 Reheat the mash, sauce, and lentils and stir parsley into the lentils. Slice the pork. Divide the lentils between 4 plates and top with pork and apple. Make quenelles of mash and drizzle sauce over to finish.

JOHN TORODE

"The lentils have to be the star of the show, with that richness of the sauce running through."

ROASTED PORK LOIN WITH CRACKLING AND PEASE PUDDING

Stacie Stewart PA and 2010 semi-finalist

PREPARATION TIME
45 minutes, plus soaking

COOKING TIME
1 hour

SERVES 4

1 tbsp fennel seed
1½ tsp sea salt
pork rind, approx. 20 x 14cm (8 x 5¾in)
2 tbsp malt vinegar
1 tenderloin pork fillet, approx.
  600g (1lb 5oz)
1 tbsp olive oil
30g (1oz) butter

FOR THE PUDDING
200g (7oz) yellow split peas,
  soaked overnight in cold water
6 rashers of streaky bacon, chopped
600ml (1 pint) ham stock
85g (3oz) walnut oil
salt and freshly ground black pepper

FOR THE JUS
2 banana shallots, finely chopped
1 small bunch of sage, roughly chopped
1 garlic clove, crushed
1 tbsp olive oil
600ml (1 pint) dry white wine
600ml (1 pint) chicken stock
1 tsp wholegrain mustard
1 tsp Dijon mustard
1 sprig of rosemary
100ml (3½fl oz) double cream
25g (scant 1oz) butter

FOR THE LEEKS
50g (1¾oz) butter
2 thin leeks or 1 thick leek, thinly sliced
4 tbsp double cream

JOHN TORODE

"Delicious pease pudding running into soft, creamy, buttery leeks and beautifully soft pork. It tastes absolutely great."

1 For the pease pudding, drain the soaked split peas and place in a pan with the bacon. Pour in the stock and bring to the boil. Skim off any scum that rises to the surface, then reduce to a simmer for 35 minutes, or until the peas are tender. Strain through a fine sieve, then leave the peas and bacon to drain in the sieve for 10 minutes. Blend the peas and bacon in a food processor until smooth. Stir in the walnut oil, then season with salt and pepper to taste.

2 For the jus, sauté the shallots, sage, and garlic in the olive oil until the shallots and garlic are translucent. Add the wine and reduce, then add the stock and reduce again. Add the mustards and rosemary and reduce on a rolling boil until a syrupy consistency is reached; the quantity should have reduced by half. Pass through a sieve, then stir in the cream and whisk in the butter. Reheat gently before serving.

3 Preheat the oven to 230°C (450°F/Gas 8). Dry fry the fennel seeds and mix with the sea salt using a pestle and mortar. To make the crackling, score the skin of the pork rind, pour boiling water over it and pat dry. Rub the malt vinegar and fennel salt into the skin. Put into the preheated oven for 15 minutes then turn it down to 200°C (400°F/Gas 6) and cook for another 45 minutes. Take the crackling out of the oven when really crisp, slice it thinly and put to one side until ready to serve. See also the MasterClass pages 208–9 for more advice on how to cook crackling.

4 Rub the fillet of pork with oil and seal in a pan for 2 minutes, adding butter for the last 30 seconds to caramelize and brown the meat. Transfer to a roasting tin and roast for 20 minutes at 200°C (400°F/Gas 6). Remove from the oven and leave to rest for 5 minutes.
5 For the creamed leeks, melt the butter in a frying pan and soften the leeks. Finish with cream and seasoning.
6 To serve, place a portion of creamed leeks on each plate with slices of pork on top. Form a round of pease pudding with a chef's ring, run the rich jus around it, and garnish with crispy crackling alongside.

SPARE RIB CHOP WITH QUICK RICE AND PEAS
Colin Jackson Olympic athlete and 2010 Celebrity quarter-finalist

PREPARATION TIME
20 minutes

COOKING TIME
2 hours

SERVES 4

2 tbsp vegetable oil
1 onion, chopped
1–2 tsp ground allspice
2 tbsp tomato purée
2 tbsp soy sauce
2 tsp thyme leaves
4 pork spare rib chops, trimmed of fat
600ml (1 pint) chicken stock
salt and freshly ground black pepper

FOR THE RICE AND PEAS
4 rashers of streaky bacon, chopped
2 shallots, finely chopped
1 Scotch bonnet chilli pepper
400g can kidney beans, drained
sprig of thyme
1 chicken stock cube
225g (8oz) long grain rice
400g can coconut milk

1 Heat the oil in a frying pan then fry the onion, stirring, for 5 minutes or until softened. Stir in the allspice, tomato purée, soy sauce, and thyme. Add the chops and pour in the stock. Season with salt and pepper and bring to the boil. Reduce the heat, cover, and simmer gently for about 50–60 minutes or until the pork is meltingly tender.
2 For the rice and peas, fry the bacon in a large frying pan for 5 minutes or until beginning to crisp. Add the shallots and cook for 2–3 minutes. Stir in the remaining ingredients except the coconut milk, then pour in 500ml (16fl oz) water and bring to the boil. Reduce the heat and simmer, uncovered. When nearly all the water has been absorbed, add the coconut milk and cook for 5–10 minutes or until the rice is tender, adding a splash of boiling water if the rice starts to stick before it is completely cooked. Remove the chilli, taking care not to burst it as the seeds are extremely hot. Add salt if needed – the stock may have already been quite salty.
3 Remove the pork from the pan and keep hot. Strain the cooking liquor into a clean pan and reduce to a jus. Check the seasoning. Serve the pork on a bed of rice and peas with a little jus poured over.

HONEY-GLAZED PORK FILET MIGNON

Jez Barfoot restoration builder and 2010 quarter-finalist

2 tbsp balsamic vinegar
1 Bramley cooking apple, peeled and
  thinly sliced
2 large onions, 1 thinly sliced,
  1 quartered
1 large carrot, chopped
1 leek, sliced
1 celery stick, chopped
5 garlic cloves, 1 chopped
2 bay leaves
bunch of thyme
10 rashers of smoked streaky bacon
2 tbsp olive oil
12 sage leaves

450g (1lb) pork filet mignon
salt and freshly ground black pepper
3 tbsp clear honey, plus 1 tsp
1 tbsp Dijon mustard
3 large Maris Piper potatoes, peeled
  and cut into chunks
1 small celeriac, about 350g (12oz),
  peeled and cut into chunks
75ml (2½fl oz) milk
100g (3½oz) butter
8 baby carrots, whole
175g (6oz) French beans
450ml (15fl oz) dry cider
200ml (7fl oz) chicken stock

PREPARATION TIME
50 minutes

COOKING TIME
1 hour

SERVES 4

1 Put the vinegar in a saucepan, add the apple and sliced onion, and cook gently, uncovered, for about 20 minutes to caramelize. Stir from time to time to prevent them from burning. Leave to cool.
2 Preheat the oven to 200°C (400°F/Gas 6). Put the carrot, leek, celery, quartered onion, 4 garlic cloves, bay leaves, thyme, and 3 rashers of bacon, roughly chopped, in a roasting tin. Drizzle the oil over them. Roast for 30 minutes, stirring from time to time.
3 Overlap the remaining bacon rashers and cover with the caramelized apple and onion and sage leaves. Place the pork on top, add pepper, and wrap tightly in the bacon. Glaze with honey and mustard. Place the pork on the vegetables and return to the oven for a further 20–25 minutes.
4 Put the potatoes and celeriac in a pan, add salt and boiling water, cover, and cook for 15 minutes. Drain and mash with the milk and 50g (1¾oz) butter, season, and keep warm. Boil the carrots until tender, about 5 minutes. Boil the beans in salted water for about 6 minutes.
5 When the pork is cooked, remove from the oven and set aside. Add the cider to the roasting tin and put over high heat. Scrape the vegetables from the bottom of the tin then transfer the contents of the tin to a sauce pan. Add the stock and boil rapidly for about 15 minutes to reduce to a thick sauce. Season and sieve into a clean pan.
6 Fry the chopped garlic lightly in 25g (scant 1oz) of butter. Add the beans and toss lightly. In a separate pan, fry the carrots lightly in 25g (scant 1oz) of butter and add 1 tsp of honey.
7 To serve, slice the pork and arrange on each plate with the selection of vegetables. Serve the sauce separately.

JOHN TORODE
"That pork with the apples and the salty bacon around the outside, is delicious."

ROAST BELLY OF PORK WITH APPLES, BLACK PUDDING, AND BUTTERNUT SQUASH, ACCOMPANIED BY PAN-FRIED LOIN OF PORK

Tim Kinnaird paediatrician and 2010 finalist

PREPARATION TIME
1 hour

COOKING TIME
2 hours

SERVES 4

800g (1¾lb) belly of pork, boned but
   with skin on
salt and freshly ground black pepper
4 fat garlic cloves, skin on
sprig of fresh thyme
1 tbsp olive oil
1 small butternut squash, peeled,
   deseeded, and cubed
8 prunes
about 4 tbsp brandy
1 pork tenderloin, approx. 450g (1lb)
4 slices of proscuitto
8 stems of white chard
4 x 1cm (½in) slices of good-quality
   black pudding, approx. 3.5cm (1½in)
   in diameter
2 apples, such as Cox's Orange Pippin,
   cored and cut into wedges

FOR THE SALSA VERDE
small bunch each of mint and basil,
   leaves picked
small bunch of parsley
2 tsp capers
2 anchovy fillets
1 garlic clove
juice of 1 small lemon
1 tbsp olive oil
1 tbsp red wine vinegar
2 tsp Dijon mustard

TO GARNISH
1 tbsp chopped parsley
microgreens

1 Preheat the oven to 180°C (350°F/Gas 4). Wipe the pork belly, making sure that the skin is thoroughly dried, and place in a roasting tin. Season and cook for about 2 hours until the meat is cooked through and the skin is crisp and golden. See also the MasterClass pages 208–9 for more advice on how to cook crackling.

2 While the pork is cooking, lay out a piece of foil, place the garlic and thyme on it, add a splash of oil, and season well. Bring up the edges of the foil and scrunch them together to make a sealed parcel. Coat the squash in oil and seasoning and place on a baking tray. Cook in the oven with the garlic parcel for 1 hour, turning occasionally. Meanwhile, soak the prunes in the brandy.

3 Blend all the ingredients for the salsa verde in a blender or a food processor. Taste and adjust the seasoning with salt and pepper. If the mixture appears too thick, loosen with a little more oil and vinegar. Spoon into a bowl, cover, and chill.

4 Wrap the pork tenderloin in the prosciutto, then wrap in cling film and put in the fridge to chill for 15–20 minutes until firm.

5 Blanch the white chard in boiling salted water for 2–3 minutes. Refresh in iced water, drain, and set aside.

6 Remove the squash, pork, and foil parcel from the oven. Purée the squash using a hand-held blender or transferring to a food processor and season to taste. Remove the crackling from the pork and break into strips – if these are not crisp enough for your liking, finish off under a hot grill.

7 Shred the meat. Pop the baked garlic cloves from their skins and drain and chop the prunes. Mix the garlic and prunes into the shredded meat with some salt and pepper. Set four 7.5cm (3in) chef's rings on a baking sheet and pack the meat mixture into each, pressing down well with the back of a spoon. Return to the oven to reheat thoroughly.

8 Unwrap the pork loin, slice into 8, and pan fry with the prosciutto in olive oil for 10–15 minutes, turning once, until the pork is cooked through and the prosciutto is crisp. In a separate pan, heat a little oil and cook the black pudding slices for 5 minutes, turning once. Pan-fry the apples in a little oil for 4–5 minutes, or until golden. Lift out and quickly pan-fry the chard. Reheat the squash.

9 To serve, carefully transfer the shredded belly pork to warmed plates and garnish with parsley. Arrange the chard on the side with the black pudding and the apple on top. Spoon the squash on the other side and arrange the pork loin slices on top. Dress the plate with salsa verde garnished with microgreens. Lift off the chef's rings and put the crackling on top just before you serve.

FLAVOUR COMBINATION

PORK, APPLE, AND BLACK PUDDING

The natural sweetness of pork is enhanced by similar sweet notes in prunes, apples, and black pudding. Cox's Orange Pippins contain a perfect balance of sweet and acid which works superbly with pork. Black pudding adds different sweetnesses and then speeds your palate off to new excitements with sharp spices and extra pork fat. Together sweet pork, apple, and black pudding then make a perfect basis for pungent and salty salsa verde. Perfect.

MONICA'S MASTERCLASS
MAKING PERFECT CRACKLING

Pork crackling has seen a resurgence in popularity in recent years but achieving a perfectly crisp, crunchy texture can be a challenge. The key to success is to dry out the skin before the meat goes in the oven, and then roast initially at a high heat.

1 Dry the skin
Remove the meat from the fridge and thoroughly pat dry the skin with a clean tea towel. Leave the meat out to return to room temperature, uncovered so the skin dries out further.

2 Score the skin
Using a heavy-duty craft knife, score the skin in diagonal lines or a criss-cross pattern (diagonal lines produce large slices of crackling for the plate), about a finger's width apart. This enables heat to penetrate the skin more easily, so that the fat bastes the crackling.

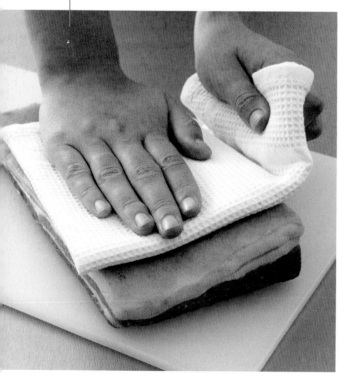

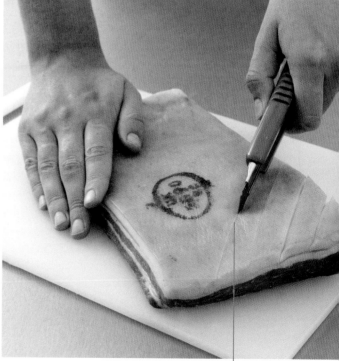

Do not cut too deeply and risk exposing the meat, which could dry out in the oven.

"Roast pork isn't complete without some crackling. Add some peeled and quartered apples to the roast along with your vegetables."

3 Rub in the salt

Take flakes of sea salt and massage them into the skin, getting the salt deep into the cracks, with a final sprinkling on top. If there's time, leave the salt to dry out the skin further, for another 30 minutes or so.

4 Roast the meat

First roast the meat at the highest temperature for 20–30 mins to give the skin an early crisping, before reducing the heat. If the crackling still looks chewy by the end, slice off in one piece, return to the top of the oven on a baking tray, and turn up the heat until done.

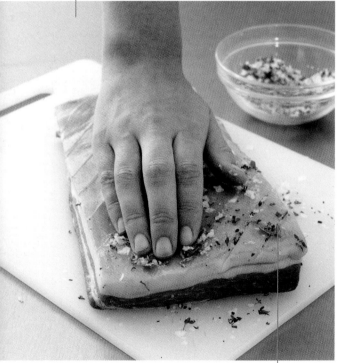

Add other flavourings, such as herbs and crushed spices, along with the salt.

BRAISED PIG'S CHEEKS WITH DEEP-FRIED EARS, APPLE JELLY, MASHED POTATO, AND BLACKBERRY SAUCE

Alex Rushmer freelance writer and 2010 finalist

PREPARATION TIME
45 minutes

COOKING TIME
4 hours 30 minutes

SERVES 4

FOR THE EARS
2 pig's ears
1 carrot, chopped
1 celery stick, chopped
1 onion, chopped
1 leek, chopped
sea salt and freshly ground black pepper
vegetable oil, for deep frying
4 tbsp plain flour, seasoned
60g (2oz) self-raising flour
2 tsp cornflour

FOR THE CHEEKS
8 pig's cheeks
2 tbsp olive oil
1 large carrot, chopped
1 large white onion, chopped
1 celery stick, chopped

1 leek, chopped
2 bay leaves
250ml (8fl oz) red wine
250ml (8fl oz) chicken stock

FOR THE JELLY
250ml (9fl oz) medium-dry apple juice
1 cinnamon stick
2 cloves
1 star anise
1 tsp agar

FOR THE SAUCE
2 tbsp blackberry jelly
1–2 tsp white wine vinegar, to taste

TO SERVE
greens such as chard, spinach, or kale
knob of butter
mashed potato

1 Remove and discard the lower third of the pig's ears (from where the ear begins to thicken). Gently simmer the ears with the vegetables and seasoning in enough water to cover for 3 hours, then remove and leave to cool.

2 Preheat the oven to 130°C (250°F/Gas ½). Season the pig's cheeks and brown in a hot pan with 1 tbsp olive oil. Remove to a casserole dish. Add the remaining olive oil to the pan and gently brown the vegetables for about 10 minutes, then add them to the cheeks. Pour in the wine and stock and cover with a circle of greaseproof paper that completely covers the surface. Cook in the oven for 3–4 hours until the cheeks are tender.

3 Remove the cheeks from the oven and leave to cool. Strain the cooking liquor through a fine sieve into a clean pan and reduce by boiling over high heat for 10–15 minutes, or until reduced in volume to a glazing consistency.

4 For the apple jelly, bring the apple juice to the boil with the cinnamon, cloves, and star anise. Simmer gently for 20 minutes to allow the flavours to infuse. Remove the spices, sprinkle the agar over and leave for 30 seconds, then whisk and bring to the boil. Boil for 2 minutes, then pour into a shallow-sided tray and leave to set in the fridge. Once set, cut the jelly into cubes and set aside.

5 For the blackberry sauce, heat the blackberry jelly and vinegar with 2 tbsp of water in a small pan over medium heat until the jelly has melted. Boil for 1–2 minutes to reduce slightly, then season with salt and pepper and adjust the vinegar to give a sweet-sharp taste. Set aside and keep warm.

6 Once the ears have cooled, heat the vegetable oil in a deep fat fryer. Cut the ears into 1cm (½in) thin strips and toss in 4 tbsp seasoned flour. Make a tempura batter by lightly mixing the self-raising flour with the cornflour, 125ml (4fl oz) iced water, and 2–3 ice cubes. Dip the ears into the tempura batter and deep fry 4 or 5 at a time for 2–3 minutes until crisp. Dry on kitchen paper and sprinkle with sea salt.

7 Wilt the greens in a little butter, season with salt and pepper, and leave to drain in a sieve.

8 To serve, halve the cheeks lengthways and return to the reduced cooking liquor. Gently heat up in a saucepan until the cheeks are warm all the way through. Serve with mashed potato, a few cubes of the apple jelly, the greens, and a few slices of the ear tempura. Finish with the blackberry sauce and serve immediately.

PIG'S EARS AND CHEEKS

Ears and cheek or jowl usually need to be ordered in advance from your butchers. Ears should be cleaned inside and out and have all the hair removed. Both ears and cheek need long, gentle simmering to tenderize, though the cartilage in ears mean they never completely soften. The crunchy texture forms part of their appeal.

GAME

ROASTED PIGEON WITH POMMES MOUSSELINE AND PANCETTA PEAS

Claire Lara lecturer and 2010 Professionals champion

PREPARATION TIME
30 minutes

COOKING TIME
1 hour

SERVES 4

4 pigeons
225g (8oz) butter, softened
250g (9oz) duck fat
4 Rooster potatoes
salt and freshly ground black pepper
200ml (7fl oz) double cream, warmed
1 tbsp olive oil
1 garlic clove, crushed

1 sprig of thyme
100g (3½oz) pancetta
175g (6oz) shelled fresh peas
300ml (10fl oz) game stock
200g (7oz) quince jelly, finely diced
2 Baby Gem lettuce, finely shredded
½ bunch of flat-leaf parsley

MICHEL ROUX JR

"It makes me salivate just looking at it. It's quite simply delicious."

1 Preheat the oven to 130°C (250°F/Gas 1) and remove the wishbone from the pigeons. Heat 75g (2½oz) of the butter in a heavy saucepan and brown the pigeons by turning the birds quickly in the hot butter. Reserve the butter.

2 Remove the pigeons from the pan, leave to cool a little and then remove the legs. Place the legs in an ovenproof dish with a close fitting lid, melt the duck fat and pour it over the legs. Cover and cook in the oven for about 45 minutes or until tender, turning the legs over once. Remove from the oven and increase the temperature to 220°C (425°F/Gas 7).

3 To make the *pommes mousseline*, cook the potatoes in a saucepan of lightly salted simmering water for about 20 minutes or until soft. Drain and skin the potatoes when they are cool enough to handle. Then put them through a vegetable mouli and gradually beat in 150g (5½ oz) of the butter and all the warmed cream. The potato purée should be very smooth and shiny. Season to taste. Keep warm.

4 For the pancetta peas, heat the oil in a heavy saucepan. Add the garlic, thyme, and pancetta and cook over medium heat for about 10 minutes or until the pancetta is crispy. Drain off excess fat and remove the thyme. Simmer the peas gently in salted water for 10 minutes until just tender. Drain and set aside.

5 To make the sauce, pour the stock into a saucepan and reduce by about half until it has reached a syrupy consistency and rich colour.

6 Put the pigeons in a roasting tin, add seasoning and brush with the butter used in step 1. Roast in the oven for 15 minutes, basting once. Leave to rest and remove the meat from the leg bones.

7 Add the peas and lettuce to the browned pancetta with 2 tbsp of sauce. Heat gently until the lettuce has wilted slightly.

8 Carve the pigeon breasts and lay on the *pommes mousseline* in 4 bowls. Scatter the pea mix, pour on the sauce, and garnish with parsley.

CHENNAI SPICED BALLOTINE OF GUINEA FOWL WITH MUSHROOM PILAU AND TOMATO CHUTNEY

Dhruv Baker sales director and 2010 champion

PREPARATION TIME
3 hours

COOKING TIME
1 hour

SERVES 4

FOR THE CHUTNEY
900g (2lb) tomatoes, chopped
2 garlic cloves, chopped
½ onion, chopped
½ red pepper, deseeded and chopped
½ large red chilli, chopped
½ tsp smoked sweet paprika
½ cinnamon stick
¼ tsp black mustard seeds
small pinch of ground cloves
85g (3oz) light soft brown sugar
25g (scant 1oz) sultanas
100ml (3½ fl oz) white wine vinegar

FOR THE CHUKKA MASALA
225g (8oz) desiccated coconut
6 tbsp vegetable oil
10 dried red chillies
3 tsp coriander seeds
2 tsp fennel seeds
2 tsp black peppercorns
2 cinnamon sticks
4 cloves
1 tsp ground turmeric
2 red onions, finely chopped

1 tsp garlic paste
1 tsp ginger paste
225g (8oz) tomatoes, finely chopped
2 sprigs of curry leaves or
   10 dried curry leaves
200g (7oz) butter

FOR THE PILAU
3 tbsp vegetable oil
2 bay leaves
1 cinnamon stick
4 green cardamom pods
1 large onion, finely chopped
150g (5½oz) chestnut or button
   mushrooms, wiped and sliced
2 garlic cloves
225g (8oz) white basmati rice
1 tsp salt
1 onion, thinly sliced
good pinch of saffron strands
   (see MasterTip, p.147)

FOR THE GUINEA FOWL
4 guinea fowl breasts with skin on
butter for frying

1 Put all the tomato chutney ingredients into a heavy saucepan, stir and bring to the boil. Reduce the heat, cover the pan and simmer for 30 minutes. Remove the lid and cook, stirring occasionally, for a further 30 minutes or until nearly all the liquid has boiled away to form a thick chutney. Remove the cinnamon stick before serving.
2 For the chukka masala, toast the coconut in 1 tbsp of the oil over gentle heat, stirring, until golden. Drain on kitchen paper. Add the chillies, coriander and fennel seeds, peppercorns, cinnamon sticks, and cloves to the pan. Cook gently for 2–3 minutes, stirring occasionally, or until the spices start to pop and release their fragrance.
3 Use a spice grinder or pestle and mortar to grind the coconut and spice to a fine paste. Stir in the turmeric.

4 Heat the remaining oil in the frying pan and cook the onions and garlic and ginger pastes for about 5 minutes or until softened. Stir in the tomatoes and curry leaves and cook for about 10 minutes. Then stir in the spice mix and cook for another 10 minutes.

5 Transfer the mixture to a bowl and leave until cold. In a separate bowl, beat the butter to soften, then beat in about 4 tbsp of the spicy paste. Divide the spiced butter into 4, shape into small sausages, wrap in cling film, and chill until solid.

6 To make the mushroom pilau, heat 2 tbsp of the oil in a large saucepan. Add the bay leaves, cinnamon, and cardamom pods and cook for 1 minute. Scatter in the onion and fry for 5 minutes or until softened. Stir in the mushrooms and garlic and cook over medium heat for 4–5 minutes, or until the juices have evaporated.

7 Add the rice and salt, stir with a fork to coat in the onion mix, then pour in the boiling water. Stir once again, cover and reduce the heat to the lowest setting. Leave for 15 minutes or until all the liquid has been absorbed. Remove the lid, cover with a clean cloth and set aside.

8 Heat the remaining 1 tbsp of the oil in another frying pan and fry the sliced onion until it is golden. Soak the saffron in hot water for 5 minutes. Divide the onions between 4 dariole moulds or tea cups and place a couple of drained saffron strands in each.

9 Flatten the guinea fowl breasts between 2 sheets of cling film, taking care not to tear the flesh. Place a piece of the spiced butter in the centre of each guinea fowl, then roll up tightly, tucking in the ends. Wrap in cling film and poach in boiling water for 10 minutes.

10 Unwrap the guinea fowl and pan-fry in butter for 5–8 minutes, turning occasionally, until evenly golden and thoroughly heated through. Remove the bay leaves, cinnamon, and cardamom pods from the rice, then pack into the dariole moulds or tea cups. Quickly turn out onto warmed serving plates. Slice each ballotine and serve with the rice and tomato chutney.

MASTER TIP
CURRY LEAVES

Curry leaves come from a small, deciduous tree that grows wild in the foothills of the Himalayas, and in India, northern Thailand, and Sri Lanka. Fresh curry leaves are used extensively in south Indian cooking; strip from the stalk just before adding to a dish.

ROASTED PHEASANT WITH POMMES ANNA, CARROTS, BREAD SAUCE, AND SLOE JELLY

Tim Kinnaird paediatrician and 2010 finalist

PREPARATION TIME
1 hour 50 minutes

COOKING TIME
1 hour

SERVES 4

2 oven-ready pheasants
4–6 sprigs of thyme
4–6 sprigs of rosemary
2 tbsp olive oil
25g (scant 1oz) butter
16 smoked streaky bacon rashers
quince jelly, cut into squares

FOR THE GAME STOCK
2 grouse or other game bird carcasses,
   chopped into 4
a little vegetable oil
1 onion, roughly chopped
1 carrot, roughly chopped
2 juniper berries
few sprigs of thyme
1 bay leaf
1.5 litres (2¾ pints) chicken stock

FOR THE SLOE JELLY
75ml (2½fl oz) sloe gin
75ml (2½fl oz) red wine
1 tbsp agar flakes
sprig of thyme
5 juniper berries, crushed
2 tsp clear honey
2 tsp caster sugar
12 blackberries

FOR THE POMMES ANNA
1kg (2¼lb) waxy potatoes
100g (3½oz) butter
salt and freshly ground black pepper

FOR THE BREAD SAUCE
500ml (16fl oz) full-fat milk
4 bay leaves
1 onion, halved
140g (5oz) white breadcrumbs
ground white pepper
¼ tsp ground mace
25g (scant 1oz) butter

FOR THE GAME SAUCE
3 banana shallots, finely chopped
2 tbsp olive oil
100g (3½oz) butter
100g (3½oz) button mushrooms, sliced
500ml (16fl oz) game stock
250ml (9fl oz) red wine
3 tbsp port
3 tbsp Cognac

FOR THE CARROTS
4 carrots, cut into batons
3 tbsp caster sugar
250ml (9fl oz) chicken stock
10g (½oz) butter
pak choi, leaves separated

1 To make the stock, fry the carcasses in the oil with the vegetables over high heat for a few minutes until lightly coloured. Add the juniper berries, thyme, bay leaf, and stock, bring to the boil and simmer gently for 1 hour, skimming occasionally. Strain through a fine sieve and set aside to use for the game sauce.

2 To make the sloe jelly, pour the gin and wine into a saucepan with all the other jelly ingredients, sprinkling the agar over the mixture. Bring to the boil, without stirring, then simmer, whisking occasionally until the flakes dissolve. Take off the heat and strain into a shallow container. Chill until firmly set.

JOHN TORODE "It's just beautiful. It's got little sweet notes that come from the jellies. It's got wonderful texture from the bird. It's got buttery bits that are coming from the potato. I think it's delicious."

3 For the pommes Anna, preheat the oven to 180°C (350°F/Gas 4). Peel the potatoes and, using a mandoline or a food processor, thinly slice. Soak in a bowl of cold water for 10 minutes, drain and pat dry. Melt the butter. Layer up the potatoes in a square baking dish with lots of butter and seasoning. Bake for about 1 hour or until tender.

4 Wipe the pheasants, inside and out. Tuck the herbs into the cavities and massage oil and butter over the skin. Wrap the birds in bacon. Roast for 40 minutes, until the meat is tender but a little pink. Rest.

5 Start the bread sauce by placing the milk, bay leaves, and onion into a small pan over low heat. Slowly bring to simmering point. Switch off the heat, cover the pan with a lid and allow to infuse.

6 For the game sauce, sauté the shallots in the oil and a knob of the butter for 10 minutes. Add the mushrooms and cook for 5 minutes, then stir in the stock and bring to the boil. Reduce by half. Stir in the wine and port and reduce by half again. Add the Cognac and boil for another 2 minutes. Dice the remaining butter and whisk into the sauce, a little at a time, until it thickens.

7 Bring the carrots, sugar, stock, and butter to the boil in a pan. Simmer until the liquid has almost evaporated and carrots are tender. Wilt the pak choi in a frying pan with a splash of water.

8 To finish the bread sauce, strain then bring to the boil. Scatter in the breadcrumbs and stir until it bubbles. Take off the heat, add butter and season.

9 Heat the game sauce. Remove the pheasant breasts from the carcass. Cut 4 portions of potatoes and place to the side of each plate. Wrap a bundle of carrots in the wilted pak choi, place in the centre of each plate and top with the pheasant. Cut squares of the sloe jelly and arrange on the plates with the squares of quince jelly. Drizzle over the game sauce and serve with bread sauce in a jug alongside.

FLAVOUR COMBINATION
PHEASANT AND SLOES

Culinary stars of the hedgerow, the fruity flavour of sloes comes with astringent bitterness that no amount of sugar can correct; only acidity balances bitterness. Here, wild and resinous juniper, a natural food of pheasants, adds a whiff of heather, and red wine underpins the regal colour sloes give to gin, vodka, or anything. Hanging pheasant develops gratifying sweetness and acidity in the flesh that cries for the wild flavours of the sparkling sloe jelly.

PHEASANT WITH APPLE AND HAGGIS RINGS

Christine Hamilton TV personality and 2010 Celebrity finalist

4 pheasant breasts, skin on
300g (10oz) baby spinach leaves
20 slices streaky bacon
1 tbsp olive oil
2 large Bramley apples
225g (8oz) cooked haggis
25g (scant 1oz) butter

4 branches cherry tomatoes on the vine
3–4 potatoes, approx. 500g (1lb 2oz), chopped
1–2 tbsp milk (optional)
200ml (7fl oz) dry cider
200ml (7fl oz) double cream

PREPARATION TIME
25 minutes

COOKING TIME
40 minutes

SERVES 4

1 Preheat the oven to 200°C (400°F/Gas 6). Remove the skin from the pheasant breasts and reserve. Cut a pocket in the thickest part of each breast and stuff each with about 10g (¼oz) of the spinach leaves. Wrap each breast in 5 slices of the bacon.

2 Heat a large ovenproof frying pan and fry the pheasant skins in the oil. Add the pheasant breasts and fry for about 2 minutes, or until the bacon is crisp all over. Transfer the pan to the oven, with the skins covering the pheasant breasts, and cook for about 15 minutes or until the pheasant is cooked through. Remove the pan from the oven, cover tightly with foil, and leave the pheasant to rest.

3 For the apple and haggis rings, core the apples, cut chunky slices from the middle of each apple (round the equator) and fill the centre of each ring tightly with about 25g (scant 1oz) of the haggis. Then pan-fry in butter, turning as they brown, for about 10 minutes or until the apple is *al dente*.

4 Gently cook the vine tomato branches for 5–6 minutes in the same pan. Remove and keep warm.

5 Meanwhile, cook the potatoes in a saucepan of salted water for about 20 minutes, or until soft. Cook the remaining spinach on a steamer above the potatoes. When the potatoes are ready, drain and lightly mash (leave the mash slightly chunky) with the remaining haggis and a little milk, if needed. Keep the spinach warm.

6 Remove the pheasant from the pan and pour away any fat, but keep the juices. Heat the pan, deglaze with the cider, and reduce the sauce by half. Add the double cream and bubble for about 5 minutes until thick.

7 To serve, cut the pheasant into slices. Put the haggis mash into chef's rings, or divide neatly between 4 plates, and place the apple and haggis circles on top. Put the pheasant slices to one side together with the spinach and tomatoes and then pour over the juices.

MASTER TIP

HAGGIS

Haggis is made by coarsely mincing sheep's liver, heart, and lights (lungs) with onion, beef suet, oatmeal, and seasonings; stuffing this into a sheep's stomach; and boiling. Bought cooked, haggis only needs to be heated through.

PAN-FRIED PIGEON BREASTS WITH RAVIOLI

Alex Rushmer freelance writer and 2010 finalist

PREPARATION TIME
2 hours

COOKING TIME
30 minutes

SERVES 4

200g (7oz) type "00" pasta flour
2 large eggs
5g (⅛oz) sodium alginate
1 litre (1¾pints) bottle still water
200g (7oz) frozen peas
a few mint leaves
10g (¼oz) calcium gluconolactate
50g (1¾oz) demerara sugar

2 thick pieces of smoked streaky bacon
8 pigeon breasts
salt and freshly ground black pepper
2 tbsp olive oil
50g (1¾oz) unsalted butter
24 thin asparagus tips
4 tbsp white wine vinegar
handful of young pea shoots

MASTER TIP

PIGEON BREAST

Wild pigeons are typically lean but "squabs", those that are raised for the table, have a fine covering of fat. The flesh of all pigeons is a very dark red. Fry or grill breasts rare and, if roasting whole squabs and young pigeons, always serve rare or medium-rare. Use the legs for soup and stock, or braise and serve with the breasts.

1 Make the pasta dough following the method in the MasterTip on p.34.
2 In a large bowl, whisk the sodium alginate with half the bottled water until it has dissolved and the mixture is slightly gluey. Set aside.
3 Bring a pan of salted water to the boil and cook the peas and mint for 2 minutes. Drain, reserving a cup of the cooking water, and plunge into iced water. Drain again. Using a hand-held blender, blend the peas and mint with a little of the reserved cooking water. Add the calcium gluconolactate and blend again. Pass through a sieve into a bowl.
4 To make pea "caviar" pearls, squeeze droplets of the pea mix from a dropper (or use a ¼ tsp measuring spoon) into the alginate bath. Leave for 30 seconds, remove, rinse, and leave to rest in spring water.
5 Cut the pasta dough into 2 pieces. Use a pasta machine to roll out the dough to the thinnest setting (see MasterTip, p.35) or roll out very thinly with a rolling pin. Lightly brush 1 sheet of pasta with water.
6 Place pea spheres onto the pasta every 5cm (2in), reserving a few. Cover with a second sheet of pasta and press around the edges to seal, squeezing out any air. Cut between the filling. (See also pp.126–7.)
7 Preheat the oven to 180ºC (350ºF/Gas 4). Cook the ravioli in boiling salted water for 3 minutes. Leave to rest under a damp cloth.
8 Sprinkle 25g (scant 1oz) sugar onto a baking tray lined with baking parchment. Press the bacon into the sugar and cover with the rest of the sugar. Bake for 20–25 minutes until crispy. Cut into small lardons.
9 Season the pigeon breasts and fry for 2 minutes in the oil. Turn and fry for 1 minute, then leave to rest. Slice each breast into 3 pieces.
10 Brown 25g (scant 1oz) butter in a frying pan. Add the ravioli and fry for 1 minute. Set aside. Use the same pan to briefly cook the asparagus in the rest of the butter. Set aside. Add the bacon to the pan. Cook briefly and deglaze with the vinegar.
11 Divide the pigeon between 4 plates and surround with the ravioli, asparagus, pea shoots, vinaigrette, and reserved pea "caviar" pearls.

ROASTED PARTRIDGE WITH POLENTA

Tim Kinnaird paediatrician and 2010 finalist

4 oven-ready partridge
8 slices prosciutto
4 sprigs of thyme, leaves chopped
4 sprigs of rosemary, leaves chopped
2 tbsp olive oil

FOR THE POLENTA

200g (7oz) quick-cook polenta
100g (3½oz) butter
3 tbsp extra virgin olive oil
salt and freshly ground black pepper

FOR THE MUSHROOM SAUCE

30g (1oz) dried porcini mushrooms
1 white onion, finely chopped
5 tbsp olive oil

1 carrot, finely chopped
1 celery stick, finely chopped
1 sprig of thyme
2 bay leaves
1 sprig of rosemary
300ml (10fl oz) red wine
300ml (10fl oz) chicken stock
100ml (3½fl oz) Marsala wine
200g (7oz) Portobello mushrooms
100g (3½oz) unsalted butter

FOR THE CELERY

400ml (14fl oz) chicken stock
100g (3½oz) butter
4 celery sticks

PREPARATION TIME
1 hour, plus soaking

COOKING TIME
2½ hours

SERVES 4

1 For the polenta, grease a 20 x 15cm (8 x 6in) baking tin with oil. Bring 800ml (1¼ pints) of water to the boil in a large saucepan, pour in the polenta and cook, stirring, according to the packet's instructions.
2 Stir in the butter and oil and season. Pour the polenta into the oiled tin and leave for about 20 minutes to set. Cut into oblong portions.
3 Soak the porcini mushrooms in 400ml (14fl oz) warm water for an hour. Drain and finely chop. For the celery, heat the stock in a pan, then whisk in the butter until melted. Poach the celery over a low heat for 20–40 minutes, depending on how tough the celery is, until tender.
4 For the partridge, preheat the oven to 180°C (350°F/Gas 4). Bone the partridge and remove the breasts and leg meat, discarding the skin. Overlap 2 slices of prosciutto on a work surface. Lay the meat from 1 partridge on the ham, season and sprinkle with the herbs. Repeat with remaining prosciutto and partridge. Roll each partridge firmly in the ham, securing, if necessary, with a cocktail stick.
5 Briefly pan-fry the rolls in oil in an ovenproof pan, turning regularly, until browned on all sides. Then cook in the oven for 20–25 minutes until tender. Leave to rest in the pan for 5 minutes.
6 For the mushroom sauce, fry the onion in 3 tbsp of the oil over medium heat for 5–10 minutes or until softened, but not browned. Then add the carrot, celery, and herbs and cook for a further 10 minutes. Add the red wine and reduce by half. Repeat with the stock and then the Marsala wine. Strain into a clean saucepan.
7 Slice and pan-fry the Portobello mushrooms in the remaining oil

MASTER TIP
PARTRIDGE

Partridge is found in most parts of the northern hemisphere on grassland and agricultural margins. Whole partridge can be roasted or braised, depending on age; and breasts can be fried, grilled, braised, or stewed. The legs can be used for soup and stock, or braised and served with roasted breasts.

over medium-high heat until softened and browned. Remove from the heat and, when cool enough to handle, chop very finely.

8 Add the finely chopped porcini and Portobello mushrooms to the sieved sauce and reheat over medium heat. Gradually whisk in the cold butter to make a smooth sauce. Keep warm over a very low heat.

9 When ready to serve, preheat a griddle pan over high heat until smoking, brush the griddle with a little oil and chargrill the polenta for about 10 minutes until marked and crisp on both sides.

10 To serve, divide the chargrilled polenta between 4 plates and place the celery at an angle on top. Cut the partridge rolls in half and place on top of the celery. Finally, dress the plates with the sauce.

POACHER'S ROAST

Dick Strawbridge TV presenter and 2010 Celebrity finalist

PREPARATION TIME
50 minutes

COOKING TIME
1 hour

SERVES 4

FOR THE FORCEMEAT
350g (12oz) venison sausagemeat
1 small leek, green part only,
  finely chopped
1 garlic clove, crushed
50g (1¾oz) fresh white breadcrumbs
1 egg, beaten
salt and freshly ground black pepper

FOR THE ROAST
1 boned saddle of rabbit
2 pheasant breasts
2 pigeon breasts
8 large slices of air-dried ham
4 tsp bramble jelly
olive oil, for brushing

FOR THE DAUPHINOISE
1 swede
1 celeriac
2 parsnips
4 carrots, approx. 700g (1lb 9oz)
  in total
500ml (16fl oz) double cream

100g (3½oz) Parmesan cheese,
  finely grated
olive oil, for brushing

FOR THE SAUCE
2 shallots, finely chopped
½ tbsp olive oil
225g (8oz) blackberries
200ml (7fl oz) port
2 tbsp bramble jelly
200ml (7fl oz) chicken stock

FOR THE CHESTNUTS
25g (scant 1oz) butter
2 Cox's apples, peeled, cored,
  and finely diced
100ml (3½fl oz) dry cider
1 tbsp cider vinegar
1 tbsp honey
2 tsp pink peppercorns in brine,
  drained
100g (3½oz) pre-cooked sweet
  chestnuts, halved

1 For the forcemeat, break the sausagemeat into a bowl. Add the remaining forcemeat ingredients and mix well to combine. Take 1 tsp of the mix and fry quickly for 4–5 minutes, or until cooked through. Taste and adjust the seasoning of the forcemeat if necessary.

2 For the roast, cut the 2 loins from the rabbit, then cut these in half. Cut the pheasant and pigeon breasts into equal-sized strips. Lay the ham out on a large board. Divide the forcemeat into 4 and roll each on a sheet of cling film to a rectangle of 20 x 15cm (8 x 6in). Place the slices of pigeon meat on top of each rectangle. Spread a little jelly over the meat, then add seasoning. Using the cling film to help, roll up to encase the filling, tucking in the ends.

3 Remove the cling film and then wrap each parcel in 2 slices of ham and secure each one with a cocktail stick or piece of string. Wrap in foil, place in a roasting tin and chill until ready to roast.

4 For the vegetable Dauphinoise, preheat the oven to 190°C (375°F/ Gas 5). Peel and slice the swede, celeriac, parsnips, and carrots into equal-sized pieces. Put into a large saucepan and par boil in salted water for 5 minutes, or until beginning to soften. Drain well.

5 Thoroughly butter a 1 litre (1¾ pints) gratin dish. Layer the vegetables in the dish, seasoning well between each layer. Pour over the cream and sprinkle over about 25g (scant 1oz) of the Parmesan cheese. Cover with a sheet of greased foil and bake for 1 hour. After 15 minutes, unwrap the meat and return it to the roasting tin. Brush with the oil and roast for about 45 minutes or until the juices run clear.

6 Meanwhile, for the sauce, soften the shallots in the oil for 5 minutes. Add the blackberries, port, and jelly, then simmer for about 10 minutes to reduce by about a quarter. Add the stock and bring to the boil. Simmer for another 8–10 minutes or until the blackberries are tender. Strain into a clean pan and reduce by about half, until the sauce is syrupy and will coat the back of a wooden spoon.

7 For the chestnuts, melt the butter in a frying pan, add the apples and cook for 2–3 minutes. Pour in the cider and cider vinegar and bring to the boil. Stir in the honey and peppercorns, and then the chestnuts.

8 Check the meat and remove it from the oven. Cover and leave to rest in a warm place. Increase the oven temperature to 200°C (400°F/ Gas 6). Uncover the vegetables. Line a baking sheet with a silicon sheet and spread out 4 small piles of the remaining grated Parmesan. Heat in the oven for 3–4 minutes or until just melted and the Dauphinoise is golden brown.

9 To serve, divide the sauce between 4 plates. Remove the cocktail stick or string from the roast and cut each parcel in half at an angle. Place on top of the sauce. Spoon the chestnuts alongside with a spoonful of the Dauphinoise. Garnish each with a Parmesan crisp.

GREGG WALLACE "It's meaty, gamey, rich. That's very good cooking and the sausage with all those meats in there was inspired."

DICK STRAWBRIDGE

"There's no doubt about it getting to the final felt great, however it's a competition and there was still lots to play for. You know it's your last chance to shine and you just have to get three plates that do you justice. The competition was an awesome experience, hard work, and for months I lived and breathed food and cooking. It was a journey and a half, and I'm really happy with what I achieved. I was making pub food before, and now I'm trying to act more like a chef."

DESSERT

RHUBARB CRUMBLE TART WITH SYLLABUB AND RHUBARB SYRUP p.254

"I liked this a lot, so beautiful in appearance and really well made. I wanted more ginger in there, but it's a really good pudding."
JOHN

STARTER

WHITING QUENELLES IN SHELLFISH BROTH p.18

"That broth was absolutely fantastic – rich and thick with a wonderful base from the prawns."
JOHN

MAIN

RABBIT WITH MUSTARD DUMPLING SERVED WITH CIDER CREAM AND MUSTARD SAUCE p.228

"This dish was Dick at his absolute best – so many little delights on the plate, very complex cooking, and subtle flavours."
GREGG

RABBIT WITH MUSTARD DUMPLING SERVED WITH CIDER CREAM AND MUSTARD SAUCE

Dick Strawbridge TV presenter and 2010 Celebrity finalist

PREPARATION TIME
50 minutes

COOKING TIME
50 minutes

SERVES 4

2 rabbits, plus 4 extra kidneys, if available (optional)
1 tbsp olive oil
60g (2oz) green leek, chopped
1 garlic clove, chopped
1 crunchy apple, peeled and cut into small dice
60g (2oz) plain flour
1 large egg, beaten
60g (2oz) breadcrumbs
groundnut oil, for frying

FOR THE DUMPLINGS
140g (5oz) self-raising flour
85g (3oz) suet

salt and white pepper
2 tbsp wholegrain mustard

FOR THE SAUCE
300ml (10fl oz) cider
300ml (10fl oz) double cream
freshly ground black pepper
1 tbsp wholegrain mustard
1 tbsp honey (optional)

FOR THE ACCOMPANIMENTS
30g (1oz) butter
1 crunchy apple
12 baby carrots, peeled
2 small parsnips, peeled

MASTER TIP

PREPARING RABBIT

Cut along the back of the rack, just above the meaty part of the rabbit. Turn the knife upwards and scrape the gristly meat off to expose the rib bones. Cut between each of the ribs, taking out the tiny amount of meat found there. Scrape away the bones until they are clean. Chop and reserve the kidneys and cut the meat off the bone on the front legs and a bit off the back legs. Dice some of the leg meat and process the rest in a blender or food processor.

1 Prepare the rabbit (see MasterTip, left).
2 Heat the oil in a pan, then add the leek and garlic and cook for about 5 minutes to soften. Add the apple and cook for 2–3 minutes until just beginning to soften. Combine in a bowl with the kidney to make a chunky forcemeat. Using your hands, squeeze the mixture around the bone of the legs to create a chicken drumstick shape. Chill.
3 Put the flour, egg, and breadcrumbs onto 3 separate plates. Roll the legs in the flour, then the egg and, finally, the breadcrumbs.
4 Preheat the oven to 200°C (400°F/Gas 6). For the dumplings, mix the flour, suet, seasoning, and mustard in a bowl. Bring together with 100ml (3½fl oz) of cold water. Grease four 6–7cm (2½–2¾in) metal rings and divide the mix between them. Bake for about 15 minutes or until golden.
5 Oil, season, and flash fry the rabbit loins and kidneys until golden all over. Fill a wok with groundnut oil and deep-fry the legs for 10 minutes. Transfer to a roasting tin and cook in the oven for 10 minutes.
6 To make the sauce, place the cider in a wide pan. Bring to the boil and reduce by half. Add the cream and bubble again until reduced and thick. Season well, adding the mustard and honey (if using).
7 For the accompaniments, heat half the butter in a frying pan. Core and slice the apple and sauté for 5–6 minutes. Boil the carrots and parsnips in lightly salted water for 10 minutes then slice lengthways and glaze with the remaining butter. Serve as shown.

ROAST RABBIT LOIN, STUFFED CABBAGE, RABBIT CAKE, AND MUSTARD SAUCE

Terry Ireland ex-factory worker and 2010 semi-finalist

PREPARATION TIME
1 hour

COOKING TIME
2 hours

SERVES 4

2 whole young rabbits, jointed and
  boned, offal chopped and reserved
salt and freshly ground black pepper
1 leek, about 150g (5½oz), sliced
½ tbsp olive oil
50g (1¾oz) hazelnuts, chopped
½ tbsp chopped sage
2 tbsp chopped parsley
50g (1¾oz) Panko breadcrumbs
6 streaky bacon rashers

FOR THE SAUCE
1 onion, roughly chopped
3 purple carrots, roughly chopped
2 celery sticks, roughly chopped
1 tsp Dijon mustard
1 tsp wholegrain mustard
1 tbsp clear honey

FOR THE VEGETABLES
4 golden beetroot
4 carrots, unpeeled but roughly
  chopped
50ml (2fl oz) cider vinegar
50ml (2fl oz) vermouth
2 star anise

FOR THE PUMPKIN PURÉE
½ pumpkin, or squash, approx.
  500g (1lb 2oz) in weight
3 tbsp milk
2 bay leaves
25g (scant 1oz) butter

FOR THE CABBAGE
2 shallots, finely chopped
1 garlic clove, peeled and chopped
1 tbsp olive oil
3 tbsp sherry
1 tbsp cider vinegar
1 tbsp redcurrant jelly
1 tsp Dijon mustard
½ tsp paprika
4 large Savoy cabbage leaves, destalked

FOR THE CAKES
1 onion, roughly chopped
3 purple carrots, roughly chopped
2 celery sticks, roughly chopped
1 tsp peppercorns
4 bay leaves
4 sprigs of thyme
25g (scant 1oz) plain flour
1 egg, beaten
50g (1¾oz) breadcrumbs

1 Preheat the oven to 200°C (400°F/Gas 6). For the sauce, chop up the remaining rabbit carcasses, place in a roasting tin, and roast for 15 minutes. Transfer to a saucepan and add the vegetables. Cover with 400ml (14fl oz) boiling water and simmer for 45 minutes. Strain and reduce the stock. Finish with the mustards and honey, and season.
2 Season the rabbit loins. Fry the leek in oil for 10 minutes, until soft. Combine with the hazelnuts, sage, parsley, and breadcrumbs and blitz in a food processor. Spoon the stuffing into the cavity of each loin. Roll the loins and tie with string. Cover with bacon and roast for 25 minutes, then remove and rest.
3 For the vegetables, wrap the beetroots in foil and cook in the oven for about 30 minutes, or until tender. Simmer the carrots in water for

about 15 minutes or until almost tender. Peel the beetroots and cut both beetroots and carrots into 1cm (½in) cubes. Meanwhile, put the cider vinegar into a pan, bring to the boil, and let it reduce by half. Add the vermouth and star anise and cook for 1 minute. Add the diced vegetables and simmer for about 5 minutes or until cooked through.

4 Dice the pumpkin or squash and add to a pan with the milk, bay leaves, and enough water to cover. Simmer for about 20 minutes, or until tender. Transfer to a food processor with a slotted spoon and purée, adding some of the cooking liquor if necessary. Pass through a sieve into a clean pan and whisk in the butter and season to taste.

5 For the cabbage, fry the shallots and garlic in oil for 5 minutes or until soft. Add the chopped offal and cook for 2–3 minutes. Add the sherry, let it bubble, and then add the cider vinegar. Follow this with the jelly, mustard, and paprika. Season to taste. Steam the cabbage leaves for 3–4 minutes until they wilt. Lay out the leaves, divide the offal mix between them, then fold up one flap to cover the mix. Fold in the sides to hold the filling, then wrap completely to form a parcel. Cover and keep warm.

6 For the rabbit cakes, place the vegetables in a pan with the pepper, bay, and thyme. Cover with 500ml (16fl oz) water and bring to a simmer. Add the rabbit legs and poach for 20 minutes, until tender. Remove the meat, coarsely chop, and add seasoning, mixing well. Shape into little patties. Toss in the flour, egg, and then the breadcrumbs, and fry for 4–5 minutes on each side or until golden.

7 To serve, spoon some pumpkin purée just off-centre on each plate. Slice the loin and place on top of the pumpkin. Place a rabbit cake opposite the loin, again off-centre, and top with the stuffed cabbage. Spoon some sauce onto the loin and drizzle a little on the plate.

JOHN TORODE

"The sauce is lovely and sweet, the loin of rabbit nice and moist, and the leek stuffing I really like."

FLAVOUR COMBINATION

RABBIT, HAZELNUT, AND MUSTARD

Rabbit is gently flavoured, in the same taste family as chicken. It behaves well with almost any ingredient but mustard is a reliable time-honoured tradition, particularly in France. Here the sweetness of hazelnuts adds creamy heft and hedgerow accents to the loin stuffing. On the plate, this is neatly balanced by mustard sauce. The potential is perfection, but mustard loses its bite rapidly when heated, so cook this minimally.

ROE VENISON WITH CRISPY POLENTA AND VANILLA SQUASH PURÉE

Gary Cooke sous chef and 2010 Professionals quarter-finalist

PREPARATION TIME
1 hour, plus resting

COOKING TIME
3 hours 15 minutes

SERVES 4

FOR THE RED WINE SHALLOTS
½ bottle of red wine
40g (1¼oz) dark soft brown sugar
150ml (5fl oz) maple syrup
1 bay leaf
1 star anise
5 mustard seeds
4 juniper berries
4 banana shallots, peeled

FOR THE RED ONION PURÉE
4 red onions, sliced
15g (½oz) butter
100ml (3½fl oz) olive oil
200ml (7fl oz) Marsala wine
100ml (3½fl oz) balsamic vinegar

FOR THE POLENTA
400ml (14fl oz) whole milk
400ml (14fl oz) chicken stock
1 garlic bulb, halved through
  the equator
5 sprigs of thyme
onion trimmings or 1 small onion,
  roughly chopped
200g (7oz) quick-cook polenta
120g (4¼oz) Parmesan cheese, grated
25g (scant 1oz) butter

FOR THE GARLIC
8 garlic cloves, peeled and left whole
150ml (5fl oz) full-fat milk, or enough
  to cover
100ml (3½fl oz) duck fat, or enough
  to cover

FOR THE SQUASH
500g (1lb 2oz) butternut squash
  (approx. 300g/10oz peeled weight),
  peeled and diced
2 banana shallots, sliced
1 garlic clove, halved
1 sprig of thyme
2 tbsp olive oil
15g (½oz) butter
60ml (2fl oz) white wine
¼ vanilla pod, split, seeds scraped
  out and reserved with the pod
  (see MasterTip p.256)
250ml (9fl oz) chicken stock

FOR THE VENISON
1 bay leaf
1 star anise
5 mustard seeds
4 juniper berries
3 espresso coffee beans
sea salt and freshly ground white
  pepper
700–800g (1lb 9oz–1¾lb) loin of
  venison, thick end if possible
  (see MasterTip, opposite)
1 tbsp olive oil

FOR THE VENISON LIVER (OPTIONAL)
½ venison liver, cut into 1cm (½in)
  thick slices
25g (scant 1oz) butter
2 tsp sherry vinegar
100ml (3½fl oz) venison or beef stock
2 bags of baby spinach, wilted, to serve

1 For the shallots, pour the wine into a saucepan and add the sugar, maple syrup, bay leaf and spices. Bring to the boil then reduce over high heat, stirring, until the sugar has dissolved.
2 Add the shallots to the liquor and cook over low–medium heat for 20 minutes, or until soft, adding a splash of water to the pan if it reduces too far. Remove from the heat and set aside.

3 For the purée, sweat the onions in the butter and oil for 5 minutes. Add the Marsala and vinegar and cook on low–medium heat for 30–40 minutes, or until very soft. Blitz using a hand-held blender or by transferring to a food processor. If you like a smoother purée, pass through a sieve. Set aside.

4 For the polenta, grease a baking tin measuring about 20 x 20cm (8 x 8in). Put the milk and stock into a saucepan with the garlic, thyme, and onion trimmings and leave to infuse for 10 minutes over medium heat. Pass through a sieve into a clean pan, then bring to the boil and pour in the polenta. Stir constantly for 5–8 minutes (or according to packet instructions) until the polenta is thick. Stir in the Parmesan and butter until thoroughly combined, then pour into the prepared tin and let set. Cut into 1cm (½in) thick slices and set aside.

5 To cook the garlic, put the garlic cloves in a saucepan with the milk. Bring to the boil, then strain through a sieve and discard the milk. Pat dry the garlic cloves. Heat the duck fat in a small saucepan over medium heat, add the garlic, reduce the heat to low and simmer gently for 15–20 minutes, or until softened. Drain and add to a small pan with a spoonful of the shallot reduction sauce to glaze.

6 Sweat the squash, shallots, garlic, and thyme in the oil and butter for 5 minutes, or until the shallots are translucent, then pour in the wine and boil over high heat for 2–3 minutes until reduced. Add the vanilla seeds and pod and the stock, bring to a boil, then reduce the heat to medium and simmer for 25 minutes or until the squash is tender. Remove the vanilla pod and thyme and blend to a purée with a hand-held blender or by transferring to a food processor. Pass through a sieve if you like a smoother purée. Keep warm.

7 For the venison, preheat the oven to 220°C (425°F/Gas 7). Blitz the spices and coffee beans in a spice grinder or use a pestle and mortar. Then mix with salt and black pepper and rub into the venison. Drizzle with the olive oil and roast the venison for 25 minutes for rare or cook for longer if you prefer. Leave to rest for at least 10 minutes and slice when needed.

8 If you are using the venison liver, sear the liver in a hot pan with the butter for 1–2 minutes on each side. Season with salt and pepper and deglaze the pan with vinegar. Glaze the liver with a little venison stock.

9 When ready to serve, lightly brush a griddle pan with olive oil, heat until hot and then griddle the polenta slices for 5 minutes on each side or until crisp and marked in places. Divide the venison between 4 plates and add the griddled polenta with the red wine shallots, the red onion and vanilla squash purées, and garlic, together with the venison liver, if using. Finally, drizzle over any juices left over from cooking the venison.

MASTER TIP
VENISON LOIN

The boned-out saddle (back) of a deer yields the venison loin and fillet muscles. These two prime cuts are often confused, but cooking times are very different, as loin (top) is at least twice as thick as fillet. The fillet muscle tapers at one end, whereas the loin does not.

JOHN TORODE'S
VENISON WELLINGTON
WITH BRAISED RED CABBAGE

Wild venison, rich and sweet, lean and tender, wrapped in buttery puff pastry, is hard to beat. Add spiced red cabbage and loads of mushrooms, and you're walking in the woods.

PREPARATION TIME
40 minutes

COOKING TIME
1 hour 20 minutes

SERVES 4

500g (1lb 2oz) venison loin, cut into 4
50g (1¾oz) butter
2 shallots, chopped
4–5 dried cèpes
150g (5½oz) chestnut mushrooms, finely chopped
2 tsp chopped parsley
375g (13oz) ready-made puff pastry, cut into 4
some milk

FOR THE RED CABBAGE
10g (¼oz) butter
1 smoked bacon rasher, chopped
½ red cabbage, approx. 400g (14oz), cored and sliced
1 Granny Smith apple, cored, peeled, and sliced
the rind of ¼ orange, in big strips
1 cinnamon stick
30g (1oz) light soft brown sugar
salt and freshly ground black pepper
2 tbsp red wine vinegar
4 tbsp red wine

1 To make the braised red cabbage, preheat the oven to 160°C (325°F/Gas 3). In a heavy ovenproof saucepan, heat the butter over high heat and add the bacon. Fry the bacon until there is just a little colour, then remove from the pan and set aside.

2 Layer the remaining ingredients in the pan starting with a quarter of the cabbage and apple. Add some of the orange rind and some cinnamon, bacon, and sugar. Season each layer well with salt and pepper. Continue the layering until all the ingredients are used.

3 Place the pan over high heat and add the vinegar and wine, bring to the boil and cook for 3–4 minutes. Cover the pan with a lid and cook in the oven for 1 hour. Do not stir at any stage, but check the liquid every 20 minutes or so to ensure that it does not evaporate. If it does, top up with water.

4 When the cabbage is cooked through, remove from the oven and keep warm. Increase the temperature to 220°C (425°F/Gas 7).

5 Put the pieces of venison on a board and season all over with salt and pepper. Melt half the butter in a large frying pan over medium heat. When foaming, put the meat in the pan and brown all over for 2 minutes only, taking care not to burn the butter. Transfer the venison to a plate and leave to cool.

6 In the same pan, melt the remaining butter, add the shallots and cook for 1 minute. Grind the dried mushrooms in a pestle and mortar and add to the pan together with the chopped mushrooms. Increase the heat and cook for about 10 minutes until the mushrooms are dry in the pan, then season and add the parsley. Set aside to cool.

7 On a lightly floured surface, roll each piece of the puff pastry to 3mm (⅛in) thick and 3 times bigger than the meat. Spoon some of the mushroom mix onto each and place the sealed meat on top. Brush the pastry edges with a little milk and then wrap the meat like a present. Transfer the parcels to a baking sheet with the seal side down, brush the top with milk and bake for 15–18 minutes or until brown and crisp.

8 Leave to stand for 5 minutes before cutting each one in half and trimming off the ends. Serve with the red cabbage.

MasterChef 2010 Finalist
ALEX RUSHMER

"I went into the final having finally worked out what my style was, and I was really happy with the three courses that I came up with. I knew I wanted to play around with both classic flavour combinations and modern techniques to bring the dishes right up to date. My final dessert is something that seems to have gone down in MasterChef history: a real love it or loathe it creation that matched a pear with spices, caramel, and a blue cheese ice cream for a 21st-century take on a classic combination. John and Gregg might not have liked it but try it for yourself and see what you think!"

STARTER

PHEASANT SALTIMBOCCA WITH BUTTERNUT SQUASH AND BEETROOT JUS p.84

"Alex is one of the bravest finalists we've ever had and this is typical of him: a modern style, big splashes of colour, and really interesting flavour combinations."
GREGG

MAIN

LOIN OF VENISON WITH CELERIAC PURÉE, BRAISED CABBAGE, AND REDCURRANT JUS p.236

"This is a lovely dish, with the beefy porcini mushrooms working so well with the soft meat and wonderful creamy earthiness of the celeriac purée."
GREGG

DESSERT

PEAR TATIN WITH STILTON ICE CREAM AND WALNUT AND TOBACCO BRITTLE p.282

"I love Alex's extraordinary style which is really daring. The flavours in the pudding were absolutely delicious – but, for me, the blue cheese ice cream didn't belong on the plate."
JOHN

LOIN OF VENISON WITH CELERIAC PURÉE, BRAISED CABBAGE, AND REDCURRANT JUS

Alex Rushmer freelance writer and 2010 finalist

PREPARATION TIME
20 minutes

COOKING TIME
1 hour 30 minutes

SERVES 4

700g (1lb 9oz) loin of venison
1 tbsp olive oil
knob of butter
100g (3½oz) porcini or wild
  mushrooms, cut into thick slices

FOR THE CABBAGE
knob of butter
1 small shallot, diced
300g (10oz) red cabbage, quartered,
  cored, and sliced
1 apple, cored, peeled, and sliced
1 tbsp clear honey
3 tbsp red wine vinegar
100ml (3½fl oz) red wine
200ml (7fl oz) chicken stock
salt and freshly ground black pepper

FOR THE CELERIAC
1 celeriac, approx. 800g (1¾lb)
juice of 1 lemon
3 tbsp double cream
25g (scant 1oz) butter
500ml (16fl oz) vegetable oil

FOR THE JUS
knob of butter
1 shallot, diced
8 juniper berries
50g (1¾oz) redcurrants
150ml (5fl oz) port
150ml (5fl oz) veal stock
2 tsp redcurrant jelly

JOHN TORODE "I like the softness of the venison with the sweetness from your red cabbage and earthiness from the celeriac."

1 For the cabbage, melt the butter in a large heavy saucepan. Add the shallot and cook for about 5 minutes to soften. Add the remaining ingredients and season. Cover with greaseproof paper and a lid and braise over very low heat for 1½ hours, stirring occasionally.
2 Peel the celeriac and shave off 4 strips to make crisps. Put in a bowl of iced lemon water and set aside. Dice the rest. Put in a pan with water to cover, salt, and lemon juice and bring to the boil. Simmer for 15–20 minutes or until soft. Drain and transfer to a blender or food processor. Add the cream, butter, and seasoning and purée. Keep warm.
3 For the jus, melt the butter in a pan. Cook the shallot for 3 minutes to soften. Add the berries and redcurrants and cook for 1 minute, then stir in the port and reduce by half. Pour in the stock and reduce again. Stir in the jelly and pass through a sieve into a pan to keep warm.
4 Season the venison and fry in the oil for 10–15 minutes, turning once. Cook longer if you prefer your meat less pink. Remove the venison from the pan, leave to rest, and then slice. Add the butter and mushrooms to the pan and fry for about 2 minutes to cook through.
5 Just before serving, drain and dry the celeriac shavings. Deep-fry in the vegetable oil for 2–3 minutes until crisp. Drain on kitchen paper. Spoon the purée and cabbage onto 4 plates and top with the venison and mushrooms. Drizzle over the sauce and garnish with the crisps.

ROAST LOIN OF VENISON WITH CHESTNUTS, VENISON JUS, AND CHILLI CHOCOLATE OIL

Dhruv Baker sales director and 2010 champion

PREPARATION TIME
20 minutes

COOKING TIME
1 hour 30 minutes

SERVES 4

700g (1lb 9oz) loin of venison (see MasterTip, p.233)
2 tsp coriander seeds, crushed
2 Maris Piper potatoes, cut into small dice
400ml (14fl oz) vegetable oil
2 tsp dried fenugreek leaves
250g (9oz) goose or duck fat
2 cinnamon sticks
8 green cardamom pods
10 whole cloves
100g (3½oz) peeled chestnuts

FOR THE JUS
250g (9oz) venison bones/trimmings
4 tbsp vegetable oil
1 carrot, chopped
3 banana shallots, chopped
1 celery stick, chopped
1 white onion, chopped
500ml (16fl oz) veal stock

FOR THE OIL
15g (½oz) dark chocolate (100% cocoa solids)
50g (1¾oz) dark chocolate (85% cocoa solids)
2 tbsp extra virgin olive oil
3 tbsp groundnut oil
pinch of chilli powder

FOR THE VEGETABLES
200g (7oz) carrots, sliced
50g (1¾oz) butter
½ tsp sugar
2 tbsp double cream
¼ tsp ground cumin
16 baby orange or purple carrots, trimmed and peeled
½ lemon
½ tsp toasted cumin seeds
150g (5½oz) curly kale, stalks removed
2 garlic cloves
salt and freshly ground black pepper

GREGG WALLACE

"I think it looks fantastic. I think it looks like a piece of Pop Art. It's a subtle dish, but I love it."

1 Coat the venison in the coriander seeds and set aside. Deep-fry the potato in the vegetable oil for 4–5 minutes until crisp and golden. Drain on kitchen paper and mix with the fenugreek leaves. Set side.
2 Melt the goose or duck fat together with the spices in a shallow pan. Add the chestnuts and cook over very low heat for about 45 minutes. Take care not to let the fat boil. Remove from the heat and drain carefully, reserving the chestnuts (and the fat for another time).
3 Meanwhile, make the jus. Put the venison bones and trimmings in a large pan and fry in the oil for 15 minutes until browned. Add the vegetables and fry for 15 minutes. Drain off the fat and pour in the stock. Bring to the boil and cook, skimming occasionally, for 45 minutes. Strain into a clean pan and return to the boil. Boil for 20–25 minutes or until the jus has reduced to a glossy liquor.
4 For the chilli chocolate oil, put the chocolates in a bowl set over a pan of simmering water. Add the oils and chilli and leave to melt without stirring. Stir once and set aside.
5 Preheat the oven to 200°C (400°F/Gas 6). Pan-fry the venison in

an ovenproof frying pan until sealed on all sides. Cook in the oven for about 15 minutes, then cover and leave to rest for 15 minutes.

6 Cook the carrots, uncovered, in 200ml (7fl oz) of water. When this has almost evaporated, add half the butter and half the sugar. Using a hand-held blender or transferring to a food processor, blend the carrots with the cream and cumin until they are smooth.

7 Cook the baby carrots in 2.5cm (1in) of water for 5 minutes or until the water has almost boiled off. Add the remaining sugar, a squeeze of lemon juice, and the toasted cumin seeds.

8 Boil the kale in lightly salted water for 7–8 minutes and drain. Melt the remaining butter in a frying pan with the whole garlic cloves. Add the kale, season well, and set aside.

9 To serve, divide the kale between 4 plates and drizzle over some of the jus. Cut the venison into slices and place on top, together with the potato and fenugreek. Then place 4 tbsp of the carrot purée on each plate and top each with a baby carrot. Place the chestnuts in between the carrots. Serve with the chocolate oil in a jug alongside.

LOIN OF VENISON WITH SPICED BEETROOT, CHERRY, AND BITTER CHOCOLATE

Conor Marron surgeon and 2010 contestant

PREPARATION TIME
30–35 minutes

COOKING TIME
1 hour

SERVES 4

2 large Maris Piper potatoes
1 tbsp olive oil
50g (1¾oz) unsalted butter, plus a knob
 for the red chard
5–6 sprigs fresh thyme
150ml (5fl oz) chicken stock
2 large beetroots
2 star anise
6 cloves
8 black peppercorns
16 juniper berries, crushed
400ml (14fl oz) full-bodied red wine
200ml (7fl oz) port
3 carrots, chopped

300ml (10fl oz) double cream
vanilla pod
salt and freshly ground black pepper
4 loin fillets of venison, approx.
 200g (7oz) per person, trimmed
 and unsliced
1 tbsp rapeseed oil
3 tbsp beef stock
1 dessert spoon dark cherry conserve
25g (scant 1oz) dark chocolate
 (70% cocoa solids)
1 large handful red chard, or baby
 spinach, washed and de-stalked

1 For the fondant potatoes, peel and cut the potatoes into 3cm (1¼in) thick discs using a pastry cutter. Heat the olive oil in a saucepan and fry the potatoes on one side for 4–5 minutes until golden in colour. Add 50g (1¾oz) of the butter and 2 sprigs of thyme, and turn the potatoes. Cook for a further 4–5 minutes, until golden.

2 Add 3 tbsp of chicken stock and reduce by half. Then add the remaining stock and reduce. Cover and cook for about 40 minutes.

3 For the spiced beetroot, preheat the oven to 170°C (350°F/Gas 4). Cut the beetroot into 1.5cm (½in) cubes, place on a baking tray and cook in the oven for 20 minutes.

4 Warm the star anise, cloves, peppercorns, and half of the juniper berries in a saucepan. Add 100ml (3½ fl oz) of the red wine and reduce by half. Add the port and reduce by half again. Strain the sauce, then add the beetroot to the liquor and place in the oven for 20 minutes.

5 Meanwhile, make the carrot and vanilla purée. Boil the carrots in salted water until tender. Place the cream in a small saucepan, scrape the seeds from the vanilla pod into the cream, then add the pod into the cream. Warm gently to let the flavours infuse.

6 When the carrots are cooked, strain and return to the saucepan. Add the cream gradually and blend with a hand-held blender or by transferring to a food processor. Add seasoning and keep warm.

7 Season the venison with salt and pepper. Rub the remaining thyme and juniper berries over the surface of the meat and wrap in cling film for 10 minutes. Heat the rapeseed oil in a pan. Remove the juniper berries and thyme from the venison (reserve for use in sauce) and sear the outside of the venison loin fillet on all sides. Cook in the oven for 10–15 minutes, then remove and let rest for 10 minutes. Return to oven to warm through immediately prior to serving.

8 For the cherry and bitter chocolate sauce, deglaze the pan from cooking the venison using the remaining red wine. Add the reserved thyme and juniper berries and reduce by half. Add the beef stock, and further reduce until to a thick sauce. Take off the heat until you are ready to serve. Strain the sauce to remove the thyme and juniper berries. Stir in the cherry conserve and then grate in chocolate to taste. Season with salt and pepper.

9 For the wilted red chard or baby spinach, melt a knob of butter in a saucepan and wilt the chard by moving it in the pan for a few minutes until it is tender. Remove from the heat and drain on kitchen paper.

10 To serve, place a spoonful of sauce at one side of each of 4 plates. Place some wilted red chard in the middle of the sauce. Slice the venison and place 3 slices on top of each pile of chard. Put fondant potato to the other side of the plate. Add the carrot and vanilla purée and then cubes of beetroot. Drizzle the beetroot with a small amount of the spiced port reduction.

GREGG WALLACE

"I love the sweet taste of the beetroot and that sauce against the rich venison. I think this is accomplished cooking with some very different, unique flavours I find very pleasing."

TEA-SMOKED VENISON WITH CABBAGE, BEETROOT PURÉE, AND A RED WINE SAUCE

Stacie Stewart PA and 2010 semi-finalist

PREPARATION TIME
20 minutes

COOKING TIME
1¼ hours

SERVES 4

50g (1¾oz) demerara sugar
50g (1¾oz) risotto rice
50g (1¾oz) Earl Grey tea leaves
700g (1lb 9oz) loin of venison
50g (1¾oz) clarified butter
salt and freshly ground black pepper
100g (3½oz) venison trimmings
1 tbsp olive oil
1 bay leaf
1 onion, chopped
1 carrot, chopped
sprig of thyme
2 banana shallots, peeled and chopped
8–10 juniper berries
2 tbsp sherry vinegar
350ml (12fl oz) full-bodied red wine
350ml (12fl oz) chicken stock
30g (1oz) dark chocolate (70% cocoa)

3 garlic cloves, lightly crushed
black peppercorns

FOR THE PURÉE
300g (10oz) baby beetroot
1 tbsp olive oil
pinch of salt
2 sprigs of thyme
2 garlic cloves, peeled and left whole
100g (3½oz) blackberries
25g (scant 1oz) caster sugar

FOR THE CABBAGE
1 small red cabbage, cored and shredded
100g (3½oz) clarified butter
150g (5½oz) dark soft brown sugar
75ml (2½fl oz) sherry vinegar
75ml (2½fl oz) port

MASTER TIP
SHERRY VINEGAR

Sherry vinegar is matured for a number of years in a series of wooden barrels. It is full of dried fruit flavours and makes an aromatic dressing for robust salads. Use to marinate pork loin for pot roasting.

1 For the purée, preheat the oven to 180°C (350°F/Gas 4). Wrap the beetroot in foil with oil, salt, thyme, and garlic and bake for 30 minutes. Poach the blackberries and sugar in simmering water for 2 minutes. Remove the beetroot from the oven, peel, and put in a blender or food processor with the blackberries and purée. Pass through a sieve.
2 For the red cabbage, put all the ingredients into a large heavy saucepan, cover, and simmer for 1 hour until the cabbage is tender. Transfer the cabbage to an ovenproof bowl and reduce the sauce until syrupy. Pour back over the cabbage and keep warm in a low oven.
3 Line a wok with foil, fill it with the sugar, rice, and tea and put over high heat until it smokes. Put the venison on a rack over the smoke, cover it tightly with foil, reduce the heat, and leave for 15 minutes. Heat a pan with the butter, season the meat, and pan-fry for 15 minutes.
4 For the sauce, brown the trimmings in a saucepan in the oil. Fry the bay leaf, onion, carrot, thyme, shallots, and juniper berries for 2 minutes. Add the vinegar and reduce by half; add the wine and reduce by half; then add the stock and reduce by half again. Pass through a sieve, return to the heat, and reduce to a syrupy sauce. Add the chocolate off the heat.
5 To serve, slice the venison. Place a layer of purée on each plate, then some cabbage and top with the venison. Drizzle with sauce.

COLLOPS OF VENISON IN A BLACKBERRY SAUCE, WITH CELERIAC MASH, AND SPROUTS

Christine Hamilton TV personality and 2010 Celebrity finalist

2 tbsp olive oil
½ tsp freshly ground black pepper
1 tsp juniper berries, crushed
700g (1lb 9oz) fillet of venison
2 large sheets of filo pastry
50g (1¾oz) butter, plus extra for brushing
1 large celeriac, approx. 800g (1¾lb), cut into dice
3 garlic cloves
2 tbsp milk
1 tbsp truffle oil
salt and freshly ground black pepper

400ml (14fl oz) red wine
2 rounded tbsp redcurrant jelly
100g (3½oz) blackberries, plus a few extra to garnish
about 10g (¼oz) dark chocolate (70% cocoa), grated
2 tbsp crème fraîche (optional)
25g (scant 1oz) pancetta
125g (4½oz) Brussels sprouts, shredded
75g (2½oz) chestnuts, cooked, peeled, and chopped
grated zest and juice of ½ lemon

PREPARATION TIME
20 minutes

COOKING TIME
1 hour 30 minutes

SERVES 4

1 In a shallow container, mix together 1 tbsp of the oil, the pepper, and juniper berries. Add the venison and leave to marinate while you make the sprout baskets.

2 To make the baskets, preheat the oven to 180°C (350°F/Gas 4). Cut the filo pastry into 8cm (3¼ in) squares. Brush the squares with melted butter, then place 3 squares on top of each other in a star shape. Push gently, but completely, into a mini muffin tin. Repeat with the rest of the pastry until you have 8 baskets. Bake in the oven for 10 minutes until golden.

3 Heat the remaining oil in a heavy frying pan on medium heat and sear the venison for about 5 minutes on each side. Remove from the pan and wrap in foil to keep it warm.

4 Boil the celeriac with the garlic in a saucepan for 10–15 minutes or until soft. Then mash with 25g (scant 1oz) of the butter together with the milk and truffle oil. Season to taste and keep warm.

5 Add the wine to the venison pan and reduce by half. Then add the jelly and blackberries and cook for about 5 minutes until the blackberries are soft. Pass the sauce through a sieve into a clean pan, return to the heat, then add the remaining butter and chocolate and season. Finally, add the crème fraîche (if using).

6 Meanwhile, sauté the pancetta in a frying pan, add the sprouts, chestnuts, and 100ml (3½fl oz) of water. Season and simmer until the water has evaporated. Then add the lemon zest and juice.

7 Slice the venison into collops (slices) and serve with the celeriac mash, sprout and chestnut baskets, and sauce. Garnish with berries.

MASTER TIP
JUNIPER BERRIES

The aroma of the small, purple-black, smooth berries is pleasantly woody, bittersweet, and like gin. The taste is clean and refreshing, sweetish with a slight burning effect, and a hint of pine and resin. Crush or grind juniper berries just before use to keep their flavour.

VENISON LIVER, RED CABBAGE AND DAUPHINOISE POTATOES, WITH A SMOKED BACON AND BRANDY CREAM SAUCE

Andrew Perry property developer and 2010 quarter-finalist

PREPARATION TIME
45 minutes

COOKING TIME
1¾ hours

SERVES 4

FOR THE POTATOES
1 large waxy potato, weighing approx.
  300g (10oz)
1 small onion, sliced
75g (2½oz) mature Cheddar cheese,
  finely grated
1 tsp milk
300ml (10fl oz) double cream
1 garlic clove, finely chopped
salt and freshly ground black pepper

FOR THE RED CABBAGE
1 small red cabbage, approx. 400g
  (14oz), quartered and cored
115g (4oz) dark soft brown sugar
500ml (16fl oz) dry cider
150ml (5fl oz) white wine vinegar

FOR THE SAUCE
1 large red onion, peeled
300g (10oz) thin-cut smoked streaky
  bacon rashers
1 tbsp olive oil
600ml (1 pint) double cream
60ml (2fl oz) brandy
small bunch of fresh sage, chopped
1 garlic clove, finely chopped
½ tsp dried mace
1 tsp mustard powder
knob of butter

FOR THE LIVER
30g (1oz) salted butter
1 tbsp olive oil
450g (1lb) venison or calf's liver,
  thinly sliced

1 Preheat the oven to 180°C (350°F/Gas 4). Lightly grease the base and sides of four 175ml (6fl oz) ramekins with a little oil or butter and line the base of each with a circle of baking parchment.

2 For the Dauphinoise potatoes, slice the potato very thinly using a mandoline or a food processor. Put the slices into a bowl of cold water to prevent them from going brown, then remove from the water and pat dry on kitchen paper.

3 Layer the potato, onion, and cheese in each ramekin, reserving about 15g (½oz) cheese. Finish with a layer of potato and gently press down into the ramekins.

4 Mix the milk, cream, and garlic together with salt and pepper in a jug. Stand the ramekins on a baking tray and slowly pour the cream mixture over the potato so it comes to the top of each container. Sprinkle on the remaining cheese. Cover each ramekin with foil and bake for 45 minutes. Reduce the temperature to 160°C (325°F/Gas 3) and bake for a further 30 minutes or until the potatoes are softened.

5 For the red cabbage, trim and shred the cabbage finely using a mandoline or a food processor and put into a large saucepan. Add the sugar, cider, vinegar, and some seasoning and stir together well.

6 Bring to the boil on high heat, then reduce the heat to simmer and cook slowly, uncovered, for about 1½ hours or until the cabbage is softened.

7 To make the sauce, slice the onion and bacon finely, reserving 4 whole rashers of bacon. Heat the oil in a large frying pan, then add the onion and bacon and fry for about 10 minutes on medium heat until brown and the onion is soft. Reduce the heat, then add the cream and brandy, stirring well. Add the sage, garlic, mace, mustard powder, knob of butter, and seasoning. Set aside until required.

8 Put the remaining rashers of bacon on a baking tray and cook in the oven at 180ºC (350º/Gas 4) for 10–15 minutes or until crisp. Keep the bacon hot while you cook the liver.

9 For the liver, put the butter and oil in a separate frying pan and heat on a high setting. Add the liver and cook for 2–3 minutes or until browned and tender, turning once and basting with the butter. Remove the liver from the pan, cover with foil and allow to rest for 5 minutes. Pour the excess juices into the sauce, reheat gently and stir well.

10 To serve, turn out each Dauphinoise by loosening the edges of the ramekin with a palette knife and inverting onto a serving plate, gently easing it out. Carefully remove the baking parchment from each. Spoon red cabbage into a serving ring, pressing down firmly and position on each plate. Add the liver, spoon on the gently reheated sauce and top each with a bacon rasher.

JOHN TORODE "That liver cooked very rare, with the bacon sauce and the brandy, tastes like a really good paté. Then the sweetness of that red cabbage is a wonderful accompaniment."

ABAGLIONE - WARM GINGER CAKE WI
HUBARB - RHUBARB CRUMBLE TART
ITH SYLLABUB AND RHUBARB SYRUP
ANILLA PANNA COTTA WITH RHUBAR
ND RASPBERRY COMPOTE - RHUBARB
ND GINGER CRUMBLE - CUSTARD TAR
ITH RHUBARB STEWED IN WHISKY AI
INGER CREAM - BEE POLLEN MOUSSE
HUBARB AND RASPBERRY JELLY - RH
RUMBLE WITH VANILLA CUSTARD - A
ND RASPBERRY FILO BASKETS WITH
OUNTRY ATHOL BROSE - STRAWBERR
ND "CHAMPAGNE" JELLY WITH ICE CR
ND SHORTBREAD WAFER FANS - RICE
RISPIE CAKE WITH CHOCOLATE MOUS
HERRY SORBET, AND CHERRIES IN KI
OOSEBERRY AND ELDERFLOWER SYL
ITH ALMOND DAQUOISE BISCUITS - A

DESSERTS

ROSÉ AND ORANGE RHUBARB WITH ZABAGLIONE

Jo Jenkins dental practice manager and 2010 quarter-finalist

PREPARATION TIME
20 minutes

COOKING TIME
25–30 minutes

SERVES 4

6 red rhubarb stalks, about 450g (1lb) in total, chopped into small pieces
3 tbsp caster sugar
grated zest of 1 orange
2 star anise
140ml (4¾fl oz) rosé wine

FOR THE ZABAGLIONE
6 egg yolks
65g (2¼oz) caster sugar
100ml (3½fl oz) Marsala wine
100ml (3½fl oz) double cream

JOHN TORODE

"There's a really deep, rich flavour of Marsala inside the zabaglione."

1 Preheat the oven to 200°C (400°F/Gas 6). Put the rhubarb in a small ovenproof dish and add the sugar, orange zest, star anise, and rosé wine. Cover the dish with foil.

2 Roast in the oven for 15–20 minutes until the rhubarb is tender, then remove the foil and cook for a further 5 minutes until the wine becomes syrupy. Remove the star anise and discard. Set the rhubarb aside to cool while you make the zabaglione.

3 Put the egg yolks, sugar, and wine into a heatproof bowl, set over a pan of gently simmering water, and whisk until thick, light, and frothy; this will take about 15 minutes using an electric whisk, but longer if using a rotary or balloon whisk. Remove the bowl from the pan and set aside.

4 Whisk the double cream until it forms soft peaks, then fold it gently and thoroughly into the whisked egg mixture.

5 To serve, divide the zabaglione between 4 large glasses and serve the rhubarb separately. Serve immediately.

FLAVOUR COMBINATION
STAR ANISE AND RHUBARB

You can't go wrong with rhubarb and orange – except by using too much juice. Here the concentrated flavour of the zest guarantees big flavour uptake. But star anise? Absolutely. Star anise includes the flavour of cinnamon more commonly used, but then provides plenty of surprises, including the mesmerizing flavours of aniseed and liquorice. The affinity of rhubarb with star anise creates a new flavour that gratifies the entire palate.

WARM GINGER CAKE WITH RHUBARB

John Calton head chef and 2010 Professionals finalist

150g (5½oz) unsalted butter at room
  temperature, plus extra for greasing
150g (5½oz) caster sugar
3 eggs
125g (4½oz) self-raising flour
75g (2½oz) ground almonds
1 tbsp ground ginger
2 tbsp chopped stem ginger in syrup

FOR THE VANILLA-SCENTED YOGURT
2 vanilla pods, split, seeds scraped out
  and reserved with their pods
200g (7oz) plain low-fat yogurt
juice of ½ lime

FOR THE POACHED RHUBARB
125g (4½oz) sugar
grated zest of 1 lemon
2 sticks of bright pink rhubarb,
  cut into batons

FOR THE RHUBARB SORBET
1 leaf of gelatine
500g (1lb 2oz) rhubarb, finely chopped
125g (4½oz) caster sugar
20ml liquid glucose
juice of ½ lemon
a couple of drops of red food
  colouring (optional)

PREPARATION TIME
1 hour

COOKING TIME
40 minutes

SERVES 4

1 Preheat the oven to 180°C (350°F/Gas 4). Generously grease and
flour 4 large ramekins. Place the butter and sugar in a large mixing
bowl and cream together until white and fluffy. Add the eggs one by
one and mix for 3 minutes. Fold in the flour and almonds until fully
incorporated. Add the ground ginger and stem ginger and transfer
the mixture to the ramekins. Bake in the oven for 20–25 minutes,
until springy to the touch.

2 Add the vanilla seeds to the yogurt. Whisk together and season
with the lime juice. Decant into a squeezy bottle.

3 Put the sugar, lemon, and vanilla pods in a medium pan with 250ml
(9fl oz) water. Bring to the boil to create a syrup. Add the rhubarb and
poach for 5–7 minutes until just tender. Set aside to cool.

4 Soak the gelatine in cold water for 10 minutes. Place the rhubarb,
sugar, glucose, and 60ml (2fl oz) water in a large pan, bring to the boil,
and cook for 4–5 minutes, until the rhubarb is tender. Add the gelatine,
stirring to dissolve, and the lemon juice. Liquidize the rhubarb using
a hand-held blender or by transferring to a food processor, adding
150ml (5fl oz) of the syrup used to cook the rhubarb batons. Pass
through a sieve and chill over ice. The sorbet should be naturally pink,
but if you want to bring up the colour, add a couple of drops of food
colouring. Churn in an ice-cream maker and freeze until required.

5 To serve, pattern the plates with the yogurt and then turn out the
sponges. Drizzle the sponges with a little of the syrup, then add a
ball of sorbet and a few batons of rhubarb to each plate.

RHUBARB CRUMBLE TART WITH SYLLABUB AND RHUBARB SYRUP

Dick Strawbridge TV presenter and 2010 Celebrity finalist

PREPARATION TIME
45 minutes, plus chilling

COOKING TIME
1 hour

SERVES 4

225g (8oz) sugar, plus 3 tbsp
450g (1lb) rhubarb, cut into
  1cm (½in) pieces
2 pieces of stem ginger, finely diced

FOR THE NUT CRUST
50g (1¾oz) blanched hazelnuts,
  toasted
25g (scant 1oz) icing sugar
100g (3½oz) plain flour
50g (1¾oz) butter
½ tsp vanilla extract
1 small egg, beaten

FOR THE CRUMBLE TOPPING
100g (3½oz) plain flour
50g (1¾oz) butter
25g (scant 1oz) demerara sugar
finely grated zest of 1 lemon

FOR THE SYLLABUB
300ml (10fl oz) double cream
1-2 tbsp ginger wine or brandy
2 tbsp ginger syrup from the stem
  ginger jar
1 piece of stem ginger, finely sliced

GREGG WALLACE

"Really good pastry, crunchy on top. Very sharp rhubarb sweetened by the fruit syrup. Hint of ginger in your well-made syllabub. Good pudding."

1 First make a syrup by dissolving 225g (8oz) of the sugar in a saucepan with 300ml (10fl oz) of boiling water. Preheat the oven to 180°C (350°F/Gas 4). Add half the rhubarb to the syrup, bring to the boil, then leave until completely cold. Put the remaining rhubarb in an ovenproof dish and sprinkle over 3 tablespoons of sugar. Bake in the oven for about 20 minutes or until softened. Allow to cool then drain and mix with the slices of stem ginger, reserving 8 slices for decoration. Strain the cold rhubarb syrup into a jug and chill.
2 For the nut crust, put the nuts and sugar in a food processor and mix briefly to combine. Add the remaining ingredients except the egg and mix on pulse setting. With the machine running, gradually pour in the egg and mix to form a ball. Wrap in cling film and chill for 30 minutes. Divide into 4 equal pieces and press into the base of four 10cm (4in) tart tins. Chill for 10 minutes.
3 Increase the oven heat to 190°C (375°G/Gas 5). Cook the tarts for about 8-10 minutes or until pale golden. Meanwhile, make the crumble. Put all the ingredients in a food processor and mix briefly to form crumbs. Spread out on a baking sheet and cook for 8-10 minutes or until pale golden. Give the crumble a stir halfway through cooking.
4 Divide the rhubarb between tart cases and top with the crumble. Bake for 10 minutes or until heated through.
5 For the syllabub, put the cream, wine, and ginger syrup into a bowl and whisk to form soft peaks. Chill for 10 minutes.
6 Serve the tarts warm with the syllabub, decorating the syllabub with slices of stem ginger. Place a cup of pink rhubarb syrup alongside.

VANILLA PANNA COTTA WITH RHUBARB AND RASPBERRY COMPOTE

Claire Lara lecturer and 2010 Professionals champion

PREPARATION TIME
30 minutes, plus setting

COOKING TIME
25 minutes

SERVES 4

5 leaves of gelatine
250ml (8fl oz) whole milk
250ml (8fl oz) double cream
1 vanilla pod, cut in half, seeds scraped out and reserved with the pod
30g (1oz) caster sugar

FOR THE COMPOTE
175g (6oz) sugar
1 vanilla pod, split, seeds scraped out and reserved with the pod
175g (6oz) raspberries
140g (5oz) rhubarb, peeled and cut into 5cm (2in) chunks

FOR THE LEMON AND OAT TUILE
50g (1¾oz) butter
85g (3oz) rolled oats
85g (3oz) icing sugar
25g (scant 1oz) plain flour
2 egg whites

FOR THE FOAM
250ml (8fl oz) whole milk
1 tbsp sugar
1 slice stem ginger, chopped
2 tbsp Sauternes wine

VANILLA PODS

Vanilla is the fruit of a perennial climbing orchid. Fresh pods have no aroma or taste, it is only after fermentation that they develop the distinctive "vanilla" flavour. Use whole or split pods to flavour creams, custards, ice cream, and sugar. Remove the tiny, sticky black seeds inside the pods by splitting in half and extracting at the point of a knife.

1 To make the panna cotta, first soak the gelatine in a little cold water for 10 minutes or until soft. Place the milk, cream, vanilla pod and seeds, and sugar in a pan and bring to a simmer. Remove from the heat and discard the vanilla pod. Squeeze the water out of the gelatine, add the gelatine to the pan, and stir until dissolved. Spoon into 150ml (5fl oz) dessert glasses, allow to cool then refrigerate for about 1 hour until set.

2 For the compote, place the sugar, vanilla pod and seeds, and 175ml (6fl oz) water in a pan. Gently heat to dissolve the sugar, then bring to the boil. Remove from the heat and transfer the syrup to a bowl, then add the raspberries and rhubarb and cover with cling film. After 10 minutes, remove the rhubarb from the syrup and cut into small dice.

3 Preheat the oven to 180°C (350°F/Gas 4) and line a baking sheet with baking parchment. For the tuile, melt the butter in a pan, then set aside. Whizz the oats in a blender or a food processor until they are finely ground but not powdery, add the icing sugar and flour and combine. Gradually add the egg whites, and the melted butter, and mix. Transfer the mixture to a bowl.

4 Place 1 tsp of the mixture on the baking parchment and spread with the back of a spoon to a 7cm (2¾in) round. Repeat with the rest of the mixture, leaving space between each biscuit. Bake in the oven for approximately 6–7 minutes until pale golden and then remove from the tray. Press over a rolling pin to make a rounded tuile shape and transfer to a wire rack to cool.

5 To prepare the foam, gently heat the milk in a pan and then dissolve the sugar in it. Add the ginger and wine and set aside to infuse. When the milk is cool, pass through a fine sieve and remove the ginger. Place the milk in a cream charger and follow the manufacturer's instruction to produce a foam.

6 To serve, drain some raspberries from the stock syrup, mix with the diced rhubarb, then place a portion on top of each panna cotta. Spoon the foam over the fruit and balance a tuile over each glass. Serve immediately.

RHUBARB AND GINGER CRUMBLE

Lisa Faulkner actress and 2010 Celebrity champion

450g (1lb) rhubarb,
  cut into 2cm (¾in) pieces
2 slices preserved stem ginger,
  finely diced
2 tbsp ginger syrup, reserved from jar
2 tbsp caster sugar

FOR THE CRUMBLE TOPPING
140g (5oz) plain flour
45g (1½oz) oats
85g (3oz) unsalted butter, diced

60g (2oz) golden caster sugar
45g (1½oz) flaked almonds

FOR THE CUSTARD
8 egg yolks
75g (2½oz) caster sugar
300ml (10fl oz) whole milk
300ml (10fl oz) double cream
1 vanilla pod, split, seeds scraped
  out and reserved with the pod
  (see MasterTip, left)

PREPARATION TIME
15 minutes

COOKING TIME
45 minutes

SERVES 4

1 Preheat the oven to 180°C (350°F/Gas 4). Put the rhubarb in a 1 litre (1¾ pint) deep pie dish. Add the ginger, syrup, and sugar and mix together.

2 For the crumble, mix the flour and oats in a bowl. Add the butter and rub into the flour mixture until the texture resembles fine breadcrumbs. Add the sugar and almonds and mix well.

3 Spoon half the crumble mixture on top of the rhubarb and pat down. Sprinkle the rest on top and leave sitting loosely. Place in the preheated oven and bake for about 45 minutes until golden.

4 To make the custard, beat the egg yolks and sugar together in a bowl until pale and thickened. Pour the milk and cream into a large saucepan, and add the vanilla seeds and pod. Bring to simmering point over medium heat, then pour through a fine sieve onto the egg mixture and whisk thoroughly. Place the bowl over a pan of simmering water and stir until the custard thickens and coats the back of a spoon. Serve the warm custard with the crumble.

GREGG WALLACE

"The big smash-hit of the day."

CUSTARD TART WITH RHUBARB STEWED IN WHISKY AND GINGER CREAM

Neil Stuke actor and 2010 Celebrity semi-finalist

PREPARATION TIME
1 hour 30 minutes, plus setting

COOKING TIME
1 hour

SERVES 4

4 leaves of gelatine
300ml (10fl oz) double cream
300ml (10fl oz) whole milk
125g (4½oz) caster sugar
1 vanilla pod
2 tbsp ginger wine
4 pieces of stem ginger, chopped
icing sugar, to finish

FOR THE TART
250g (9oz) ready-made sweet pastry
500ml (16fl oz) double cream
8 eggs

1 egg yolk
75g (2½oz) caster sugar
freshly grated nutmeg

FOR THE RHUBARB
125g (4½oz) caster sugar
500g (1lb 2oz) rhubarb,
   roughly chopped
grated zest of 2 lemons
grated zest of 2 oranges
60ml (2fl oz) whisky
1 tsp ground ginger
4 leaves of gelatine

1 To make the ginger cream, soak the gelatine in cold water for 10 minutes. Gently heat together the cream, milk, sugar, and vanilla pod. Stir to dissolve the sugar and bring to the boil for 2 minutes, then remove from the heat. Squeeze out as much water as possible from the gelatine before adding it to the cream mix. Stir until the gelatine is dissolved, then stir in the ginger wine.

2 Divide the stem ginger between four 150ml (5fl oz) dariole or pudding moulds. Remove the vanilla pod and strain the cream mixture into a jug. Pour into the moulds and leave to cool before putting into the fridge to set. This will take about 3 hours.

3 To make the custard tart, grease a 23cm (9in) pastry ring (or loose-bottomed tart tin), and place on a baking sheet lined with baking parchment. Roll out the pastry and use to line the pastry ring. Chill for 30 minutes. Meanwhile, preheat the oven to 180°C (350°F/Gas 4).

4 Remove the pastry from the fridge, place some greaseproof paper on the base, add baking beans and bake blind for about 10 minutes, or until the edges begin to brown.

5 Meanwhile, put the cream in a medium saucepan and bring to the boil, then turn down to a simmer. Whisk the eggs and sugar in a bowl, then add the hot cream. Sieve into a jug and set aside to cool.

6 Remove the beans and greaseproof paper from the tart case. Whisk the egg yolk, brush onto the pastry, and bake for a further 5 minutes. Repeat once more to ensure there are no cracks.

7 Open the oven, pull out a shelf, and place the pastry case on the shelf. Pour in the filling then grate on some nutmeg. Bake for 45–50 minutes – the middle should still be a bit wobbly.

8 To cook the rhubarb, heat 150ml (5fl oz) water and the caster sugar together in a large pan until the sugar has dissolved. Add the rhubarb and lemon and orange zest and bring to the boil. After a while, turn it down to a simmer, add the whisky and ground ginger and cook for 10 minutes. Meanwhile, put the gelatine to soak in cold water.

9 Remove the rhubarb from the heat, add the drained leaves of gelatine, and stir to dissolve. After about 10 minutes, pour into a bowl and cool in the fridge until ready to serve.

10 To serve, cut a slice of the tart and lay on the plate. Take the cream moulds out of the fridge, remove the cream from the mould, and place on the plate as well. Add the stewed rhubarb as desired. Sieve some icing sugar over to finish.

BEE POLLEN MOUSSE
WITH RHUBARB AND RASPBERRY JELLY

Alice Churchill chef de partie and 2010 Professionals semi-finalist

PREPARATION TIME
1 hour 30 minutes, plus setting

COOKING TIME
1 hour 15 minutes

SERVES 4

5 leaves of gelatine
3 eggs, separated
85g (3oz) caster sugar
50g (1¾oz) bee pollen powder
250ml (9fl oz) double cream

FOR THE JELLY
225g (8oz) raspberries
225g (8oz) rhubarb, chopped
85g (3oz) caster sugar
1 tsp agar powder or 1 tbsp agar flakes

FOR THE RHUBARB BATONS
225g (8oz) rhubarb, cut into 16 batons,
    about 7cm (2¾in) long
60g (2oz) caster sugar
115g (4oz) raspberries
1 cinnamon stick
2 star anise

1 Lightly oil the base and sides of a 20cm (8in) square, 6cm (2½in) deep cake tin and line with cling film. Break the gelatine into pieces, put in a bowl with 3 tbsp cold water and soak for 10 minutes. Set the bowl over a pan of gently simmering water and allow the gelatine to dissolve, stirring once or twice. Remove the bowl from the heat and allow to cool but not set – if need be, gently reheat until liquid again.
2 Put the egg yolks, sugar, and bee pollen in a large bowl. Set the bowl over a pan of gently simmering water and whisk for about 10 minutes until thick and creamy. Remove the bowl from the pan and whisk until cool. Slowly pour the gelatine into the mixture, whisking well.
3 In a separate bowl, whip the cream until it just holds its shape but is still light and floppy. Whisk the egg whites to soft peaks. Using a metal spoon, fold the cream into the bee pollen mixture and, once it is incorporated, fold in the egg whites a little at a time. Stop folding as soon as the egg whites are fully combined. Pour the mousse into the tin, smooth the top and put in the fridge for 2–3 hours to set.
4 To make the jelly, put the raspberries, rhubarb, sugar, and 500ml (16fl oz) water into a large pan. Bring to a simmer, stirring well to dissolve the sugar. Cover the pan and cook for about 10 minutes until the rhubarb is soft. Strain the liquid and discard the solids. Return the juice to the pan and stir in the agar powder. Bring to a rolling boil for 1 minute. Remove from the heat and allow to cool for about 10 minutes, then pour into 4 glasses. Put in the fridge to set – about 1–2 hours.
5 For the batons, put the rhubarb in a pan. Add the sugar, raspberries, cinnamon, star anise, and 150ml (5fl oz) water. Cover the pan and poach for 5–10 minutes until the rhubarb is softened but still holding its shape. Remove the rhubarb from the cooking liquor and allow to

drain on kitchen paper. Strain the liquor and return the juice to the pan. Boil for about 3 minutes until reduced and slightly thickened.

6 To assemble, put a piece of cling film on top of the mousse and invert the tin on to a chopping board so that the mousse is encased in cling film. Peel it away from the top and sides, then cut the mousse into 4 pieces and lift onto the serving plates. Arrange 4 rhubarb batons on each plate and pour the syrup over. Add the jelly glasses and serve.

RHUBARB CRUMBLE WITH VANILLA CUSTARD

Terry Ireland ex-factory worker and 2010 semi-finalist

50g (1¾oz) plain flour
90g (3¼oz) caster sugar
30g (1oz) unsalted butter, cubed
75g (2½oz) whole hazelnuts, blanched and skinned
150ml (5fl oz) ginger wine

600g (1lb 5oz) pink rhubarb, cut into 2.5cm (1in) batons
150ml (5fl oz) double cream
150ml (5fl oz) whole milk
1 vanilla pod, split, seeds scraped out and reserved with the pod
3 egg yolks

PREPARATION TIME
1 hour

COOKING TIME
40 minutes

SERVES 4

1 Preheat the oven to 160°C (325°F/Gas 3). Put the flour and 15g (½oz) sugar in a food processor and whizz together. Gradually add the butter followed by the hazelnuts. Process until a breadcrumb consistency is reached. Spread the crumble evenly on a greased baking tray and bake for 20–30 minutes until it is cooked but not brown. Remove from the oven and increase the heat to 220°C (425°F/Gas 7).

2 Put the wine and 60g (2oz) sugar in a pan. Bring slowly to the boil to dissolve the sugar. Add the rhubarb and simmer gently, uncovered, until it is softened but still holds its shape – about 10–15 minutes.

3 Slowly heat the cream and milk in a pan with the vanilla pod and seeds. Beat the egg yolks with 15g (½oz) sugar. Just before the mixture boils, remove from the heat and pour a little onto the eggs and sugar, whisking. Gradually add the rest, discarding the vanilla pod and whisking all the time. Return the mixture to the pan and heat slowly, stirring with a wooden spoon. Cook the custard for 10 minutes until it coats the back of the spoon, then strain it into a jug.

4 Grease 4 pastry rings, 10cm (4in) in diameter and 4cm (1½in) deep, and place them on a greased baking tray. Arrange the rhubarb at the bottom of each ring. Pile the crumble on top, press down tightly and bake in the oven for 8–10 minutes or until golden brown.

5 When the crumbles are cooked, remove from the baking tray with a spatula and transfer each to a plate. Carefully remove the ring from each. Serve with individual jugs of custard.

JOHN TORODE

"A little bit of ginger wine to give warmth to the rhubarb, sweetness from the topping, and a really gutsy full-of-flavour custard. It tastes great!"

APPLE AND RASPBERRY FILO BASKETS WITH A WEST COUNTRY ATHOL BROSE

Dick Strawbridge TV presenter and 2010 Celebrity finalist

PREPARATION TIME
50 minutes

COOKING TIME
1 hour

SERVES 4

150g (5½oz) unsalted butter
1 tsp ground cinnamon
4 crisp English apples, such as Golden
   Delicious, Discovery, or Granny Smith
4 sheets of filo pastry
icing sugar, for dusting
200g (7oz) raspberries

2 tbsp golden caster sugar
1 tsp vanilla extract
4 tbsp medium oatmeal
2 tbsp apple brandy or Calvados
3 tbsp dry cider
2 tbsp clear honey
300ml (10fl oz) double cream

GREGG WALLACE

"That's probably one of the best dishes I've tasted in a long, long time. Sharp, sweet, bit of cinnamon, and quality honey running through it. Exceptional."

1 Make beurre noisette by melting 100g (3½oz) of the butter in a saucepan over low heat and allow it to separate into butter fat and milk solids. The milk solids will sink to the bottom of the pan and, if left over gentle heat, begin to brown. As the milk solids reach a toasty hazelnut colour, remove the pan from the heat. Stir in the cinnamon.

2 Preheat the oven to 200°C (400°F/Gas 6). Peel and core the apples and toss in the beurre noisette and cinnamon. Place the apples in a muffin tray and cook in the oven for 30–45 minutes until they are soft, turning and basting once. Allow to cool.

3 Make the filo baskets by melting the rest of the butter and using it to butter 4 holes of a muffin tin. Unroll the filo pastry and keep covered with a damp tea towel. Cut the filo into 15cm (6in) squares, big enough to line the holes of the muffin tin with a bit of an overlap. Brush the squares with butter and dust with icing sugar. Take one square and overlap with another square placed diagonally on top, so you end up with a star shape. Press this shape gently into the muffin tin. Repeat with the remaining pastry to make 4 baskets. Bake for about 5 minutes until golden. Allow to cool.

4 Simmer the raspberries in a pan with 2 tbsp water and the golden caster sugar for 5–10 minutes until softened. Add the vanilla extract, and allow to cool. Save some raspberries for decoration and liquidize the rest, pass through a sieve and set the coulis aside.

5 Toast the oatmeal in a dry frying pan for 5–10 minutes, stirring frequently until slightly golden. Allow to cool. Stir together the apple brandy or Calvados, cider, and honey in a small jug. Softly whip the cream and fold in the brandy mix, to taste.

6 Place a filo basket on each plate. Insert a cooked apple into each basket topped with a reserved raspberry. Serve with a spoonful of the brandy cream, sprinkle with a little oatmeal, then a drizzle of raspberry coulis with more reserved raspberries.

STRAWBERRY AND "CHAMPAGNE" JELLY WITH ICE CREAM AND SHORTBREAD WAFER FANS

Dhruv Baker sales director and 2010 champion

PREPARATION TIME
1 hour 15 minutes, plus freezing

COOKING TIME
15 minutes

SERVES 4

FOR THE ICE CREAM
300ml (10fl oz) clotted cream
150ml (5fl oz) whole milk
5 egg yolks
100g (3½oz) caster sugar

FOR THE SHORTBREAD
225g (8oz) strong white flour
175g (6oz) unsalted butter
50g (1¾oz) icing sugar

FOR THE JELLY
6 leaves of gelatine
500ml (16fl oz) English sparkling wine
  or Cava

75g (2½oz) caster sugar
3 x 85g (3oz) punnets wild strawberries,
  briefly washed

FOR THE STRAWBERRY CREAM
100g (3½oz) wild strawberries, briefly
  washed and chopped
2 tsp caster sugar
2 tbsp Grand Marnier
200ml (7fl oz) double cream
finely grated zest of ½ small orange

1 Preheat the oven to 180°C (350°F/Gas 4). Heat the cream and milk in a pan until almost boiling. Whisk the egg yolks and sugar in a bowl until pale.

2 Slowly whisk in the cream mixture. Pour back into the pan and stir over low heat until the mixture coats the back of a wooden spoon. Churn in an ice-cream maker and freeze.

3 To make the shortbread, sift the flour. Cream the butter and sugar until pale and fluffy, then work in the flour to form a dough. Wrap in cling film and chill for 30 minutes.

4 Line 2 baking sheets with baking parchment. Remove the shortbread dough from the fridge and roll out on a lightly floured surface. Using a fan-shaped biscuit cutter or cutter of your choice, stamp out biscuits and place them spaced apart on the baking sheets. Chill for 5 minutes.

5 Bake the biscuits in the oven for 12–15 minutes, or until pale golden. Leave on the tray for 5 minutes to firm before transferring to a wire rack.

6 To make the jelly, soak the gelatine leaves in cold water for at least 10 minutes to soften. Pour the wine into a medium pan. Stir in the sugar and heat gently without boiling until dissolved. Lift out the gelatine, shake off the excess water, and add to the wine, stirring until dissolved. Leave to cool.

7 Pour a layer of jelly into the base of 4 tall sundae glasses. Chill until set, then put in half the strawberries. Spoon over a layer of jelly and chill until set. Repeat the layers so that the glasses are just over half full, ending with a jelly layer.

8 Remove the ice cream from the freezer and allow to soften at room temperature for about 15–20 minutes.

9 To make the cream, sprinkle the strawberries with sugar and Grand Marnier and leave to macerate for 15 minutes. Whip the cream until soft peaks form, then fold in the strawberry mixture and orange zest.

10 To serve, scoop a ball of ice cream on top of the jellies and swirl strawberry cream on top. Push the wafers lightly into the cream and serve immediately.

MASTER TIP
WILD STRAWBERRIES

Also known as *fraises des bois*, these are found both in the wild and cultivated. Their tiny, fragile red or white fruit has an exquisitely fragrant taste. Use in tarts or as a special dessert. Ripe strawberries are highly perishable, so use quickly.

MAIN

CHICKEN AND MUSHROOM "PIE" p.142

"This pie is lovely! The strong, meaty morels match the chicken beautifully and it's soft, creamy and lovely. I think it's delicious." GREGG

STARTER

MACKEREL TARTARE AND SMOKED MACKEREL
PATÉ, WITH CUCUMBER PAPARDELLE p.68

"David is a talented chef, and this has great
flavour combinations, especially using pickle
with raw fish. Very clever indeed." MICHEL

DESSERT

RICE CRISPIE CAKE WITH
CHOCOLATE MOUSSE, CHERRY SORBET,
AND CHERRIES IN KIRSCH p.268

"I enjoyed this. Chocolate
with cherries steeped in
booze and crunchy toffee
bits at the bottom was
lovely. Visually it lacked
elegance but it tasted
absolutely great!"
GREGG

RICE CRISPIE CAKE WITH CHOCOLATE MOUSSE, CHERRY SORBET, AND CHERRIES IN KIRSCH

David Coulson head chef and 2010 Professionals finalist

PREPARATION TIME
50 minutes, plus freezing

SERVES 4

FOR THE SORBET
100g (3½oz) caster sugar
400g jar of griotines or 390g jar of
 black cherries in Kirsch

FOR THE CAKE
50g (1¾oz) plain chocolate
 (68% cocoa solids)
30g (1oz) rice crispies
1 tbsp golden syrup
100g (3½oz) condensed milk
1 packet of crackle crystals

FOR THE MOUSSE
75g (2½oz) plain chocolate
 (68% cocoa solids)
2 eggs, separated
100ml (3½fl oz) double cream

FOR THE POACHING SYRUP
150ml (5fl oz) reserved Kirsch syrup
 from the jar of cherries
1 tbsp caster sugar
1 star anise
1 cinnamon stick

GREGG WALLACE
"I think it
tastes great."

1 To make the sorbet, put the sugar in a saucepan with 100ml (3½fl oz) of water, gently heat to dissolve the sugar, then boil for 1 minute to make a stock syrup. Drain the jar of cherries. Set aside 4 cherries and reserve the Kirsch syrup for poaching them.
2 Add the remaining cherries to the stock syrup and blend in a liquidizer or food processor until smooth. Pour into an ice-cream maker and churn. Transfer to a suitable container and freeze.
3 To make the cake, melt the chocolate in a glass bowl set over a pan of simmering water. Stir in the rice crispies, syrup, and condensed milk and add the crackle crystals. Divide the crispie cake between 4 glass dessert dishes and set aside, but not in the fridge.
4 For the mousse, melt the chocolate and stir in the egg yolks. Softly whip the cream and fold into the chocolate mix. Beat the egg whites until stiff and fold into the mix until well combined. Spoon the mousse into the glasses on top of the crispie mixture.
5 Put the reserved Kirsch in a pan and stir in the sugar. Add the reserved cherries, the star anise, and the cinnamon stick. Simmer for 5 minutes. Remove the cherries and spices with a slotted spoon and reduce the sauce to a syrup. Reserve the cherries and discard the spices.
6 To finish, use a melonball scoop to put a small scoop of the sorbet on top of the mousse and decorate with a poached cherry. Serve immediately and with the syrup in a jug alongside.

GOOSEBERRY AND ELDERFLOWER SYLLABUB WITH ALMOND DAQUOISE BISCUITS

Tim Kinnaird paediatrician and 2010 finalist

PREPARATION TIME
30 minutes

COOKING TIME
15–20 minutes

SERVES 4

100g (3½oz) gooseberries, topped and tailed
60ml (2fl oz) elderflower syrup or cordial
2 egg yolks
100g (3½oz) caster sugar
½ vanilla pod, split, seeds scraped out and reserved (see MasterTip, p.256)
240ml (8fl oz) double cream
grated zest of 1 unwaxed lemon

2 tbsp dessert wine such as Brown Brothers Orange Muscat and Flora
2 egg whites

FOR THE BISCUITS
50g (1¾oz) ground almonds
1 tbsp cornflour
100g (3½oz) caster sugar
1 egg white
icing sugar, to dust

GREGG WALLACE

"It's sweet, but just sweet enough. It's sharp, but just sharp enough. Yummy."

1 Put the gooseberries in a small saucepan, add the elderflower syrup or cordial, and stew gently on medium heat for 10 minutes, or until soft. Set aside and leave to cool while you make the syllabub.

2 Put the egg yolks and 50g (1¾oz) sugar in a medium bowl and whisk until thick and creamy. This will take about 10–15 minutes using an electric whisk, but longer with a rotary or balloon whisk. Add the vanilla seeds to the whisked eggs and sugar. Pour in the double cream and whisk again until thick and creamy, but not stiff. Add the lemon zest and wine and whisk again to combine.

3 In a separate bowl, whisk the egg whites until they form soft peaks, then whisk in the remaining sugar. Gently fold the whisked egg whites and sugar into the cream mixture and combine thoroughly. Spoon the syllabub evenly into 4 martini glasses and put in the fridge.

4 To make the biscuits, preheat the oven to 150°C (300°F/Gas 2) and line a baking tray with baking parchment. Have ready a large food piping bag fitted with a plain nozzle. Put the almonds, cornflour, and 50g (1¾oz) of the sugar in a medium bowl. Stir together until all the ingredients have combined.

5 In a separate bowl, whisk the egg white until it forms stiff peaks. Slowly whisk in the remaining sugar. Fold the dry ingredients into the whisked egg white mixture, making sure they are well combined.

6 Spoon the mixture into the piping bag and pipe 8 sticks 7.5cm (3in) long onto the baking tray. Bake for 15–20 minutes until lightly golden. Remove from the oven, leave to cool on the tray until firm, then dust with icing sugar and carefully remove from the tray. Serve the gooseberry syllabub with the biscuits.

APPLE AND GINGER TART WITH RUBY GRAPEFRUIT SABAYON

Christine Hamilton TV personality and 2010 Celebrity finalist

FOR THE BASE
25g (scant 1oz) plain flour
15g (½oz) butter
4 amaretti biscuits

FOR THE TOPPING
15g (½oz) butter
2 pieces of preserved stem ginger,
  finely chopped
2 Granny Smith apples
25g (scant 1oz) light soft brown sugar
½ tsp ground cinnamon
apricot jam, melted, to glaze

FOR THE SABAYON
1 egg yolk
2 tsp caster sugar
3 tbsp blood orange or ruby
  grapefruit juice
juice of 1 lemon

TO DECORATE
ground cinnamon
4 physalis

PREPARATION TIME
50 minutes

COOKING TIME
25 minutes

SERVES 4

1 Preheat the oven to 180°C (350°F/Gas 4). Lightly grease four 6cm (2½in) ring moulds and place on a greased baking sheet. To make the base, rub the flour and butter together until a fine breadcrumbs texture is achieved. Crush the amaretti biscuits in a mortar with the pestle and stir into the flour and butter. Press the mixture well into the ring moulds.

2 For the topping, melt the butter in a small saucepan. Sprinkle the ginger over the base. Peel, core, quarter, and finely slice the apples. Fan them out on top of the ginger and brush generously with the melted butter. Mix the sugar and cinnamon together and sprinkle on top. Bake for 20 minutes. Brush with the melted apricot jam and return to the oven for 5 minutes. Allow to cool.

3 To make the sabayon, whisk together the egg yolk and sugar in a heatproof bowl. Slowly add the fruit juices and continue to whisk until frothy. Sit the bowl on a pan of simmering water and continue whisking until the sauce thickens.

4 Serve the tarts in a pool of sabayon lightly sprinkled with cinnamon. Garnish with physalis.

JOHN TORODE "That dessert is fantastic. Crunchy at the bottom and then that cloud of sabayon sitting underneath. I think it's brilliant."

MASTER TIP
PHYSALIS

Also known as Cape gooseberries, physalis fruits are juicy with tiny seeds, and have a lively sweet-tart taste. They can be eaten raw, poached, or preserved. Ripe fruits will have straw-coloured husks and should look firm and waxy with no bruising.

WENSLEYDALE AND APPLE PUDDING WITH A 17TH-CENTURY POSSET AND CARAMELIZED WALNUTS

Dick Strawbridge TV presenter and 2010 Celebrity finalist

PREPARATION TIME
50 minutes

COOKING TIME
50–60 minutes

SERVES 8

115g (4oz) butter
115g (4oz) caster sugar
2 eggs, beaten
140g (5oz) self-raising flour
550g (1¼lb) Bramley, Cox, and Russet
  apples, peeled, cored, and chopped
115g (4oz) walnuts, chopped
225g (8oz) Wensleydale cheese,
  crumbled
icing sugar, to dust

FOR THE POSSET
4 eggs
600ml (1 pint) double cream
1 cinnamon stick
¼ tsp grated nutmeg
150ml (5fl oz) Madeira
  or Marsala wine
85g (3oz) caster sugar

MASTER TIP
WENSLEYDALE CHEESE

Wensleydale is one of Britain's oldest cheeses. It has a dense yet flaky texture, and a subtle wild-honey flavour balanced by refreshing acidity. Wensleydale compliments sweet dishes, and in Yorkshire, they like to pair the cheese with a slice of apple pie.

1 Preheat the oven to 180°C (350°F/Gas 4) and grease and line a 23–25cm (9–10in) diameter cake tin.

2 Using an electric beater, whisk the butter and sugar in a large bowl until light and fluffy. Continuing to beat, gradually add the eggs to the mixture. Fold in the self-raising flour, followed by the apples, walnuts, and cheese.

3 Transfer the mixture to the cake tin and cook for 50–60 minutes, or until a skewer inserted in the top of the sponge comes out clean. Leave the cake to cool, then turn it out of the tin.

4 To make the posset, beat the eggs and pour into a large saucepan. Heat the cream with the cinnamon and nutmeg in a separate saucepan until just boiling. Strain the cream into a clean pan and then, stirring continuously, gradually add to the eggs. Stand over a low heat and continue to stir constantly until the sauce thickens.

5 In a separate saucepan, heat the Madeira or Marsala and sugar until just boiling and the sugar has dissolved. Add the cream and eggs sauce and stir to mix.

6 Cut the cake into wedges and serve with the posset poured around the plate.

APPLE, VANILLA, AND BAY LEAF TARTE TATIN WITH CALVADOS CREAM

Alex Rushmer freelance writer and 2010 finalist

3 sweet apples, such as Braeburn or Pink Lady
50g (1¾oz) unsalted butter
50g (1¾oz) caster sugar
2 star anise
2 bay leaves

1 cinnamon stick
1 vanilla pod, split (see MasterTip, p.256)
250g (9oz) ready-made puff pastry
150ml (5fl oz) double cream
1–2 tsp Calvados

PREPARATION TIME
15 minutes

COOKING TIME
20–25 minutes

SERVES 4–6

1 Preheat the oven to 180°C (350°F/Gas 4). Peel, core, and slice the apples into eighths.
2 Cube the butter and melt it in a 20cm (8in) diameter, heavy ovenproof pan. Then add the sugar and continuously stir until it begins to turn golden brown and caramelize. Add the star anise, bay leaves, cinnamon, and vanilla pod and stir together. Lay the apples in a single layer over the caramel and turn to coat. Cook over low-medium heat for 5 minutes.
3 Roll out the pastry slightly larger than the diameter of the pan and cut out a circle. Remove the pan from the heat and place the pastry on the apples, tucking it down the sides of the fruit.
4 Cook in the oven for 20–25 minutes, or until the apples are soft and the pastry is nicely browned. Carefully turn out onto a waiting plate and leave to cool. Before serving, remove the spices and discard.
5 Whip the cream, stir in a generous dribble of Calvados, and serve with a slice of the tarte Tatin.

GREGG WALLACE

"Cor! Sweet apple, bags of vanilla, hint of cinnamon. I really like that."

MASALA TEA ICE CREAM AND SPICED SAUTERNES-POACHED PEAR WITH A CHOCOLATE TRUFFLE

Dhruv Baker sales director and 2010 champion

PREPARATION TIME
1 hour 20 minutes

COOKING TIME
40 minutes

SERVES 4

FOR THE MASALA
6 black peppercorns
5 cloves
5 green cardamom pods
2 cinnamon sticks
1 tsp dried ginger
½ tsp finely grated nutmeg

FOR THE ICE CREAM
250ml (8fl oz) whole milk
1 tsp Ceylon tea leaves
250ml (8fl oz) double cream
4 egg yolks
50g (1¾oz) caster sugar

FOR THE PEARS
4 Comice pears, peeled and cored
  but stalks left intact

400ml (14fl oz) Sauternes dessert wine
1 vanilla pod, split
1 star anise
2 cinnamon sticks

FOR THE TRUFFLES
35g (1¼oz) dark chocolate (at least
  90% cocoa solids)
50g (1¾oz) dark chocolate
  (75% cocoa solids)
25g (scant 1oz) caster sugar
85ml (3fl oz) double cream
2–3 tbsp brandy
cocoa powder, for dusting

TO DECORATE
1 sheet gold leaf (optional)

1 For the masala, put the whole spices into a dry frying pan and roast over medium heat for 2 minutes, or until they begin to release their aromas. Tip into a pestle and pound with a mortar or, if you have one, grind to a powder in a spice machine. Sift into a bowl and set aside.
2 To make the ice cream, heat the milk with the tea leaves and ½ tsp of the masala mixture in a saucepan. Gradually bring to the boil. Stir in the cream and bring to a simmer for 1 minute. Leave to cool, then chill.
3 Whisk the egg yolks and sugar until pale. Strain the masala tea milk and gradually stir about a third into the egg yolks. Pour in the remainder and transfer to a pan. Stirring continuously, cook over low heat until the custard coats the back of a spoon. Take the pan off the heat and leave until cold. Churn in an ice-cream maker and freeze.
4 For the pears, cut a thin slice from the base of each pear so they sit evenly. Place the wine, vanilla pod, and spices in a pan with 300ml (10fl oz) water and bring to the boil. Add the pears, reduce the heat, and poach gently for 30 minutes or until very soft. Check after 20 minutes that the pears are not collapsing. Allow to cool, then chill.

5 Put all the truffle ingredients, except the cocoa powder, and adding the brandy to taste, into a bowl set over a pan of simmering water and allow to melt. Stir gently, then leave until cold enough to mould. Using 2 spoons or your hands, shape truffles, coat with cocoa, and set aside.
6 Remove the ice cream from the freezer about 15 minutes before serving. Lift the pears from their cooking liquor. Strain this liquor into a clean pan and reduce until syrupy.
7 To serve, sit 1 pear on each of 4 plates together with a truffle and a quenelle of ice cream. Decorate the pear with a little gold leaf (if using) and dust on some extra cocoa powder.

GREGG WALLACE "That is delicious. There is almost a pepper flavour in that ice cream. When that's gone, you've got the juiciness of the pear. When that cleans your palate out, you are left with the sticky cocoa of that wonderful chocolate. That is brilliant."

PEAR AND VANILLA SPONGE WITH DARK CHOCOLATE SAUCE

Ben Piette hospitality chef and 2010 Professionals semi-finalist

50g (1¾oz) marzipan
2 ripe pears, about 250g (9oz),
 peeled, cored, and diced
1 tbsp sugar

FOR THE SPONGE
115g (4oz) butter, softened
115g (4oz) caster sugar
1 vanilla pod, split, seeds
 scraped out and reserved
2 eggs
125g (4½oz) self-raising flour

1 tbsp honey, warmed
2 tbsp flaked almonds

FOR THE SAUCE
50g (1¾oz) dark chocolate
 (at least 60% cocoa solids)
50g (1¾oz) unsalted butter
50g (1¾oz) light brown sugar
50g (1¾oz) double cream

TO DECORATE
100g (3½oz) clotted cream
handful of mint

PREPARATION TIME
25 minutes

COOKING TIME
30 minutes, plus cooling

SERVES 4

1 Preheat the oven to 190°C (375°F/Gas 5). Grease 4 dariole pudding moulds with butter and line the bases with a circle of greaseproof paper. Roll out the marzipan thinly and cut into 4 circles the same size as the dariole moulds.

2 Simmer the pears with the sugar and 1 tablespoon water over low to medium heat for 5–10 minutes until softened. Drain excess moisture through a sieve. Reserve half the pear and push the rest through a sieve into a clean bowl to make a purée.

3 For the sponge, cream the butter, sugar, and vanilla seeds together until light and fluffy. Gradually beat in the eggs, then sift in the flour and fold in.

4 Spoon half the sponge mixture between the pudding moulds. Top with a circle of marzipan, the reserved pear and the pear purée, then top with the remaining sponge mixture. The moulds should be no more than half full.

5 Place the moulds on a baking tray and bake in the oven for 15–20 minutes until golden and a skewer comes out clean. Leave to cool in the moulds for 5 minutes, then run a knife round the edge and turn them out. Brush the tops with honey and sprinkle with almonds.

6 To make the sauce, place the chocolate, butter, sugar, and cream in a saucepan. Bring to the boil and whisk continuously until the chocolate has melted.

7 To serve, place a sponge on each plate and pool the sauce around it. Decorate with a quenelle of clotted cream and a sprig of mint.

MASTER TIP
CLOTTED CREAM

A traditional delicacy from the West Country, clotted cream is a rich, thick-textured, and slightly sweet treat, varying from pale to golden cream. Made by heating cow's cream, it has a high fat content of 55–60 per cent. Qashtah and kaymak are similar products from the Middle East.

MasterChef 2010 Finalist
TIM KINNAIRD

"I tried to choose dishes that reflected what I'd learnt during the programme and how far I'd come. I thought about the time of year and the seasons, and I used a couple of extra-special ingredients including quince and squash grown in our garden at home. I was a bit overwhelmed by John and Gregg's comments about my main course, but my favourite dish was the dessert. I adore the combination of coffee and chestnut. The day of the final was such a special moment in time. Everything changed at that point, and life will never be the same."

MAIN

ROASTED PHEASANT WITH POMMES ANNA, CARROTS, BREAD SAUCE, AND SLOE JELLY p.218

"This dish set my toes on fire. The flavour that bursts out of the jellies, with a little bit of fruitiness and spiciness, is just a delight."
GREGG

STARTER

OPEN LASAGNE OF ROASTED SQUASH AND WILD MUSHROOMS WITH SAGE BUTTER p.36

"Tim is a brilliant cook, and this dish is elegant, sophisticated and really moreish. The sweet pumpkin with woody mushrooms and sage is just lovely."
JOHN

DESSERT

MONT BLANC WITH COFFEE-POACHED PEAR p.280

"For Tim to deliver this dessert in the final was incredible, the skill and thought that went into it was extraordinary and showed just how far he'd come." JOHN

MONT BLANC WITH COFFEE-POACHED PEAR
Tim Kinnaird paediatrician and 2010 finalist

PREPARATION TIME
50 minutes

COOKING TIME
45 minutes

SERVES 4

250ml (8fl oz) fresh coffee
3 William or Packham pears
400ml (14fl oz) double cream
435g can unsweetened chestnut purée
50g (1¾oz) icing sugar, or to taste
200g (7oz) blackberries
1–2 tbsp caster sugar

FOR THE MERINGUES
2 egg whites
100g (3½oz) caster sugar
50g (1¾oz) ground almonds
1 tbsp cornflour

GREGG WALLACE "That is stunning. It is sweet, but not too sweet. There is just the hint of almond in there as well. And all that lovely, sweet juice. Fantastic."

1 For the meringue, preheat the oven to 160°C (325°F/Gas 3) and line 2 baking sheets with non-stick baking parchment. Whisk the egg whites to soft peaks in a clean bowl. Whisk in half the sugar, a spoonful at a time, whisking well between each addition to form a smooth, glossy meringue. Carefully fold in the remaining sugar with the almonds and cornflour.

2 Spread the meringue in a thin layer measuring about 28 x 14cm (11 x 5½in) on one of the baking sheets. Cook for 10 minutes or until beginning to firm. Using a 7cm (2¾in) square cutter, stamp out 8 meringues and place on the second baking sheet. Return to the oven for 10–15 minutes, or until the meringues are dry and crisp.

3 Heat the coffee in a saucepan. Peel and core the pears and slice them into thick chip-shaped batons. Poach in the coffee for 6–8 minutes (firm pears may take up to 10 minutes) or until soft, but still retaining their shape. Leave to cool.

4 Meanwhile, whip the double cream to soft peaks and fold in the chestnut purée and icing sugar to taste. Chill until required.

5 Just before serving, push about half of the blackberries through a sieve set over a small pan. Stir in the sugar and dissolve it over a low heat, ensuring the juice doesn't come to the boil or it will become jam-like in consistency. Drain the pears and discard the coffee.

6 To serve, sandwich the meringues with the chestnut filling and place on 4 serving plates. Decorate with a blackberry and arrange a stack of pear batons to one side with more blackberries placed over them. Drizzle the plates with a little sweetened blackberry juice.

Note The chestnut filling makes more than you need for the meringue. It will freeze for another time. Simply stir in 1 teaspoon of cornflour to stabilize it and to prevent it from splitting on thawing.

PEAR TATIN WITH STILTON ICE CREAM AND WALNUT AND TOBACCO BRITTLE

Alex Rushmer freelance writer and 2010 finalist

PREPARATION TIME
40 minutes, plus freezing

COOKING TIME
1 hour 25 minutes

SERVES 4

FOR THE ICE CREAM
½ vanilla pod, split, seeds scraped out, and reserved with the pod (see MasterTip, p.256)
160ml (5½fl oz) double cream
1.5 litres (2¾ pints) milk
2 egg yolks
35g (1oz) caster sugar
50g (1¾oz) Stilton cheese, chopped
pickled walnuts, chopped

FOR THE TATIN
4 pears, peeled
100g (3½oz) caster sugar
100g (3½oz) unsalted butter, cubed
4 star anise
250g (9oz) ready-made puff pastry

FOR THE BRITTLE
100g (3½oz) caster sugar
pinch of smoky tobacco such as Drum
25g (scant 1oz) dried walnuts, finely chopped

JOHN TORODE

"That pear inside the pastry: sticky and sweet. And the flavour of that rich tobacco inside the caramel and walnuts is absolutely delicious. But blue cheese? Please no."

1 Place the vanilla pod and seeds in a pan with the cream and milk. Slowly bring to the boil, then remove from the heat and, leave to infuse for 5 minutes. Meanwhile, whisk the egg yolks together with the sugar until pale and creamy. Strain the cream and milk into the egg yolks, whisking all the time. Return to the pan and heat gently, stirring, until the custard is thick enough to coat the back of a spoon. Stir in the cheese, then churn in an ice-cream maker, and freeze.

2 Preheat the oven to 190°C (375°F/Gas 5). Remove the narrowed part of the pears to make neat spheres, then core them. Heat the sugar in a dry pan until it is a pale caramel colour. Pour into 10cm (4in) metal ring moulds or individual tart tins, divide the butter between them, then add a star anise and pear to each. Place on a baking tray and bake in the oven for 20 minutes.

3 Roll out the puff pastry to 5mm (¼in) thick, then cut into four 12cm (5in) rounds. Prick with a fork. Remove the pears from the oven and add the pastry lids, tucking the sides of the pastry down inside the tins. Cook for a further 15–20 minutes until the pastry is golden brown.

4 To make the walnut brittle, heat the sugar with 3 tbsp water and add the tobacco. Leave to infuse for 20 minutes. Strain, then boil hard to create the caramel. Add the walnuts to the caramel and turn out onto a silicone mat. Spread thinly and allow to harden slightly before cutting into strips, or breaking into shards.

5 To serve, turn the tarts out onto 4 plates, then add a spoonful of ice cream. Top the ice cream with a shard of brittle and decorate the plate with some chopped pickled walnuts. Serve immediately.

BAKED PEARS IN WINE WITH AN ORANGE AND WALNUT CREAM

Alex Fletcher actress and 2010 Celebrity quarter-finalist

PREPARATION TIME
30 minutes

COOKING TIME
50 minutes

SERVES 4

4 pears with good stems strip of peel and juice of 1 orange
125g (4½oz) light soft brown sugar
300ml (10fl oz) fruity white wine
1 vanilla pod, split, seeds scraped out and reserved
100g (3½oz) peeled walnut halves

FOR THE CREAM
125g (4½oz) mascarpone cheese
50g (1¾oz) peeled walnut halves, crushed
juice of 1 orange, plus grated zest
approx. 2 tsp light soft brown sugar

GREGG WALLACE

"That's got an almost toffiness from the nuts, and the pears are giving loads of juice. Lovely."

1 Preheat the oven 220°C (425°F/Gas 7). Peel the pears and place in a tight-fitting ovenproof pan. Pour the orange juice over the pears and then add the sugar, wine, orange peel, and vanilla pod and seeds and bring to the boil.

2 Sprinkle half the walnuts over the pears and cook in the oven for about 30 minutes, or until the pears are soft. Remove and allow to cool while you roast the remaining walnuts for 5 minutes on a baking tray, taking care not to burn them.

3 Remove the pears from the juice with a slotted spoon and set aside. Sieve the juice, letting it drain into a clean pan. Discard the orange peel and vanilla pod and set aside the walnuts. Bring the juice to the boil and reduce by half to a syrup. Return the walnuts to the syrup and stir to coat.

4 To make the orange and walnut cream, beat the mascarpone cheese to soften, then gradually stir in the orange juice and walnuts until smooth. Sweeten to taste.

5 To serve, place each pear on a plate with some of the orange and walnut cream, drizzle the syrup around and over the pear, and sprinkle a little orange zest over the cream.

FLAVOUR COMBINATION
WALNUT AND ORANGE

Orange naturally stimulates bigger flavour in every fruit and nut from banana to mango, peanut to Brazil nut. Combining orange with roasted walnuts gives an array of complementary but edgy flavours and tastes that are then calmed and made noble by the richness of the mascarpone.

CARAMELIZED PEAR AND ROSEMARY TARTE TATIN WITH STAR ANISE ICE CREAM

Lee Groves head chef and 2010 Professionals semi-finalist

200g (7oz) caster sugar
2 sprigs of rosemary, leaves picked
200g (7oz) unsalted butter
4–6 semi-ripe William pears, approx.
  750g (1lb 10oz) in total, peeled, cored,
  and cut into neat quarters
6 sheets filo pastry
100g (3½oz) butter, melted
2 tbsp icing sugar

FOR THE ICE CREAM
8 whole star anise
170ml (6fl oz) double cream
170ml (6fl oz) milk
1 vanilla pod, split, seeds scraped out
  and reserved (see MasterTip, p.256)
4 large egg yolks
70g (2¼oz) caster sugar

PREPARATION TIME
35 minutes, plus cooling, churning,
  and freezing

COOKING TIME
45 minutes

SERVES 4

1 To make the ice cream, coarsely crush the star anise using a pestle and mortar. Put the anise, cream, milk, and vanilla pods and seeds into a saucepan and bring to the boil. Take the pan off the heat and leave to infuse for 15 minutes.

2 Whisk the egg yolks and sugar in a large bowl until light and creamy. Gradually pour the cream mixture onto the eggs and whisk. Pour into a clean pan and stir over medium heat (do not allow the mixture to boil), until the cream coats the back of a wooden spoon.

3 Strain into a clean bowl and set over ice to cool. Churn in an ice-cream maker and freeze.

4 To make the tarte Tatin, preheat the oven to 180°C (350°F/Gas 4). Heat the sugar in a heavy frying pan over medium heat, until it forms a caramel. Stir in the rosemary and butter until melted. Add the pears, coat in the caramel and cook for 2 minutes. Arrange the pears in 4 mini frying pans or ovenproof dishes small enough for a snug fit. Pour over some of the caramel.

5 Brush a sheet of filo pastry with melted butter and sprinkle with icing sugar. Put another sheet on top and repeat until all 6 sheets have been used.

6 Cut the pile of filo pastry into quarters. Take one of the quarters and lay it on top of the pears in one of the pans or dishes, tucking in the edges like a blanket. Repeat with the remaining filo and pears. Bake for 10–15 minutes, until the pastry is golden and crisp and the pears have slightly softened.

7 Remove from the oven and turn out onto 4 serving plates. Place a neat ball of ice cream in the middle of each tart and serve.

GREGG WALLACE

"Good flavours. You've got juicy pear and sticky caramel, and that star anise ice cream is very nice."

CINNAMON SPONGE PUDDING WITH PEAR PURÉE AND HONEY AND VANILLA MASCARPONE

Daniel Howell sous chef and 2010 Professionals quarter-finalist

PREPARATION TIME
50 minutes

COOKING TIME
1 hour 10 minutes

SERVES 4-6

FOR THE SPONGE
350g (12oz) golden syrup
175y (6oz) unsalted butter, plus
  extra for greasing
175g (6oz) muscovado sugar
250g (9oz) self-raising flour
1 tbsp ground cinnamon
225ml (8fl oz) milk
3 large eggs, lightly beaten

FOR THE PURÉE
4 large pears, peeled and diced
50g (1¾oz) unsalted butter
200g (7oz) caster sugar, or to taste

FOR THE MASCARPONE
250g (9oz) mascarpone cheese
1–2 tbsp clear honey, or to taste
1 vanilla pod, split, seeds scraped out
  and reserved

1 Preheat the oven to 180°C (350°F/Gas 4). Butter a baking dish measuring about 25 × 18cm (10 × 7in) and 6cm (2½in) deep.
2 Prepare the mix for the sponge by putting the syrup, butter, and sugar in a saucepan and heating over medium-low heat until melted.
3 In a large bowl, sift together the flour and ground cinnamon. Mix in the milk and beaten egg, then stir in the melted ingredients. Do not worry about a few lumps as these will disappear during cooking.
4 Once the mix is prepared, fill the baking dish and place it in the oven for 45 minutes, or until the sponge is just firm to the touch and a skewer inserted in the middle comes out clean.
5 Meanwhile, tip the diced pear into a saucepan with the butter and cook gently over medium heat for 10–15 minutes, or until softened (this will depend on the ripeness of the pears). Stir in caster sugar to taste, then pass the mixture through a sieve to make a purée.
6 Beat the mascarpone lightly and fold in honey to taste and the seeds from the vanilla pod.
7 Serve the warm sponge with the warm pear purée and cold mascarpone cream alongside.

QUINCE POACHED IN ROSEWATER

Dick Strawbridge TV presenter and 2010 Celebrity finalist

FOR THE QUINCE
4 tbsp rosewater
115g (4oz) caster sugar
4 quince, peeled and sliced

FOR THE SHORTBREAD
175g (6oz) plain flour
115g (4oz) butter, softened

50g (1¾oz) caster sugar
finely grated zest of 1 lemon
1 tsp poppy seeds

FOR THE ELDERFLOWER CREAM
300ml (10fl oz) double cream
3 tbsp elderflower cordial
icing sugar, to taste (optional)

PREPARATION TIME
30 minutes

COOKING TIME
55 minutes

SERVES 4

1 For the poached quince, put the rosewater and sugar in a shallow saucepan with 100ml (3½fl oz) of water. Bring the syrup to the boil then add the quince in a single layer. Reduce the heat and allow the quince to cook for 30–35 minutes, or until tender. Leave to cool in the syrup.
2 For the shortbread, preheat the oven to 160°C (325°F/Gas 3) and line a baking sheet with baking parchment. Put the flour, butter, and sugar in a blender or food processor and mix briefly on pulse setting. Tip into a bowl and add the lemon and poppy seeds. Bring the mixture together into a ball.
3 Roll out the shortbread mix to a thickness of about 5mm (¼in) and, using a 7.5cm (3in) diameter fluted round cutter, stamp out rounds. Gather together the offcuts and roll again to make more rounds. Place the biscuits, a little spaced apart, on the baking sheet and cook for 15–20 minutes, or until pale golden. Leave to cool on the tray for a few minutes and then transfer to a wire rack.
4 For the elderflower cream, mix together the cream and elderflower cordial in a bowl. Taste and add the icing sugar if desired. Whip until the cream forms soft peaks.
5 Divide the quince between 4 bowls, add spoonfuls of the elderflower cream, and serve with the shortbread biscuits alongside.

GREGG WALLACE
"This is Dick at his best, nothing wild. Beautiful simplicity. Just wonderful flavour combinations."

FLAVOUR COMBINATION

ROSES AND QUINCE
Start with quinces so highly perfumed they scent a room. Sniff deeply and you'll discover rose among their compelling fragrance; and rosewater is the distilled essence of the most fragrant red roses. Thus quinces and roses are a perfect combination, something cooks in the Middle East have known about for a long time.

GREEN TEA AND LEMON DELICE

Tim Kinnaird paediatrician and 2010 finalist

PREPARATION TIME
1 hour, plus chilling

COOKING TIME
1 hour

SERVES 4

2 tbsp cooking grade matcha powder,
 plus extra for soaking and garnish
50g (1¾oz) plain flour
2 eggs, separated
160g (5¾oz) caster sugar, plus 1 tbsp
fresh raspberries, to decorate

FOR THE LEMON CURD
2 leaves of gelatine
2 eggs
3 egg yolks
110g (3¾oz) caster sugar
grated zest and juice of 2½ lemons
100g (3½oz) unsalted butter

FOR THE WHITE CHOCOLATE MOUSSE
2 leaves of gelatine
100ml (3½fl oz) milk

seeds of 8 green cardamom pods,
 crushed
3 bay leaves
200g (7oz) white chocolate
300ml (10fl oz) double cream
3 egg whites

FOR THE CHOCOLATE MOUSSE CUBES
3 medium egg whites
100g (3½oz) caster sugar
225g (8oz) dark chocolate
 (70% cocoa solids)
450ml (15fl oz) double cream

FOR THE WHITE CHOCOLATE SAUCE
100g (3½oz) white chocolate
200ml (7fl oz) double cream

GREEN CARDAMOM

Cardamom is the fruit of a
large, perennial bush that
grows wild in the rainforests of
the Western Ghats in southern
India. Green pods from Kerala
are considered to be the best.
Cardamom enhances both
sweet and savoury flavours.
Look for hard, plump, and
green pods, with dark brown or
black seeds that feel sticky.

1 Preheat the oven to 180°C (350°F/Gas 4) and oil a 20cm (8in) square
cake tin. Sieve the matcha and flour together. Whisk the egg whites
with 30g (1oz) sugar until stiff and glossy, then the egg yolks with 30g
(1oz) sugar until thick and pale. Fold the whites into the yolks, then
fold in the flour and matcha. Pour into the tin and bake in the oven for
10–12 minutes until the sponge is firm to a gentle touch. Using ½ tsp
matcha and 90ml (3fl oz) water, make tea and sweeten with 1 tbsp
sugar. Remove the sponge from the oven and soak it with the tea.
2 For the lemon curd, soak the gelatine in cold water for 10 minutes.
Add the eggs, egg yolks, sugar, and lemon juice and zest to a pan
and whisk over low heat until the mixture is hot and just starting to
thicken. Remove from the heat. Squeeze the water out of the softened
gelatine and stir in until dissolved. Over very low heat, whisk in the
butter in 2 stages and cook for 5 minutes, taking care not to let it boil,
until thickened. Allow to cool, then pour on top of the sponge.
3 For the mousse, soak the gelatine as before. Simmer the milk with
the cardamom seeds and bay leaves for 5 minutes, then leave to
infuse for 10 minutes. Melt the chocolate in a bowl placed over a pan
of simmering water, making sure the bowl is clear of the water. Whip
the cream to form soft peaks, then whip the egg whites to form stiff
peaks. Sieve the milk, warm it again, and stir in the gelatine, off the

heat, until dissolved. Add to the chocolate and stir to combine. Pour the chocolate on to the egg whites and fold in, then fold in the cream. Pour on to the lemon layer and chill for at least 5 hours until set.

4 For the cubes, whisk the egg whites with the sugar until glossy and at soft peak stage. Melt the chocolate as before and stir in 300ml (10fl oz) cream. Whisk the remaining cream to form soft peaks. Fold the meringue and then the cream into the chocolate mix. Pour into a 15cm (6in) square tin and refrigerate for at least 2 hours or until set.

5 In a small pan, heat 100g (3½oz) sugar over gentle heat until deep golden brown. Pour onto a sheet of greased foil on a baking sheet and spread thinly, using an oiled palette knife. Once it is semi-set, use a pizza wheel cutter to cut neat squares of caramel. To make the sauce, melt the chocolate with the cream in a bowl over simmering water.

6 To assemble, layer the caramel squares with the raspberries and the sauce on one side of each plate. Place a square of delice on the other side and a smaller square of chocolate mousse alongside. Make a thick paste with water and matcha and brush onto the plate next to the delice.

SPICED PLUM CRUMBLE
Stacie Stewart PA and 2010 semi-finalist

50g (1¾oz) plain flour
50g (1¾oz) demerara sugar
75g (2½oz) butter, softened
50g (1¾oz) ground almonds
50g (1¾oz) small oats
5–6 dark plums, halved and stoned
1 vanilla pod

1½ tbsp caster sugar
1 star anise
generous grating of nutmeg
1 cinnamon stick
3 tbsp red wine
2 tbsp golden syrup
250g tub mascarpone cream

PREPARATION TIME
25 minutes

COOKING TIME
50 minutes

SERVES 4

1 Preheat the oven to 190°C (375°F/Gas 5). For the topping, rub the flour, demerara sugar, 50g (1¾oz) of the butter, and almonds together until the mixture resembles crumbs, then mix in the oats.

2 Fry the plums in a saucepan in the remaining butter until soft. Halve the vanilla pod and reserve the seeds. Add the caster sugar, 1½ tablespoons of water, spices, vanilla pod, and half the seeds, and stir. Add the wine and syrup, and reduce until the plums are slightly soft.

3 Drain the plums, discarding the cinnamon stick and star anise, and reduce the sauce until syrupy. Put the plums in an ovenproof dish, spread the crumble evenly on top, and bake for 30–35 minutes, or until the crumble is crisp and golden. Serve with the mascarpone cream infused with the rest of the vanilla seeds.

JOHN TORODE

"Sweet on top, sour underneath, and rich with spices."

CITRUS MERINGUE TART WITH CINNAMON CREAM AND PASSION FRUIT

Christine Hamilton TV personality and 2010 Celebrity finalist

PREPARATION TIME
30 minutes

COOKING TIME
1 hour

SERVES 4

1 egg white
60g (2oz) caster sugar
½ tsp cornflour

FOR THE PASTRY
60g (2oz) butter
grated zest of 1 lime and ½ tbsp
  lime juice
85g (3oz) plain flour
30g (1oz) ground almonds
½ tbsp icing sugar
pinch of ground cinnamon

FOR THE FILLING
1 egg
40g (1¼oz) caster sugar
grated zest and juice of 1 lemon
75ml (2½fl oz) double cream

FOR DECORATION
100ml (3½fl oz) double cream
pinch and a sprinkle of ground
  cinnamon
seeds of 2 passion fruit
grated zest of 1 lime

1 Preheat the oven to 160°C (325°F/Gas 3) and line a baking tray with greaseproof paper. To make the meringues, whisk the egg white until fairly stiff, then add the caster sugar a little at a time, whisking it in well after each addition. Add the cornflour and whisk until fully incorporated and the mixture is stiff and glossy. Transfer to a piping bag and form 4 meringues, about 6cm (2½in) in diameter, by piping in a swirl on to the lined baking tray. Cook in the oven for 20 minutes, then remove and leave to cool.

2 To make the pastry, melt the butter and add the lime juice and zest, flour, almonds, icing sugar, and cinnamon. Mix together until it forms a dough, then turn it out, divide into 4, and roll out to line four 8cm (3¼in) tart tins. Chill for 30 minutes. Prick the base and sides of the dough, line with greaseproof paper and baking beans, and bake blind for 10 minutes. Remove the beans and paper and return to the oven for 5 minutes to crisp up.

3 Meanwhile, whisk together the filling ingredients and pour into the pastry cases. Bake in the oven for about 20–25 minutes. Allow to cool.

4 The cinnamon cream can either be served on the side or as a pool of cream under each tart. Place the cream in a bowl, add a pinch of cinnamon, and either whip until it just starts to thicken for a pool, or until it forms soft peaks to serve on the side.

5 To serve, place a pool or dollop of cream on each plate and sprinkle with a little extra cinnamon. Position the tarts, place a meringue on top, and decorate the plate with the passion fruit and lime zest.

Note These lemon tarts would also work well with Italian meringue piped on top. See the MasterClass on pages 292–3 for how to do this.

MAKING ITALIAN MERINGUE

Italian meringue involves adding sugar syrup, rather than granulated sugar, to the whipped egg; you will need a sugar thermometer. 250g (9oz) caster sugar and 4 egg whites makes enough to cover a 24cm (9½in) or four 6cm (2½in) tarts.

1 Whisk in the syrup

Dissolve the sugar in 75ml (2½fl oz) water over a low heat to precisely 121°C (248°F). Meanwhile, whisk the egg whites on medium until they form soft peaks. When the sugar syrup reaches the correct heat, pour into the egg whites, whisking all the time, in a thin stream.

2 Transfer when cold

Continue to whisk until the meringue is cold, with a very stiff, smooth, and satiny consistency; Italian meringue can be cooked as soon as it is cold. Transfer the meringue mixture into a piping or pastry bag fitted with a metal tip.

Start whisking the egg whites on medium speed when the syrup reaches 115°C (239°F).

Squeeze the meringue mixture towards the tip to get rid of any air pockets.

"Use a clean saucepan to prevent the syrup crystallizing, and make sure you practise your piping before attempting to decorate your dish."

3 | Pipe on the meringue

Twist off the loose end of the bag then, squeezing with one hand, pipe the meringue over the surface of the tart in an attractive pattern. You may find it easier to hold the tip end with your other hand to keep it steady.

4 | Brown the top

Italian meringue is far easier and quicker to cook than traditional meringue. Simply place under a preheated grill for a few minutes to lightly brown the top.

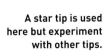

A star tip is used here but experiment with other tips.

SAUCY LEMON PUDDING WITH RASPBERRIES

Matt Edwards music executive and 2010 semi-finalist

PREPARATION TIME
5 minutes

COOKING TIME
30–35 minutes

SERVES 6

25g (scant 1oz) unsalted butter
2 large eggs, separated
250ml (8fl oz) milk
250g (9oz) caster sugar
3 tbsp flour, sifted
a pinch of sea salt

grated zest and juice of
 1 unwaxed lemon
100g (3½oz) raspberries

TO DECORATE
250ml (8oz) double cream
sprigs of mint

GREGG WALLACE

"That's very soft, very yummy, and it's a lot lighter than it looks. It's bordering on a soufflé."

1 Preheat the oven to 200°C (400°F/Gas 6). Grease six 200ml (7fl oz) ramekins or teacups with the butter and set aside.
2 Beat the egg yolks with the milk. Combine the sugar, flour, and salt, then pour in the milk and egg mixture and fold in the lemon juice and zest.
3 With an electric beater, whisk the egg whites to stiff peaks and fold through the lemon mixture.
4 Pour into the ramekins and poke 4–5 raspberries into the batter. Place the ramekins in a roasting tin, pour enough boiling water around them to reach about 3cm (1¼ in) deep and bake for 30–35 minutes until the tops are golden and set.
5 Serve with the double cream and raspberries, decorated with mint.

FLAVOUR COMBINATION
LEMON AND RASPBERRIES

You would not normally think to combine sharp lemon with fragrant raspberries; lemon seems too robust, too brutal for the fruit to survive. The secret of this recipe is the soothing flavour bridge of the buttery, sweetened sponge mixture. As it is served warm, the scent of the lemon sponge and cooked raspberries also blend in your nose – crucial to the best flavour experiences. Fresh raspberries cleverly expand cooked flavours to seal success.

LEMON TART

Nargis Chaudhary physiotherapist and 2010 semi-finalist

250g (9oz) digestive biscuits
100g (3½oz) ground almonds
100g (3½oz) roasted chopped hazelnuts
250g (9oz) unsalted butter
600ml (1pint) double cream
400g can condensed milk
pared zest and juice of
  6 unwaxed lemons
freshly grated nutmeg
1 jar of lemon curd

PREPARATION TIME
30 minutes, plus chilling

SERVES 8

1 Place the biscuits in a sealed bag and crush them to a breadcrumb consistency with a rolling pin. Add the almonds and hazelnuts and place the mixture in a bowl.
2 Melt the butter, pour it into the biscuit mixture and mix until evenly combined. Tip into a 24cm (9½in) and 2.5cm (1in) deep flan tin and press into a smooth base for the tart. Place in the fridge to chill.
3 Place the cream in a mixing bowl, add the condensed milk and mix well. Add the lemon juice and stir until thick and creamy.
4 Take the biscuit base out of the fridge, pour the filling in, and replace in the fridge to chill.
5 Once the tart is set, sprinkle the nutmeg on top and decorate with the lemon zest. Swirl the curd on the plates to give colour.

GREGG WALLACE "Beautiful. Sharp lemon then turns creamy, then goes into a buttery biscuit base. That is lovely."

EXPLODING LEMON MACAROONS
Tim Kinnaird paediatrician and 2010 finalist

PREPARATION TIME
55 minutes, plus standing
  and chilling

COOKING TIME
25 minutes

SERVES 4

FOR THE MACAROONS
180g (6oz) caster sugar
3 tbsp water
4 egg whites near their sell-by date
180g (6oz) ground almonds
180g (6oz) icing sugar
1 tsp yellow food colouring

FOR THE LEMON CURD
4 egg yolks
grated zest and juice of 6 lemons
70g (2¼fl oz) caster sugar
70g (2¼fl oz) salted butter

TO SERVE
popping candy (optional)

JOHN TORODE

"They are
perfectly made.
Very impressive.
I think they
are fantastic."

1 Preheat the oven to 150°C (300°F/Gas 2) and line 2–3 baking sheets with baking parchment.

2 To make the macaroons, dissolve the sugar in 3 tbsp of water over low heat for about 8 minutes, stirring occasionally. Increase the heat and allow the sugar to boil for about 10 minutes, without stirring, until it reaches 118°C (244°F) – "soft boil" temperature.

3 Whisk the egg whites in a free-standing mixer until they start to foam. Still mixing, gradually add the sugar syrup in a steady stream until the sugar is incorporated and the egg whites form stiff peaks.

4 In a separate bowl, mix together the ground almonds, icing sugar, 165g (5½oz) of the egg whites, and the food colouring. Mix together until the meringue flows like lava.

5 Pipe 5cm (2in) circles of the meringue mixture onto the baking parchment with at least 2cm (¾in) gaps between each circle. Leave for 45 minutes for the shells to dry a little and a crust to form.

6 Bake in the oven for about 15 minutes. Remove from the oven to cool and then gently remove from the paper.

7 While the biscuits are resting, make the lemon curd. Put the egg yolks, lemon zest and juice, and caster sugar into a saucepan and heat gently with half the butter for about 10 minutes until the curd thickens.

8 Strain the lemon curd into a bowl to remove the zest and whisk in the remaining butter. Chill in the fridge until the curd is firm and the biscuits are cool.

9 Sandwich pairs of macaroons with lemon curd and put them back in the fridge to chill, preferably overnight.

10 Remove the macaroons from the fridge an hour before serving. Slightly moisten them by lightly brushing them with a moistened pastry brush and sprinkle with popping candy (if using).

LIME POSSET WITH CARAMELIZED PINEAPPLE AND BASIL CREAM

Lee Groves head chef and 2010 Professionals semi-finalist

PREPARATION TIME
40 minutes, plus chilling

COOKING TIME
20 minutes

SERVES 4–6

600ml (1 pint) double cream
200g (7oz) caster sugar
zest and juice of 4 limes
200g (7oz) caster sugar
1 small pineapple, peeled, cored,
  and drained of juice
1 bunch of basil

1 Put 450ml (15fl oz) of the cream, sugar, and lime juice and zest into a medium saucepan. Bring to the boil, stirring to dissolve the sugar, then cook gently for 5 minutes. Pour into a clean bowl, cool and chill.
2 Dice the pineapple into 1cm (½in) cubes. Melt the sugar until golden and caramelized, which will take about 10 minutes. Toss the pineapple through the caramel, then cook for 10 minutes until golden and slightly softened.
3 Whip the remaining cream until stiff. Chop the basil at the last minute and fold into the cream.
4 Put a spoonful of pineapple in the bottom of serving glasses. Gently pour the posset into the glasses and chill.
5 To serve, put a small spoonful of pineapple mix on the posset and top with a neat quenelle of basil cream.

LEMON CREAM WITH AMARETTI BISCUITS

Tim Kinnaird paediatrician and 2010 finalist

FOR THE BISCUITS
100g (3½oz) ground almonds
60g (2oz) caster sugar
finely grated zest of ½ lemon
1 drop of almond extract
1 egg white
pinch of salt
1 tsp clear honey
icing sugar, for dusting

FOR THE CREAM
2 leaves of gelatine
2 eggs, separated

75g (2½oz) icing sugar
finely grated zest and juice of 1 lemon
1 tbsp Amaretto di Sarrono
2–3 drops of Angostura bitters
200ml (7fl oz) double cream

FOR THE SPONGE
100g (3½oz) caster sugar
4 tsp Limoncello
about 12 sponge finger biscuits, halved

PREPARATION TIME
15 minutes, plus resting
and chilling

COOKING TIME
15–20 minutes

SERVES 4

1 Preheat the oven to 180°C (350°F/Gas 4) and line 2 baking sheets with baking parchment.

2 For the biscuits, mix together the almonds, sugar, and lemon zest in a bowl. Sprinkle over the almond extract. Whisk the egg white and salt in a separate bowl until soft peaks form. Add the honey and whisk again. Fold into the almond mixture to form a sticky paste.

3 Dust a work surface with lots of icing sugar. With more icing sugar on your hands to prevent sticking, divide the mixture into 8 pieces. Roll each biscuit into a ball then flatten slightly to make rounds. Place on the baking sheets, spaced apart, and leave for 20 minutes before baking for 15–20 minutes, or until pale golden. Leave to cool slightly, then carefully lift off with a palette knife and cool on a wire rack.

4 Make a syrup for the sponge. Put the sugar into a bowl and add 100ml (3½fl oz) boiling water. Stir to dissolve, then pour into a shallow dish and stir in the Limoncello. Set aside to cool.

5 Meanwhile, make the lemon and almond cream. Put the gelatine into a bowl of water and leave to soak for 10 minutes. Whisk the egg yolks and icing sugar until pale. Add the lemon zest and juice, Amaretto, and Angostura bitters. Drain the gelatine, leaving 1 tbsp of the soaking water and dissolve it gently over a pan of hot water. Stir into the egg yolk mixture. Softly whip the cream in a clean bowl and gently fold into the egg mix. In another bowl whip the egg whites until soft peaks form. Gently fold into the lemon cream.

6 To assemble, dip the sponge fingers into the Limoncello syrup. Put 6 halves in the bottom of each of 4 glass dishes. Spoon over the lemon cream and chill for an hour before serving with the amaretti biscuits.

MICHEL ROUX JR'S
SESAME CRISPS WITH MARINATED GRAPES AND TIPSY CREAM

I created this dessert to match Napoleon Bonaparte's favourite dessert wine. Take your time when you make it, as it's the attention to detail that makes all the difference.

PREPARATION TIME
50 minutes, plus marinating

COOKING TIME
12–15 minutes

SERVES 6

400g (14oz) seedless white grapes
60ml (2fl oz) sweet white wine
1 tbsp grappa
100g (3½oz) caster sugar
75g (2½oz) unsalted butter
pinch of sea salt
25g (scant 1oz) liquid glucose

1½ tbsp milk
125g (4½oz) sesame seeds
25g (scant 1oz) black sesame seeds
175ml (6fl oz) double cream
1 tbsp crème fraîche
25g (scant 1oz) icing sugar, sifted
2 tbsp grappa or brandy

1 Using a small, sharp knife, peel the grapes over a bowl to collect any juice as you work. Place the grapes in the bowl. Mix together the wine, grappa, and 2 tbsp of the sugar, pour over the grapes, and leave to marinate for at least 1 hour or overnight if possible.

2 Preheat the oven to 200°C (400°F/Gas 6). To make the sesame crisps, put the butter, the remaining sugar, salt, glucose, and milk into a saucepan and warm over low heat, stirring continuously, until completely melted. Fold in the sesame seeds, then spread the mixture thinly on a large greased baking tray. Bake for 8- 10 minutes until golden.

3 Remove the sesame mix from the oven and leave to cool for 1–2 minutes until it has firmed up but is not solid, then cut out 18 discs, using a 6cm (2½in) round metal cutter. If the mix becomes brittle, return the baking tray to the oven for a few seconds. Using a palette knife, transfer the crisps to a wire rack to cool completely. Keep in a dry place until ready to serve; you can make them the day before and store them in an airtight container in a cool place, layered with baking parchment in between to prevent them from sticking together.

4 Drain the grapes and pour the marinade into a saucepan. Boil uncovered until syrupy, pour over the grapes, then set aside to cool.

5 For the tipsy cream, whisk the cream until soft peaks form. Add the crème fraîche, icing sugar, and grappa or brandy, and whisk until firm. Transfer to a piping bag with a star tip.

6 Assemble the dish by piping cream on a sesame crisp, adding 3–4 grapes and repeating, finishing with a third crisp topped with grapes. Drizzle some of the syrup onto the plate and serve the remaining cream on the side.

SPICED PINEAPPLE WITH COCONUT RICE, FRUIT SALSA, CANDIED LIME, AND CORIANDER CRESS

Christine Hamilton TV personality and 2010 Celebrity finalist

PREPARATION TIME
20 minutes

COOKING TIME
1 hour

SERVES 4

100g (3½ oz) pudding rice
400ml can coconut milk
250ml (8fl oz) double cream
1 vanilla pod, split, seeds scraped out and reserved (see MasterTip, p.256)
100g (3½oz) caster sugar
3 limes
1 large pineapple, peeled and sliced into 4 rings

1 papaya, peeled and chopped
3 passion fruits, halved, pulped, and seeds scraped out
100g (3½oz) butter
pinch each of ground cinnamon, ginger, and cloves
100g (3½oz) soft brown sugar
200ml (5fl oz) brown rum
1 punnet coriander cress

1 Tip the rice into a saucepan and stir in the coconut milk, cream, vanilla seeds, and half the sugar. Bring to a boil, then reduce the heat to low and simmer gently for 45 minutes, stirring occasionally, until the rice is cooked.

2 While the rice is cooking, pare the zest from the limes. Cut it into thin julienne strips, boil in water for 2 minutes to soften, then drain. Add the remaining caster sugar and 2 tablespoons water, and simmer over medium heat for 2–3 minutes until soft and sticky, then remove the lime zest with a fork and separate the strips on baking parchment. Leave to harden.

3 Continue to boil the sugar syrup until it forms a caramel, brushing down the sides of the pan with a pastry brush dipped in water to prevent crystallization. Pour the caramel onto a baking tray lined with baking parchment. Leave to harden then crush or break into thin shards.

4 Place the pineapple rings in a saucepan. Add the juice from the zested limes, plus enough water to cover the slices, and simmer gently for about 5 minutes. Drain, reserving the cooking liquid, and keep warm.

5 Mix together the papaya and passion fruit to form a fruit salsa.

6 Melt the butter in a pan and add the cinnamon, ginger, cloves, and brown sugar. Add the reserved cooking liquid and the rum and boil until reduced to a thickish pouring syrup.

7 Place a pineapple ring on each serving plate. Spoon the rice on top, using metal rings to help shape it to the diameter of the pineapple. Arrange the salsa, candied lime, and caramel shards over the rice, and spoon the rum and butter sauce around. Sprinkle with coriander cress to decorate.

CARAMELIZED WARM BERRIES COOKED IN STAR ANISE AND VANILLA, TOPPED WITH COCONUT CREAM

Dean Macey Olympic decathlete and 2010 Celebrity quarter-finalist

1 vanilla pod, split, seeds scraped out and reserved with the pod (see MasterTip, p.256)
10 star anise
150g (5½oz) blueberries
300g (10oz) strawberries, halved

170g (6oz) raspberries
2 tbsp caster sugar
2 tbsp kirsch
4 tbsp coconut yogurt

PREPARATION TIME
5 minutes

COOKING TIME
5 minutes

SERVES 4

1 Put the vanilla seeds, pod, and star anise in a dry hot pan, and heat for 1 minute, until they start to smoke.

2 Add the blueberries and cook for 1 minute. Add the strawberries and raspberries and cook for a further minute until they start to release their juices. Sprinkle the sugar over them.

3 Warm up the kirsch in a ladle, then set it alight with a match. Once it is lit, add to the berries and leave until the flames die out. Remove the vanilla and star anise, reserving 4 of the star anise. Divide the berries between 4 plates and top each with a spoonful of coconut yogurt. Add a star anise for decoration and serve.

ALMOND PANNA COTTA WITH POACHED TAMARILLOS AND BERRIES

Lisa Faulkner actress and 2010 Celebrity champion

PREPARATION TIME
30 minutes, plus chilling

COOKING TIME
40 minutes

SERVES 4

4 leaves of gelatine
250ml (9fl oz) whole milk
250ml (9fl oz) double cream
1 vanilla pod
50g (1¾oz) caster sugar
few drops of almond extract

FOR THE TAMARILLOS
100g (3½oz) caster sugar
1 vanilla pod

1 cinnamon stick
1 bay leaf
4 tamarillos, halved lengthways

FOR THE BERRIES
50g (1¾oz) caster sugar
60ml (2fl oz) cassis
50g (1¾oz) raspberries
50g (1¾oz) blueberries

MASTER TIP
TAMARILLOS

The tough, bitter skin of the tamarillo or tree tomato is inedible. The dark red variety is best eaten fresh, while the milder, yellow variety is suitable for preserving. The attractive flushed flesh has swirls of dark edible seeds, and a tangy, sweet-sour taste. When ripe, tamarillos should smell like a mix of tomatoes and apricots.

1 To make the panna cotta, first soak the gelatine in cold water for 10 minutes to soften. Pour the milk and cream into a saucepan, split the vanilla pod, and add to the pan. Bring to the boil, remove from the heat, and allow to infuse for few minutes. Shake off excess water from the gelatine and stir into the pan. Add the sugar, then continue to stir over low heat until completely melted. Take out the vanilla pod and stir in the almond extract.

2 Lightly oil 4 individual pudding basins that will hold 135ml (4½fl oz) of panna cotta then set them on a tray. Pour the mixture into each. Chill for at least 2 hours, or until completely set.

3 For the tamarillos, pour 200ml (7fl oz) water into a saucepan and add the sugar, vanilla, cinnamon, and bay leaf. Cook over low heat until the sugar has dissolved. Increase the heat and, when simmering, add the tamarillos and poach for about 5–10 minutes. Remove from the heat and leave to cool in the syrup.

4 For the berries, pour 100ml (3½fl oz) water into a saucepan, add the sugar and cassis and bring to the boil. Add the berries and cook slowly for about 30 minutes, stirring occasionally. The mixture should appear syrupy.

5 Dip the pudding basins in hot water for a couple of seconds then turn out onto the centre of each serving plate. Top with a berry and serve alongside 2 halves of a tamarillo and a spoonful of the poached berries.

GREGG WALLACE "That is a pudding man's heaven. Absolute heaven. That is just lovely. Cor!"

SPICY PINEAPPLE CARPACCIO WITH MASCARPONE AND MEDJOOL DATE MOUSSE, AND KIWI COULIS

Renaud Marin head chef and 2010 Professionals quarter-finalist

PREPARATION TIME
30 minutes

COOKING TIME
20 minutes

SERVES 4

250ml (9fl oz) mineral water
110g (3¾oz) caster sugar
10g (¼oz) whole allspice
1 clove
½ cinnamon stick
½ pineapple, peeled and cored
125g (4½oz) mascarpone cheese
2 tbsp whipping cream
50g (1¾oz) pitted Medjool dates
3 kiwis, peeled and roughly chopped

MASTER TIP
MEDJOOL DATES

Large, crinkled, purple-brown Medjool dates are soft, fleshy, and sticky-sweet. Fresh dates are usually best from November to January; they should look plump, smooth, and glossy. Whether sold on the stem or in boxes, they should smell of honey.

1 Put the mineral water, 50g (1¾oz) of the sugar, and all the spices into a saucepan and slowly bring to the boil. Once the sugar has dissolved, increase the heat and leave over medium heat to boil for 15 minutes.

2 Meanwhile, finely slice the pineapple with a mandoline or a very sharp knife. When the syrup is ready, pour over the pineapple slices in a large tray and leave to rest in the fridge until cool.

3 For the mousse, whip the cheese, cream, and 50g (1¾oz) of the sugar until smooth.

4 Finely dice the dates and add to the mousse and whip again until the mix is even. Leave to set and rest in the fridge.

5 To make the kiwi coulis, put the kiwi pieces in a blender or food processor with the final 10g (¼oz) of sugar and mix until smooth. Pass through a fine sieve into a clean bowl.

6 To serve, drain the pineapple slices and arrange on 4 plates. Drizzle over some of the kiwi coulis and add a quenelle of mascarpone mousse in the middle.

MICHEL ROUX JR "It's actually delicious. The pineapple is sweet, and the date mousse works really well with it."

MANGO AND CARDAMOM RUM SYLLABUB SPOONS

Dhruv Baker sales director and 2010 Champion

75g (2½oz) flesh of ½ small mango
2 cardamom pods (see MasterTip,
 p.288)
75ml (2½fl oz) double cream
grated zest of ½ lime, plus 1 tsp juice
1 tbsp dark rum
tiny mint leaves, to decorate

PREPARATION TIME
20 minutes

SERVES 4

1 Have ready about 20 identical teaspoons. Put 50g (1¾oz) of the mango flesh in a blender or food processor and purée until smooth. Finely dice the remaining flesh and set aside.
2 Shell the cardamom pods and grind the seeds to a powder in a pestle and mortar.
3 Using an electric whisk, whip the cream until soft peaks form. Add the lime zest and juice, rum, and ground cardamom and whip again until thick, but not overly so. Stir in the mango purée, then spoon into a piping bag. Snip off the end so it is nearly the same width as the teaspoons and pipe neatly into each spoon.
4 Arrange 5 spoons per person in a shallow bowl, then decorate the syllabub with a little diced mango and mint leaves before serving.

GREGG WALLACE

"Oh, that's lovely."

FLAVOUR COMBINATION
MANGO AND CARDAMOM

A perfect tropical combination that relies on the mango being succulent and highly scented. With an array of flavours that can run from pineapple to coconut, mango reaches new heights when lime juice and dark rum from similar climes are added. But then spicing with cardamom is inspired; this spice is highly charged with exotic perfumes and definite aniseed/caraway overtones that enhance the excitements already in your mouth. Heady proof small really is beautiful.

FLAMBÉED BANANAS WITH GINGER PANNA COTTA, DARK RUM ICE CREAM, AND COOKIES

Ben Piette hospitality chef and 2010 Professionals semi-finalist

PREPARATION TIME
50 minutes, plus churning
and freezing

COOKING TIME
30 minutes

SERVES 4

FOR THE COOKIES
60g (2oz) self-raising flour
15g (½oz) butter
15g (½oz) caster sugar
25ml (1½ tbsp) milk
30g (1oz) dry raisins, finely chopped

FOR THE ICE CREAM
300ml (10oz) whole milk
4 large egg yolks
100g (3½oz) sugar
1 tsp vanilla extract
150ml (5fl oz) dark rum
300ml (10fl oz) extra-thick
  double cream

FOR THE PANNA COTTA
600ml (1 pint) double cream
4 pieces of stem ginger, finely
  chopped
3 leaves of gelatine

FOR THE BANANAS
2 ripe bananas
1 tbsp sugar
20g (¾oz) butter
4 tbsp rum
dash of vanilla extract
½ bunch of mint, to decorate

MICHEL ROUX JR "The rum ice cream is beautiful, with a big punch of rum there – it really is lovely."

1 Place the flour, butter, and sugar in a blender or food processor and blend for 2 minutes. Alternatively, rub them together until a breadcrumb consistency is reached. Add the milk and bring the mixture together to form a dough.

2 Lay the dough on a floured surface and roll to 3mm (⅛in) thick. Spread the raisins on one half and fold over the other half. Roll again to 3mm (⅛in) thick, then cut out the biscuits with a 6cm (2½in) pastry cutter. Rest in the fridge for 20 minutes.

3 Preheat the oven to 180°C (350°F/Gas 4). Bake the biscuits for 18–20 minutes until they are golden brown.

4 To make the ice cream, bring the milk to the boil in a pan. Remove from the heat and leave to cool slightly. Put the egg yolks in a bowl, add the sugar and vanilla, and beat with a wooden spoon until pale. Pour in the milk and rum. Return to the pan and cook until the custard coats the back of the spoon. Remove from the heat and leave to cool. Stir in the cream then churn in an ice-cream maker and freeze.

5 For the panna cottas, place the cream and ginger in a pan, bring to the boil then take off the heat and leave to infuse for 30 minutes. Meanwhile, soak the gelatine in cold water for at least 10 minutes. Add the gelatine to the cream then strain through a fine sieve. Pour into 4 oiled dariole moulds, or ramekins, and place in the fridge to set.

6 Finely slice one of the bananas, roll the slices in sugar then blow torch the tops. Leave to set. Slice the remaining banana lengthways and then in half crossways. Place in a hot frying pan, sprinkle with the remaining sugar then add the butter. Colour both sides then, when the caramel starts to form, add the rum and ignite it. Reduce the heat and continue to cook for 2 minutes, basting the bananas all the time and adding a splash of vanilla.

7 Serve the panna cottas topped with the slices of banana and lean the cookies against them. Arrange the flambéed banana and ice cream on the plate around the panna cottas and garnish with mint.

FLOATING ISLANDS WITH MANGO

Neil Mackenzie sous chef and 2010 Professionals quarter-finalist

4 eggs, separated
130g (4½oz) sugar
¼ tsp cream of tartar
250ml (8fl oz) milk
250ml (8fl oz) double cream

1 vanilla pod, split, seeds scraped out and reserved (see MasterTip p.256)
2 Alphonso mangoes, peeled and roughly diced
juice of 1 lime

PREPARATION TIME
40 minutes

COOKING TIME
15 minutes

SERVES 4

1 Whisk 2 of the egg whites until stiff, then gradually add 100g (3½oz) sugar and cream of tartar, whisking as you do so. Whisk until the mixture is glossy and stiff.

2 In a shallow pan, heat the milk and cream with the scraped out vanilla pod until just warm.

3 Using 2 large spoons, make 8 quenelles with the meringue. Add to the milk and cream mixture and poach gently for 5 minutes. Meanwhile, line a tray with cling film. Remove the meringues from the pan, transfer them to the tray, and place in the fridge. Strain the milk mixture through a sieve.

4 In a bowl, whisk the egg yolks with the vanilla seeds and 30g (1oz) sugar. Pour in the milk mixture. Transfer to a pan and cook over low heat, stirring, until thickened and the mixture coats the back of a spoon. Cool and then chill in the fridge.

5 Place the mango in a bowl and add the lime juice and a little sugar to sweeten if desired.

6 To serve, take 4 clean glasses and place some mango in the bottom of each. Spoon on the chilled crème anglaise. Apply a blow torch to the meringues and place on top.

MASTER TIP

ALPHONSO MANGOES

The dark green "king of mangoes" has a brief summer season. The buttery flesh has a saffron hue, the aroma is heady, and the sweetness is enhanced by a dash of tartness. Choose fruit that gives slightly all over when gently squeezed and has a perfumed aroma at the stem end.

BANANA SOUFFLÉ WITH BLUEBERRY COULIS

Natalie Brenner student and 2010 quarter-finalist

PREPARATION TIME
30 minutes

COOKING TIME
25 minutes

SERVES 4

FOR THE COULIS
150g (5½oz) blueberries
50g (1¾oz) sugar

FOR THE SOUFFLÉS
15g (½oz) unsalted butter
4 tsp sugar
1 large, ripe banana, roughly chopped

1 tbsp clear honey
2 large eggs, whites only
1 tbsp caster sugar

TO SERVE
icing sugar
1 tbsp double cream

1 For the coulis, place the blueberries and sugar in a saucepan with 100ml (3½fl oz) water and bring to the boil. Take off the heat and allow to cool, then blend, using a hand-held blender or by transferring to a food processor, and pass through a sieve. Put back on the hob, bring to the boil, and reduce until syrupy. Set aside to cool.
2 Preheat the oven to 200°C (400°F/Gas 6) and place a baking sheet in the oven to heat up. Evenly grease 4 ramekins with the butter, then coat the inside with a layer of sugar.
3 Place the banana in a food processor, add the honey, and blend until smooth.
4 Place the egg whites in a clean, dry bowl and whisk until the whites form soft peaks. Gradually add the caster sugar, whisking all the time, until soft peaks are formed.
5 Using a spatula, fold one-third of the egg whites into the banana mixture relatively vigorously, then very gently fold in the remainder. Spoon the soufflé mix into the ramekins, tap on the work surface to expel any air and run a finger around the rim to create a "top hat" effect. See also the MasterClass pages 312–13 for more advice on making soufflés.
6 Put the soufflés on the preheated baking sheet and place in the oven and bake them for 10–12 minutes until risen.
7 To serve, put the coulis in a small jug on each plate. Place the soufflés in the ramekins on the plate, and sprinkle icing sugar on them just before serving.

GREGG WALLACE "I like the light banana flavour that comes from the soufflé, with the sharper sweetness of the blueberry."

MONICA'S MASTERCLASS
BAKING A SOUFFLÉ

Crisp on top and light on the inside, versatile enough to be used for sweet or savoury, as a starter or dessert, the soufflé is arguably the pinnacle of egg cookery – and it really isn't too difficult to achieve a perfect rise.

1 Coat with crumbs

Grease the inside of each soufflé dish and then coat with sugar, biscuit crumbs, or grated cheese. Use sugar or biscuit crumbs for a sweet soufflé and grated cheese for a savoury soufflé.

2 Whisk and fold

Whisk the egg whites until holding stiff peaks: if under-whisked the soufflés will not rise. Use a gentle folding action to mix the whites into the base, to retain as much air as possible. Add a pinch of salt before mixing for savoury soufflés.

Coating with sugar gives the mix something to grip, to help it rise properly and not sink back down.

Folding in the first third of the whites more vigorously makes it easier to incorporate the rest.

"To make the egg whites whip up nicely, leave them to reach room temperature before use."

3 Form the "top hat"
Run a finger around the soufflé mix, along the top edge of each ramekin just inside the rim, to give a professional "top hat" effect and help the soufflés rise up straight.

4 Cook to perfection
Cook the soufflés straight away, placing them on a preheated baking tray, which will heat immediately the base of the ramekins so that the soufflés begin to rise as soon as you put them in the oven.

The perfect soufflé should have a light and fluffy, but still moist, consistency.

BANANA BREAD, BUTTERSCOTCH SAUCE, AND BROWN BUTTER ICE CREAM

David Coulson head chef and 2010 Professionals finalist

PREPARATION TIME
20 minutes, plus churning
and freezing

COOKING TIME
1 hour

SERVES 4

FOR THE ICE CREAM
150g (5½oz) sugar
300ml (10fl oz) milk
300ml (10fl oz) double cream
150g (5½oz) butter, cut into chunks
5 egg yolks
1 tsp cornflour
1 tbsp liquid glucose

FOR THE BANANA BREAD
60g (2oz) butter
80g (2¾oz) dark soft brown sugar

1 egg
2 very ripe bananas, mashed
110g (3¾oz) self-raising flour
½ tsp ground allspice

FOR THE SAUCE
25g (scant 1oz) dark soft brown sugar
25g (scant 1oz) butter
3 tbsp double cream
½ vanilla pod, split, seeds scraped out,
and pod discarded

1 To make the ice cream, slowly bring the sugar, milk, and cream up to simmering point in a large saucepan. Remove from the heat.
2 Melt the butter in a large frying pan and continue heating until it starts foam, turns brown, and smells nutty.
3 Meanwhile, combine the egg yolks, cornflour, and glucose in a blender or food processor. With the motor running, pour in the browned butter in a slow, steady stream. If you do this too fast, it will not emulsify. Add the scalded milk mixture and combine. Churn in an ice-cream maker and freeze.
4 For the banana bread, preheat the oven to 180°C (350°F/Gas 4). Line a 750ml (1¼ pint) loaf tin with baking parchment.
5 In a large bowl, beat the butter and sugar until well combined. Beat in the egg, bit by bit, then add the bananas and beat to combine. Sift in the flour and allspice and beat again until well mixed.
6 Pour the mix into the prepared tin and bake in the oven for 40–45 minutes or until golden and a skewer comes out clean. Allow to cool in the tin for 5 minutes and then remove and leave to cool on a wire rack.
7 For the butterscotch sauce, place all the ingredients in a pan over low heat. Once the butter has melted and the sugar dissolved, turn up the heat and let it bubble for 1 minute. Reheat when needed.
8 To serve, place a slice of banana bread on each of plate. Top with a scoop of ice cream and drizzle over some butterscotch sauce.

BEAUMES DE VENISE ICE CREAM WITH BRANDY SNAPS AND SALTED CARAMEL SAUCE

Christine Hamilton TV personality and 2010 Celebrity finalist

FOR THE ICE CREAM
300ml (10fl oz) carton double cream
50g (1¾oz) caster sugar
3 tbsp Beaumes de Venise
2 tbsp thick Greek-style yogurt

FOR THE BRANDY SNAPS
30g (1oz) unsalted butter
30g (1oz) brown caster sugar
1 tbsp golden syrup
60g (2oz) plain flour
½ tsp ground ginger
vegetable oil, for greasing

FOR THE SAUCE
60g (2oz) caster sugar
40g (1¼oz) butter
⅛ tsp fine sea salt
1½ tbsp lime juice

TO SERVE
grated zest of 1 lime
6 squares of plain chocolate
  (70% cocoa solids), grated

PREPARATION TIME
20 minutes, plus churning
  and freezing

COOKING TIME
15 minutes

SERVES 4

1 To make the ice cream, whip the cream to form soft peaks. Add the sugar and wine and mix, then fold in the yogurt. Churn in an ice-cream maker and freeze.

2 For the brandy snaps, preheat the oven to 180°C (350°F/Gas 4). Melt the butter, sugar, and syrup in a heavy saucepan over medium heat. Sift in the flour and ginger and mix to a smooth paste. Remove from the heat and leave to cool.

3 Line a baking tray with greaseproof paper and grease with a little vegetable oil. Drop teaspoons of the ginger paste onto the baking sheet, spaced well apart. Bake for 6–8 minutes or until golden and bubbling. Remove from the baking sheet while they are still warm and before they set. Immediately drape over 2 wooden spoon handles laid side by side about 1cm (½in) apart to create a wavy effect. Leave to cool.

4 Make the sauce by gently dissolving the sugar in a saucepan over low heat for about 5 minutes or until it has melted and become light golden, stirring continuously with a spatula. Remove the pan from the heat and add 1½ tbsp water, taking care as it will splutter. Then add the butter and stir to combine before returning to the heat so that any caramel that has set can melt again. Stir in the salt and lime juice and reduce to a sauce-like consistency.

5 To serve, put a brandy snap and a spoonful of ice cream on each plate and pour the caramel sauce around. Decorate with the grated zest of lime and chocolate.

MICHEL ROUX JR'S
NOUGATINE BASKET WITH CHANTILLY CREAM AND BERRIES

This is an intricate recipe, but produces a beautiful dessert. Be careful with your timings when you make the baskets – you need to mould the nougatine into shape before it sets.

PREPARATION TIME
25 minutes

COOKING TIME
10 minutes

SERVES 4

FOR THE BASKET
½ tbsp peanut or groundnut oil
75g (2½oz) flaked almonds
165g (5¾oz) caster sugar
15g (½oz) butter

FOR THE CREAM
300ml (10fl oz) double cream
1 tbsp icing sugar

1 vanilla pod, split, seeds scraped out
  and reserved

TO DECORATE
300g (10oz) mixture of berries
icing sugar, to taste
squeeze of lemon juice

1 For the nougatine basket, preheat the oven to 180°C (350°F/Gas 4). Lightly oil a baking sheet and a ramekin or dariole mould.
2 Spread the almonds over another baking sheet and cook for about 5 minutes or until lightly browned. Remove from the oven but keep it switched on.
3 Gently dissolve the sugar in a saucepan over low heat for about 5 minutes or until it has melted and become light golden, stirring continuously with a spatula. Stir in the almonds. Add the butter and mix until absorbed.
4 Pour the mixture onto the oiled baking sheet and roughly divide it into 4 discs. Place the baking sheet near the warm oven, keeping the oven door half open; if it is not placed near a source of heat, the nougatine will become difficult to work with. Taking 1 piece at a time, quickly roll out the nougatine and place the ramekin or dariole mould in the centre. Fold up the sides of the nougatine around it. If the nougatine becomes too difficult to work with, reheat it in the oven for 1–2 minutes.
5 Make the chantilly cream by whisking up the cream, icing sugar, and seeds from the vanilla pod to form soft peaks.
6 Put 100g (3½oz) of the berries in a blender or food processor and blitz to a purée. Sweeten to taste with icing sugar and add the lemon juice, then pass through a sieve.
7 To serve, spoon the cream into the nougatine baskets and decorate with the remaining berries and fruit coulis.

STICKY TOFFEE PUDDING WITH CLOTTED CREAM
Stacie Stewart PA and 2010 semi-finalist

200g (7oz) dried or fresh dates, pitted
90g (3¼oz) butter, softened
a little plain flour, for dusting
170g (6oz) dark brown sugar
1 tbsp golden syrup
2 tbsp black treacle
½ tsp vanilla extract
2 large eggs
200g (7oz) self-raising flour
1 tsp bicarbonate of soda

FOR THE SAUCE
200ml (7fl oz) double cream
80g (2¾oz) butter
80g (2¾oz) dark soft brown sugar
4 tbsp black treacle
2 tbsp golden syrup

TO SERVE
clotted cream
strawberries (optional)

PREPARATION TIME
10 minutes

COOKING TIME
20–25 minutes

SERVES 8

1 Preheat the oven to 200ºC (400°F/Gas 6) and generously grease eight 150ml (5fl oz) dariole moulds with butter and dust with flour.
2 Place the dates and 300ml (10fl oz) of water in a saucepan and bring to the boil. Remove from the heat.
3 Using an electric beater, whisk the butter and sugar in a large bowl until light and fluffy. Gradually add the syrup, treacle, vanilla extract, and eggs to the mixture and continue beating. Add the self-raising flour and beat until well combined.
4 Purée the hot water and date mixture in a blender or food processor and add the bicarbonate of soda. Quickly add this to the mixture in the bowl while it is still hot. Stir to combine and fill the moulds. Bake in the oven for 20–25 minutes until the top is just firm to the touch.
5 Meanwhile, make the sauce. Place all the sauce ingredients in a pan and bring to the boil. Simmer for 3–4 minutes until glossy.
6 To serve, gently unmould the puddings onto 8 plates, pour over the sauce and serve with clotted cream and strawberries, if using.

JOHN TORODE
"Lovely deep flavours. A majestic, wonderful little pudding."

FLAVOUR COMBINATON
DATES AND BLACK TREACLE

The natural sweetness and satiny texture of dates are vital in a Sticky Toffee Pudding; any acidity in their skins is removed by the bicarb. Black treacle is more unusual but its acidic, mineral background and hints of bitterness pick up the darker flavours of date.

PANETTONE PUDDING
Christine Hamilton TV personality and 2010 Celebrity finalist

PREPARATION TIME
15 minutes, plus soaking

COOKING TIME
40 minutes

SERVES 4

60g (2oz) butter, melted, plus extra greasing 60g (2oz) sultanas
1 tbsp brandy
300g (10oz) panettone, torn into chunks
grated zest and juice of 1 orange
2 tbsp candied peel

2 large eggs
200ml (7fl oz) double cream
200ml (7fl oz) rice milk
2 tbsp demerara sugar
icing sugar, to dust

1 Thoroughly grease a 1.2 litre (2 pints) ovenproof dish. Put the sultanas and brandy in a small saucepan and warm through for a few minutes to plump up. Drain and set aside.
2 Spread half the panettone over the bottom of the dish. Then pour over half the melted butter and sprinkle over half the orange zest and juice, sultanas, and candied peel.
3 Repeat step 2 with the remaining panettone, butter, orange zest and juice, sultanas, and candied peel.
4 Mix together the eggs, cream, and milk in a jug and pour over the panettone. Set aside for at least 30 minutes and meanwhile preheat the oven to 180°C (350°F/Gas 4).
5 Just before baking, sprinkle the demerara sugar over the top of the panettone and cook for about 35 minutes or until puffed up, golden, and just set throughout but with a slight wobble in the centre. To finish, place under a hot grill or use a blow torch to crisp the top. Sprinkle icing sugar over the top just before serving.

MICHEL ROUX JR'S
BOULES DE BERLIN

These classic German doughnuts are always a hit whenever I serve them. Make sure your oil is good and hot before frying, so that you get a nice crisp exterior with a soft, pillowy inside.

15g (½oz) fresh yeast, or 7g sachet fast-action dried yeast
2 tbsp warm milk (optional)
250g (9oz) bread flour
1 tsp salt
2 large eggs, beaten
50g (1¾oz) butter, softened
25g (scant 1oz) caster sugar

sugar, to sprinkle
vegetable oil, for deep frying

FILLING OPTIONS
seedless raspberry jam
1 ripe banana
Nutella

PREPARATION TIME
15 minutes, plus rising and chilling

COOKING TIME
15 minutes

MAKES 16 DOUGHNUTS

1 If using fresh yeast, mix it with the warm milk and set aside for 10 minutes to become frothy. Put the flour, salt, yeast mixture (or dried yeast sachet), eggs, and 1 tbsp warm water into a mixer fitted with a dough hook. Slowly mix to combine adding a dash more water if it is on the dry side, then increase the speed and mix for about 10 minutes or until the dough is smooth and elastic.
2 Beat together the softened butter and caster sugar in a separate bowl. Then, at a low speed, add this mixture to the dough, a little at a time, making sure that it is completely amalgamated each time. Continue to mix for about 5 minutes or until the dough is perfectly smooth and fairly elastic. Tip the dough into an oiled bowl, cover with oiled cling film and leave in a warm place for 1 hour or until doubled in size.
3 Punch the dough to knock out the air, knead briefly on a floured surface. Roll out until about 2cm (¾in) thick and cut out 16 circles using a 5cm (2in) plain cutter; re-roll trimmings to cut them all. Save scraps to test oil temperature later. Place on 2 large, floured baking sheets, spaced apart. Chill for 15 minutes in the fridge, then cover with oiled cling film and leave in a warm place for 1 hour or until doubled in size.
4 Cover a baking sheet with the sugar. Fill a deep, wide pan just over half full with the oil. Heat over high heat until a scrap of doughnut mix turns golden in 1 minute. Carefully drop 5 doughnuts into the oil and cook for 3–4 minutes, turning halfway, until deep golden and cooked through. Remove with a slotted spoon, drain on kitchen paper, then roll in the sugar and set aside. Repeat to cook all of the doughnuts and fill with your choice of fillings (see MasterTip, right).

MASTER TIP
FILLING THE BOULES

For the fillings, mix the jam until smooth, then put it into a piping bag fitted with a small nozzle. With a small, sharp knife make a hole in the side of each doughnut and pipe in the jam. For the banana, mash it until it is fairly smooth and pipe in as for the jam. For the Nutella, mix until softer, then pipe as before. Keep the doughnuts for up to 1 day in an airtight tin in a cool place or freeze, unfilled, for up to 1 month. Thaw, warm in the oven, fill, and serve.

DARK CHOCOLATE MOUSSE, GREEN TEA FINANCIER, AND MILK ICE CREAM

John Calton head chef and 2010 Professionals finalist

PREPARATION TIME
1 hour 30 minutes, plus freezing and chilling

COOKING TIME
1 hour 20 minutes

SERVES 8

FOR THE ICE CREAM
500ml (16fl oz) whole milk
500ml (16fl oz) ewe's or goat's milk
50g (1¾oz) caster sugar
100g (3½oz) condensed milk
1 tsp liquid glucose
1 leaf of gelatine

FOR THE MOUSSE
3 eggs and 3 egg yolks
300g (10oz) granulated sugar
3 leaves of gelatine
150ml (5fl oz) double cream
300g (10oz) dark chocolate buttons
  (60% cocoa solids)
3 tbsp vodka
650ml (1 pint 2fl oz) whipping cream

FOR THE FINANCIER
125g (4½oz) egg whites
125g (4½oz) caster sugar
250g (9oz) butter
1 tsp matcha green tea powder
45g (1½oz) plain flour, sieved
45g (1½oz) ground almonds, sieved
1 tsp baking powder, sieved

FOR THE CHOCOLATE LEAVES
400g (14oz) dark chocolate
  (70% cocoa solids)

FOR THE COFFEE ESSENCE
300g (10oz) caster sugar
½ tsp liquid glucose
100g (3½oz) instant coffee granules

GREGG WALLACE

"That's absolutely lovely. The milk ice cream going into the chocolate is just a delight."

1 First make the milk ice cream. Heat the whole milk, ewe's or goat's milk, and sugar in a large, high-sided saucepan until the sugar is dissolved, then boil until the liquor has reduced to 375ml (13fl oz).
2 Mix the condensed milk and glucose in a bowl and pour over the hot milk. Mix well and pass through a fine sieve.
3 Cool quickly over ice then churn in an ice-cream maker until frozen.
4 To make the dark chocolate mousse, whisk the eggs in a bowl over a pan of hot water for 10–15 minutes or until thickened and doubled in volume.
5 Put 150g (5½oz) of the granulated sugar in a pan. Heat slowly to melt and then heat it to 110°C (230°F) or "soft ball" stage on a sugar thermometer. Pour the hot sugar into the eggs, whisking as it is added. Continue whisking until the eggs form soft peaks.
6 Soak the gelatine in cold water. Put the cream in a saucepan and bring to the boil. Then add the soaked gelatine and the chocolate. Stir until smooth and add the vodka.
7 Whisk together the chocolate and egg mixtures. Leave to cool until the mixture is around 20°C (68°F). Then whip the whipping cream and gently fold through until the mix is well incorporated. Leave to cool, then transfer the mousse to a piping bag with a small nozzle.

8 For the green tea financier, preheat the oven to 160°C (325°F/Gas 3) and grease a 23cm (9in) square baking tray. Put the egg whites and sugar in a bowl and lightly whisk to blend.

9 Melt the butter in a small pan, bring to the boil, and cook for a few minutes. Then stir in the green tea powder, remove from the heat, and leave to infuse for 10 minutes.

10 Fold the flour, almonds, and baking powder through the egg whites and sugar, and then add the butter and green tea mixture. Pour onto the baking tray and bake for 8–10 minutes until it has set and is just very lightly golden on top. Leave to cool on a rack.

11 To make the chocolate leaves, break the dark chocolate into a bowl and heat over a saucepan of simmering water. When melted and smooth, pour onto a sheet of baking parchment on a baking sheet and allow to cool.

12 To make the coffee essence, put the caster sugar in a saucepan with the liquid glucose and 4 tbsp cold water. Dissolve slowly over low–medium heat, stirring occasionally and brushing the pan sides down with water if crystals start to appear. When every grain has dissolved, stop stirring and boil the syrup steadily until it begins to caramelize. Remove from the heat and carefully mix in the coffee granules. Leave to cool and then pour into a squeezy bottle.

13 To assemble, cut the green tea financier into 8 equal-sized rectangles. Cut the chocolate into 16 rectangles, the same size as the sponge. Put 1 piece of the sponge on to each plate. Pipe 3 rows of the mousse on to each piece of sponge and top with a chocolate leaf. Pipe on a further 3 rows of the mousse and finish with a second chocolate leaf. Place a scoop of milk ice cream alongside and finish with some of the coffee essence.

MICHEL ROUX JR "That's great. Chocolatey, rich, yet still light."

CHOCOLATE TRUFFLE MOUSSE WITH POPPY SEEDS AND ORANGE TUILES

Roz Anslow clothes shop owner and 2010 quarter-finalist

100g (3½oz) dark chocolate
  (70% cocoa solids)
300ml (10fl oz) double cream
2 tbsp Frangelico
1 large egg white
50g (1¾oz) caster sugar

FOR THE TUILES
1 large egg white
50g (1¾oz) caster sugar
25g (scant 1oz) unsalted butter, melted
15g (½oz) poppy seeds
25g (scant 1oz) plain flour
grated zest of 1 small orange

PREPARATION TIME
20 minutes

COOKING TIME
15 minutes

SERVES 4

1 Put 4 serving cups in the fridge to chill. Break the chocolate into small pieces and set aside.

2 In a small, heavy saucepan, heat half of the cream until it begins to boil, then remove the pan from the heat and leave the cream to cool slightly. Add the chocolate pieces and stir until the chocolate has melted into a smooth ganache.

3 Pour the mixture into a bowl and set over a larger bowl of iced water, taking care not to let the iced water splash into the chocolate and cream. Add the rest of the cream and the Frangelico and mix together.

4 Whisk the egg white into stiff peaks. Add the sugar, a tablespoon at a time, and continue to whisk until smooth. Fold the egg mix through the chocolate cream, spoon into chilled serving cups, and set aside in the fridge.

5 For the tuiles, preheat the oven to 190°C (375°F/Gas 5). Line 2 large baking sheets with baking parchment and grease the parchment with oil.

6 Whisk the egg white to a loose texture. Then whisk in the sugar followed by the butter, poppy seeds, and flour. Put 12 teaspoonfuls of the mixture onto the prepared baking sheets, spaced well apart. Spread thinly in a circle using the back of a spoon, then sprinkle over the orange zest.

7 Bake for 8–10 minutes or until pale golden. Remove from the oven and leave to cool for 1 minute before lifting off the paper with a palette knife and draping over an oiled rolling pin to set in a tuile shape. Remove and leave to cool on a wire rack.

8 Before serving, remove the mousse pots from the fridge and allow them to come to room temperature. Serve each one with 1–2 tuiles (the rest will store in an airtight container for up to 2 days).

MASTER TIP
DARK POPPY SEEDS

The flavour of dark poppy seeds is stronger than that of white. The blue-grey seeds are commonly used in Europe, added to breads and cakes. They do not grind easily, but dry roasting followed by a whizz in a coffee grinder can help to break them down.

CHOCOLATE POTS, COFFEE ESPUMA, AND SHORTBREAD BISCUITS

Alex Rushmer freelance writer and 2010 finalist

PREPARATION TIME
50 minutes, plus setting

COOKING TIME
1 hour

SERVES 4

FOR THE ESPUMA
2 leaves of gelatine
325ml (11fl oz) espresso coffee
75g (2½oz) caster sugar
175ml (6fl oz) double cream

FOR THE CHOCOLATE POTS
325ml (11fl oz) double cream
175ml (6fl oz) whole milk
4 egg yolks

50g (1¾oz) caster sugar
200g (7oz) dark chocolate
  (70% cocoa solids)

FOR THE SHORTBREAD
100g (3½oz) butter
50g (1¾oz) caster sugar
150g (5½oz) plain flour
1 tbsp rice flour

1 To make the espuma, soften the gelatine in a bowl of cold water for 2–3 minutes. Heat 100ml (3½fl oz) of the coffee in a saucepan, then add the sugar and stir to dissolve. Lift the gelatine out of the water, shaking off any excess water, and add to the coffee. Stir over a very low heat until completely dissolved. Stir in the remaining coffee and cream. Pour into a cream whipper and charge as described in the manufacturer's instructions. Shake well, then chill until needed.

2 For the chocolate pots, heat the cream and milk in a heavy pan until almost boiling. In a separate bowl, cream the egg yolks and sugar until pale. Melt the chocolate in a bowl over a pan of simmering water. Remove the pan from the heat once the chocolate has melted.

3 Slowly whisk the cream into the eggs, then stir this mixture into the melted chocolate. Divide the chocolate mixture between 4 cappuccino cups and chill for at least 1 hour or until set.

4 To make the shortbread, cream the butter and sugar together in a bowl, then stir in the flours, bringing the mixture together into a smooth dough. Wrap the dough in cling film and chill for 30 minutes.

5 Preheat the oven to 160°C (325°F/Gas 3) and line a baking sheet with baking parchment. Unwrap the dough and form it into a sausage shape of about 5cm (2in) diameter. Slice off rounds and place them on the baking sheet, spaced apart. Bake for 20–30 minutes or until the biscuits are crisp and pale golden. Leave to cool on the baking sheet for about 5 minutes before lifting off.

6 Top each chocolate cup with a generous layer of coffee espuma and serve with the shortbread.

WHITE CHOCOLATE SOUP WITH RASPBERRY PURÉE

John Calton head chef and 2010 Professionals finalist

FOR THE WHITE CHOCOLATE SOUP
210g (7½oz) white chocolate
450ml (15fl oz) whipping cream
150ml (5fl oz) whole milk
190g (7oz) plain low-fat yogurt

FOR THE RASPBERRY PURÉE
250g (9oz) raspberries
3 tbsp raspberry liqueur
50g (1¾oz) caster sugar

PREPARATION TIME
10 minutes, plus cooling

COOKING TIME
10 minutes

SERVES 4

1 To make the white chocolate soup, melt the chocolate in a bowl over a saucepan of simmering water. In a separate saucepan, bring the cream and milk to the boil.

2 Pour the milk in a slow steady stream onto the chocolate, whisking continuously as if you were making mayonnaise. This must be done slowly to fully emulsify.

3 Cool the mixture over ice and then mix in the yogurt. Place in the fridge to keep cold.

4 To make the raspberry purée, blend the raspberries in a blender or food processor. Add the liqueur and caster sugar to taste and pass through a fine sieve.

5 Serve the chocolate soup in 4 bowls with a good dollop of the purée placed in the middle of each one.

Professionals 2010 Champion
CLAIRE LARA

"MasterChef was an amazing experience for me and I learnt so much at every stage. I wanted my dishes in the final to reflect this and I'm really pleased with how they came out. Cooking at Noma was just incredible, I took so much away from it and this starter definitely reflects the simplicity and respect for natural flavours that I learnt there. I don't think the competition has changed my style as a chef – it's just made me better and my food is now more refined. It's inspired me to keep on improving as a chef and achieve as much as I can with my cooking."

MAIN

ROASTED PIGEON WITH POMMES MOUSSELINE AND PANCETTA PEAS p.214

"This is wonderful. The sort of dish where the waiters would be trying to take the plate away and I'd still be picking up the sauce with my finger!"
GREGG

STARTER

MI-CUIT SEA TROUT WITH APPLE PURÉE AND CIDER BEURRE BLANC p.70

"Claire's food is so beautiful, elegant and appealing. This dish is wonderfully balanced and the butter sauce with the cider works perfectly." MICHEL

DESSERT

WHITE CHOCOLATE MOUSSE WITH RASPBERRY AND ELDERFLOWER JELLY p.328

"I love this, the textures are wonderful with the crisp pastry and smooth chocolate alongside the raspberry. I would definitely, definitely wipe the plate clean!" MICHEL

WHITE CHOCOLATE MOUSSE WITH RASPBERRY AND ELDERFLOWER JELLY

Claire Lara lecturer and 2010 Professionals champion

PREPARATION TIME
1 hour, plus chilling

COOKING TIME
30 minutes

SERVES 4

5 leaves of gelatine
200ml (7fl oz) double cream
150g (5½oz) Valrhona white chocolate
400g (14oz) raspberries
150g (5½oz) caster sugar, plus extra
  for scattering over the filo sheets

3 tbsp elderflower cordial
4 sheets of filo pastry
50g (1¾oz) butter, melted
2 tsp chopped freeze-dried raspberries

MASTER TIP
ELDERFLOWER

A common hedgerow and woodland tree, elder was once regarded as a complete medicine chest. Today, the flowers are commonly used to make refreshing cordials and "champagne", and the berries can be added to jams and compotes. Wrapped in muslin, the flowers can also be used directly to flavour fruit compotes, jellies, and panna cotta. Look out for the blooms in early summer and the berries in early autumn.

1 Soak 2 of the leaves of gelatine in cold water for at least 10 minutes to soften. Whip the cream until soft peaks form.
2 Melt the chocolate in a bowl set over a pan of barely simmering water, making sure the bowl is clear of the water. Remove the bowl from the pan. While the chocolate is still warm (not hot), squeeze the excess water from the gelatine and stir the gelatine into the chocolate. Whisk the chocolate into the whipped cream and transfer to a piping bag with a plain nozzle. Place in the fridge for 20 minutes to set.
3 Meanwhile, place the remaining leaves of gelatine in cold water to soften. Reserving 12 raspberries, whizz the rest of the raspberries to a purée with the sugar in food processor, then pass through a sieve.
4 Place the raspberry purée and elderflower cordial in a pan and heat gently, then stir in the gelatine. Warm over low heat until the gelatine is dissolved. Pour into mini muffin tins, sit a raspberry on top of each and put in the fridge to set.
5 Preheat the oven to 200°C (400°F/Gas 6). Cut each sheet of filo pastry into 4 rectangles. Brush with melted butter and sugar and bake in the oven for 3 minutes until crispy, then remove and cool. Scatter with freeze-dried raspberries.
6 To serve, on each plate pipe 3–4 lines of mousse on top of a filo rectangle and top with another piece of filo. Repeat twice, finishing with a piece of filo pastry. Serve with the jellies alongside.

MICHEL ROUX JR "It's good because there are lots of textures. It's damned good and I would definitely wipe the plate clean."

CHOCOLATE AND BANANA BRÛLÉE WITH BRIOCHE SOLDIERS

David Coulson head chef and 2010 Professionals finalist

PREPARATION TIME
15 minutes, plus setting

COOKING TIME
15 minutes

SERVES 4

350ml (12fl oz) double cream
125ml (4fl oz) whole milk
3 ripe bananas, mashed
100g (3½oz) dark chocolate, broken
  into chunks
1 vanilla pod, split

3 tbsp Tia Maria
6 large egg yolks
75g (2½oz) caster sugar,
  plus extra for the brulée
2 slices of brioche

1 Place the cream, milk, bananas, chocolate, and vanilla pod in a pan and bring just to the boil. Take off the heat, add the Tia Maria and leave to infuse for at least 30 minutes.

2 In a bowl, whisk together the egg yolks and sugar. Stir in the cream mixture then return to the pan and cook, stirring constantly, until it coats the back of a spoon. Strain through a sieve and pour into 4 ramekins. Leave to set in the fridge for at least 8 hours.

3 When nearly ready to serve, preheat the oven to 180°C (350°F/Gas 4). Cut the brioche into soldier shapes and dust with sugar. Bake for 5 minutes until golden.

4 Remove the ramekins from the fridge. Sprinkle the top of each with a thin, even layer of sugar and apply a blow torch to create the brulée top, before serving on plates with the brioche soldiers.

CHOCOLATE PAVÉ WITH A PEANUT TUILE

John Calton head chef and 2010 Professionals finalist

220ml (7½fl oz) double cream
130ml (4¼fl oz) whole milk
350g (12oz) dark chocolate (minimum
   67% cocoa solids), broken into pieces
3 large eggs
sprig of thyme, leaves only,
   finely chopped
finely grated zest of ½ orange

FOR THE COOKIE CRUMBS
50g (1¾oz) caster sugar
60g (2oz) ground almonds

35g (1¼oz) plain flour
20g (¾oz) cocoa powder
30g (1oz) butter, melted

FOR THE TUILE
100ml (3½fl oz) liquid glucose
100g (3½oz) caster sugar
50g (1¾oz) salted peanuts
½ tsp sea salt

PREPARATION TIME
35 minutes

COOKING TIME
1 hour

SERVES 8–10

1 Take a baking tray about 25cm (10in) square and 5cm (2in) deep and line with baking parchment. Preheat the oven to 130°C (250°F/Gas ½).
2 Heat the cream and milk in a saucepan until almost boiling. Melt the chocolate in a bowl set over simmering water, making sure the base of the bowl is clear of the water. Gradually pour the milk and cream mixture onto the chocolate, mixing all the time until emulsified, then beat in the eggs. Stir in the thyme and orange zest. Place in the lined baking tin and cook in the oven for 20–25 minutes until slightly set. Leave to cool in the tin.
3 To make the cookie crumbs, preheat the oven to 180°C (350°F/Gas 4). Mix all the dry ingredients together. Pour the melted butter over and mix well; the mixture will look like damp sand. Spread on a baking tray and cook in the oven for 15–20 minutes. Check every 5 minutes and stir gently so the mixture at the edges of the tray does not burn.
4 For the tuile, lightly oil a baking tray. Put the glucose, sugar, and 2 tbsp water in a small saucepan. Heat gently to dissolve the sugar then bring to the boil and bubble for about 5 minutes until a caramel colour is obtained, periodically brushing the inside of the pan with a pastry brush dipped in water to stop sugar crystals forming. Add the peanuts and stir so that they are evenly coated. Pour onto the baking tray and leave to cool until firm.
5 Preheat the oven to 220°C (425°F/Gas 7). Break the peanut caramel into rough pieces then place in a blender or food processor and grind to a coarse powder. Sprinkle the powder in a thin layer onto a baking tray lined with baking parchment and cook in the oven for 2–4 minutes. Cut into squares as it cools, before it becomes too hard.
6 To serve, cut the pavé into squares, sprinkle with the cookie crumbs, and top with a peanut tuile.

CHOCOLATE AND PRALINE GATEAU WITH PEANUT BRITTLE

Alice Churchill chef de partie and 2010 Professionals semi-finalist

PREPARATION TIME
25–30 minutes

COOKING TIME
50 minutes, plus 1 hour chilling

SERVES 4

FOR THE MOUSSE
100g (3½oz) hazelnuts
200ml (7fl oz) milk
1 vanilla pod, split
  (see MasterTip, p.256)
75g (2½oz) icing sugar
400g (14oz) milk chocolate
1 tsp agar flakes
300ml (10fl oz) double cream

FOR THE SPONGE
175g (6oz) butter
175g (6oz) caster sugar
3 large eggs
175g (6oz) self-raising flour

FOR THE BRITTLE
400g (14oz) caster sugar
200g (7oz) unsalted roasted peanuts

FOR THE TUILE
2 egg whites
85g (3oz) plain flour
100g (3½oz) caster sugar

FOR THE CHOCOLATE GANACHE
300ml (10fl oz) double cream
300g (10oz) dark chocolate
  (70% cocoa solids)

TO SERVE
100g (3½oz) good quality white chocolate
100ml (3½fl oz) double cream

1 For the hazelnut and chocolate mousse, first make a hazelnut purée. Tip the hazelnuts into a saucepan with the milk, vanilla pod, and icing sugar. Bring to the boil and simmer for 15 minutes. Discard the vanilla pod. Transfer the hazelnuts to a blender or food processor and blend, gradually adding the hot milk, to a purée.

2 Melt the chocolate in a bowl set over a saucepan of simmering water. Stir in the agar flakes.

3 Meanwhile, whip the cream in a large bowl until medium peaks form. Fold the purée into the cream. Then add the melted chocolate and mix. Pour into a Swiss roll tin and freeze for about 1 hour to set.

4 For the sponge, preheat the oven to 180°C (350°F/Gas 4) and grease and line a second Swiss roll tin with baking parchment.

5 Cream together the butter and caster sugar until pale and fluffy. Beat in the eggs, one at a time, then fold in the flour. Spoon the mix into the prepared tin and spread out with a spatula. Bake for 20 minutes, or until golden brown. Remove from the oven and set aside.

6 For the peanut brittle, gently heat the sugar in a heavy pan until it liquifies and turns golden. Mix in the peanuts. Pour onto a baking mat and allow to cool. Break the peanut brittle into smaller pieces.

7 To make the tuile biscuits, mix all the ingredients together to form a smooth paste. Spread small circles of the paste very thinly onto a

baking mat and bake for 4–6 minutes, or until slightly golden. Remove from the oven and immediately curl over an oiled rolling pin to set in a tuile shape. Set aside and leave to cool.

8 For the ganache, pour the cream into a small milk pan and bring to the boil. Remove from the heat, break up the chocolate and stir in gently until it is smooth. Return to the heat and bring to the boil, then remove from heat and allow to cool. Keep at room temperature.

9 Melt the white chocolate in a bowl set over a saucepan of simmering water. Add the double cream.

10 Cut the sponge into 12 rectangles. Repeat with the mousse. Place a layer of mousse onto each plate, and top with a layer of sponge. Repeat the layering twice more. Cover with chocolate ganache, reserving some for decoration, and leave in the fridge to chill. To serve, top each gateau with a tuile biscuit, place pieces of peanut brittle alongside and decorate with the reserved ganache (warmed to help trail on the plate) and the melted white chocolate and cream.

GOLDEN SYRUP CHOCOLATE FONDANTS WITH THICK VANILLA CREAM
Andrew Fletcher graphics designer and 2010 contestant

PREPARATION TIME
15 minutes

COOKING TIME
12–15 minutes

SERVES 4

100g (3½oz) butter, cubed, plus extra
  for greasing
cocoa powder for dusting
100g (3½oz) dark chocolate
  (70% cocoa solids)
2 large eggs

50g (1¾oz) golden caster sugar
50g (1¾oz) golden syrup
20g (¾oz) plain flour
1 vanilla pod, split, seeds scraped out
  and reserved (see MasterTip, p.256)
225ml (7½fl oz) extra thick double cream

JOHN TORODE

"A wonderful crust coating a sticky centre. I admire your bravery cooking something so delicate, so well."

1 Preheat the oven to 170°C (340°F/Gas 3–4). Grease four 150ml (5fl oz) pudding moulds and dust them with cocoa powder.

2 Melt the chocolate and butter in a bowl over a pan of simmering water.

3 In a separate bowl, whisk together the eggs and sugar until pale. Pour the melted chocolate and butter into the eggs and add the golden syrup, then mix well.

4 Sift the flour into the bowl and gently fold in. Divide the mixture between the pudding moulds and place them on a baking sheet.

5 Bake for 12–15 minutes, or until the puddings are set on the outside but still soft and runny inside.

6 Stir the vanilla seeds into the extra thick cream. Turn out the warm puddings and serve with the cream.

FLOURLESS SPICED GINGER AND CHOCOLATE TORTE WITH A GINGER SCENTED CREAM

Aliya Holland nutritionist and 2010 quarter-finalist

100g (3½oz) butter, plus extra
  for greasing
100g (3½oz) dark chocolate
  (70% cocoa solids)
1 tsp vanilla extract
¼ tsp ground cardamom seeds (see
  MasterTip, p.288)
¼ tsp ground ginger

¼ tsp cinnamon powder
2 large eggs, separated
100g (3½oz) caster sugar
50g (1¾oz) ground almonds
25g (scant 1oz) cocoa powder
2 pieces of stem ginger in syrup,
  chopped, plus 2 tbsp of the syrup
100ml (3½fl oz) whipping cream

PREPARATION TIME
30 minutes

COOKING TIME
25–30 minutes

SERVES 4

1 Preheat the oven to 170°C (325°F/Gas 3). Grease and line the bases of two 12.5cm (5in) fluted or plain round loose-bottomed cake or flan tins with baking parchment.
2 Melt the chocolate and butter in a bowl over a pan of simmering water. Then carefully stir in the vanilla and spices.
3 In a separate bowl, whisk together the egg yolks with half the sugar until pale. Fold in the melted chocolate and butter.
4 Sift the almonds and cocoa powder into the bowl and gently fold in.
5 In another clean bowl, whisk the egg whites until they are stiff. Then gradually whisk in the rest of the sugar until it is combined and the whites are glossy and firm.
6 Add one-third of the egg white to the chocolate mixture relatively vigorously and then gently fold in the rest. Divide the mixture between the prepared tins, then sprinkle the stem ginger over the top.
7 Bake for 25–30 minutes, or until slightly soft in the centre but cooked on the outside. Leave to cool slightly in the tins, then turn the cakes out of the tins.
8 Whip the cream with 2 tablespoons of the ginger syrup. Cut each cake in half and serve on plates with the ginger syrup.

GREGG WALLACE

"Wow! I really love that. Your food is so unusual."

CHOCOLATE AND HAZELNUT SOUFFLÉ
John Calton head chef and 2010 Professionals finalist

PREPARATION TIME
35 minutes

COOKING TIME
17 minutes

MAKES 8 SOUFFLÉS

125g (4½oz) butter, plus extra
  for greasing
100g (3½oz) dark chocolate
  (70% cocoa solids)
3 egg whites
40g (1¼oz) caster sugar

FOR THE CRÈME PÂTISSIÈRE
250ml (9fl oz) full-fat milk
1 vanilla pod
3 egg yolks

50g (1¾oz) caster sugar
15g (½oz) plain flour
15g (½oz) cornflour

FOR THE HAZELNUT GANACHE
100g (3½oz) dark chocolate
  (70% cocoa solids)
100ml (3½fl oz) whipping cream
2 tbsp hazelnut paste
  or hazelnut spread
2 tbsp Frangelico

HAZELNUT

The rounded nut, which may also be called cobnut or filbert, has a sweet flavour and pleasantly crunchy texture. Fresh "green" hazelnuts are juicier and milder in taste than the mature, ripe hazelnuts. Roasting hazelnuts enhances their flavour; use in cakes, biscuits, and desserts as well as savoury dishes.

1 For the crème pâtissière, put the milk and vanilla pod in a saucepan and bring to the boil. In a separate bowl, whisk the egg yolks and sugar until thick and creamy. Fold the flour and cornflour into the egg yolk mixture, then add the hot milk, whisking continuously. Return the sauce to the pan, bring up to the boil and cook for 1 minute, whisking all the time. Pass through a fine sieve and leave to cool.
2 To make the ganache, break the chocolate into a bowl. Put the cream in a saucepan and bring to the boil. Pour onto the chocolate and whisk well until fully emulsified. Whisk in the hazelnut paste and Frangelico and leave to cool.
3 For the soufflé, preheat the oven to 200°C (400°F/Gas 6) and place a baking sheet on the middle shelf to preheat. Grease eight 125ml (4fl oz) ramekins with a small knob of butter. Place in the fridge for 5 minutes, remove and re-grease. Dust the insides of each with a little sugar and return them to the fridge until needed.
4 Melt together the butter and chocolate in a bowl standing over a pan of barely simmering water. In a separate bowl, whisk the egg whites until soft peaks form, and then whisk in the sugar until glossy. Once the butter and chocolate have melted, fold in the crème pâtissière and 100g (3½oz) of the ganache. Then fold in the egg whites.
5 Spoon the mixture into the ramekins. Lightly tap the dishes to level the mixture and fill to the top. Run your finger around the edge of each ramekin to help achieve an even rise. Cook in the oven for 15–17 minutes or until well risen (they should be about 2–3cm/¾–1¼in over the top of the dish) and firm on the top, but still slightly wobbly when moved. Serve immediately. See also the MasterClass pages 312–13 for more advice on making soufflés.

ORANGE AND CHOCOLATE BAKED MERINGUE

Tim Kinnaird paediatrician and 2010 finalist

butter, for greasing
5 eggs, separated
250g (9oz) caster sugar
280ml (9½fl oz) double cream
60g (2oz) plain chocolate (70% cocoa
    solids), broken into pieces

½ vanilla pod, split, seeds scraped out
    and reserved (see MasterTip, p.256)
100ml (3½fl oz) full fat milk
10g (¼oz) ginger, peeled and sliced
200ml (7fl oz) orange juice

PREPARATION TIME
50 minutes, plus infusing

COOKING TIME
45 minutes

SERVES 4–6

1 Preheat the oven to 150°C (300°F/Gas 2). Grease a 20cm (8in) springform cake tin and wrap the base in foil to prevent water getting in. Also base-line an 18cm (7in) cake tin with greaseproof paper.
2 For the meringue, put the egg whites into a mixing bowl with 200g (7oz) of the sugar. Discard 3 of the yolks and put the other 2 in a separate bowl and set aside. Place the bowl of egg whites over a pan of simmering water and whisk by hand until the sugar has dissolved. Remove from the heat and whisk until soft peaks form.
3 Set aside 70g (2¼oz) of the meringue in a bowl and pour the rest into the foil-wrapped cake tin, ensuring there are no air pockets in the meringue, and place it in a roasting tray. Pour 1cm (½in) of water into the tray and cook in the oven for 20 minutes or until the meringue is just set and without any colour. Remove the roasting pan from the oven and leave the meringue to cool in the fridge.
4 For the mousse, pour 120ml (4fl oz) of the cream into a pan and gently warm it. Melt the chocolate in a bowl set over simmering water, then add the cream. Leave to cool. In a separate bowl, whisk 60ml (2fl oz) of the cream to just less than soft peaks. Fold 70g (2¼oz) of the meringue into the chocolate and cream. Then fold in 60ml (2fl oz) of the whipped cream. Pour into the remaining cake tin and put in the freezer.
5 For the custard, add the vanilla pod and seeds to the remaining 100ml (3½fl oz) of cream and 100ml (3½fl oz) of milk in a saucepan. Bring to a simmer, then leave to infuse for 30 minutes.
6 Add 25g (scant 1oz) of sugar to the 2 egg yolks. Remove the pod from the milk and cream, pour the warmed milk onto the yolks and whisk. Return to the milk pan and put on gentle heat, stirring constantly. When thickened, strain into a jug and cover in cling film.
7 Put the ginger, juice, and remaining sugar into a pan. Gently heat to dissolve the sugar. Bring to the boil and reduce to a syrup.
8 To serve, remove the meringue from its tin and turn out onto the chocolate mousse. Cut into wedges. Pour the custard onto plates, place a pool of ginger orange syrup in the middle and a wedge of meringue and mousse on top. Decorate with caramel shards, if using.

MASTER TIP

CARAMEL SHARDS

For an optional decoration, make a hard caramel to break into shards. Gently heat 50g (1¾oz) caster sugar in a small saucepan until it turns a golden caramel. Pour it onto a sheet of greased foil and, when cooled, break into shards.

JOHN TORODE

"The softness of the baked meringue on top and then going into this really rich chocolate mousse sitting underneath, is fantastic."

DARK CHOCOLATE AND ALMOND TORTE WITH AMARETTO CREAM, RASPBERRIES, AND PASSION FRUIT

Dhruv Baker sales director and 2010 champion

PREPARATION TIME
30 minutes

COOKING TIME
30 minutes

MAKES 8 SLICES

150g (5½oz) dark chocolate
  (70% cocoa solids)
125g (4½oz) unsalted butter
5 eggs, separated
175g (6oz) light soft brown sugar
175g (6oz) ground almonds

100ml (3½fl oz) amaretto, plus 1 tbsp
  for amaretto cream
100ml (3½fl oz) double cream
1 punnet raspberries
2 passion fruit, peeled, cut in half,
  and seeds scooped out
icing sugar

1 Preheat the oven to 150°C (300°F/Gas 2). Line the base of a 23cm (9in) diameter springform baking tin with baking parchment and butter the sides.

2 Melt the chocolate and butter in a large bowl placed over a saucepan of simmering water. Once melted, remove from heat and leave to cool slightly.

3 In a separate bowl, whisk the egg whites with a whisk until they form peaks.

4 Mix the sugar and almonds in the chocolate mixture, then stir in the egg yolks and the 100ml (3½fl oz) of amaretto.

5 Finally, fold the egg whites into the chocolate mixture using a metal spoon. Pour the mixture into the prepared tin and bake for about 30 minutes or until firm on top and a skewer comes out clean. Remove the torte from the oven and allow to cool for a few minutes.

6 Whip the cream with a whisk and pour in the remaining amaretto.

7 Put the passion fruit flesh into a blender or food processor and whisk to a pulp. Push through a sieve and add icing sugar to taste.

8 To serve, place a slice of the torte on each plate. Drizzle over some passion fruit coulis and add a spoonful of the cream and a few raspberries.

GREGG WALLACE "That cake is so full of all the flavours that I love. And it is so moist. Mate, that is just majestic."

BITTER CHOCOLATE AND ORANGE BREAD AND BUTTER PUDDING WITH VANILLA CUSTARD

Jez Barfoot restoration builder and 2010 quarter-finalist

PREPARATION TIME
25 minutes

COOKING TIME
40 minutes

SERVES 4

FOR THE PUDDING
8 thick slices of white bread
grated zest and juice of 1 orange
50g (1¾oz) butter, softened, plus extra
  for greasing
100g (3½oz) dark chocolate
  (70% cocoa solids), broken into pieces
150g (5½oz) demerara sugar
150ml (5fl oz) double cream
150ml (5fl oz) full-fat milk
¼ tsp ground cinnamon
¼ tsp ground nutmeg or pinch
  of freshly grated nutmeg

1 egg
3 tbsp Cointreau

FOR THE CUSTARD
150ml (5fl oz) double cream
150ml (5fl oz) whole milk
1 vanilla pod, split, seeds scraped out
  and reserved (see MasterTip, p.256)
1 egg, plus 1 egg yolk
1 tbsp demerara sugar

GREGG WALLACE

"A hint of orange, then the warmth of liqueur and the cosiness of chocolate, all in a sponge with vanilla cream on top. It's heaven. That is delicious!"

1 Preheat the oven to 170°C (340°F/Gas 3–4). Butter 4 individual 10cm (4in) springform cake tins.

2 Cut the bread into circles using a pastry cutter slightly smaller than the size of the cake tins. Mix the orange zest and butter and spread onto each slice of bread. Put 1 circle of bread in each cake tin and top with the chocolate and 100g (3½oz) of the sugar.

3 Mix the cream, milk, cinnamon, nutmeg, egg, and Cointreau together with 1 tbsp of the orange juice in a bowl. Pour over the bread and then sprinkle the remaining sugar on top. Bake in the oven for 25 minutes until golden brown. Let the puddings cool slightly before releasing them from the tins.

4 Make the custard by heating the cream and milk in a saucepan with the vanilla seeds. Mix together the whole egg and egg yolk with the sugar. Gradually whisk the hot milk and cream into the egg and sugar, then return to the pan and heat gently, stirring, over low heat until thickened slightly to a pouring consistency like single cream. Do not let it boil.

5 To serve, put each pudding on a serving plate and pour the custard around the edge.

MICHEL ROUX JR'S
WARM BITTER CHOCOLATE TART WITH BITTER ORANGE SAUCE

This tart has a soft, crumbly pastry with a rich, chocolately centre. The bitter orange sauce offsets the sweetness perfectly for a well-balanced slice of indulgence.

FOR THE SWEET PASTRY
115g (4oz) plain flour
50g (1¾oz) butter, slightly softened
50g (1¾oz) caster sugar
2 large egg yolks

FOR THE FILLING
2 eggs
3 egg yolks
120g (4¼oz) caster sugar

250g (9oz) dark chocolate (70% cocoa solids), broken into pieces
160g (5¾oz) unsalted butter

FOR THE SAUCE
150ml (5fl oz) orange juice
50g (1¾oz) caster sugar
50g (1¾oz) bitter orange marmalade

TO SERVE
double cream, whipped or poured

PREPARATION TIME
40 minutes

COOKING TIME
55 minutes

SERVES 4

1 To make the pastry, tip all the ingredients into a food processor and pulse until just combined, like very wet sand. Tip out onto the work surface and knead briefly, about 5 times, until it comes together. Wrap the pastry in cling film and rest in the fridge for at least an hour before rolling out.

2 Preheat the oven to 180°C (350°F/Gas 4). Roll out the pastry and use to line a 25cm (10in) flan ring. Cover the base of the pastry with a circle of greaseproof paper and some dried beans and bake blind for 15–20 minutes until the pastry is crisp and golden. Remove the baking beans and greaseproof paper and set the case aside. Reduce the oven temperature to 140°C (275°F/Gas 1).

3 For the filling, whisk the eggs, yolks, and sugar in an electric mixer until thick, very pale, and frothy. Place the chocolate and butter in a bowl over simmering water to melt, then fold into the egg mixture. Pour into the pastry base and bake in the oven for 20 minutes, or until set. Remove from the oven and leave to cool until tepid.

4 Make the orange sauce by boiling the orange juice and sugar for about 5 minutes until reduced by about half. Add the marmalade and pass through a sieve before serving.

5 To serve, cut the tart into slices, pour the orange sauce in a pool alongside, and serve with double cream.

CHOCOLATE AND GINGER TART WITH CARAMELIZED ORANGES, GRAND MARNIER SAUCE, RED BERRY SOUP, AND TUILES

Christine Hamilton TV personality and 2010 Celebrity finalist

PREPARATION TIME
2 hours

COOKING TIME
1 hour

SERVES 8

115g (4oz) butter
1 tbsp icing sugar
pinch of ground ginger
175g (6oz) plain flour
125g (4½oz) dark chocolate
   (70% cocoa solids)
85g (3oz) unsalted butter
1 large egg
2 large egg yolks
20g (¾oz) caster sugar
4 pieces of stem ginger, finely chopped

FOR THE ORANGES
2 oranges
icing sugar

FOR THE SAUCE
grated zest and juice of 4 oranges
2 tsp cornflour

2 tbsp Grand Marnier
caster sugar, to taste

FOR THE ORANGE AND ALMOND TUILES
30g (1oz) butter, plus extra for greasing
1 egg white
60g (2oz) caster sugar
30g (1oz) plain flour, sifted
zest of 1 orange
2 tbsp toasted flaked almonds

FOR THE SOUP
75g (2½oz) caster sugar
500ml (16fl oz) red grape juice
75g (2½oz) crème fraîche
225g (8oz) mixed berries, such as
   raspberries, blueberries,
   and redcurrants

1 To make the pastry, melt the butter until it is hot, but not boiling. Add 1 tsp of water with the icing sugar and ginger and mix. Then mix in the flour. While the pastry is still warm, press it into the base and up the sides of a 23cm (9in) round loose-bottomed tart tin. Leave to chill for 30 minutes. Preheat the oven to 190°C (375°F/Gas 5). For a more delicate look, do not take the pastry up the sides of the tin and, once the tart is cooled, cut it into a heart or any other shape.
2 Prick the pastry and cover the base of the pastry with a circle of greaseproof paper. Add some baking beans and bake blind for 12–15 minutes until lightly golden. Remove the beans and paper and bake for another 5–10 minutes until the pastry feels sandy to the touch. Leave to cool and reduce the oven temperature to 150°C (300°F/Gas 2).
3 To make the filling, melt the chocolate and butter in a bowl set over simmering water until smooth and just warm. In a separate bowl, whisk the egg, egg yolks, and sugar until thick, light, and frothy.
4 Mix the stem ginger into the chocolate and then fold the chocolate and butter into the egg mixture. Spoon into the pastry case and bake for about 10 minutes until lightly set.

5 For the caramelized oranges, cut the top and bottom off the oranges and slice off the peel. Cut out the segments and lay on a sheet of baking parchment. Dust liberally with the icing sugar and then caramelize under a hot grill or with a blow torch. Repeat with another layer of icing sugar.

6 For the sauce, mix 2 tbsp of the orange juice with the cornflour. Put the remaining juice in a saucepan and bring to the boil. Stir in the cornflour mix and cook for about 2 minutes. Remove from the heat and stir in the Grand Marnier and orange zest, adding sugar to taste.

7 For the tuiles, preheat the oven to 190°C (375°F/Gas 5) and grease a baking sheet. Melt the butter in a saucepan. In a separate bowl, whisk the egg white until stiff and then add the sugar, continuing to beat until smooth and stiff. Still whisking, slowly add the melted butter to the eggs and then add the flour. Finally, fold in the orange zest. Spread out teaspoonfuls of the mixture, well spaced, on the baking sheet and top with toasted almonds. Bake in the oven for 5 minutes or until just cooked.

8 To make the red berry soup, put the sugar and grape juice in a saucepan. Bring to the boil and continue to boil for 5 minutes. Reduce the heat, allow to settle, add the crème fraîche and leave to simmer gently for 5 minutes. Add the berries to the soup at the last minute and gently heat them. Serve warm or at room temperature.

9 To serve, pour the red berry soup into 8 small glasses and stand each in the middle of a serving plate. Add a pool of orange sauce on one side and top with 2 orange segments. Finish with a slice of tart, (or cut-out shapes, see above) on the other side with 2 of the tuiles.

GREGG WALLACE

"The chocolate is absolutely lovely and I love the oranges and the Grand Marnier. Absolute typical Christine, this is. Set out to do one dessert, end up with twelve."

FLAVOUR COMBINATION
CHOCOLATE, GINGER, AND ORANGE

Of course chocolate combines wondrously with ginger and with orange. But some ways are better than others. Butter, eggs, and chocolate make a truffle-like mixture with chopped stem ginger, and this velvet creaminess subdues any ginger-burn potential, ensuring subtle delivery to the palate. The accompaniments offer orange in different guises, all picking up and enhancing the tart's scents and flavours.

BAKED CHOCOLATE MOUSSE CAKE WITH POACHED WHISKY PEARS AND VANILLA CREAM

Will Adams tailor and 2010 quarter-finalist

PREPARATION TIME
50 minutes

COOKING TIME
20–25 minutes

SERVES 4

300g (10fl oz) plain chocolate
 (70% cocoa solids)
150g (5½oz) butter
50g (1¾oz) caster sugar
6 eggs, separated
150g (5½oz) mascarpone cheese
1 vanilla pod, split, seeds scraped
 out and reserved with the pod
 (see MasterTip, p.256)

1 piece of stem ginger in syrup,
 finely chopped
icing sugar, for sweetening and dusting
2 William or Packham pears
2 tbsp clear honey
2 tbsp Scotch whisky

GREGG WALLACE

"I like the way the cake's made. Really light, much lighter than it looks. Putting that with pear and a little bit of mascarpone, that's a joy!"

1 Preheat the oven to 180°C (350°F/Gas 4) and grease a 23cm diameter, deep springform cake tin.
2 Melt the chocolate and butter in a bowl over barely simmering water.
3 Put 30g (1oz) of the sugar and the egg yolks into a bowl and whisk until combined. Clean the whisk and then whisk the egg whites with the remaining sugar in a separate bowl until stiff peaks form.
4 Pour the melted chocolate into the egg yolks and mix well. Then fold in the egg whites and pour into the cake tin. Bake for 20 minutes, or until set but still slightly moist. Remove from the oven, leave to cool in the tin, and then turn out and cut into slices.
5 For the cream, put the mascarpone cheese into a bowl and stir in the vanilla seeds. Then add the stem ginger and add icing sugar to taste if you feel the cream is not sweet enough.
6 Peel one of the pears, then core, and dice it. Put the pear pieces into a saucepan and add the honey, split vanilla pod, whisky, and 1 tablespoon of water. Stir together and simmer gently for 10–15 minutes, or until the pear is tender. Set aside.
7 Preheat the grill to hot. Peel the second pear and cut 4 thin slices from the centre. Place on a baking sheet, dust with icing sugar and grill (or use a blow torch) for about 1 minute until lightly browned.
8 To serve, put a slice of cake on each plate. Drain the pears in syrup and spoon the pears to one side of the cake, adding the mascarpone to the other, decorated with a pear slice.

STEAMED CHOCOLATE PUDDING WITH VANILLA ICE CREAM AND COGNAC CHOCOLATE SAUCE

Nargis Chaudhary physiotherapist and 2010 semi-finalist

FOR THE ICE CREAM
300ml (10fl oz) double cream
300ml (10fl oz) whole milk
115g (4oz) golden caster sugar
1 vanilla pod (see MasterTip, p.256)
3 large eggs

FOR THE PUDDING
100g (3½oz) dark chocolate
　(55% cocoa solids)
100g (3½oz) butter
2 tsp instant coffee granules
45g (1½oz) plain flour

45g (1½oz) self-raising flour
⅛ tsp bicarbonate of soda
100g (3½oz) dark soft brown sugar
100g (3½oz) golden caster sugar
15g (½oz) cocoa powder
2 eggs

FOR THE SAUCE
100g (3½oz) dark chocolate
　(55% cocoa solids)
150ml (5fl oz) double cream
1 tbsp golden caster sugar
2 tbsp Cognac

PREPARATION TIME
45–50 minutes, plus freezing

COOKING TIME
1 hour 30 minutes

SERVES 4–6

1   To make the ice cream, heat the cream and the milk in a pan. Add half the sugar and the vanilla pod and heat until almost boiling. Set aside for 10 minutes for the vanilla to infuse.
2   In a separate bowl, whisk the egg yolks and remaining sugar until pale and the mixture leaves a trail when the blades are lifted out of it.
3   Strain the cream and remove the vanilla pod. Then add the cream to the egg and reheat over low heat, stirring constantly, until a thick custard consistency is achieved and it coats the back of a spoon. Leave to cool, then churn in an ice-cream maker, and freeze.
4   For the pudding, preheat the oven to 200°C (400°F/Gas 6). Butter a 1 litre (1¾ pints) pudding basin and line the base with greaseproof paper. Melt the chocolate and butter in a bowl over simmering water. Mix the coffee in 4 tbsp of cold water and stir into the chocolate.
5   Sift the flours, bicarbonate of soda, sugars, and cocoa into a bowl. In a separate bowl, beat the eggs. Whisk the eggs into the melted chocolate and then fold in the dry ingredients. Pour into the pudding bowl and cover with a piece of greased foil. Secure it with string and place in a roasting tin. Put the tin on the oven shelf and pour in boiling water coming half way up the sides of the basin. Cook for 1½ hours or until a skewer comes out clean. Turn out onto a serving dish.
6   For the sauce, melt the chocolate, pour in the cream, and add the sugar. Once melted, add the Cognac, to taste. Pour over the pudding and serve with a ball of the ice cream.

JOHN TORODE "The pudding is stodgy and beautiful, the chocolate sauce is rich with booze and smooth."

CHEFS' BIOGRAPHIES

On these pages are listed all the chefs featured in the book with short biographies and a list of their recipes. Chefs are listed in alphabetical order by surname.

MITRA ABRAHAMS
MASTERCHEF 2010: SEMI-FINALIST

Living in Edinburgh and loving Scottish produce, Mitra enjoys creating new dishes for her friends whenever time allows.

STARTER Cauliflower and barberry fritters with yogurt sauce p.22

MAIN Lamb stew with apple and sour plums p.176

WILL ADAMS
MASTERCHEF 2010: QUARTER-FINALIST

Still working as a tailor in London, Will hasn't yet given up his dreams of becoming a chef one day.

STARTER Broad bean and prosciutto ravioli with a red pepper sauce p.34

DESSERT Baked chocolate mousse cake with poached pears and whisky cream p.344

ROZ ANSLOW
MASTERCHEF 2010: QUARTER-FINALIST

Off the back of the show Roz is now the food critic on her local paper, and hopes to publish her own cookbook.

DESSERT Chocolate truffle mousse with poppy seeds and orange tuiles p.323

NIHAL ARTHANAYAKE
CELEBRITY 2010: CONTESTANT

TV presenter and award-winning radio host for his shows on BBC Radio 1 and the BBC Asian Network.

STARTER Butternut squash soup p.16

DHRUV BAKER
MASTERCHEF 2010: CHAMPION

Since winning the show Dhruv has worked in several Michelin-starred kitchens, and plans to open his own restaurant in 2011.

STARTERS Gazpacho shots with tiger prawns p.14, Saffron glazed scallops with apple and pistachio purée p.44, Spiced lobster with fennel, celeriac purée, and a fennel chilli mayonnaise p.50, Spiced battered fish and chips p.97

MAINS Pan-fried halibut with sauté potatoes, and a creamy clam sauce p.108, Ballotine of chicken with girolles and Madeira sauce p.140, Spiced duck poori and saffron raita p.146, Pan-roasted duck in pickling spices with carrot purée and plum sauce p.152, Soy braised duck with parsnip and turmeric purée p.154, Musallam lamb two-ways p.174, Herb-crusted rump of lamb with balsamic-roasted beetroot and a tomato herb jus p.182, Chennai spiced ballotine of guinea fowl p.216, Roast loin of venison with chestnuts, venison jus, and chilli chocolate p.240

DESSERTS Strawberry and "Champagne" jelly p.264, Mango and cardamom rum syllabub spoons p.307, Dark chocolate and almond torte with amaretto cream p.338

JEZ BARFOOT
MASTERCHEF 2010: QUARTER-FINALIST

Jez is currently working as a head chef in Dorset, and is looking to open his own restaurant in 2011.

MAIN Honey-glazed pork filet mignon p.205

DESSERT Bitter chocolate and orange bread and butter pudding p.340

NATALIE BRENNER
MASTERCHEF 2010: QUARTER-FINALIST

Natalie works for a sports marketing and events firm and still loves cooking in her spare time.

DESSERT Banana soufflé with blueberry coulis p.310

JOHN CALTON
PROFESSIONALS 2010: FINALIST

John is working at a new restaurant in the North East, and continues to enjoy learning about cooking and the restaurant business.

STARTERS Pan-fried sea scallops with peas, crispy bacon, and quail's egg p.39, Tartare of scallops with oyster beignet p.40

MAINS Pan-fried fillets of seabass with citrus fruits, fennel, and coriander p.98, Pan-fried turbot with langoustines and truffled celeriac purée p.104, Pan-roasted breast of duck, rainbow chard, carrots, and polenta p148, Roast lamb, with olive sauce and anchovy tempura p.178

DESSERTS Warm ginger cake with rhubarb p.253, Dark chocolate mousse and green tea financier p.320, White chocolate soup p.325, Chocolate pavé with a peanut tuile p331, Chocolate and hazelnut soufflé p.336

NARGIS CHAUDHARY
MASTERCHEF 2010: SEMI-FINALIST

Still working as a physiotherapist, Nargis is also making plans to open a bakery in the near future.

STARTER Fish pakoras with raita p.54

MAINS Sea bream with ratatouille and crispy potato and cheese balls p.106, Murg saag on pilau rice p.145, Thai green chicken curry p.146

DESSERTS Lemon tart p.295, Steamed chocolate pudding with Cognac chocolate sauce p.345

ALICE CHURCHILL
PROFESSIONALS 2010: SEMI-FINALIST

Since the show Alice has moved to London and is now working in a Michelin-starred restaurant in the capital.

MAIN Roasted salmon with clams, broad bean purée, and horseradish broth p.122

DESSERTS Bee pollen mousse with rhubarb and raspberry jelly p.260, Chocolate and praline gateau with peanut brittle p.332

GARY COOKE
PROFESSIONALS 2010: QUARTER-FINALIST

Gary continues to work as a professional chef and is still striving to open his own restaurant one day.

STARTER Seared Orkney scallops and glazed pork belly with sweetcorn p.43

MAIN Roe venison with crispy polenta p.232

DAVID COULSON
PROFESSIONALS 2010: FINALIST

Having left his previous job just before MasterChef, David is now working in a new restaurant in the North East.

STARTERS Scallops with potato pancakes and a salsa verde dressing p.42, Grilled smoked haddock, black pudding, fried quail's egg p.67, Mackerel tartare and smoked mackerel paté with cucumber papardelle p.68

MAIN Chicken and mushroom pie p.142

DESSERTS Rice crispy cake with hot chocolate mousse and cherry sorbet p.268, Banana bread and brown butter ice cream p.314, Chocolate and banana brulée with brioche soldiers p.330

MATT EDWARDS
MASTERCHEF 2010: SEMI-FINALIST

Matt has left the music industry behind and is now chef de partie at the new St John hotel and restaurant in London.

STARTER Salad of wood pigeon with a warm blackberry vinaigrette p.83

MAIN Black bream with mussels p.107

DESSERT Saucy lemon pudding p.294

LISA FAULKNER
CELEBRITY 2010: CHAMPION

Actress Lisa is best known for her roles in Holby City and Spooks, and is now looking to continue her culinary adventures!

STARTERS Goat's cheese and red onion tarts p.32, Mackerel with smoked beetroot p.66, Smoked salmon and dill soufflé p.74

MAINS Fish stew with almonds, rosemary, and aïoli p.93, Monkfish with butternut squash fondant and sauce vierge p.94, Pan-fried sea trout with crushed new potatoes and baby leeks p.117, Chicken braised in cider and chorizo p.130

DESSERTS Rhubarb and ginger crumble p.257, Almond panna cotta with poached tamarillos and berries p.304

ALEX FLETCHER
CELEBRITY 2010: QUARTER-FINALIST

Stage and screen actress Alex was a key member of the Brookside team, playing the role of Jacqui Farnham (née Dixon) for over a decade, and she is now appearing in Hollyoaks.

STARTER Smoked haddock Florentine p.64

DESSERT Baked pears in wine p.284

ANDREW FLETCHER
MASTERCHEF 2010: CONTESTANT

Now a creative director in Leeds, Andrew cooks whenever he can – and his Mum always makes him do lunch when he goes home!

DESSERT Golden syrup chocolate fondants p.334

LEE GROVES
PROFESSIONALS 2010: SEMI-FINALIST

Lee continues to run the kitchen at Headland Hotel in Newquay.

STARTER Roast red mullet with plum tomatoes and tapenade p.61

DESSERT Pear and rosemary tarte Tatin with star anise ice cream p285, Lime posset with caramelised pineapple and basil cream p298

CHRISTINE HAMILTON
CELEBRITY 2010: FINALIST

Self-confessed Battleaxe and Media Butterfly, Christine is a regular of TV and radio, writes for national newspapers, and is in demand as an after-dinner speaker.

STARTERS Scallops with mint and pea risotto p.38, Smoked haddock timbale p.62

MAINS Halibut in a chervil cream sauce with minted peas p.109, Ragout of fish with basil cream sauce and Parmesan twists p.114, Pancetta-wrapped chicken with tomato, pine nut, and basil stuffing p.134, Moroccan spiced lamb with wild rice p.173, Fillet of beef with twice-baked cheese and leek soufflé p.192, Pheasant with apple and haggis rings p.221, Collops of venison in a blackberry sauce p.245

DESSERTS Apple and ginger tart with ruby grapefruit sabayon p.271, Citrus meringue tart with cinnamon cream and passion fruit p.290, Spiced pineapple with coconut rice p.302, Beaumes de Venise ice cream with brandy snaps p.315, Panettone pudding p.318, Chocolate and ginger tart with caramelised oranges and Grand Marnier sauce p.342

ALIYA HOLLAND
MASTERCHEF 2010: QUARTER-FINALIST

Aliya and family have moved to South Africa where she's getting her local community involved in cooking healthy food.

DESSERT Flourless spiced ginger and chocolate torte p.335

DANIEL HOWELL
PROFESSIONALS 2010: QUARTER-FINALIST

Daniel is still working at the Olive Tree in Penarth and loving it!

MAIN Roast rack of lamb with a curry-scented sauce p.172

DESSERT Warm cinnamon sponge pudding with pear purée and honey mascarpone p.286

TERRY IRELAND
MASTERCHEF 2010: SEMI-FINALIST

Since the show Terry has moved down to Dorset and is working as a sous chef in 2009 MasterChef champion Mat Follas' restaurant The Wild Garlic.

MAIN Roast rabbit loin, rabbit cake, and mustard sauce p.230

DESSERT Rhubarb crumble p.261

COLIN JACKSON
CELEBRITY 2010: QUARTER-FINALIST

Former 110m Hurdles world record holder and Olympic silver medallist Colin is now a broadcaster and presenter.

MAIN Spare rib chop with rice and peas p.204

JO JENKINS
MASTERCHEF 2010: QUARTER-FINALIST

Jo continues to be practice manager of their very busy dental practice, and caters for charity dinners when she can.

DESSERT Rosé and orange rhubarb with zabaglione p.252

TIM KINNAIRD
MASTERCHEF 2010: FINALIST

Since the show Tim has left his job as a paediatrician and now runs a cake business specializing in macarons.

STARTERS Celeriac soup with curried scallops p.20, Tomato salad in a tuile basket with basil sorbet p.26, Open lasagne of roasted squash and wild mushrooms with sage butter p.36

MAINS Pan-fried sea bass with langoustines and fennel p.99, Hake with lemon and anchovy potatoes p.101, Chicken roulade with a honey, walnut, and pine nut sauce p.138, Roast belly of pork with apples, black pudding, and butternut squash p.206, Roasted pheasant with pommes Anna, bread sauce, and sloe jelly p.218, Roasted partridge with polenta p.223

DESSERTS Gooseberry and elderflower syllabub p.270, Mont Blanc with coffee-poached pear p.280, Green tea and lemon delice p.288, Exploding lemon macaroons p.296, Lemon cream with amaretti biscuits p.299, Orange and chocolate baked meringue p.337

CLAIRE LARA
PROFESSIONALS 2010: CHAMPION

Claire is enjoying motherhood after the birth of her first child, and is working with husband Marc on plans to open a restaurant together.

STARTERS Goat's cheese ravioli with raisin and almond beurre noisette p.35, Pan-fried red mullet with buttered spider crab and fennel and orange salad p.60, Mi-cuit sea trout with apple purée and cider beurre blanc p.70

MAINS Pan-fried mackerel, shallot purée, and à la grecque vegetables p.116, Lamb with liver and sweetbreads p.163, Rump of hogget with lentil ravigot and stuffed baby artichokes p.184, Pan-roasted calf's liver with spring broth p.200, Roasted pigeon with pommes mousseline and pancetta peas p.214

DESSERTS Vanilla panna cotta with rhubarb and raspberry compote p.256, White chocolate mousse with raspberry and elderflower jelly p.328

MARK LITTLE
CELEBRITY 2010: CONTESTANT

TV and stage actor as well as stand-up comedian, Mark is best known for his rissoles on MasterChef.

STARTER Butternut squash soup with sage and Parmesan damper p.17

DEAN MACEY
CELEBRITY 2010: QUARTER-FINALIST

Olympic decathlete and Commonwealth Gold medallist, Dean now works as a sports broadcaster.

MAIN Pan-fried cod with Provençal vegetables in a Roquefort cheese sauce p.91

DESSERT Caramelised warm berries cooked in star anise and vanilla, topped with coconut cream p.303

NEIL MACKENZIE
PROFESSIONALS 2010: QUARTER-FINALIST

Neil has moved back up to Scotland and is working in a Michelin-listed restaurant in Edinburgh.

MAIN Rump of new seaon lamb with crushed spring vegetables p.180

DESSERT Floating islands with mango p.309

RENAUD MARIN
PROFESSIONALS 2010: QUARTER-FINALIST

Renaud is still working as a head chef, now in Hong Kong in the fine dining restaurant at a boutique hotel.

MAIN Roasted beef fillet with a black olive emulsion, confits, and a socca and Swiss chard millefeuille p.190

DESSERT Spicy pineapple carpaccio with mascarpone and Medjool date mousse p.306

CONOR MARRON
MASTERCHEF 2010: CONTESTANT

Still working as a training vascular surgeon, since the show Conor has run several cookery courses and consulted for a local restaurant.

MAIN Loin of venison with cherry and bitter chocolate sauce p.242

ANDREW PARRY
MASTERCHEF 2010: QUARTER-FINALIST

Since MasterChef Andrew has opened a restaurant and still enjoys cooking game and foraging.

MAIN Venison liver and red cabbage with a smoked bacon and brandy cream sauce p.246

BEN PIETTE
PROFESSIONALS 2010: SEMI-FINALIST

Continues to love working as head of hospitality at the McLaren Technology Centre, looking after all the visitors and team.

MAINS John Dory and cockles on spiced lentils p.96, Chaud-froid of salmon on peas and broad beans with lemon hollandaise p.123, Chargrilled rack of lamb and confit of shoulder with sautéed potatoes, tomatoes, and garlic mayonnaise p.168

DESSERTS Pear and vanilla sponge with dark chocolate sauce p.277, Flambée of bananas with ginger panna cotta, dark rum ice cream and cookies p.308

ALEX RUSHMER
MASTERCHEF 2010: FINALIST

Still a food writer, Alex is currently working on his first book and will be opening a restaurant in Cambridgeshire in Spring 2011.

STARTERS Lime and chilli salmon with crème fraîche on black pepper oatcakes p.73, Pheasant saltimbocca with butternut squash and beetroot jus p.84

MAINS Sea trout with beetroot purée p.118, Roasted chicken breast with thyme risotto and pan-fried chanterelles p.139, Duck with spiced tobacco caramel, potato rosti, pickled cucumber, and duck heart salad p.150, Tea-smoked duck with lobster, apple purée, maple jelly, and bitter leaves p.156, Pan-fried lamb sweetbreads with hazelnut brittle, and blackberry coulis p.164, Osso buco, saffron fondant potato and pea gremolata p.195, Braised pig's cheeks with deep-fried ears, apple jelly, mashed potato, and blackberry sauce p.210, Pan-fried pigeon breast with ravioli p.222, Loin of venison with braised cabbage and redcurrant jus p.238

DESSERTS Apple, vanilla, and bay leaf tarte Tatin with Calvados cream p.273, Pear tatin with Stilton ice cream and walnut and tobacco brittle p.282, Chocolate pots, coffee espuma, and shortbread biscuits p.324

DANIEL SAVAGE
PROFESSIONALS 2010: QUARTER-FINALIST

Daniel continues to work as head chef at Caistor Hall Hotel.

STARTER Confit of salmon and roasted baby beetroots p.72

ALAN SIMPSON
MASTERCHEF 2010: CONTESTANT

A medical underwriter from Falkirk in Scotland, 2010 was topped off by the birth of his son.

MAIN Sea bass with crispy prosciutto ham and crushed new potatoes p.100

STACIE STEWART
MASTERCHEF 2010: SEMI-FINALIST

Still working as a PA, Stacie also now runs the Beehive Bakery offering a mail order cakes service.

MAINS Poached chicken with spinach, mushrooms, and broad beans in a creamy Somerset cider sauce p.131, Roasted pork loin with crackling and pease pudding p.202, Tea-smoked venison with cabbage, beetroot purée, and a red wine sauce p.244

DESSERTS Spiced plum crumble p.289, Sticky toffee pudding with clotted cream p.31

DICK STRAWBRIDGE
CELEBRITY 2010: FINALIST

Television presenter, eco-engineer, retired army colonel and proud owner of the best moustache in showbusiness.

STARTERS Whiting quenelles in broth p.18, Lamb's kidney with a Vermouth sauce on celeriac rosti p.78, Carpaccio of beef salad with horseradish tuile, oyster emulsion, and "Champagne" caviar p.80, Creamy mushrooms with haggis, potato cakes, and black velvet sauce p.82, Cornish seafood ravioli with a crab sauce and samphire p.124

MAINS Fig and chilli lamb with champ, cabbage, and sweet chestnuts p.162, Beef and chorizo with horseradish mash and roasted rosemary dumplings p.199, Poacher's roast p.224, Rabbit with mustard dumpling served with cider cream and mustard sauce p.228

DESSERTS Rhubarb crumble tart with syllabub and rhubarb syrup p.254, Apple and raspberry filo baskets with a West Country athol brose p.262, Wensleydale and apple pudding with a 17th-century posset p.272, Quince poached in rosewater p.287

NEIL STUKE
CELEBRITY 2010: SEMI-FINALIST

Actor Neil has starred in many much-loved television series such as Game-On, Grafters, Trust, The Sins and Reggie Perrin.

STARTERS Beetroot, walnut, and goat's curd salad, with a sherry vinegar and lemon dressing p.28, Langoustine risotto with courgette and roasted cherry tomatoes p.46, Monkfish wrapped in pancetta with beurre blanc p.58

MAINS Fried sea bass and clams with green sauce and rice p.92, Beef wrapped in coppa di Parma with swiss chard and soft polenta p.186

DESSERT Custard tart with rhubarb stewed in whisky and ginger cream p.258

CHRIS WALKER
CELEBRITY 2010: SEMI-FINALIST

Actor Chris has appeared on our TV screens in many guises, most notably for his award-winning role in Doctors.

STARTER Salmon with caviar velouté and poached quail's egg p.76

MAINS Fillet of beef with wild mushrooms and Madeira sauce p.189, Loin of pork in a black pudding crust p.201

STACEY WARR
PROFESSIONALS 2010: SEMI-FINALIST

Since appearing on the show Stacey has moved to a new restaurant in Leicestershire where she is now head chef.

MAIN Roasted fillet of beef with vanilla mash and shallot jus p.188

MATTHEW WORSWICK
PROFESSIONALS 2010: SEMI-FINALIST

Matthew is still working towards his goal of cooking in the best kitchens in the country at the highest level he can.

STARTER Seared pavé of brill on parsnip purée with raisin butter sauce p.55

London, New York, Munich, Melbourne, and Delhi

First published in Great Britain in 2011
by Dorling Kindersley Limited
80 Strand, London WC2R 0RL

Penguin Group (UK)

MasterChef
www.masterchef.com

Senior Editor Alastair Laing
Project Art Editor William Hicks
Editorial Assistant Roxanne Benson-Mackey
Managing Editor Dawn Henderson
Managing Art Editor Marianne Markham
Senior Creative Nicola Powling
Production Editor Ben Marcus
Senior Production Controller Man Fai Lau
Creative Technical Support Sonia Charbonnier

Editors Emma Callery, Diana Vowles

DK India
Editor Alicia Ingty
Assistant Editor Tina Jindal
Art Editor Devika Dwarkadas
Managing Editor Glenda Fernandes
Senior Art Editor (Lead) Navidita Thapa
Production Manager Pankaj Sharma
DTP Manager Sunil Sharma
Assistant DTP Designer Sourabh Challariya

Recipe photography William Reavell
Photography art direction Nicky Collings
Food stylists Fergal Connolly and Penny Stephens
Props stylist Sue Rowlands

Cover photography
Front: main image © John Wright, styling by Boo Attwood,
make-up by Katie Reedman; recipe photography: William Reavell
Back (and throughout the book): images of judges © John Wright,
except Michel Roux Jr by Peter Kindersley

Image of John Torode and Gregg Wallace, p1
Photographed exclusively for Radio Times by John Wright
© BBC Magazines Limited

Proofing Alta Images, London
Printed and bound by Tien Wah Press, Singapore

Acknowledgements

Shine would like to thank
David Ambler, Michelle Bennett, Cody Burridge, Jessica Boydell, Holly Brooks, Martin Buckett,
Jo Carlton, Nico Chirlando, Bev Comboy, Greg Comboy, Cosmetic Ink, Lynsie Drewett, Simone Foots,
John Gilbert, Simon Goodman, Jessica Hannan, Alex Mahon, Sam Michel, Jamie Munro, Elisabeth
Murdoch, Claire Nosworthy, Lou Plank, Lyndsey Posner, Franc Roddam, Karen Ross, Rosemary Scoular,
Caroline Stott, Clare Watkinson, Gordon Wise, John Wright, and Samantha Wright.

A massive thank you must go to all the creative and production teams who have worked on the 2010 series
of MasterChef that these recipes have been selected from. Without your exceptional talents none of this
would have been possible. And finally to the contestants who have shared their skill, their passion, their
ambition, and their cooking dreams with us – you have been an inspiration! Thank you.

Dorling Kindersley would like to thank
Divya PR, Era Chawla, Nand Kishor Acharya, Nicola Erdpresser, and Tessa Bindloss for design help; Kokila
Manchanda and Ekta Sharma for editorial help; Lakeland for props (www.lakeland.co.uk); recipe testers
Lesley Ball, Diane van Bueren, Anna Burges-Lumsden, Louisa Carter, Sonja Edridge, Jan Fullwood, Laura
Fyfe, Clare Greenstreet, Katy Greenwood, Anne Harnan, Jill Joynson, Sarah King, Bren Parkins-Knight,
Vicky Pettipher, Kate Pring, Natalie Seldon, Cathy Seward, Deirdre Taylor, Jill Weatherburn, and Jane
Milton; Sarah Fassnidge for quote-noting; Nicola Hodgson for proofreading; and Sue Bosanko for indexing.